MANAGEMENT

FOR UGC - NET

(Paper II & III)

MANAGEMENT
FOR UGC - NET
(Paper II & III)

(VOLUME - I)

Debasish Biswas

First Edition, 2019

KALPAZ

First Published, 2019

Published by

Kalpaz Publications
C-30, Satyawati Nagar,
Delhi – 110052
Ph.: 011-47034999, 9811692060
www.kalpazpublications.com
E-mail: kalpaz@hotmail.com

Printed at: G. Print Process, Delhi

Cataloging in Publication Data—DK
Courtesy: D.K. Agencies (P) Ltd. <docinfo@dkagencies.com>

Biswas, Debasish, author.
Management for UGC-NET (paper II & III) / Debasish Biswas.
pages cm
ISBN 9789353240653 (Set)
9789353240660 (Vol. I) (HB)

1. Management—Examinations—Study guides. I. Title.

LCC HD30.413.B57 2018 | DDC 658.0076 23

In Memory of My Father
Whose Blessings are
My Fountain of Spirit and Inspiration

Contents

(Volume - I)

(Volume - II)

Preface

I feel great pleasure in placing the first edition of this book before my esteemed readers. It is the outcome of a great deal of encouragement from my colleagues and request from students.

This book is appropriate for management students for appearing NET and all other competitive examinations in the field of Management.

My sincere and deliberate efforts have been devoted to give the book comprehensive form.All units have been discussed in a very simple and lucid language so as to make the subject easily understandable to my beloved students.

I am grateful to the esteemed teachers who always provided me with their valuable suggestions from time to time. I am thankful to my students who always shown a keen interest in my publication. I offer my heartfelt congratulations to......Publications, New Delhifor quick publication of the book.

I welcome suggestions from esteemed teachers and my students for enrichment and improvement of the book in the future.

This book provides detailed information about the management related areas with simple language along with easy examples.

Dr. D. Biswas

M.Com, M.B.A, M.Phil, DLL, PGDHM,
PGDE, PGDMM, GDCA, PGDFM, Ph.D.
Assistant Professor&Head
Dept. of Business Administration
Vidyasagar University
Midnapore

Acknowledgements

First of all, I would like to express my sincere gratitude to Dr. Debabrata Mitra, Professor of Commerce, North Bengal University, who has been my motivator since the beginning of my write up. He provided me with many helpful suggestions, important advice and constant encouragement during the course of this work.

I am also grateful to Prof.Dr. Ajit Kumar Ghosh, Department of Commerce, Burdwan University for his valuable suggestions.

A special note of appreciation is due to Prof. Dr.Susanta Mitra, Professor of Commerce, Kaji Nazrul University, West Bengal for his valuable contributions towards enhancing the standard of the book.

I also thank to Mr. Nirmal Chandra Roy, Dr. Keya Das and Dr.Sudin Bag for extending their help in conducting the task. I am also indebted to all of my beloved students and colleagues for their whole hearted co-operation for this book.

I owe a deep gratitude to the authorities of Vidyasagar University, different librarians and all those who inspired and helped me in this work. I must thank Mr. Subhasish Khan for preparing a neat typed copy of the book.

Finally, my sincere thanks to my publisher,.....Publications, New Delhi, for their untiring effort and support in bringing out this book.

The responsibility for errors remains me alone.

Dr. D. Biswas

M.Com, M.B.A, M.Phil, DLL, PGDHM,
PGDE, PGDMM, GDCA, PGDFM, Ph.D.
Assistant Professor&Head
Dept. of Business Administration
Vidyasagar University

Unit - I

Managerial Economics

Demand Analysis

Demand is the amount of goods that consumers or buyers are willing and capable to buy for a specific price in a specific time period while everything else remains the same. Demand is an economic principle that describes the willingness and desire of consumers to purchase specific goods or services at a specific **ceteris paribus** (all other things being unchanged or constant).

It is necessary to estimate the demand for the goods or services before they are produced and provided. The producers, for this purpose, heavily depend upon the data relating to the pattern of consumption of these goods and services. The demand analysis provides them the basis to take decisions relating to volume of production, capital to be invested and so on.

Demand for a commodity refers to the quantity of the commodity which an individual consumer is willing to purchase at a particular time at a particular price.

A product or service is said to have demand when three conditions are satisfied.

(a) Desire to acquire: Desire of the consumer to buy the Product

(b) Willingness to pay: His willingness to buy the product and

(c) Ability to pay: Ability to pay the specified price for it.

Nature and Types of Demand

Demand for the product is determined by its nature. Demand for such commodities which use indispensable for the consumer is not affected significantly by changes in their market conditions. In other words, a product with more number of uses is naturally more in demand than one with a single use, the nature of demand is better understood when we see these variations given below:

(1) Consumer Goods V/S Producer Goods

Consumer Goods

Consumer goods refer to such products and services which are satisfying consumer need. Consumer goods are those which are available for **ultimate consumption**. Consumer goods are needed for direct consumption and gives direct and immediate satisfaction.

Example: Bread, Rice, etc.

Producer Goods

Producer goods are those which are used for **producing other goods**. Producer goods are those which are used for further processing or production of goods or services to generate income. These goods give satisfaction indirectly.

Example: Machines, Steel, Tools, etc.

There could be cases where a given product may be both producer and also consumer goods. Example: A farmer having twenty bags of paddy may use ten bags for his personal consumption and other ten bags as seeds for the next crop. In such a case, paddy is **both producer goods and consumer goods**.

2. Autonomous Demand V/S Derived Demand

Autonomous Demand

Autonomous demand refers to the demand for products and services directly and independently. Example: Demand for four wheelers is autonomous demand.

Derived Demand

In case of derived demand, the demand for a product arises due to **purchase of another product**. Example: **(1)** Demand for petrol due to purchase of two wheelers; **(2)** If there is a demand for house then there is a demand for cement, iron and bricks.

3. Durable Goods V/S Perishable Goods

Durable Goods

Durable Goods are those which give service relatively for a **long period**. Example: T.V., Washing Machine, etc.

Perishable Goods

Perishable Goods are those which give service relatively for a **short period**. Example: Milk, Vegetables, Fish, Rice, etc.

4. Firm Demand V/S Industry Demand

Firm Demand

The firm is a single business unit. The term 'Firm Demand' denotes demand for a particular product of a particular firm. Example: The demand of LG TVs is referred as Firm Demand or Company Demand.

Industry Demand

Industry refers to the group of companies producing same type of product. Industry Demand refers to the total demand for the product of a particular industry. Example: Demand for TVs produced by all companies is referred as Industry Demand.

5. New Demand V/S Replacement

New Demand refers to the demand for the new products and it is addition to the existing stock.

Replacement Demand

Replacement demand may also refer to the demand resulting out of replacing the existing asset with the new ones. Example: Purchasing a new TV and replacing with old is referred as replacement demand.

6. Total Market and Segment Market Demand

Total Market Demand

Total market demand means the total demand for a product in a given total market.

Segment Market Demand

Segment market demand refers to the demand of product in **particular market segment** of a total market. Example: If a product selling in Andhra Pradesh then total demand means that total demand to that product in A.P.

Factors Determining the Demand

The demand for a particular product depends on several factors. The following factors determine the demand for a given product.

1. Price of the product
2. Income of the consumer

3. Taste and preference of the consumer
4. Price of related goods (Substitute or complementary)
5. Expectations about the prices in future
6. Expectations about the income in future
7. Size of the population
8. Distribution of consumers over different regions
9. Advertising effort

1. Price of the Product

The most important factor which influences the demand is price. A decrease in the price of a normal good leads to rise in demand of a product. Similarly, an increase in the price will reduce the demand for a commodity. The relation between price and demand is **inversely related**.

2. Income of the Consumer

When the income of the consumer is increased, the consumers purchase more quantity of goods. When the income of consumer is decreased, the consumers purchase less quantity of goods. The income of the consumer and demand of a product moves in the **same direction**.

3. Tastes and Preference of the Consumer

We know it quite well that the change in tastes and preferences of a consumer in favour of a commodity results in increasing demand for a commodity, while if this change is against the commodity it results in smaller demand for the commodity.

4. Price of the Related Goods (Substitute and Complementary Goods)

When a change in the price of one commodity influences the demand for **other commodity**. The related commodities are two types:

(a) Substitutes
(b) Complements

(a) Substitute Goods: When the price of **one commodity increases**, then the demand for **another product will increase**. Example: In case of Tea and Coffee, when coffee price increased then the demand for tea will also increase and vice versa. Demand for a given commodity varies directly with the price of a substitute good. For example, if price of a substitute good (say, coffee) increases, then demand for given commodity (say, tea) will rise as tea will become relatively cheaper in comparison to coffee.

(b) Complementary Goods: When the price of one commodity will increase then the demand for another commodity will decrease. Complementary goods are those goods which are **used together** to satisfy a particular want. Demand for a given commodity varies inversely with the price of a complementary good. For example, if price of a complementary good (say, sugar) **increases**, then demand for given commodity (say, tea) will **fall** as it will be relatively costlier to use both the goods together.

(5) Expectations about Future Price of the Product

If the consumer expects future price of the product will increase then the consumer purchases more quantity of goods at present. Similarly, if the price of the product in the future will decrease then the demand at present will decrease.

(6) Expectations about Future Income of the Consumer

In case, the consumer expects a higher income in future, he spends more at present to purchase more quantity of goods. Similarly, the consumer expects a lower income in future; he spends less at present to purchase less quantity of goods.

(7) Size of the Population

(8) Distribution of Consumers over Different Regions

(9) Advertisement

If we can spend more amounts on advertisement to influence the consumer, the demand will increase, if advertisement expenditure is less, then the demand will decrease.

Law of Demand

The law of demand describes the inverse relationship of price and the quantity demanded all else remaining constant. If the price is high, the quantity demand decreases and if the price decreases, then the quantity demand will increase.

Exceptions to the Law of Demand

There are certain exceptions to the law of demand. These are stated below:

(1) Giffen Goods: Giffen goods are a special type of **inferior goods** whose **demand increases** as the **price of the goods increases**. An example could be rice which is a staple food of a region and majority of the food consumption is rice that cannot be substituted. What will happen? Even if the price of rice increases, there is no substitute for rice in the food basket, so its demand does not fall. This disobeys the fundamental law of demand, i.e. demand decreases as price increases.

(2) Veblen Goods: Veblen goods violate the law of demand because people actually prefer goods to be **more expensive** as a status symbol. Such goods are called Veblen Goods. Example: Products such as Jewels, Gold, etc.

(3) Inferior Goods: An inferior goods is a good whose **demand increases** when the consumer's **income decreases** and whose demand decreases as the consumer's income increases. For example, second hand cars are cheaper. If my income is low, I would buy a second hand car, and as my income rises, I would prefer a brand new car that I can afford. So, inferiority, in a sense, refers to the easy affordability of the goods at lower consumer income, compared to the costly substitute.

(4) Where there is a Shortage of Necessities: If the consumers fear that these could be shortage of necessities, then this law of demand does not applicable. They may tend to buy more than what they require immediately, even if the price of the product increases.

(5) In Case of Ignorance of Price Changes: When the customer is not familiar with the changes in the price, he tends to buy even if there is increase in price.

Production Functions

A production function shows the relationship between inputs of **capital and labour** and other factors and the outputs of goods and services.

Production function expresses the relationship between inputs and outputs. Production function is an equation, a table, a graph, which express the relationship between **inputs and outputs**. Production function explains that the maximum output of goods or services that can be produced by a firm in a specific time with a given amount of inputs or factors of production.

Production Function: $Q = f(K, L)$

We are producing Q quantities of goods by employing K capital and L labour.

Here,

Q represents quantity of goods

K represents capital employed

L represents labour employed

One way to measure returns to scale is to use a coefficient of output elasticity.

EQ = Percentage change in Q/ Percentage change in all inputs

Thus,

If **E > 1**, we have **increasing returns to scale** (IRTS).

If **E = 1**, we have **constant returns to scale** (CRTS).

If **E < 1**, we have **decreasing returns to scale** (DRTS).

Cobb-Douglas Production Function

In economics, the Cobb-Douglas functional form of production function is widely used to represent the relationship of an output to inputs. It was proposed by Knut Wicksell (1851 - 1926), and tested against statistical evidence by Charles Cobb and Paul Douglas in 1928.

In 1928, Charles Cobb and Paul Douglas published a study in which they modeled the growth of the American economy during the period 1899 - 1922. They considered a simplified view of the economy in which production output is determined by the amount of labour involved and the amount of capital invested. While there are many other factors affecting economic performance, their model proved to be remarkably accurate.

The function they used to model production was of the form:

$$P(L, K) = b\,L\,\alpha\,K\,\beta$$

Where:

- P = Total production (the monetary value of all goods produced in a year)
- L = Labour input (the total number of person-hours worked in a year)
- K = Capital input (the monetary worth of all machinery, equipment, and buildings)
- b = Total factor productivity
- α and β are the output elasticities of labour and capital respectively. These values are constants determined by available technology.

Output elasticity measures the responsiveness of output to a change in levels of either labour or capital used in production, ceteris paribus. For example, if α = **0.15**, it implies that **1% increase in labour** would lead to approximately **0.15% increase in output**.

Further, if $\alpha + \beta$ = **1** then the production function has **constant returns to scale**. That is, if L and K are each increased by 20% then production increases by 20%.

If output increases by less than that proportional change, there are decreasing returns to scale (DRS). If output increases by more than that proportion, there are increasing returns to scale (IRS)

However, if $\alpha + \beta < 1$, returns to scale are **decreasing**, and if $\alpha + \beta > 1$, returns to scale are **increasing**.

Cost Output Relation (Short Term)

TC = TFC + TVC

ATC = TC / Output

ATC = AFC + AVC

FC in short term is constant.

MC = TVCn – TVCn-1

MC is independent of the FC in the short term.

Fixed cost is constant in the short term and thus average fixed cost keeps on reducing till infinity.

Cost Output Relation (Long Term)

Every component is variable in the long term, even the fixed cost.

In Increasing Returns to Scale, the firm's efficiency is increasing but is not optimum.

In Constant Returns to Scale, the firm is at the most effective phase of their operations.

In Decreasing Returns to Scale, the firm's effectiveness starts to decrease and cost increases.

Market Structures

A market is the area where buyers and sellers contact each other and exchange goods and services. Market structure is said to be the characteristics of the market. Market structures are basically the number of firms in the market that produce identical goods and services. Market structure influences the behaviour of firms to a great extent. The market structure affects the supply of different commodities in the market.

When the competition is high there is a high supply of commodity as different companies try to dominate the markets and it also creates barriers to entry for the companies that intend to join that market. A monopoly market has the biggest level of barriers to entry while the perfectly competitive market has zero percent level of barriers to entry. Firms are more efficient in a competitive market than in a monopoly structure.

Classification of Market Structure Based on the Nature of Competitor:

(1) Perfect Market

(2) Imperfect Market

The imperfect market in turn can be classified as

(a) Monopoly Market

(b) Duopoly Market

(c) Oligopoly Market
(d) Monopolistic Market

Pricing Theories

Determinants of Price under Perfect Competition

Perfect competition is a situation prevailing in a market in which buyers and sellers are so numerous and well informed that all elements of monopoly are absent and the market price of a commodity is beyond the control of individual buyers and sellers.

Market price is determined by the equilibrium between demand and supply in a market period. The market period is a period in which the maximum that can be supplied is limited by the existing stock. The market period is so short that more cannot be produced in response to increased demand. The firms can sell only what they have already produced. This market period may be an hour, a day or a few days or even a few weeks depending upon the nature of the product.

Market Price of a Perishable Commodity

In the case of perishable commodity like fish, the supply is limited by the available quantity on that day. It cannot be stored for the next market period and therefore the whole of it must be sold away on the same day whatever the price may be.

Market Price of Non-Perishable and Reproducible Goods

In case of non-perishable but reproducible goods, some of the goods can be preserved or kept back from the market and carried over to the next market period. There will then be two critical price levels.

The first, if price is very high the seller will be prepared to sell the whole stock. The second level is set by a low price at which the seller would not sell any amount in the present market period, but will hold back the whole stock for some better time. The price below which the seller will refuse to sell is called the **Reserve Price**.

Determinants of Price under Imperfect Competition

Monopoly Market

Monopoly is said to exist when one firm is the sole producer or seller of a product which has no close substitutes. According to this definition, there must be a single producer or seller of a product. If there are many producers producing a product, either perfect competition or monopolistic competition will prevail depending upon whether the product is homogeneous or differentiated.

In a monopoly market the following things are essential:

(i) Only one firm produces and sells a particular commodity or a service.

(ii) There are no rivals or direct competitors of the firm.

(iii) No other seller can enter the market.

(iv) Monopolist is a price maker. He tries to take the best of whatever demand and cost conditions exist without the fear of new firms entering to compete away his profits.

Duopoly Market

A **duopoly** is a form of oligopoly occurring when **two companies** control all or most of the market for a product or service.

There are two kinds of *duopolies*. In the first, the **Cournot** duopoly, competition between the two companies is based on the **quantity of products** supplied. The duopoly members essentially agree to split the market. The price each company receives for the product is based on the quantity of items produced, and the two companies react to each other's production changes until equilibrium is achieved.

In a **Bertrand** duopoly, the two companies compete on **price** because consumers will purchase the cheaper of two identical products, this leads to a zero-profit price as the two competitors attempt to attract more customers through price cuts.

Oligopoly Market

Oligopoly is a situation in which only a **few firms** are competing in the market for a particular commodity. The distinguishing characteristics of oligopoly are such that neither the theory of monopolistic competition nor the theory of monopoly can explain the behaviour of an oligopolistic firm.

Two of the main characteristics of Oligopoly are briefly explained below:

(i) Under oligopoly the number of competing firms being small, each firm controls an important proportion of the total supply. Consequently, the effect of a change in the price or output of one firm upon the sales of its rival firms is noticeable and not insignificant. When any firm takes an action its rivals will in all probability react to it. The behaviour of oligopolistic firms is interdependent and not independent or at optimistic as is the case under perfect or monopolistic competition.

(ii) Under oligopoly new entry is difficult. It is neither free nor barred. Hence the condition of entry becomes an important factor determining the price or output decisions of oligopolistic firms and preventing or limiting entry of an important objective.

Monopolistic Market

Monopolistic competition is a form of market structure in which a **large number of independent firms** are supplying products that are slightly differentiated from the point of view of buyers. Thus, the products of the competing firms are close but not perfect substitutes because buyers do not regard them as identical. This situation arises when the same commodity is being sold under different brand names, each brand being slightly different from the others.

For Example— Lux, Liril, Dove, etc.

In addition to product differentiation, the other three basic characteristics of monopolistic competition are as follows:

(i) There are large number of independent sellers and buyers in the market.

(ii) The relative market shares of all sellers are insignificant and more or less equal.

(iii) There are neither any legal nor any economic barriers against the entry of new firms into the market. New firms are free to enter the market and existing firms are free to leave the market.

(iv) In other words, product differentiation is the only characteristic that distinguishes monopolistic competition from perfect competition.

Advertising

Advertising is a means of communication with the users of a product or service. Advertisements are messages paid for by those who send them and are intended to inform or influence people who receive them, as defined by the Advertising Association of the UK.

Advertising is always present, though people may not be aware of it. In today's world, advertising uses every possible media to get its message through. It does this via television, print (newspapers, magazines, journals, etc), radio, press, internet, direct selling, hoardings, mailers, contests, sponsorships, posters, clothes, events, colours, sounds, visuals and even people.

A company that needs to advertise itself and/or its products hires an advertising agency. The company briefs the agency on the brand, its imagery, the ideals and values behind it, the target segments and so on. The agencies convert the ideas and concepts to create the visuals, text, layouts and themes to communicate with the user.

Macro Economics

Macroeconomics is the branch of economics that studies the behaviour and performance of an **economy as a whole**. It focuses on the aggregate changes in the economy such as unemployment, growth rate, gross domestic product and inflation.

Macroeconomics analyzes all aggregate indicators and the microeconomic factors that influence the economy. Government and corporations use macroeconomic models to help in formulating of **economic policies and strategies**.

NI Concepts

There are various concepts of National Income. The main concepts of NI are: GDP, GNP, NNP, NI, PI, DI, and PCI. These different concepts explain about the phenomenon of economic activities of the various sectors of the economy.

Gross Domestic Product (GDP)

The most important concept of national income is Gross Domestic Product. Gross domestic product is the **money value of all final goods and services** produced within the domestic territory of a country during a year.

Algebraic expression under product method is,

GDP = (P*Q)

Where,

GDP = Gross Domestic Product

P = Price of goods and service

Q = Quantity of goods and service

According to expenditure approach, GDP is the sum of consumption, investment, government expenditure, net foreign exports of a country during a year.

Algebraic expression under expenditure approach is,

GDP = C + I + G + (X-M)

Where,

C=Consumption

I=Investment

G=Government expenditure

(X-M)=Export minus import

GDP includes the following types of final goods and services. These are:

1. Consumer goods and services.
2. Gross private domestic investment in capital goods.
3. Government expenditure.
4. Exports and imports.

Gross National Product (GNP)

Gross National Product is the total market value of **all final goods and services produced annually in a country plus net factor income from abroad**. Thus, GNP is the total measure of the flow of goods and services at market value resulting from current production during a year in a country including net factor income from abroad. The GNP can be expressed as the following equation:

GNP = GDP+NFIA (Net Factor Income from Abroad)

Or, **GNP=C+I+G+(X-M)+NFIA**

Hence, GNP includes the following:

1. Consumer goods and services.
2. Gross private domestic investment in capital goods.
3. Government expenditure.
4. Net exports (exports-imports).
5. Net factor income from abroad.

Net National Product (NNP)

Net National Product is the **market value of all final goods and services after allowing for depreciation**. It is also called National Income at market price. When charges for depreciation are deducted from the gross national product, we get it. Thus,

NNP = GNP-Depreciation

Or, NNP = C + I + G + (X-M) + NFIA - Depreciation

National Income (NI)

National Income is also known as National Income at factor cost. National income at factor cost means the sum of all incomes earned by resources suppliers for their contribution of land, labour, capital and organizational ability which go into the year's net production. Hence, the sum of the income received by **factors of production** in the form of rent, wages, interest and profit is called National Income. Symbolically,

NI = NNP + Subsidies - Interest Taxes

Or, **GNP- Depreciation + Subsidies - Indirect Taxes**

Or, **NI = C + G + I + (X-M) + NFIA - Depreciation - Indirect Taxes + Subsidies**

Personal Income (PI)

Personal Income is the total money income received by individuals and households of a country from all possible sources before direct taxes. Therefore, personal income can be expressed as follows:

PI = NI - Corporate Income Taxes - Undistributed Corporate Profits- Social Security Contribution + Transfer Payments

Disposable Income (DI)

The income left after the payment of direct taxes from personal income is called Disposable Income. Disposable income means actual income which can be spent on consumption by individuals and families. Thus, it can be expressed as:

DI = PI - Direct Taxes

From consumption approach,

DI = Consumption Expenditure + Savings

Per Capita Income (PCI)

Per Capita Income of a country is derived by dividing the national income of the country by the total population of a country. Thus,

PCI = Total National Income/Total National Population

Methods of Calculating National Income

There are three methods by which national income can be calculated. These are as follows:

1. Product Method

This is also called the **output method, the inventory method or the census method**. It consists of finding out the market value of all the goods and services produced during a year.

According to this method the economy is classified into different sectors, namely

Direct Sector: In this sector, the value of services of such professions like doctors, dramatics, soldiers, politicians, etc., are taken by equating to their services.

Agriculture Industry

International Transaction Sector: In this sector, we take into account the value of goods exported and imported payment from abroad, payments to other countries.

In each sector, we make an inventory of goods produced and find out the end product making an addition to the value of goods. The value added method can be followed in order to avoid double counting. The value added of a firm is its output less whatever it purchases from other firms such as raw materials, and other inputs.

This method has a merit because it helps us to have a comparative idea of the importance of various activities in economy like agriculture, manufacturing, trade, etc. However in advanced countries this method may be successful as it is very easy to get data from government records. But in under developed countries, this method may give rise to various problems like imputation of money values to non- monetized sector.

2. Income Method

This method refers to the gross national income obtained by adding together wages and salaries, interests, profits and rents of persons and institution and including government incomes are earned either from property or through work. To arrive at the totality of income of nation, the following procedure will be adopted:

(a) Net rents include the rental value of owner occupied houses.

(b) Wages, salaries and all such earnings of person employed, pensions are excluded.

(c) Earnings by way of interest.

(d) Income of joint stock companies.

(e) Income from overseas investment.

This method gives national income at factor cost.

3. Expenditure Method

This method is also called the **flow of product approach** (by American economist Samuelson) or the **outlay method**.

Here, we take into account the expenditure on finished products-

- Expenditure by consumers on goods and services.
- Expenditure by producers on investment of goods.
- Expenditure by government on consumption as well as capital goods.

To this we add money received from abroad through trade and other payments. This figure thus arrived at will give us G.N.P.

The merit of this method is that it believes in the identity between national expenditure, income and total product.

Whichever method we use the result should be more or less the same. In other words, they can be used to cross-check reliability of each other.

Infrastructure – Management and Policy

Infrastructure is the basic physical systems of a business or nation; transportation, communication, sewage, water and electric systems are all examples of infrastructure. These systems tend to be high-cost investments; however, they are vital to a country's economic development and prosperity. Projects related to infrastructure improvements may be funded publicly, privately or through public-private partnerships.

Infrastructure Management is the planning, design, delivery and control of the basic facilities, structures, equipment, services and information technologies that serve as a foundation for economic activity.

Infrastructure management is the management of operation component, policies, processes, data and external contacts. Infrastructure management divided into three categories:-

- Systems Management
- Network Management
- Storage Management

There are some benefits of using Infrastructure management:

- Cost Reduction
- Enhanced Security
- Improved Customer Satisfaction
- Maximize Productivity
- Reduced Downtime

Rather than describing infrastructure through a single definition, it might be more helpful to describe infrastructure through a set of characteristics that are attributed to it. Some of these characteristics that are popularly associated with infrastructure are:

(i) Infrastructure facilities are generally available to large groups of people.

(ii) Infrastructure helps to deliver essential services for the functioning of an organization or society.

(iii) Infrastructure helps to achieve economic and social objectives.

(iv) Infrastructure is the base upon which society and its activities rest.

The importance of infrastructure is two-fold. These are as follows:

(i) Infrastructure is instrumental in promoting economic growth.

(ii) Infrastructure also plays a role in alleviating poverty.

Despite the importance of infrastructure for economic and social well-being, we are faced with several problems. These are stated below:

(i) Infrastructure in developed countries is old, unreliable, inefficient and in need of replacement. The USA is embarking on a major plan relating to infrastructure spending.

(ii) In developing countries, infrastructure is often not available. Large portions of urban and rural populations in developing countries have inadequate access to water and sanitation.

(iii) Power supply is non-existent or unreliable and people are faced with frequent power-cuts.

(iv) Quality of road infrastructure is often bad, leading to long travel times and increased vehicle maintenance costs. Width of roads is also often a constraining factor leading to traffic jams and blocks.

We list out a few of the causes for the failure to provide adequate infrastructure. These are as follows:

(i) Lack of funds;

(ii) Lack of implementation and management capabilities;

(iii) Corruption, bureaucracy and unfair competition;

(iv) Land acquisition issues involving dealing with displaced people and special interest groups.

Business Environment

A. Internal Environment

Internal environment includes all those factors which influence business and which are present within the business itself. These factors are usually under the **control of business**. The study of internal factors is really important for the study of internal environment. These factors are:

(i) Objectives of Business, **(ii)** Policies of Business, **(iii)** Production Capacity, **(iv)** Production Methods, **(v)** Management Information System, **(vi)** Participation in Management, **(vii)** Composition of Board of Directors, **(viii)** Managerial Attitude, **(ix)** Organisational Structure, **(x)** Features of Human Resource, etc.

Confining business environment to uncontrollable external factors, it may be classified as **1.** Economic environment; and **2.** Non-economic environment.

The economic environment includes **economic conditions, economic policies and economic system** of the country. Non-economic environment comprises **social, political, legal, technological, demographic and natural environment**. All these have a bearing on the strategies adopted by the firms and any change in these areas is likely to have a far-reaching impact on their operations.

Let us have a brief idea about each of these areas of business environment.

1. Economic Environment: The survival and success of each and every business enterprise depend fully on its economic environment. The main factors that affect the economic environment are:

(a) Economic Conditions: The economic conditions of a nation refer to a set of economic factors that have great influence on business organizations and their operations. These include gross domestic product, per capita income, markets for goods and services, availability of capital, foreign exchange reserve, growth of foreign trade, strength of capital market, etc. All these help in improving the pace of economic growth.

(b) Economic Policies

All business activities and operations are directly influenced by the economic policies framed by the government from time to time. Some of the important economic policies are:

(i) Industrial policy
(ii) Fiscal policy
(iii) Monetary policy
(iv) Foreign investment policy
(v) Export –Import policy (**Exim policy**)

The government keeps on changing these policies from time to time in view of the developments taking place in the economic scenario, political expediency and the changing requirement. Every business firm has to function strictly within the policy framework and respond to the changes therein.

Important Economic Policies

(i) Industrial Policy: The Industrial policy of the government covers all those principles, policies, rules, regulations and procedures, which direct and control the industrial enterprises of the country and shape the pattern of industrial development.

(ii) Fiscal Policy: It includes government policy in respect of public expenditure, taxation and public debt.

(iii) Monetary Policy: It includes all those activities and interventions that aim at smooth supply of credit to the business and a boost to trade and industry.

(iv) Foreign Investment Policy: This policy aims at regulating the inflow of foreign investment in various sectors for speeding up industrial development and take advantage of the modern technology.

(v) **Export–Import Policy:** It aims at increasing exports and bridges the gap between export and import. Through this policy, the government announces various duties/levies. The focus now-a-days lies on removing barriers and controls and lowering the custom duties.

(c) Economic System

The world economy is primarily governed by three types of economic systems, viz., **(i)** Capitalist economy; **(ii)** Socialist economy; and **(iii)** Mixed economy. India has adopted the **mixed economy system** which implies co-existence of **public sector and private sector**.

2. Non-Economic Environment: The various elements of non-economic environment are as follows:

(a) Social Environment

The social environment of business includes social factors like customs, traditions, values, beliefs, poverty, literacy, life expectancy rate, etc.

The social structure and the values that a society cherishes have a considerable influence on the functioning of business firms. For example, during festive seasons there is an increase in the demand for new clothes, sweets, fruits, flower, etc. Due to increase in literacy rate the consumers are becoming more conscious of the quality of the products. Due to change in family composition, more nuclear families with single child concepts have come up. This increases the demand for the different types of household goods. It may be noted that the consumption patterns, the dressing and living styles of people belonging to different social structures and culture vary significantly.

(b) Political Environment

This includes the political system, the government policies and attitude towards the business community and the unionism. All these aspects have a bearing on the strategies adopted by the business firms. The stability of the government also influences business and related activities to a great extent. It sends a signal of strength, confidence to various interest groups and investors. Further, ideology of the political party also influences the business organisation and its operations.

For example, the trade union activities influence the operation of business enterprises. Most of the labour unions in India are affiliated to various political parties. Strikes, lockouts and labour disputes, etc. also adversely affect the business operations. However, with the competitive business environment, trade unions are now showing great maturity and started contributing positively to the success of the business organisation and its operations through workers participation in management.

(c) Legal Environment

This refers to set of laws, regulations, which influence the business organizations and their operations. Every business organisation has to obey, and work within the framework of the law. The important legislations that concern the business enterprises include:

(i) Companies Act, 1956
(ii) Foreign Exchange Management Act, 1999
(iii) The Factories Act, 1948
(iv) Industrial Disputes Act, 1972
(v) Payment of Gratuity Act, 1972
(vi) Industries (Development and Regulation) Act, 1951
(vii) Prevention of Food Adulteration Act, 1954
(viii) Essential Commodities Act, 2002
(ix) The Standards of Weights and Measures Act, 1956
(x) Monopolies and Restrictive Trade Practices Act, 1969
(xi) Trade Marks Act, 1999
(xii) Bureau of Indian Standards Act, 1986
(xiii) Consumer Protection Act, 1986
(xiv) Environment Protection Act, 1986
(xv) Competition Act, 2002

Besides, the above legislations, the following are also form part of the legal environment of business.

(i) Provisions of the Constitution: The provisions of the Articles of the Indian Constitution, particularly directive principles, rights and duties of citizens, legislative powers of the central and state government also influence the operation of business enterprises.

(ii) Judicial Decisions: The judiciary has to ensure that the legislature and the government function in the interest of the public and act within the boundaries of the constitution. The various judgments given by the court in different matters relating to trade and industry also influence the business activities.

(d) Technological Environment

Technological environment includes the methods, techniques and approaches adopted for production of goods and services and its distribution. The varying technological environments of different countries affect the designing of products. For example, in USA and many other countries, electrical appliances are designed for 110 volts. But when these are made for India, they have to be of 220 volts. In the modern competitive age, the pace of technological changes is very fast. Hence, in order to survive and grow in the market, a business has to adopt the technological changes from time to time. It may be noted that scientific research for improvement and innovation in products and services is a regular activity in most of the big industrial organizations. Now a day in fact, no firm can afford to persist with the outdated technologies.

(e) Demographic Environment

This refers to the size, density, distribution and growth rate of population. All these factors have a direct bearing on the demand for various goods and services. For example, a country where population rate is high and children constitute a large section of population then there is more demand for baby products. Similarly, the demand of the people of cities and towns are different than the people of rural areas. The high rise of population indicates the easy availability of labour. These encourage the business enterprises to use labour intensive techniques of production. Moreover, availability of skill labour in certain areas motivates the firms to set up their units in such area. For example, the business units from America, Canada, Australia, Germany, UK, are coming to India due to easy availability of skilled manpower. Thus, a firm that keeps a watch on the changes on the demographic front and reads them accurately will find opportunities knocking at its doorsteps.

(f) Natural Environment

The natural environment includes geographical and ecological factors that influence the business operations. These factors include the availability of natural resources, weather and climatic condition, location aspect, topographical factors, etc. Business is greatly influenced by the nature of natural environment. For example, sugar factories are set up only at those places where sugarcane can be grown. It is always considered better to establish manufacturing unit near the sources of input. Further, government's policies to maintain ecological balance, conservation of natural resources, etc. put additional responsibility on the business sector.

Capital Budgeting

Capital Budgeting is the process of making investment decision in fixed assets or capital expenditure. Capital Budgeting is also known as investment, decision making, planning of capital acquisition, planning and analysis of capital expenditure, etc.

Objectives of Capital Budgeting

The following are the objectives of capital budgeting.

1. To find out the profitable capital expenditure;
2. To know whether the replacement of any existing fixed assets gives more return than earlier;

3. To decide whether a specified project is to be selected or not;
4. To find out the quantum of finance required for the capital expenditure;
5. To assess the various sources of finance for capital expenditure;
6. To evaluate the merits of each proposal to decide which project is the best.

Features of Capital Budgeting

The features of capital budgeting is briefly explained below:

1. Capital budgeting involves the investment of funds currently for getting benefits in the future.
2. Generally, the future benefits are spread over several years.
3. The long term investment is fixed.
4. The investment made in the project is determining the financial condition of business organization in future.
5. Each project involves huge amount of funds.
6. Capital expenditure decisions are irreversible.
7. The profitability of the business concern is based on the quantum of investments made in the project.

Limitations of Capital Budgeting

The following are the limitations of capital budgeting.

1. The economic life of the project and annual cash inflows are only estimation. The actual economic life of the project is either increased or decreased. Likewise, the actual annual cash inflows may be either more or less than the estimation. Hence, control over capital expenditure cannot be exercised.
2. Capital budgeting process does not take into consideration of various non-financial aspects of the projects while they play an important role in successful and profitable implementation of them. Hence, true profitability of the project cannot be highlighted.
3. It is also not correct to assume that mathematically exact techniques always produce highly accurate results.
4. All the techniques of capital budgeting presume that various investment proposals under consideration are mutually exclusive which may not be practically true in some particular circumstances.

Unit - II

Human Resource Management

Concepts and Perspectives of HRM

Concept of Human Resource Management

Human resources are the most valuable and unique assets of an organization. The successful management of an organization's human resources is an exciting, dynamic and challenging task, especially at a time when the world has become a global village and economies are in a state of flux. The scarcity of talented resources and the growing expectations of the modern day worker have further increased the complexity of human resource function. Even though specific human resource functions are the responsibility of the human resource department, the actual management of human resources is the responsibility of all the managers in an organization. It is therefore necessary for all managers to understand and give due importance to the different human resource policies and activities in the organization. It examines the various human resource processes that are concerned with attracting, managing, motivating and developing employees for the betterment of the organization. It has several goals:

(i) To meet the needs of the business and management;

(ii) To link human resource strategies to the business goals and objectives;

(iii) To find ways for human resources to 'add value' to a business;

(iv) To help a business to gain the commitment of employees to its values, goals and objectives.

Human Resource Management (HRM) may be defined as a **set of policies, practices and programmes** designed to maximize both personal and organizational goals. Human Resource Management is a way of management that links people-related activities to the strategy of a business or organization. HRM is often referred to as "strategic HRM".

According to Flippo, Human Resource Management is "the planning, organizing, directing, and controlling of the **procurement, development, compensation, integration, maintenance and reproduction** of human resources to the end that individual, organizational and societal objectives are accomplished."

Perspectives of HRM

Five different perspectives of human resource management (HRM) include the normative perspective, the critical perspective, behavioural perspective, systems perspective, and agency or transaction cost perspective.

1. The Normative Perspective

The concept of "Hard HRM" is the basis for the traditional approach toward human resource management. This concept traces its origins to the **Harvard model** that links workforce management to organizational strategy. **Hard HRM** stresses the linkage of functional areas such as manpower planning, job analysis, recruitment, compensation and benefits, performance evaluations, contract negotiations, and labour legislations to corporate strategy. This enforces organization's interests over the employees' conflicting ambitions and interests. It views the workforce as passive resources that the organization can use and dispose at will.

Soft HRM is synonymous with the **Michigan model** of human resources and is the bedrock of the modern approach to strategic human resource management. This model considers human capital as "assets" rather than "resources" and lays stress on organizational development, conflict management, leadership development, organizational culture, and relationship building as a means of increasing trust and ensuring performance through collaboration. This approach works under the assumption that what is good for the organization is also good for the employee.

2. The Critical Perspective of Human Resource Management

The critical perspective of human resource management is a reaction against the normative perception. This highlights some inherent contradictions within the normative perspective. This perspective espouses a gap between rhetoric, as organizations claim to follow soft HRM policies when they actually enforce hard HRM. A study by Hope-Hailey et al. (1997) finds that while most organizations claim employees to be their most important assets and make many commitments for their welfare and development, in reality employers enforce a hard HRM-based strategic control, and the interests of the organization always take priority over the individual employee.

3. The Behavioural Perspective of Human Resource Management

The behavioural perspective of human resource management has its roots in the contingency theory that considers employee behaviour as the mediator between **strategy and organizational performance**. This theory holds that the purpose of human resource intervention is to control employee attitudes and behaviours to suit the various strategies adopted to attain the desired performance. This perspective thus bases itself on the **role behaviour** of employees instead of their skills, knowledge, and abilities.

For instance, an organization aiming to innovate will require a workforce that demonstrates a high degree of innovative behaviour such as long-term focus, cooperation, concern for quality, creativity, propensity for risk taking, and similar qualities. The role of human resource management in such a context is to inculcate and reinforce such behavioural patterns in the workforce.

4. The Systems Perspective of Human Resource Management

The systems perspective describes an organization in terms of input, throughput, and output, with all these systems involved in transactions with a surrounding environment. The organized activities of employees constitute the input, the transformation of energies within the system at throughput, and the resulting product or service the output. A negative feedback loop provides communications on discrepancies.

The role of human resource management in the systems perspective is

(i) Competence management to ensure that the workforce has the required competencies such as skills and ability to provide the input needed by the organization.

(ii) Behaviour management through performance evaluation, pay systems, and other methods to ensure job satisfaction, so that employees work according to the organizational strategy, ultimately boosting productivity.

(iii) Setting up mechanisms to buffer the technological core from the environment in closed systems.

(iv) Facilitating interactions with the environment in open systems.

5. Agency or Transaction Cost Perspective of Human Resource Management

The agency or transaction cost perspective, which holds the view that the strong natural inclination of people working in groups is to reduce their performance and rely on the efforts of others in the group. When one person delegates responsibility to another person, conflicts of interests invariably arise. The major role of human resource management in such a context is to promote alternative ways of controlling behaviour to reduce the effects of such conflicts and minimize the cost to the organization. The two major approaches include:

(i) Monitoring employee behaviour and preventing shrink of work by establishing effective control systems and improving productivity.

(ii) Providing employees with incentives such as rewards, motivation, and job satisfaction to increase their individual performance.

The human resource department needs to adopt the approach that minimizes transaction cost to the organization.

HRM in Changing Environment

The five factors involved in the changing environment of HRM are as follows: 1. Work Force Diversity 2. Economic and Technological Change 3. Globalization 4. Organisational Restructuring 5. Changing Nature of Work.

1. Work Force Diversity

Diversity has been defined as any attribute that humans are likely to use to tell them, that person is different from me and, thus, includes such factors as race, sex, age, values, and cultural norms. The Indian work force is characterized by such diversity that is deepening and spreading day by day.

It is likely to be more diverse as women, minority- group members, and older workers flood the work force. With the increasing number of women entering the work force due to a combination of factors like women's emancipation, economic needs, greater equality of sexes, education and so on, additional pressures of managing a different set of problems at the work place have arisen. As such, the number of women is on increase in all walks of life i.e., teachers, lawyers, doctors, engineers, accountants, pilots, parliamentarians and so on.

However, increasing number of women in the work force has been necessitating the implementation of more flexible work scheduling, child care facilities, maternity and now paternity leave also and transfer to location of husband's place of posting.

Also, as the work force ages, employers will have to grapple with greater health care costs and higher pension contributions. On the whole, the increased diversity of work force will place tremendous demands on the HR management function.

Further, creating unanimity from a diverse work force has also become a challenge for HR manager. This is because, as several experts' put it; diversity is marked by two fundamental and inconsistent realities operating today with it. One is that organizations claim they seek to maximize diversity in the work place, and maximize the capabilities of such a diverse work force.

The other is that traditional human resources system will not allow diversity, only similarity. These experts emphasize that employers traditionally hire, appraise, and promote people who fit a particular employer's image of what employees should believe and act like. At the same time, there is corresponding tendency to screen out those who do not fit.

2. Economic and Technological Change

Along with time, several economic and technological changes have occurred that have altered employment and occupational pattern. In India too, there is a perceptible shift in occupational structure from agriculture to industry to services.

The New Economic Policy, 1991 has led to liberalization and globalization giving genesis to multinational organizations with their multicultural dimensions having certain implications for HRM. The implications of globalization for HRM are discussed subsequently. The Indian economy has already become an open economy but it will be more so from April 2003 with the complete lifting of quantitative restrictions on imports in India.

Technology has become the hallmark of the modem organizations. As such, modem organizations have become the technology-driven organizations. So, men are replaced by machinery. Manufacturing technology, for example, has changed to automation and robotisation.

Manufacturing advances like these will eliminate many blue-collar jobs, replacing them with fewer but more highly skilled jobs. Similar changes are taking place in office automation, where personal computers, word processing, and management information system (MIS) continue to change the nature of office work.

The explosive growth of information technology linked to the internet has ushered in many changes throughout the organisation. One of the major changes led by information technology is that it has hastened what experts call the "**fall of hierarchy**", i.e., managers depend less and less on yesterday's "stick-to-the -chain-of-command approach," to their organizing function.

This is so because earlier it used to be, if one wanted information, one had to go up, over and down through the organisation. Now, one just taps in. That's what broke down the hierarchy. Now, employees do not need to be present a definite work place.

Instead, they can work from their own places/ residences through the net. This has given genesis to a new breed of organizations, called '**virtual organizations**.'

3. Globalization

The New Economic Policy, 1991 has, among other things, globalised the Indian economy. There has been a growing tendency among business firms to extend their sales or manufacturing to new markets aboard. The rate of globalization in the past few years in India has been nothing short of phenomenal.

Globalization increases competition in the international business. Firms that formerly competed only with local firms, now have to compete with foreign firms/competitors. Thus, the world has become a global market where competition is a two-way street.

Globalization has given genesis to the multinational corporations (MNCs). The MNCs are characterised by their cultural diversities, intensified competition, variations in business practices and so on. As an international business expert puts it, 'the bottom line is that the growing integration of the world economy into a single, huge market place is increasing the intensity of competition in a wide range of manufacturing and service industries.

Given these conditions, from tapping the global labour force to formulating selection, training and compensation policies for expatriate employees have posed major challenges for HRM in the next few years. This has underlined the need for studying and understanding HRM of multinational organizations or international organizations separately.

4. Organisational Restructuring

Organisational restructuring is used to make the organisation competitive. From this point of view, mergers and acquisitions of firms have become common forms of restructuring to ensure organisational competitiveness. The mega-mergers in the banking, telecommunications and petroleum companies have been very visible in our country. Downsizing is yet another form of organisational restructuring.

As a part of the organisational changes, many organizations have "right sized" themselves by various ways like eliminating layers of managers, closing facilities, merging with other organizations, or out placing workers. There has been a practice to flatten organizations by removing several layers of management and to improve productivity, quality, and service while also reducing costs. Whatever is the form of restructuring, jobs are redesigned and people affected.

One of the challenges that HRM faces with organisational restructuring is dealing with the human consequences of change. For example, the human cost associated with downsizing has been much debated and discussed in the popular press. As such, HRM needs to focus on the changed scenario uniquely and that is not so simple. Thus, management of HR activities has become crucial for HR managers.

5. Changing Nature of Work

Along with changes in technology and globalization, the nature of jobs and work has also changed. For example, technological changes like introduction of fax machines, information technology, and personal computers have allowed companies to relocate operations to locations with lower wages. There is also a trend toward increased use of temporary or part-time workers in organizations.

One most significant change in the nature of work is that it has changed from manual to mental/ knowledge work. In this context, the management expert Peter Drucker's views are worth citing. He said that the typical business will soon bear little resemblance to the typical manufacturing company of 30 years ago.

The typical business will be knowledge-based, an organisation composed largely of specialists who direct and discipline their own performance through organized feedback from colleagues, customers, and headquarter. For this reason, it will be what he calls an information-based organization.

As a result, the organizations are giving and will give growing emphasis on their human capital i.e., the knowledge, education, training, skills, and expertise of employees, the expense of physical capital like equipment, machinery and physical plants This growing emphasis on education and human capital has, among other things, changed the nature of economy as service-oriented economy.

In the changed economic scenario, jobs demand a certain level of expertise that is far beyond that required of most workers 20 or 30 years ago. This means that companies are relying more on employee's creativity and skills, i.e., employee's brain power.

HRP- Objectives, Process & Techniques

Human Resource Planning

HRP is the process by which an organization ensures that it has the **right number** and **kinds of people**, at the **right places**, at the **right time** and that these people are capable of performing their tasks effectively and efficiently. This helps the organization to achieve its overall objectives.

According to Geisler, "Human resource planning is the process which includes forecasting, developing and controlling by which a firm ensures that it has the right number of people, the right kind of people, at the right places, at the right time, doing work for which they are economically most useful."

According to Beach, "Human resource planning is a process of determining and assuming that the organization will have an adequate number of qualified persons, available at the proper time, performing jobs which meet the needs of the enterprise and which provide satisfaction for the individuals involved."

Objectives of Human Resource Planning

Human Resource Planning is the process by which a management determines how an organization should move from its current manpower position to its desired manpower position. Through it, management strives to have the right number and the right kind of people at the right places at the right time. The main objectives of Human Resource Planning are as follows:

(i) To make an inventory of present manpower resources;

(ii) Manpower planning is needed in order to identify areas of surplus personnel or areas in which there is shortage of personnel;

(iii) To forecast future manpower requirements;

(iv) Planning the necessary programs of recruitment, selection, training & development to ensure that future manpower requirements are properly met;

(v) Human Resource Planning is essential because of frequent labour turnover that arises from social & economical factors like voluntary quits, marriage, promotions, etc;

(vi) The present workforce has to be changed in relation to the challenging needs of technology & production;

(vii) To facilitate productivity bargaining;

(viii) To meet the needs of expansion and diversification programmes;

(ix) To link human resource planning with organizational planning;

(x) To ensure higher labour productivity.

Process and Techniques of Human Resource Planning

Human resource planning is a process consisting of five steps. These are analyzing organizational plan, demand forecasting, forecasting supply of human resources, estimating human resource gaps and action planning. These are mentioned below:

1. Analyzing Organizational Plans: First of all, the objectives of the company are analyzed. Plans' relating to production, marketing, finance, mergers and acquisitions give an estimate of man power requirement of future work in an organization. It is also necessary to decide the time horizon for which human resource planning is to be made. Our man power planning must be consistent with organizational planning in order to achieve overall organizational objectives.

2. Demand Forecasting: The common demand forecasting techniques of manpower planning are managerial judgement, ratio trend analysis, work-study method, work force analysis, Delphi method, etc. These are discussed below:

(a) **Managerial Judgement:** Managerial judgement technique is very common technique of demand forecasting. This approach is applied by small as well as large scale organizations. This technique involves two types of approaches i.e. 'bottom-up approach' and 'top-down approach'. Under the **'bottom-up approach'**, line mangers send their departmental requirement of human resources to top management. Top management ultimately forecasts the human resource requirement for the overall organisation on the basis of proposals of departmental heads. Under the **'Top-down approach'**, top management forecasts the human resource requirement for the entire organisation and various departments. This information is supplied to various departmental heads for their review and approval. However, a combination of both the approaches i.e. **'Participative Approach'** should be applied for demand forecasting. Under this approach, top management and departmental heads meet and decide about the future human resource requirement.

(b) **Ratio Trend Analysis:** Under this method future ratios are calculated on the basis of calculated past ratio from past data of a company. Then on the basis of past ratios manpower requirement is estimated. The following example illustrates this method:

Example:

Produced unit in 2009-10	60000 units
Workers worked 2009-10	60
Past ratio	60:60000 or 1: 1000
Estimated production in 2010-11	80000 units
Estimated number of workers in 2010-11	80000 x 1/ 1000 = 80

(c) **Work-Study:** In this method, standard time required per unit of work is determined with the help of time and motion study. This technique can be used when it is possible to apply work measurement to calculate the length of operations and the amount of labour required.

Example:

Planned output for next year: 50000 units

Standard hours per unit: 2

Planned hours required: 50000 x 2 = 100000

Productive hours per worker in the year: 2000

Number of workers required = 100000/ 2000 = 50

(d) **Work Force Analysis:** All the employees may not be available throughout the year due to absenteeism and turnover. Therefore, it is very necessary to make some provision for loss of manpower to avoid the unwarranted situation. If from the work load analysis it is estimated that manpower requirement in a year is 1000, then the actual number of workers needed will be 1000 + 1000 x.10 = 1100. Here 10% has been taken as loss of manpower due to absenteeism and turnover.

(e) **Delphi Method:** It seeks estimates of personnel needs from a group of experts. The HRP experts act as intermediaries, summarize the various responses and report the findings back to the experts. Summaries and surveys are repeated until the experts opinions begin to agree. The agreement reached is the forecast of the personnel needs. There will be no interaction among experts.

(f) **Econometrics Models:** These models are based on mathematical and statistical techniques for estimating future demand. Under these models relationship is established between the dependent variable to be predicted (e.g. manpower/human resources) and the independent variables (e.g., sales, total production, work-load, etc.). Using these models, estimated demand of human resources can be predicted.

3. Supply Forecasting: There are mainly two sources where from organization can get required number of human resources. These are internal source and external source. If the number of requirements is less then organization can fulfill the vacant posts through internal source like promotion, transfer, demotion, etc. If the number of requirements is more then organization can fulfill the vacant posts through external source of recruitment.

4. Estimating Manpower Gaps: Manpower gaps can be identified by comparing demand and supply of manpower after forecast. There may be surplus or deficit of human resources in future. Action plan has to be taken depending upon the situation.

5. Action Planning: Once the manpower gaps have been identified, plans are prepared to bridge these gaps. Plans to meet the surplus manpower may be redeployment, retrenchment, transfer, etc. On the other hand deficit can be checked by selection, promotion, etc.

Job Analysis

In simple terms, job analysis may be understood as a process of collecting information about a job. The process of job analysis results in two sets of data:

(i) Job description and

(ii) Job specification.

Specifically, job analysis involves the following steps:

1. Collecting and recording job information
2. Checking the job information for accuracy.
3. Writing job description based on the information
4. Using the information to determine the skills, abilities and knowledge that are required on the job.
5. Updating the information from time to time.

Methods of Job Analysis

Methods of collecting job analysis information include direct observation, work method analysis, critical incident technique, interview and questionnaire method. These are discussed below:

1. Direct Observation Method: Direct Observation is a method of job analysis to observe and record behaviour / events / activities / tasks / duties when the worker or group engaged in doing the job. Observation method can be effective only when the job analyst is skilled enough to know what is to be observed and how to analyze what is being observed.

2. Work Method Analysis: Work methods analysis is used to describe manual and repetitive production jobs, such as factory or assembly-line jobs. Work methods analysis includes time and motion study and micro-motion analysis.

3. Critical Incident Technique: Critical incident technique is a method of job analysis used to identify work behaviours that classify in good and poor performance. Under this method jobholders are asked to describe critical incidents concerning the job and the incidents so collected are analyzed and classified according to the job areas they describe.

4. Interview Method: Interview method is a useful tool of job analysis to ask questions to both incumbents and supervisors in either an individual or a group setting. Interview includes structured interviews, unstructured interview, and open-ended questions.

5. Questionnaire Method: It includes 6 techniques, which are as follows:

(a) Position Analysis Questionnaire (PAQ Model)

PAQ model is a questionnaire technique of job analysis. It developed by **McCormick**, Jeanneret, and Mecham (1972), is a structured instrument of job analysis to measure job characteristics and relate them to human characteristics. It consists of **195 job elements** that describe generic human work behaviours.

(b) Functional Job Analysis (FJA Model)

FJA model is a technique of job analysis that was developed by the Employment and Training Administration of the United States Department of Labour. It includes 7 scales. Out of seven scales, 3 worker-function scales: measure percentage of time spent with: data, people, things; 1 worker-instruction scale; and remaining 3 scales that measure reasoning, mathematics, and language.

(c) Work Profiling System (WPS Model)

WPS model is a questionnaire technique of job analysis. It is a computer-administered system for job analysis, developed by Saville & Holdsworth, Ltd.

(d) MOSAIC Model

MOSAIC model is a questionnaire technique of job analysis used to collect information from incumbents and supervisors. It contains 151 job tasks rated in terms of importance for effective job performance and 22 competencies rated in terms of importance, and needed proficiency at entry.

(e) Common Metric Questionnaire (CMQ Model)

CMQ model is a technique of job analysis that was developed by Harvey as a "worker-oriented" job analysis instrument designed to have applicability to a broad range of exempt and nonexempt jobs. It includes 41 general questions of background section, 62 questions of contacts with people, 80 items of decision making, 53 items of physical and mechanical activities, 47 items of work setting.

(f) Fleishman Job Analysis System (FJAS Model)

FJAS model is a technique of job analysis that describes jobs from the point of view of the necessary capacities. It includes 52 cognitive, physical, psycho-motor, and sensory ability; each of the categories consists of two parts – an operational and differential definition and a grading scale.

Job Specification

Job specification is a **written statement of qualifications, traits, physical and mental characteristics** that an individual must possess to perform the job duties and discharge responsibilities effectively.

Job Specification Information

The first step in the programme of job specification is to prepare a list of all jobs in the company and where they are located. The second step is to secure and write up information about each of the jobs in a company. Usually this information includes:

1. **Physical Specifications:** Physical specifications include the physical qualifications or physical capacities that vary from job to job. Physical qualifications or capacities include physical features like height, weight, chest, vision, hearing, ability to lift weight, ability to carry weight, health, age, capacity to use or operate machines, tools, equipment, etc.
2. **Mental Specifications:** Mental specifications include ability to perform, arithmetical calculations, to interpret data, information blue prints, to read electrical circuits, ability to plan, reading abilities, scientific abilities, judgment, ability to concentrate, ability to handle variable factors, general intelligence, memory, etc.
3. **Emotional and Social Specifications:** Emotional and social specifications are more important for the post of managers, supervisors, foremen, etc. These include emotional stability, flexibility, social adaptability in human relationships, personal appearance including dress, posture, etc.
4. **Behavioural Specifications:** Behavioural specifications play an important role in selecting the candidates for higher-level jobs in the organizational hierarchy. This specification seeks to describe the acts of managers rather than the traits that cause the acts. These specifications include judgments, research, creativity, teaching ability, maturity trial of conciliation, self-reliance, dominance, etc.

Job Description

Job Description is an important document, which is basically descriptive in nature and contains a statement of job Analysis. It provides both organizational information's (like location in structure, authority, etc.) and functional information (what the work is).

It gives information about the scope of job activities, major responsibilities and positioning of the job in the organization. This information gives the worker, analyst, and supervisor with a clear idea of what the worker must do to meet the demand of the job.

Contents of Job Description

Following are the main content of a job description. It usually consists of following details or data. A statement containing items such as

Job Identification or Organization Position: This includes the job title, alternative title, department, division and plant and code number of the job.

The job title identifies and designates the job properly. The department, division, etc., indicate the name of the department where it is situated and the location give the name of the place.

Job Summary: This serves two important purposes. Firstly it gives additional identification information when a job title is not adequate; and secondly it gives a summary about that particular job.

Job Duties and Responsibilities: This gives a total listing of duties together with some indication of the frequency of occurrence or percentage of time devoted to each major duty.

Relation to Other Jobs: This gives the particular person to locate job in the organization by indicating the job immediately below or above in the job hierarchy.

Supervision: This will give an idea the number of person to be supervised along with their job titles and the extent of supervision.

Machine: It gives information about the tool, machines and equipment to be used.

Working Conditions: It gives us information about the environment in which a jobholder must work.

Hazards: It gives us the nature of risks of life and limb, their possibilities of occurrence, etc.

Selecting Human Resources

Selection

Selection is the process of choosing the best candidate from the numbers of candidate. It is a process of collecting the all necessary information and matching the desired skills with the available skill. It is a process which helps to distinguish best candidate from the normal one. It comes after recruitment.

In the opinion of Koontz et.al, Selection is the process of choosing from among the candidates from within the organizations or from the outside, the most suitable person for the current position or for the future position."

Selection Test

Tests may be classified as follows:

Aptitude Tests: These tests measure the latent ability of a candidate to learn a new job or skill. Such tests are of the following types:

Intelligence Test: This test measures the intellectual capacity of a person. It helps to determine a person's memory, reasoning skill, comprehension, perception, etc.

Mechanical Test: This test measures a person's capacity to learn a particular type of mechanical work. Capacity for spatial visualization, specialized knowledge of techniques, problem solving ability, technical vocabulary, etc. are judged in this test.

Psycho-motor Test: This test measures a person's ability to perform a specific job. It helps to determine mental dexterity or motor ability of a person.

Achievement Tests: These tests measure what a person can do. Such tests are of the following types:

Job Knowledge Test: These are used to judge proficiency in typing, shorthand, adding machines, dictating and transcribing machines, etc. Such tests are useful in the selection of typists, stenographers, office workers and the alike.

Work Sample Tests: In this test, a candidate is given a piece of work to perform in order to judge the efficiency of the candidate.

Personality Tests: These are used to judge the psychological makeup of a person. These are of three types:

Objective Test: This test measures neurotic tendencies, dominance-submission and self confidence.

Projective Test: In this test, a candidate is asked to project his own interpretation on to a certain stimuli like ambiguous pictures, figures, etc. There ways he responds to these stimuli reflect his own values, motives and personality.

Situation Test: This test measures a candidate's reaction when placed in a peculiar situation. It determines the ability to under grow stress and his demonstration under pressure.

Interest Test

This test determines a candidate's likes and dislikes in relation to work. This test is used to discover a person's areas of interest and to identify the kind of work that will satisfy him.

Process / Steps in Selection

1. Preliminary Interview: The purpose of preliminary interviews is basically to eliminate unqualified applications based on information supplied in application forms. The basic objective is to reject misfits. On the other hands preliminary interviews is often called a courtesy interview and is a good public relations exercise.

2. Selection Tests: Jobseekers who past the preliminary interviews are called for tests. There are various types of tests conducted depending upon the jobs and the company. These tests can be Aptitude Tests, Personality Tests, and Ability Tests and are conducted to judge how well an individual can perform tasks related to the job. Besides this there are some other tests also like **Interest Tests (activity preferences), Graphology Test (Handwriting)**, Medical Tests, Psychometric Tests, etc.

3. Employment Interview: The next step in selection is employment interview. Here interview is a formal and in-depth conversation between applicant's acceptability. It is considered to be an excellent selection device. Interviews can be One-to-One, Panel Interview, or Sequential Interviews. Besides there can be Structured and Unstructured interviews, Behavioural Interviews, Stress Interviews.

4. Reference & Background Checks: Reference checks and background checks are conducted to verify the information provided by the candidates. Reference checks can be done through formal letters, telephone conversations. However it is merely a formality and selections decisions are seldom affected by it.

5. Selection Decision: After obtaining all the information, the most critical step is the selection decision is to be made. The final decision has to be made out of applicants who have passed preliminary interviews, tests, final interviews and reference checks. The views of line managers are considered generally because it is the line manager who is responsible for the performance of the new employee.

6. Physical Examination: After the selection decision is made, the candidate is required to undergo a physical fitness test. A job offer is often contingent upon the candidate passing the physical examination.

7. Job Offer: The next step in selection process is job offer to those applicants who have crossed all the previous hurdles. It is made by way of letter of appointment.

Selection Error

The False Positive Error

An organization that makes a false positive error incurs three types of costs. The first type of costs are those incurred while the person is employed. These can be the result of production or profit losses, damaged public relations or company reputation, accidents due to ineptitude or negligence, absenteeism, etc. The second types of costs are those associated with training, transfer, or terminating the employee. Costs of replacing the employee, the third type of cost, include costs of recruiting, selecting, and training a replacement. Generally, the more important the job, the greater the costs of the selection error.

The False Negative Error

In the case of false negative error, an applicant who would have succeeded is rejected because failure was predicted. Most false negative selection errors go unnoticed, except when the applicant is a member of a protected class and files a discrimination charge. Costs associated with this type of error are generally difficult to estimate.

A situation in which the impact of both false positive and false negative selection errors can be detected and measured, however, is in professional sports such as football and basketball. Here, coaches and scouts analyze game films, physical statistics, scouting reports, and other data and decide whether they wish to draft a particular player. If they draft the player and his performance fails to meet expectations, a false positive selection error has occurred. Suppose, however, a team decides against drafting a player and another team chooses the individual. If the player subsequently turns out to be a star, the first team's rejection represents a false negative selection error.

Induction, Training & Development

Concept of Induction

Once an employee is selected and placed on an appropriate job, the process of familiarizing him with the job and the organization is known as induction or orientation.

"Induction is the process of receiving and welcoming an employee when he first joins the company and giving him basic information he needs to settle down quickly and happily and starts work."

Objectives of Induction

An induction programme is designed to achieve the following objectives:

(i) To help the new comer to overcome his shyness and overcome his nervousness in meeting new people in a new environment.

(ii) To give new comer necessary information such as location of a café, rest period etc.

(iii) To build new employee's confidence in the organization.

(iv) It helps in reducing labor turnover and absenteeism.

(v) It reduces confusion and develops healthy relations in the organization.

(vi) To ensure that the new comer do not form false impression and negative attitude towards the organization.

(vii) To develop among the new comer a sense of belonging and loyalty to the organization.

Training Programmes for Workers

Training is a process of learning a sequence of programmed behaviour. It is the application of knowledge & gives people an awareness of rules & procedures to guide their behaviour. It helps in bringing about positive change in the **knowledge, skills & attitudes** of employees.

According to Jucious, "training is any process by which the aptitudes, skills and abilities of employees to perform specific jobs are increased".

Training plays a significant role in human resource development. The most widely used methods of training used by organizations are classified into two categories: on the job training & off the job training.

On the Job Training

On the job training methods are those which are given to the employees within the everyday working of a concern. It is a simple and cost-effective training method. The inproficient as well as semi- proficient employees can be well trained by using such training method. The employees are trained in actual working scenario. The motto of such training is "learning by doing." Instances of such on-job training methods are job-rotation, coaching, temporary promotions, etc.

1. Coaching: Coaching is learning by doing. In this, the superior guides his sub-ordinates & gives him/her job instructions. The superior points out the mistakes & gives suggestions for improvement.

2. Job Rotation: In this method, the trainees move from one job to another, so that he/she should be able to perform all types of jobs. E.g. In banking industry, employees are trained for both back-end & front-end jobs. In case of emergency, (absenteeism or resignation), any employee would be able to perform any type of job.

3. Special Projects: Under this method, a trainee is assigned a project that is closely related to the objectives of his department. The trainee will study the problem and make recommendations upon it.

4. Committee Assignments: Under this method, an adhoc committee is constituted and is assigned a subject to discuss and make recommendations. The committee will make a study of the problem and present its suggestions to the departmental head.

Off the Job Training

Off the job training methods are those in which training is provided away from the actual working condition. It is generally used in case of new employees. Instances of off the job training methods are workshops, seminars, conferences, etc. Such method is costly and is effective if and only if large number of employees have to be trained within a short time period. Off the job training is also called as vestibule training, i.e., the employees are trained in a separate area (may be a hall, entrance, reception area, etc. known as a vestibule) where the actual working conditions are duplicated. These are stated below:

1. Role Playing: It is just like acting out a given role as in a stage play. In this method of training, the trainees are required to enact defined roles on the basis of oral or written description of a particular situation. Role playing is a useful method of developing interpersonal or human relations skills. It helps to bring out desired changes in attitudes and behaviour. Role playing creates an environment similar to real work situation. This is also known as simulation. Two other methods based on simulation are in basket and management games.

2. In basket Exercise: In this method, the trainee is given a basket or tray of papers related to his functional area. Trainee is expected to give his recommendations after studying all papers. The recommendations of different trainees are compared and conclusions are arrived at.

3. Management Games: Management games are designed to be representative of real life situations. These are classroom exercise in which teams of individuals compete against one another in order to achieve a given objective. In these exercises, the participants play a dynamic role and enrich their skills through involvement and simulated exercise.

4. Sensitivity Training: This method is also called T-Group training. The purpose of this method is to develop interpersonal competence, increase self awareness and sharpen teamwork skills. According to Chris Argyris, "sensitivity training is a group experience designed to provide maximum possible opportunity for the individuals to expose their behaviour, give and receive feedback, experiment with new behaviour and develop awareness of self and of others".

5. Lectures or Conferences: This approach is well adapted to convey specific information, rules, procedures or methods. This method is useful, where the information is to be shared among a large number of trainees. The cost per trainee is low in this method.

6. Case Study Method: It presents an in depth description of a particular problem an employee might encounter on the job. The employee attempts to find and analyze the problem, evaluate alternative courses of action & decide what course of action would be most satisfactory.

Identifying Training Needs

In order to identify training needs, the gap between the existing and required levels of knowledge, skills, performance and aptitudes should be specified. Training needs can be identified through the following types of analysis.

1. Organizational Analysis: It involves a study of the entire organization in terms of its objectives, its resources and the utilization of these resources in order to achieve stated objectives and its interaction pattern with environment. The important elements that are closely examined in this connection are:

(a) Analysis of Objectives

This is a study of short term and long term objectives and the strategies followed at various levels to meet these objectives.

(b) Resource Utilization Analysis

How the various organizational resources are put to use is the main focus of this study. The contributions of various departments are also examined by establishing efficiency indices for each unit. This is done to find out comparative labour cost, whether a unit is under manned or over manned.

(c) Environmental Scanning

Here the economic, political, socio-cultural and technological environment of the organization is examined.

(d) Organizational Climate Analysis

The climate of an organization speaks about the attitudes of members towards work, company policies, supervisors, etc. Absenteeism, turnover ratios generally reflect the prevailing employee attitudes.

2. Task Analysis: This is a detailed examination of a job, its components, its various operations and conditions under which it has to be performed. The focus is given on the roles played by an individual and the training needed to perform such roles. The objective is to find out how the various tasks be performed and what kind of skills, knowledge and attitudes are needed to the job needs. Questionnaire, interviews, reports, tests and observation method are generally used to collect job related information from time to time.

3. Manpower Analysis: Here the focus is on the individual in a given job. There are three issues to be resolved through manpower analysis. First, we try to find whether performances are satisfactory and training is required. Second, whether the employee is capable of being trained and the specific areas in which training is required. Finally, we need to state whether poor performances on the job need to be replaced by those who can do the job. Other options to training such as modifications in the job or processes should also be looked into. Personal observation, performance reviews, supervisory reports, diagnostic tests help in collecting the required information and select particular training options that try to improve the performance of individual workers.

Management Development Programmes

Management Development: Any attempt to improve current or future management performance by imparting knowledge, changing attitudes, or increasing skills. The ultimate aim is of course, to enhance the future performance of the company itself.

Managerial On-The-Job Training

Job Rotation: A management training technique that involves moving a trainee from department to department to broaden his or her experience and identify strong and weak points. It is a process of moving management trainees from department to department to broaden their understanding of all parts of the business and to test their abilities. The trainee often a recent college graduate may spend several months in each department, but more commonly gets fully involved in its operations. The trainee thus learns the department's business by actually doing it, while discovering what jobs he or she prefers.

Coaching/Understudy Approach: Here the trainee works directly works directly with a senior manager or with the person he or she is to replace; the latter is responsible for the trainee's coaching. Normally, the understudy relieves the executive of certain responsibilities, giving the trainee a chance to learn the job.

Action Learning: These programs give managers and others released time to work full time on projects, analyzing and solving problems in departments other than their own. Trainees meet periodically in four or five person's project groups to discuss their findings. Several trainees may work together as a project group, or compare notes and discuss each other's projects.

Off-The-Job Training and Development Techniques

The Case Study Method: As most everyone knows, the case study method presents a trainee with a written description of an organizational problems. Case study is a developmental method in which the manager is presented with a written description of an organizational problem to diagnose and solve. The person then analyses the cause, diagnoses the problem, and presents his or her findings and solutions in a discussion with other trainees. The script of the case study includes themes, background stories, detailed personnel histories and role playing instructions.

Management Games: A development technique in which teams of managers compete by making computerized decisions regarding realistic but simulated situations. Here trainees are split in to five to ten groups and each should compete with others in a stimulated market place. These things help trainees to develop their problem solving skills, as well as to focus attention on planning rather than just putting out fires.

Outside Seminars: Many companies and universities offer web based and traditional management development seminars and conferences.

Role Playing: A training technique in which trainees act out parts in a realistic management situations. Role playing is to create a realistic situation and then have the trainees assume the parts or roles of specific persons in that situation.

Behaviour Modeling: A training technique in which trainees are first shown good management techniques in a film , are asked to play roles in a simulated situation , and are then given feedback and praise by their supervisor. These modeling involves **1)** showing trainees the right (model) way of doing something **2)** letting trainees practice that way and then **3)** giving feedback on the trainees on the trainee's performance. The basic behavior modeling procedure is **a)** Modeling **b)** Role playing **c)** Social reinforcement **d)** Transfer of training.

Corporate Universities and In-House Development Centers: Many firms, particularly larger ones, establish in house development centers. A company based method for exposing prospective managers to realistic exercises to develop improved management skills.

Evaluation of Training

The process of examining a training program is called training evaluation. Training evaluation checks whether training has had the desired effect. Training evaluation ensures that whether candidates are able to implement their learning in their respective workplaces, or to the regular work routines

The various methods of training evaluation are:

- Observation
- Questionnaire
- Interview
- Self diaries
- Self recording of specific incidents

Types of Evaluation

Evaluating the Training addresses how one determines whether the goals or objectives were met and what impact the training had on actual performance on the job.

Generally there are four kinds of standard training evaluation:

1. Formative
2. Process
3. Outcome
4. Impact

1. Formative evaluation provides ongoing feedback to the curriculum designers and developers to ensure that what is being created really meets the needs of the intended audience.
2. Process evaluation provides information about what occurs during training. This includes giving and receiving verbal feedback.
3. Outcome evaluation determines whether or not the desired results (e.g., what participants are doing) of applying new skills were achieved in the short-term.
4. Impact determines how the results of the training affect the strategic goal

Kirkpatrick's Four-Level Training Evaluation Model

Donald Kirkpatrick, Professor Emeritus at the University of Wisconsin and past president of the American Society for Training and Development (ASTD), first published his Four-Level Training Evaluation Model in **1959**, in the **US Training and Development Journal**.

The model was then updated in 1975, and again in 1994, when he published his best-known work, "Evaluating Training Programs."

The four levels are:

1. Reaction
2. Learning
3. Behaviour
4. Results

Let's look at each level in greater detail.

Level 1: Reaction

This level measures how your trainees (the people being trained), reacted to the training. Obviously, you want them to feel that the training was a valuable experience, and you want them to feel good about the instructor, the topic, the material, its presentation, and the venue.

It's important to measure reaction; because it helps you understand how well the training was received by your audience. It also helps you improve the training for future trainees, including identifying important areas or topics that are missing from the training.

Level 2: Learning

At level 2, you measure what your trainees have learned. How much has their knowledge increased as a result of the training?

When you planned the training session, you hopefully started with a list of specific learning objectives: these should be the starting point for your measurement. Keep in mind that you can measure learning in different ways depending on these objectives, and depending on whether you're interested in changes to knowledge, skills, or attitude.

It's important to measure this, because knowing what your trainees are learning and what they aren't will help you improve future training.

Level 3: Behaviour

At this level, you evaluate how far your trainees have changed their behaviour, based on the training they received. Specifically, this looks at how trainees **apply** the information.

It's important to realize that behaviour can only change if conditions are favourable. For instance, imagine you have skipped measurement at the first two Kirkpatrick levels and, when looking at your group's behaviour, you determine that no behaviour change has taken place. Therefore, you assume that your trainees have not learned anything and that the training was ineffective.

However, just because behaviour has not changed, it doesn't mean that trainees have not learned anything. Perhaps their boss won't let them apply new knowledge. Or, maybe they have learned everything you taught, but they have no desire to apply the knowledge themselves.

Level 4: Results

At this level, you analyze the final results of your training. This includes outcomes that you or your organization have determined to be good for business, good for the employees, or good for the bottom line.

Training & Development

The major differences between training and development are as under:

(i) Training is a learning process for new employees in which they get to know about the key skills required for the job. Development is the training process for the existing employees for their all round development.

(ii) Training is a short-term process i.e. 3 to 6 months, but development is a continuous process, and so it is for the long term.

(iii) Training focuses on developing skill and knowledge for the current job. Unlike, the development which focuses on the building knowledge, understanding and competencies for overcoming with future challenges.

(iv) Training has a limited scope; it is specific job oriented. On the other hand, development is career oriented and hence its scope is comparatively wider than training.

(v) In training, the trainees get a trainer who instructs them at the time of training. In contrast to development, in which the manager self-directs himself for the future assignments.

(vi) Many individuals collectively attend the training program. Development is a self-assessment procedure, and hence, one person himself is responsible for one's development.

Exit Policy & Implications

The term 'exit' is the obverse of the term 'entry' into industry. It refers to the right or ability of an industrial unit to withdraw from or leave an industry or in other words to close down. The proposal to introduce an exit policy was first mooted in 1991 when it was felt that without labour market flexibility, efficient industrialization would be difficult to achieve. The need for such a policy arises as a result of modernization, technology up gradation, restructuring as well as closure of industrial units. Such a policy will allow employers to shift workers from one unit to another and also retrench excess labour. In India, the Industrial Disputes Act, 1947 puts restrictions on employers in the matter of reducing excess staff by retrenchment, by closure of establishments and the retrenchment process involved lot of legalities and complex procedures. Any plans of retrenchment and reduction of staff and workforce are subjected to strong opposition by trade unions.

Implications of Exit Policy

The rationale for a proper exit policy is based on the following considerations:

(i) In the liberalized regime, freedom to enter and exit will attract more investment. Higher investment implies more employment.

(ii) If employer enjoys the right to streamline – technological and organizational – the enterprise productivity levels will improve.

(iii) Low labour productivity and over manning are attributable factors for rampant industrial sickness. This can be overcome with a judicious exit policy.

(iv) With exit policy, government will be in a position to reduce the fiscal burden on its exchequer thereby divert those funds create productive employment opportunities.

Performance Appraisal

According to Flippo, a prominent personality in the field of Human resources, "performance appraisal is the systematic, periodic and an impartial rating of an employee's excellence in the matters pertaining to his present job and his potential for a better job." Performance appraisal is a systematic way of reviewing and assessing the performance of an employee during a given period of time and planning for his future.

Process of Performance Appraisal

The steps in the performance appraisal process are discussed below:

1. Establishing Performance Standards: The first step in the process of performance appraisal is the setting up of the standards which will be used to as the base to compare the actual performance of the employees. This step requires setting the criteria to judge the performance of the employees as successful or unsuccessful and the degrees of their contribution to the organizational goals and objectives. The standards set should be clear, easily understandable and in measurable terms. In case the performance of the employee cannot be measured, great care should be taken to describe the standards

2. Communicating the Standards: Once set, it is the responsibility of the management to communicate the standards to all the employees of the organization. The employees should be informed and the standards should be clearly explained to them. This will help them to understand their roles and to know what exactly is expected from them. The standards should also be communicated to the appraisers or the evaluators and if required, the standards can also be modified at this stage itself according to the relevant feedback from the employees or the evaluators.

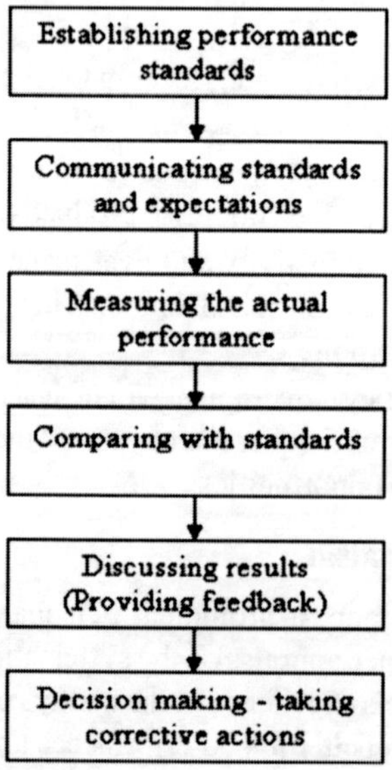

Performance Appraisal Process

3. Measuring the Actual Performance: The most difficult part of the Performance appraisal process is measuring the actual performance of the employees that is the work done by the employees during the specified period of time. It is a continuous process which involves monitoring the performance throughout the year. This stage requires the careful selection of the appropriate techniques of measurement, taking care that personal bias does not affect the outcome of the process and providing assistance rather than interfering in an employees work.

4. Comparing the Actual with the Desired Performance: The actual performance is compared with the desired or the standard performance. The comparison tells the deviations in the performance of the employees from the standards set. The result can show the actual performance being more than the desired performance or, the actual performance being less than the desired performance depicting a negative deviation in the organizational performance. It includes recalling, evaluating and analysis of data related to the employees' performance.

5. Discussing Results: The result of the appraisal is communicated and discussed with the employees on one-to-one basis. The focus of this discussion is on communication and listening. The results, the problems and the possible solutions are discussed with the aim of problem solving and reaching consensus. The feedback should be given with a positive attitude as this can have an effect on the employees' future performance. The purpose of the meeting should be to solve the problems faced and motivate the employees to perform better.

6. Decision Making: The last step of the process is to take decisions which can be taken either to improve the performance of the employees, take the required corrective actions, or the related HR decisions like rewards, promotions, demotions, transfers etc.

Errors in Performance Appraisal

The common errors in performance are as follows:

(i) Central Tendency Error: Some supervisors tend to rank all employees at about average, regardless of an employee's performance. A supervisor who believes in never rating an employee as excellent is demonstrating central tendency error.

(ii) Contrast Error: Supervisors who rate subordinates as they compare against each other rather than how they compare against the performance standards commit contrast error. This error can cause an employee who is performing average against performance standards to rate high because his peers are under performing.

(iii) False Attribution: False attribution is the tendency to attribute bad performance to internal causes and good performance to external causes. In other words, if an employee performs well, it's because the employee had help, such as a good leader; and if the employee performs badly, it's because the employee did something wrong, such as procrastinate.

(iv) Halo Effect: The halo effect is when a supervisor forms a positive impression of an employee's skill in one area and then gives her high ratings across all rating criteria. Humans tend to view some traits as more important than other traits. When a supervisor rates employees with the traits that he deems more important higher in all rating areas than employees who do not possess those traits, the supervisor is committing the halo effect error.

(v) Leniency Error: Leniency error is the tendency of a supervisor to rate an employee higher than what his performance warrants. Reasons that a supervisor might do this could include avoiding confrontations, or feeling that by giving the employee a high rating, he will work harder to live up to the rating.

(vi) Perceived Meaning: Perceived meaning becomes an issue when appraisers do not agree on the meaning of the rating criteria. For example, one supervisor may perceive an employee's constant reporting of problems as initiative, while another supervisor may feel this behaviour demonstrates dependence on supervisory assistance instead of initiative.

(vii) Recency Error: Recency error happens when a supervisor uses recent events to rate the employee. This usually occurs due to a lack of documentation of the employee's performance over the course of the entire performance appraisal period. An employee who performed highly over the course of the appraisal period may be rated low if the most recent events where negative.

(viii) Severity Error: Severity error is the opposite of leniency error. In severity error, a supervisor tends to rate an employee lower than what her performance warrants. A potential cause of the error could be the use of unrealistic standards of comparison, such as the supervisor rating a new employee against himself. In this scenario, the supervisor forgets that it took time to reach the level of performance he operates at, and a new employee would not have had enough time to develop to that level.

(ix) Stereotyping: Stereotyping is the tendency to apply the same generalizations to all members of specific social groups. One of the more common types of stereotyping that occur in the workplace is gender stereotyping. Research conducted by Madeline Heilman, a professor of psychology at NYU, suggests that women are often evaluated more negatively than men, even when both are trained to do a job the same way.

(x) Horn Effect: In this case only the negative qualities of the employee are considered and based on this appraisal is done. This again will not help the organization because such appraisal may not present a true picture about the employee.

(xi) Spillover Effect: In this case the employee is judged positively or negatively by the boss depending upon the past performance. Therefore although the employee may have improved performance, he may still not get the benefit.

Methods of Performance Appraisal

As such, there is no single appraisal method accepted and used by all organizations to measure their employees' performance. All the methods of appraisal devised so far have been classified differently by different authors. A more widely used classification of appraisal methods into two categories, viz., traditional methods and modern methods, is given by Strauss and Sayles. The methods of performance appraisal can be classified into two categories:

(i) Traditional methods and

(ii) Modern methods

(i) Traditional Methods

Traditional methods of performance appraisal are discussed below:

1. Essay Method: This traditional form of appraisal, also known as "Free Form method" involves a description of the performance of an employee by his superior. The description is an evaluation of the performance of any individual based on the facts and often includes examples and evidences to support the information. A major drawback of the method is the inseparability of the bias of the evaluator.

2. Straight Ranking Method: This is one of the oldest and simplest techniques of performance appraisal. In this method, the appraiser ranks the employees from the best to the poorest on the basis of their overall performance. It is quite useful for a comparative evaluation. The disadvantages of this method are that i) the task of ranking is difficult when a large number of employees are rated, ii) it does not tell that how much better or worse one is than another.

3. Paired Comparison Method: A better technique of comparison than the straight ranking method, this method compares each employee with all others in the group, one at a time. After all the comparisons on the basis of the overall comparisons, the employees are given the final rankings. One major disadvantage of this method is that the method can become unwieldy when large numbers of employees are being compared.

4. Critical Incidents Method: In this method of Performance appraisal, the evaluator rates the employee on the basis of critical events and how the employee behaved during those incidents. It includes both negative and positive points. The drawback of this method is that the supervisor has to note down the critical incidents and the employee behaviour as and when they occur.

5. Field Review Method: In this method, a senior member of the HR department or a training officer discusses and interviews the supervisors to evaluate and rate their respective subordinates. A major drawback of this method is that it is a very time consuming method. But this method helps to reduce the superiors' personal bias.

6. Checklist Method: The rater is given a checklist of the descriptions of the behaviour of the employees on job. The checklist contains a list of statements on the basis of which the rater describes the on the job performance of the employees.

7. Graphic Rating Scale: In this method, an employee's quality and quantity of work is assessed in a graphic scale indicating different degrees of a particular trait. The factors taken into consideration include both the personal characteristics and characteristics related to the on the job performance of the employees. For example a trait like Job Knowledge may be judged on the range of average, above average, outstanding or unsatisfactory.

8. Forced Distribution Method: This method was evolved by Tiffen to eliminate the central tendency of rating most of the employees at a higher end of the scale. To eliminate the element of bias from the rater's ratings, the evaluator is asked to distribute the employees in some fixed categories of ratings like on a normal distribution curve. The rater chooses the appropriate fit for the categories on his own discretion.

(ii) Modern Methods

Modern methods of performance appraisal are discussed below:

1. Assessment Centres: An assessment centre typically involves the use of methods like social/informal events, tests and exercises, assignments being given to a group of employees to assess their competencies to take higher responsibilities in the future. Generally, employees are given an assignment similar to the job they would be expected to perform if promoted. The trained evaluators observe and evaluate employees as they perform the assigned jobs and are evaluated on job related characteristics.

The major competencies that are judged in assessment centres are interpersonal skills, intellectual capability, planning and organizing capabilities, motivation, career orientation etc. assessment centres are also an effective way to determine the training and development needs of the targeted employees.

2. Behavioural Anchored Rating Scale: Behaviorally Anchored Rating Scales (BARS) is a relatively new technique which combines the graphic rating scale and critical incidents method. It consists of predetermined critical areas of job performance or sets of behavioral statements describing important job performance qualities as good or bad (for e.g. the qualities like inter personal relationships, adaptability and reliability, job knowledge, etc). These statements are developed from critical incidents.

In this method, an employee's actual job behaviour is judged against the desired behaviour by recording and comparing the behaviour with BARS. Developing and practicing BARS requires expert knowledge.

A behaviorally anchored rating scale is a rating scale that is anchored with specific behavioral examples of good or poor performance. Because of the anchors, which are based on the dimensions of performance illustrated by critical incidents, a BARS combines the benefits of narratives, critical incident, and quantified scales. There are five steps required for developing a BARS. Each step is explained below.

Step 1: Generate Critical Incidents: In this step, people who know the job are asked to describe specific illustrations of effective and ineffective performance.

Step 2: Develop Performance Dimensions: The people who know the job are then asked to cluster the incidents into a smaller set of performance dimensions and to define each dimension with a name.

Step 3: Reallocate Incidents: Another group of people, who also know the job, should reallocate the original critical incidents. They will receive the cluster definitions and the list of critical incidents. They will then reassign each incident into the cluster they think it fits best. If the assignments made by the first group and second group match well, then that critical incident is retained.

Step 4: Scale the Incidents: The second group then rates the behavior described by the incident as to how effectively or ineffectively it represents performance on the dimension.

Step 5: Develop a Final Instrument: Six or seven of the incidents as the dimension's behavioural anchors.

3. Human Resource Accounting Method: Human resources are valuable assets for every organization. Human resource accounting method tries to find the relative worth of these assets in the terms of money. In this method the Performance appraisal of the employees is judged in terms of cost and contribution of the employees. The cost of employees include all the expenses incurred on them like their compensation, recruitment and selection costs, induction and training costs etc whereas their contribution includes the total value added (in monetary terms). The difference between the cost and the contribution will be the performance of the employees. Ideally, the contribution of the employees should be greater than the cost incurred on them.

4. 360° Performance Appraisal Method: 360 degree feedback, also known as 'multi-rater feedback', is the most comprehensive appraisal where the feedback about the employees' performance comes from all the sources that come in contact with the employee on his job.

360 degree respondents for an employee can be his/her peers, managers (i.e. superior), subordinates, team members, customers, suppliers/ vendors - anyone who comes into contact with the employee and can provide valuable insights and information or feedback regarding the "on-the-job" performance of the employee.

360 degree appraisal has four integral components:

1. Self appraisal
2. Superior's appraisal
3. Subordinate's appraisal
4. Peer appraisal.

Self appraisal gives a chance to the employee to look at his/her strengths and weaknesses, his achievements, and judge his own performance. Superior's appraisal forms the traditional part of the 360 degree performance appraisal where the employees' responsibilities and actual performance is rated by the superior. Subordinates appraisal gives a chance to judge the employee on the parameters like communication and motivating abilities, superior's ability to delegate the work, leadership qualities etc. Also known as internal customers, the correct feedback given by peers can help to find employees' abilities to work in a team, co-operation and sensitivity towards others.

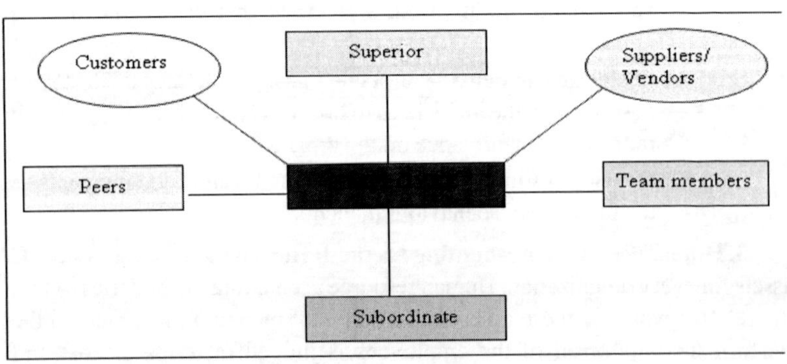

360 degree Performance Appraisal Technique

Self assessment is an indispensable part of 360 degree appraisals and therefore 360 degree Performance appraisal have high employee involvement and also have the strongest impact on behavior and performance. It provides a "360-degree review" of the employees' performance and is considered to be one of the most credible performance appraisal methods.360 degree performance appraisal is also a powerful developmental tool because when conducted at regular intervals (say yearly) it helps to keep a track of the changes others' perceptions about the employees. A 360 degree appraisal is generally found more suitable for the managers as it helps to assess their leadership and managing styles. This technique is being effectively used across the globe for performance appraisals. Some of the organizations following it are Wipro, Infosys, and Reliance Industries etc.

5. Management by Objectives Method: According to George Odiome, MBO is "a process whereby superior and subordinate managers of an Organisation jointly define its common goals, define each individual's major areas of responsibility in terms Of results expected of him and use these measures as guides for operating the unit and assessing the contribution of each of its members." According to John Humble, MBO is "a dynamic system which seeks to integrate the company's needs to clarify and achieve its profits and growth goals with the manager's need to contribute and develop himself. It is a demanding and rewarding style of managing a business."

6. 720° Performance Appraisal Method: In this system, we provide a feedback after the original / main 360 degree appraisal. This is only performed in exceptional cases. Some managers feel that doing "one" comprehensive 360 degree is not complete in itself in some cases.

These managers feel that an effective procedure to measure improvements and receive feedback is essential for the success of an appraisal.

This gives a pre and a post intervention results. The pre-intervention results set the baseline. The development program is then carried out to improve the participants' behaviour through training / development/ education.

The post intervention appraisal then shows the amount of improvement in the participant. This pre and post intervention in the performance appraisal system is the 720 degree system.

Potential Assessment

The potential appraisal refers to the appraisal i.e. identification of the **hidden talents and skills** of a person. The person might or might not be aware of them. Potential appraisal is a future oriented appraisal whose main objective is to identify and evaluate the potential of the employees to assume higher positions and responsibilities in the organizational hierarchy. Many organizations consider and use potential appraisal as a part of the performance appraisal processes. Potential appraisal helps to identify what can happen in future so that it can be guided and directed towards the achievement of individual and organizational growth and goals. Therefore, potential should be included as a part of the Performance appraisal in organizations.

The purposes of a potential review are:

(i) To inform employees of their future prospects;

(ii) To enable the organisation to draft a management succession programme;

(iii) To update training and recruitment activities;

(iv) To advise employees about the work to be done to enhance their career opportunities.

Techniques of Potential Appraisal

Self – appraisals

Peer appraisals

Superior appraisals

MBO

Psychological and psychometric tests

Management games like role playing

Leadership exercises, etc.

The following are some of the requirements and steps to be followed when introducing a potential appraisal system:

Role Description: A good potential appraisal system would be based on clarity of roles and functions associated with the different roles in an organisation. This requires extensive job descriptions to be made available for each job. These job descriptions should spell out the various functions involved in performing the job.

Qualities Required: Besides job descriptions, it is necessary to have a detailed list of qualities required to perform each of these functions. These qualities may be broadly divided into four categories -

(i) Technical knowledge and skills,

(ii) Managerial capabilities and qualities,

(iii) Behavioural capabilities, and

(iv) Conceptual capabilities.

Indicators of Qualities: A good potential appraisal system besides listing down the functions and qualities would also have various mechanisms for judging these qualities in a given individual. Some of the mechanisms for judging these qualities are -

(i) Rating by others,

(ii) Psychological tests,
(iii) Simulation games and exercises,
(iv) Performance appraisal records.

Organizing the System: Once the functions, the qualities required to perform these functions, indicators of these qualities, and mechanisms for generating these indicators are clear, the organisation is in a sound position to establish and operate the potential appraisal system. Such establishment requires clarity in organisational policies and systematization of its efforts.

Feedback: If the organisation believes in the development of human resources, it should attempt to generate a climate of openness. Such a climate is required for helping the employees to understand their strengths and weaknesses and to create opportunities for development. A good potential appraisal system should provide an opportunity for every employee to know the results of assessment. He should be helped to understand the qualities actually required for performing the role for which he thinks he has the potential, the mechanisms used by the organisation to appraise his potential, and the results of such an appraisal.

A good potential appraisal system provides opportunities continuously for the employee to know his strengths and weaknesses. These are done through periodic counseling and guidance sessions by either the personnel department or the managers concerned. This should enable the employee to develop realistic self-perceptions and plan his own career and development.

Potential Appraisal VS. Performance Appraisal

Potential Appraisal is forward looking process. It includes the possible knowledge, skills, and attitudes the employee may possess for better performance.

Performance appraisal is backward looking process. Any good or worse assessment results of performance appraisal may not be a good factor for potential appraisal. But current performance of an employee could show evidence somewhere whether he/she is flexible for new working conditions.

Job Evaluation

Job evaluation is the output given by job analysis. **Job analysis** illustrates the duties of a job, skills required, authority relationship, conditions of work, and extra pertinent information. Job evaluation in contrast, makes use of information in job analysis to assess each job, determining the relative job value and valuing its components.

In other words, it involves an organized and formal assessment of jobs so as to ascertain the value of one job in relation to another, consequently a wage or salary hierarchy results. It is a procedure by which jobs in an organization are assessed.

When jobs are evaluated, the relative importance of a given set of duties and responsibilities to the organization is assessed. This process is implemented to assist a management to uphold high levels of employee efficiency and employee contentment. If job values are not accurately studied, it is expected that jobs would not be correctly priced. When employees recognize that this is happening, they become discontented. They may leave the organization, or trim down their efforts. Thus, in present world, a huge attention is paid to the worth of the job. According to the International Labour Office (ILO), "job evaluation is an attempt to determine and compare the demands which the normal performance of a particular job makes on normal workers, without taking into account the individual abilities or performance of the workers concerned".

In the words of Kimball and Kimball, "Job evaluation is an effort to determine the relative value of every job in a plant to determine what the fair basic wage for such a job should be".

Methods of Job Evaluation

Job evaluation is the systematic process of assessing and determining the value of jobs performed within the organization and the relative value or worth of the employee's efforts. The four major methods of job evaluations are job ranking, job classification, factor comparison, and the point method.

Job Ranking: The job ranking method is the simplest and easiest job evaluation method; jobs and the employees who perform those jobs are ranked from highest to lowest depending on their quality and value to the organization.

The variation in payment of salaries depends on the variation of the nature of the job performed by the employees. The ranking method is simple to understand and practice and it is best suited for a small organization. Its simplicity, however, works to its disadvantage in big organizations because rankings are difficult to develop in a large, complex organization. Moreover, this kind of ranking is highly subjective in nature and may offend many employees. Therefore, a more scientific and fruitful way of job evaluation is called for.

Job Classification: The job classification method uses job classes or job groups to provide more customization in the evaluation. This method also uses scales to measure performance rather than comparing and ranking employees.

Factor Comparison: The factor comparison method is more scientific and complex than any other method. Each job is ranked according to a specific set of factors, such as physical effort, mental effort, or responsibility, all of which have predetermined weights indicating their importance to success.

The **steps** involved in factor comparison method may be briefly stated thus:

- Select key jobs (say 15 to 20), representing wage/salary levels across the organization. The selected jobs must represent as many departments as possible.
- Find the factors in terms of which the jobs are evaluated (such as skill, mental effort, responsibility, physical effort, working conditions, etc.).
- Rank the selected jobs under each factor (by each and every member of the job evaluation committee) independently.
- Assign money value to each factor and determine the wage rates for each key job.
- The wage rate for a job is apportioned along the identified factors.
- All other jobs are compared with the list of key jobs and wage rates are determined.

Point Method: The point method measures performance through scales and job factors rather than focusing on entire job functions and ranking employees against each other. The point method is usually seen as the most reliable and valid evaluation method by employees compared to more subjective methods such as the job ranking method.

Example:

Conversion of Job Grade Points into Money Value

Point range	Daily wage rate (Rs)	Job grades of key bank officials
500-600	300-400	1. Officer
600-700	400-500	2. Accountant
700-800	500-600	3. Manager I Scale
800-900	600-700	4. Manager II Scale
900-1,000	700-800	5. Manager III Scale

Wage Determination

Wages and salary incomes in India are fixed through several institutions. These are as follows:

1. Pay Commission
2. Wage Boards
3. Adjudication

4. Market Rate Analysis
5. Collective Bargaining

1. Pay Commission

It is an administrative system that the Government of India set up in1946 to determine the salaries of government employees. The first pay commission was established in 1946, and since then, every decade has seen the birth of a commission that decides the salaries of government employees for a particular time-frame. The commission, besides looking into the pay structure, allowances and other benefits of the Central staff, has also been directed to recommend new pay structures for personnel of the armed forces and officers and employees of regulatory bodies set up under Acts of Parliament. The commission will also look into the desirability and need to sanction interim relief, if any, till the time its recommendations are submitted and accepted by the Government. A brief description of several pay commissions is given here:

First Pay Commission

The first pay commission was constituted in May 1946. Srinivasa Varadachariar was the chairman of the first pay commission. The commission gave emphasis on the idea of the living wages and stated that the government which is going to implement the minimum wages legislation for the workers working in the private industry should also follow the same principle for its own employees. The commission recommended that the lowest rung employee should get the minimum wages.

Second Pay Commission

The second pay commission was constituted in August 1957 and submitted its report after two years. The chairman of the second pay commission was Jaganath Das. It recommended that the pay structure and the working conditions of the government employee should be designed in such a way so as to ensure efficient and effective functioning of the system. The second pay commission recommended the fair wages for the employees. It had a financial impact of Rs. 396 million to the government.

Third Pay Commission

The third pay commission was constituted in April 1970 and submitted its report after three years. The chairman of the third pay commission was Raghubir Dayal. It had a financial impact of Rs. 1.44 billion to the government. The third pay commission considered three important concepts of inclusiveness, comprehensibility and adequacy for pay structure in order to retain and satisfy the employees.

Fourth Pay Commission

The fourth pay commission was constituted in June 1983 and submitted its report within four years. The chairman of the fourth pay commission was P. N. Singhal. It had a financial impact of Rs. 12.82 billion to the government.

Fifth Pay Commission

The fifth pay commission was constituted in 1994. The chairman of the fifth pay commission was Justice S. Ratnavel Pandian. It had a financial impact of Rs. 17,000 crores to the government. One of its recommendations was to slash government work force by about 30%. It also recommended to reduce the number of pay scale from 51 to 34. None of these recommendations were implemented.

Sixth Pay Commission

The fifth pay commission was constituted in July 2006. The chairman of the sixth pay commission was Justice B.N. Srikrishna. It had a financial impact of Rs. 20,000 crores to the government. The sixth pay commission mainly focused on removing ambiguity in respect of various pay scales and mainly focused on reducing number of pay scales and brings the idea of pay bands.

2. Wage Boards

The institution of wage boards has come to be widely accepted in India as a viable wage determination mechanism. The boards have been successful in fulfilling their primary object of promoting industry-wise negotiations and active participation by the parties in determination of wages and other conditions of employment. Wage boards are set up by the Government, but in selection of members of wags boards, the government cannot appoint members arbitrarily. Members to wage boards can be appointed only with the consent of employers and employees. The representatives of employers on the wage boards are the nominees of employers' organization and the workers' representatives are the nominees of the national center of trade unions of the industry concerned. The composition of wage boards is as a rule tripartite, representing the interests of labour, Management and Public. Labour and management representatives are nominated in equal numbers by the government, with consultation and consent of major Central Organizations. These boards are chaired by government nominated members representing the public. Wage board function industry-wise with broad terms of reference, which include recommending the minimum wage differential, cost of living, compensation, regional wage differentials, gratuity, hours of work, etc.

Objectives of Wage Boards

(a) To work out wage structure based on the principles of fair wages as formulated by the Committee on Fair Wages. **(b)** To work out a system of payment by results.**(c)** To evolve a wage structure based on the requirements of social justice.**(d)** To evolve a wage structure based on the need for adjusting wage differentials in a manner to provide incentives to workers for advancing their skill.

Growth and Development of Wage Boards

The history of wage boards in India dates back to the 1930's. The Royal Commission on Labour recommended the setting up of tripartite boards in Indian industries. It said: We would call attention to certain cardinal points in the setting of (wage– fixing) machinery of this kind. The main principle is the association of representatives of both employers and workers in the constitution of the machinery. Such representatives would be included in equal members, with an independent element, chosen as far as possible in agreement with or, after consultation with, the representatives of both the parties. Take decisions regarding wage adjustments suo motu or on reference from parties or from the government. No action was taken during that plan period. However, the Second Plan emphasized the need for determining wages through industrial wage boards. It observed the existing machinery for the settlement of wage disputes has not given full satisfaction to the parties concerned. More acceptable machinery for settling wage disputes will be the one which gives the parties themselves a more responsible role in reaching decisions. An authority like a tripartite wage board, consisting of an equal number of representatives of employers and workers and an independent chairman, will probably ensure more acceptable decisions. Such wage boards should be instituted for individual industries in different areas. This recommendation was subsequently reiterated by the Indian Labour conference in 1957 and various industrial committees. The government decision to setup the first wage board in cotton textile and sugar industries in1957 was also influenced by the Report of the ILO. The appointment of a wage board often results from the demands for labour unions. It has been reported: The formation of wage boards in all industries has been the result of demands and pressures on the part of trade unions. In their efforts to secure the appointment of wage boards, trade unions have to re pressurize not only the government but also the employers whose formal or informal consent to their establishment must be obtained. In India, the Bombay Industrial Relations (Amendment) Act of 1948 may be regarded as perhaps the earliest legislation included a provision for the establishment of wage boards in any industry covered by the act. Accordingly, the first wage board was set up in Bombay for the cotton textile industry. The principal purpose of starting wage boards was to relieve the Industrial Courts and Labour Courts of a part of their adjudication work.

Industries Covered

The first non – statutory wage board was set up for the cotton textile and sugar industries in 1957. Since then, 24 wage boards covering most of them major industries have been setup by the Centre: cotton textiles, sugar, cement, working journalists and non – working journalists (twice each), jute, tea, coffee and rubber plantations, iron ore, coal mining, iron and steel, engineering, ports and docks, leather and leather goods, limestone and dolomite. On July1985, three wage boards were constituted, one each for working journalists, non – working journalists and the sugar industry. But no central act contains any provision for setting up wage boards. They are set up by a resolution of the government; and they come to an end with the submission of their reports.

Composition and Functions of Wage Boards

The wage board is, as a rule, tripartite body representing the interest of labour, management and the public. Labour and management representatives are nominated in equal numbers by the government, after consultation with and with the consent of major central organizations. Generally, the labour and management representatives are selected from the particular industry which is investigated. These boards are chaired by government – nominated members representing the public. Any person who is or has been or is eligible to be appointees as a judge of the High Court shall be qualified for appointment as the Chairman. It has been the practice to nominate a Member of Parliament to represent the interests of the consumer. They function industry – wise with broad terms of reference, which include recommending the minimum wage, differential cost of living compensation, regional wage differentials, gratuity hours of work, etc. Wage boards are required to: a. Determine which categories of employees (manual, clerical supervisory, etc.) are too brought within the scope of wage fixation. b. Work out a wage structure based on the principles of fair wages formulated by the committee on fair wages. c. Suggest a system of payment by results. d. Work out the principles that should govern bonus to workers in industries. In addition to these common items, some wage boards may be asked to deal with the question of Bonus (like that of the wage boards for cement, sugar and jute industries); gratuity (like that of the wage boards for iron ore mining, limestone and dolomite mining industries) and the second wage board on cotton textile industry; demands for payments other than wages (wage boards for jute and iron and steel industry); hours of work (rubber plantation industry); interim relief (wage boards for jute industry and post and dock workers). Some wage boards (Wage boards for sugar, jute, iron ore, rubber, tea and coffee plantations, limestone and dolomite mining industries) have been required to take into account the 'special features of the industry'. Thus, wage boards have had to deal with a large number of subjects. Of these, the fixation of wage – scales on an industry wise basis constitutes the biggest of all the issues before them. In evolving a wage structure, the board takes into account: **(a)** the needs of the industry in a developing economy including the need for maintaining and promoting exports: **(b)** the requirements of social justice, which ensures that the workman who produces the goods has a fair deal, is paid sufficiently well to be able at least to sustain himself and his family in a reasonable degree of comfort, and that he is not exploited; **(c)** the need for adjusting wage differentials (which is in relation to occupational differentials; inter-firm differentials; regional or inter-area differentials; inter-industry differentials and differentials based on sex) in such a manner as to provide incentives to workers for improving their skills. For the determination of fair wages, the board has to take into consideration such factors as the degree of skill required for his work, the fatigue involved, the training and experience of the worker, the responsibility under-taken, the mental and physical requirements for work, the disagreeableness or otherwise of the work and the hazards involved in it. The board is required to make due allowances for a fair return on capital, remuneration to management and fair allocation to reserve and depreciation.

Working of the Wage Boards

Although wage boards are set up by the government, the basic reason for their establishment is the pressure brought to bear on the government, by the trade unions, industrial federations and national organizations. Pressure has been used for the appointment of wage boards for the jute industry by the jute workers association and for the coal mining industry by their trade union. The formation of wage boards in other industries has been the result of similar demands and pressures on the part of trade unions – such as plantations, iron and steel, engineering, sugar, and electricity. The government cannot appoint members of the wage boards in an arbitrary way. Independent members can be appointed only with the consent of employers and employees. The representatives of employers on wage boards are the nominees of the employer's organisation and the workers representatives are the nominees of the national organisation of trade unions of the industry concerned. However, before their actual appointment, a great deal of negotiations takes place not only between the two main reluctant interests but also among different groups representing particular interests. Item to be included for the consideration of the wage boards are the outcome of the negotiations between the parties. The issues are unanimously determined by trade unions and employers; but these invariably relate to gratuity, bonus, hours of work and grant of interim relief. The quantum of interim relief is also decided by negations and bargaining which have sometimes resulted in temporary deadlocks. The board functions in three steps:

1. The first step is to prepare a comprehensive questionnaires designed

to collect information on the prevailing wage rates and skill differentials, means of assessing an industry paying capacity and workloads, prospects for industry in the immediate future, and regional variations in the prices of widely consumed consumer goods. The questionnaire is sent out to labour unions, employers associations, interested individuals, academic organizations and government agencies.

2. The second step is to give a public hearing at which leaders of labour unions and employers associations, not represented on the board, as well as others interested in the industry in question are given a verbal or oral bearing on issues dealing with wages, working conditions and other items.

3. The third step is to convene secret sessions at which members of the board make proposals and counter – proposals regarding the items covered under the terms of reference. In the case of failure to reach a unanimous decision on the issues, each party has the right to veto the others decision. The role of independent members on the board is limited to conciliation and mediation; they try to prevent deadlocks by promoting communication between labour and management representatives. They also offer advice and suggestions to the parties, but the final decision must result from the parties' give– and – take attitudes and compromises. The decision – unanimous recommendations – is written down in the form of a report and submitted to the government, which usually accepts unanimous agreements, although it may modify any provisions thereof. Then the report is to be complied with by the parties. The government has no legal powers to enforce the board's recommendations. It tries to persuade the parties to narrow their differences and aim to unanimity. Wage boards like their own time in the submission of reports, e.g., the second wage board for cement and the first wage board for cotton textiles and sugar took a little less than 3 years; while the wage board for coal mining, non journalists, jute, iron and steel took a little over 3 years; that for tea plantations took 5 ½ years and for coffee plantation 4 years and iron ore mining 5 years. Some of the wage boards constituted in 1964 did not submit reports even by1969, e.g., heavy chemicals, fertilizers, engineering industries and ports and docks. The average time taken by wage boards in the finalization of their deliberations varies from 3 years to 5 ½ years. The main reasons for the delay in the completion of wage boards' work have been: **1.** Routine delays in the recruitment of staff; preparation and printing of questionnaires; **2.** Getting replies to questionnaires; **3.** Time involved in public hearings and **4.** Lack of accord among members in arriving at a decision.

3. Adjudication

Since independence adjudication has been one of the main instruments for settlement of disputes, improvement in wage scales and standardization of wages and allowances. If the collective bargaining and conciliation fail to bring any amicable settlement between labour and management then the cases may be referred for voluntary or compulsory arbitration. If any party is not satisfied with the award given by arbitrator may go to the Supreme Court. In such cases, the Supreme Court is the final arbiter.

Numerous wage disputes in many industries have been referred for adjudication to labour courts and tribunals during past ten decades. The High Courts and Supreme Court have also adjudicated upon such disputes. The awards given by these authorities not only helped in formulation of a body of principles governing wage fixation but laid foundation for present wage structure in many of major industries.

Some major legislations which govern the principles of wage fixation are as follows:

> Minimum Wages Act, 1948, Payments of Wages Act, 1936, Equal Remuneration Act, 1976, Industrial Disputes Act, 1947, and Companies Act 1956.

4. Market Rate Analysis

Market rate analysis is the process of collecting and comparing data on the rates and benefits provided for similar jobs in other organizations and the rates at which pay is increasing elsewhere. It is conducted by means of surveys that review published data and/or collect data from various sources.

Decision on levels of pay following market rate analysis will be guided by the pay policy of the organization or its market stance – that is, how it and its pay levels relate to market levels.

Objectives of Market Rate Analysis

The objectives are stated below:

(i) Obtain relevant, accurate, representative and up-to-date data on levels of pay and benefits for specified jobs within the organization.
(ii) Maintain a competitive pay and benefit position in relation to the market place, thus enabling the organization to attract and retain people of the quality it needs.
(iii) Inform decisions on levels of pay for individual jobs and pay brackets or scales for pay structure grades.
(iv) Provide guidance on pay review decisions concerning any adjustments required to general or individual pay levels.

(v) Support a market pricing approach to valuing jobs.

(vi) Offer guidance on internal differentials by reference to the differentials in the external labour market.

5. Role of Collective Bargaining in Wage Determination

Collective bargaining relates to those arrangements under which wages and conditions of employments are generally decided by agreements negotiated between the parties.

Broadly speaking the following factors affect the wage determination by collective bargaining process.

(a) Alternate choices & demands

(b) Institutional necessities

(c) The right and capacity to strike

In a modern democratic society wages are determined by collective bargaining in contrast to individual bargaining by working.

In the matter of wage bargaining, unions are primarily concerned with

(a) General level of wage rates

(b) Structure of wages rates (differential among occupations)

(c) Bonus, incentives and fringe benefits, Administration of wages

Industrial Relations & Trade Unions

Concept of Industrial Relations

Industrial relations is a post-industrial revolution term that replaced the expression **"master-servant"** used to define the relationship between a worker and an employer.

Industrial relations has become one of the most delicate and complex problems of modern industrial society. Industrial progress is impossible without cooperation of labours and harmonious relationships. Therefore, it is in the interest of all to create and maintain good relations between employees (labour) and employers (management).

By "relations" we mean "the relationships that exist within the boundary wall of the industry between the employer and his workmen. On the other hand, "Industry" refers to any productive activity in which an individual (or a group of individuals) is (are) engaged".

The term Industrial relations is basically the interactions between employers, employees and the government, and the institutions and associations.

The term 'industrial relations' has been variously defined. **J.T. Dunlop** defines industrial relations as "the complex interrelations among managers, workers and agencies of the governments".

Dale Yoder defines it as a "whole field of relationships that exists because of the necessary collaboration of men and women in the employment process of an industry."

"Industrial relation is an art of living together for the purpose of production" – **J. Henry**

Industrial relation do not function in a vacuum but multi-dimensional in nature and are conditioned with three determinants **(i) Institutional factors (ii) Economic factors (iii) Technological Factors.** Institutional factors are included items such as state policy, labour laws, voluntary codes, collective agreements, worker's unions and employer's organisation, social institution like the community, caste, joint family, creed, system of beliefs, etc, attitudes of work, systems of power status, relative nearness to the centers of power; motivation and influence and industrial relations.

Economic factors are included economic organisation (socialist, capitalist, communist, individual ownership, company ownership, government ownership), power of labour and employers, the nature and composition of the labour force and the sources of supply and demand in the labour market.

Technological factors include the techniques of production, modernization and rationalization schemes, capital structures, etc.

Industrial Relations versus Employee Relations

Industrial relations commonly involves three parties: the employee, employer and the union. With employee relations, just the employee and employer are parties to the working relationship.

Objectives of Industrial Relations System

1. To safeguard the interest of labour and management by securing the highest level of mutual understanding and goodwill among all those sections in the industry which participate in the process of production.
2. To avoid industrial conflict or strife and develop harmonious relations, which are an essential factor in the productivity of workers and the industrial progress of a country.
3. To raise productivity to a higher level in an era of full employment by lessening the tendency to high turnover and frequency of absenteeism.
4. To establish and promote the growth of an industrial democracy based on labour partnership in the sharing of profits and of managerial

decisions, so that an individual's personality may grow its full stature for the benefit of the industry and of the country as well.

5. To eliminate or minimize the number of strikes, lockouts by providing reasonable wages, improved living and working conditions, fringe benefits, etc.
6. To improve the economic conditions of workers in the existing state of industrial management and political government.
7. Vesting of a proprietary interest of the workers in the industries in which they are employed.

Scope of IRs

The cordial and healthy labour management relations could be brought in- By safeguarding the interest of the workers; By fixing reasonable wages; By providing good working conditions; By providing other social security measures; By maintaining healthy trade unions; By collective bargaining. The industrial peace could be attained – By setting industrial disputes through mutual understanding and agreement; By evolving various legal measures and setting up various machineries such as Works Committee, Boards of Conciliation, Labour Courts, etc. The industrial democracy could be achieved – By allowing workers to take part in management; and by recognition of human rights.

Actors in the IR system

Three main parties are directly involved in industrial relations:

Employers: Employers possess certain rights. They have the right to hire and fire them. Management can also affect workers' interests by exercising their right to relocate, close or merge the factory or to introduce technological changes.

Employees: Workers seek to improve the terms and conditions of their employment. They exchange views with management and voice their grievances. They also want to share decision making powers of management. Workers generally unite to form unions against the management and get support from these unions.

Government: The central and state government influences and regulates industrial relations through laws, rules, agreements, awards of court and the like.

Approaches to Industrial Relations

The three popular approaches to industrial relations are unitary approach, pluralistic approach and Marxist approach. The details of the approaches are discussed as follows:

1. Unitary Approach: In unitary approach, the organization is taken as an integrated and harmonious system. A core assumption of unitary approach is that management and workers, and all members of the organization share the same objectives, interests and purposes; thus working together, hand-in-hand, towards the **shared mutual goals**. In this approach the union co-operates with the management and works for a common goal. The assumption of this approach is that everyone benefits when the focus is on a common interest.

2. Pluralistic Approach: Pluralistic approach is opposite to unitary approach. In pluralism approach, the organization is divided into sub-groups - management and trade unions. In this approach, the **conflict** between the managers and the workers over the distribution of profits is unavoidable. Union plays an important role in this approach. Employees join union to protect their interest and influence the decision making by the management. Trade unions are viewed as legitimate representatives of employees. Conflict is dealt by collective bargaining and industrial tribunals, conciliation and arbitration.

3. Marxist Approach: According to Marxist approach, the conflict in an organisation arises not because of the employees and the employer. The conflict takes place due to the division in the society between the **capital** (i.e. with those who own resources) and **labour** (i.e. who has only labour to offer). Conflict is therefore seen as inevitable and trade unions are a natural response of workers to their exploitation by capital.

Other Approaches

4. Psychological Approach: The problems of IR have their origin in the perceptions of the management, unions and the workers. The conflicts between labour and management occur because every group negatively perceives the behaviour of the other i.e. even the honest intention of the other party so looked at with suspicion. The problem is further aggravated by various factors like the income, level of education, communication, values, beliefs, customs, goals of persons and groups, prestige, power, status, recognition, security, etc. Industrial peace is a result of proper attitudes and perception of the two parties.

5. Sociological Approach: Industry is a social world in miniature. The management goals, workers' attitudes, perception of change in industry, are all, in turn, decided by broad social factors like the culture of the institutions, customs, structural changes, status-symbols, rationality, acceptance or resistance to change, tolerance, etc. Industry is, thus inseparable from the society in which it functions. Through the main function of an industry is economic, its social consequences are also important such as urbanization, social mobility, housing and transport problem in industrial areas, disintegration of family structure, stress and strain, etc. As industries develop, a new industrial-cum-social pattern emerges, which provides general new relationships, institutions and behavioural pattern and new techniques of handling human resources. These do influence the development of industrial relations.

6. Human Relations Approach: Human resources are made up of living human beings. They want freedom of speech, thought of expression, movement, etc. When employers treat them as inanimate objects, encroach on their expectations, throat-cuts, conflicts and tensions arise. In fact major problems in industrial relations arise out of a tension which is created because of the employer's pressures and workers' reactions, protests and resistance to these pressures through protective mechanisms in the form of workers' organization, associations and trade unions.

In resolving conflicts, understanding of human behaviour – both individual and groups – is a pre-requisite for the employers, the union leaders and the government. Conflicts cannot be resolved unless the management must learn and know what the basic needs of men are and how they can be motivated to work effectively.

7. The System Approach: The system approach was developed by **J. T. Dunlop** of Harvard University in **1958**. According to this approach, individuals are part of an ongoing but independent social system. The behaviour, actions and role of the individuals are shaped by the cultures of the society. The three elements of the system approach are input, process and output. Society provides the cue (signal) to the individuals about how one should act in a situation. The institutions, the value system and other characteristics of the society influence the process and determine the outcome or response of the individuals. The basis of this theory is that group cohesiveness is provided by the common ideology shaped by the societal factors.

According to **Dunlop,** the industrial relations system comprises **certain actors**, **certain contexts**, and an **ideology**, which binds them together and a **body of rules** created to govern the actors at the workplace and work community. The actors in the system are the managers, the workers and their representatives, and the government agencies. The rules in the system are classified into two categories: **Substantive rules and Procedural rules.**

The substantive rules determine the conditions under which people are employed. Such rules are normally derived from the implied terms and conditions of employment, legislations, agreements, practices and managerial policies and directives.

The procedural rules govern how substantive rules are to be made and understood. Ultimately, the introduction of new rules and regulations and revisions of the existing rules for improving the industrial relations are the major outputs of the industrial relations system. These may be substantive rules as well as procedural rules. The context in the system approach refers to the environment of the system which is normally determined by the technological nature of the organization, the financial and other constraints that restrict the actors of industrial relations, and the nature of power sharing in the macro environment, namely, the society.

8. Gandhian Trusteeship Approach: Gandhi's views on industrial relations are based on his fundamental principles of truth, non-violence and non-possession. Out of these principles evolved the concept of trusteeship on which his philosophy of industrial relations rests. This philosophy presumes the peaceful co-existence of capital and labour, which calls for the resolution of conflict by non-violent, non-cooperation (i.e., Satyagraha), which actually amounts to peaceful strikes in ordinary parlance. Gandhi accepted the workers' right to strike, but cautioned that this right is to be exercised in a just cause, and in a peaceful and non-violent manner; and it should be resorted to only after employers fail to respond to their moral appeals.

9. Weber's Social Action Approach: The social action approach of Weber has laid considerable importance to the question of control in the context of increasing rationalization and bureaucratization. Closely related to Weber's concern related to control in organizations was his concern with "power of control and dispersal". Thus a trade union in the Weber's scheme of things has both economic purposes as well as the goal of involvement in political and power struggles. Some of the major orientations in the Weberian approach have been to analyze the impact of techno-economic and politico-organizational changes on trade union structure and processes to analyze the subjective interpretation of workers' approaches to trade unionism and finally to analyze the power of various components of the industrial relations environment – Government, employers, trade unions and political parties. Thus the Weberian approach gives the theoretical and operational importance to "control" as well as to the power struggle to control work organizations – a power struggle in which all the actors in the industrial relations drama are caught up.

10. The Oxford Approach: According to this approach, the industrial relations system is a study of institutions of job regulations and the stress is on the substantive and procedural rules as in Dunlop's model. Flanders, the exponent of this approach, considers every business enterprise as a social system of production and distribution, which has a structured pattern of relationship. The "institution of job regulation" is categorized by him as internal and external-the former being an internal part of the industrial relations system such as code of work rules, wage structure, internal procedure of joint consultation, and grievance procedure. He views trade unions as an external organization and excludes collective agreements from the sphere of internal regulation. According to him, collective bargaining is central to the industrial relations system.

Causes of Poor Industrial Relations

The main causes of industrial disputes are:

(i) **Wages:** Low wages of industrial workers constitute a major cause of industrial disputes in the country. Wages have not been rising in proportion to the rise in prices. This has forced the labourers to demand higher wages, consequently leading to disputes.

(ii) **Bonus:** The demand for bonus or increase in bonus has been the second major cause of industrial disputes. The workers feel that they should have a greater share in the profits of the industrial concern. Non-acceptance of this fact by the employers has been a source of friction among the employers and the workers.

(iii) **Working Conditions:** The demand for improvement in working conditions such as lesser working hours, security of job, better safety measures in the factory, leave, canteen, gratuity facilities, etc., are also responsible for many industrial disputes.

(iv) **Other Causes:** Among other causes that lead to disputes are failure of employers to recognize trade unions, conflict between rival unions for representation, insult to trade union leadership by the employer, introduction of rationalization in the factory, the fear of retrenchment of workers, sympathetic strikes with fellow employees in other establishments, general discontent and sense of frustration among labourers, political issues, etc.

Effects of Poor Industrial Relations

Industrial relations are of great importance in industrial life. These relations have great bearing on the economic, social and political spheres of our society. If in an organisation, relations between labour and management are cordial, there will be industrial peace and interests of both the parties will be automatically safeguarded. However, organizations where industrial relations are strained, the organizations have to face lot of problems. The atmosphere of such organizations is always surcharged with industrial unrest leading either to strikes or lockouts. Organizations which ignore the importance of industrial relations face high cost of production. Adverse effect on efficiency, low-grade production, negligence in the execution of work, absenteeism among the workers, high rate of labour turnover, etc. are the evils that result from poor industrial relations.

Lack of cordiality in industrial relations not only adversely affects the interests of the labourers and employers but also cause harm to different sections of society. They are faced with lot of difficulties and problems. Demerits of poor industrial relations can be expressed as under:

Effect on Workers: (i) Loss of wages, **(ii)** Physical injury or death on account of violence during labour unrest, **(iii)** Excesses by employers, **(iv)** Economic losses, **(v)** Bitterness in relations, **(vi)** Adverse affect on career.

Effect on Employers / Industrialists: **(i)** Less production, **(ii)** Less Profit, **(iii)** Bad affect on organisation, **(iv)** Bad effect on human relations, **(v)** Damage to machines and equipments, **(vi)** Adverse effect on development of companies, **(vii)** Burden of fixed expenses.

Effect on Government: **(i)** Loss of revenue (less recovery of income tax, sales tax, etc.), **(ii)** Lack of order in society, **(iii)** Blame by different parties.

Effect on Consumers: **(i)** Rise in prices, **(ii)** Scarcity of goods, **(iii)** Bad affect on quality of goods.

Other Effects: **(i)** Adverse affect on International Trade (Fall in exports and rise in imports), **(ii)** Hindrance in Economic Development of the country, **(iii)** Uncertainty in economy.

Meaning of Trade Union

The Trade Union Act 1926 defines a trade union as a combination, whether temporary or permanent, formed primarily for the purpose of regulating the relations between workmen and employers or between workmen and workmen, or between employers and employers, or for imposing restrictive condition on the conduct of any trade or business, and includes any federation of two or more trade unions.

Objectives

Trade unions are formed to protect and promote the interests of their members. Their primary function is to protect the interests of workers against discrimination and unfair labor practices. Trade unions are formed to achieve the following objectives:

1. **Representation:** Trade unions represent individual workers when they have a problem at work. If an employee feels he is being unfairly treated, he can ask the union representative to sort out the difficulty with the manager or employer. Unions also offer their members legal representation. Normally this is to help people to get financial compensation for work-related injuries or to assist people who have to take their employer to court.
2. **Negotiation:** Negotiation is where union representatives, discuss with management, the issues which affect people working in an organization. There may be a difference of opinion between management and union members. Trade unions negotiate with the employers to find out a solution to these differences. Pay, working hours, holidays and changes to working practices are the sorts of issues that are negotiated. In many workplaces there is a formal

agreement between the union and the company which states that the union has the right to negotiate with the employer. In these organizations, unions are said to be recognized for collective bargaining purposes.

3. **Voice in Decisions Affecting Workers:** The economic security of employees is determined not only by the level of wages and duration of their employment, but also by the management's personal policies which include selection of employees for layoffs, retrenchment, promotion and transfer. These policies directly affect workers. The evaluation criteria for such decisions may not be fair. So, the intervention of unions in such decision making is a way through which workers can have their say in the decision making to safeguard their interests.
4. **Member Services:** During the last few years, trade unions have increased the range of services they offer their members. These include:
   (a) **Education and Training: -** Most unions run training courses for their members on employment rights, health and safety and other issues. Some unions also help members who have left school with little education by offering courses on basic skills and courses leading to professional qualifications.
   (b) **Legal Assistance: -** As well as offering legal advice on employment issues, some unions give help with personal matters, like housing, wills and debt.
   (c) **Financial Discounts: -**People can get discounts on mortgages, insurance and loans from unions.
   (d) **Welfare benefits: -** One of the earliest functions of trade unions was to look after members who hit hard times. Some of the older unions offer financial help to their members when they are sick or unemployed.

Functions

Trade unions perform a number of functions in order to achieve the objectives. These functions can be broadly classified into three categories:

1. Militant Functions and
2. Fraternal Functions

1. Militant Functions

One set of activities performed by trade unions leads to the betterment of the position of their members in relation to their employment. The aim of such activities is to ensure adequate wages, secure better conditions of work and employment get better treatment from employers, etc. When the unions fail to accomplish these aims by the method of collective bargaining and negotiations, they adopt an approach and put up a fight with the management in the form of go-slow tactics, strike, boycott, gheraos, etc. Hence, these functions of the trade unions are known as militant or fighting functions. Thus, the militant functions of trade unions can be summed up as:

(i) To achieve higher wages and better working conditions;
(ii) To raise the status of workers as a part of industry;
(iii) To protect labours against victimization and injustice.

2. Fraternal Functions

Another set of activities performed by trade unions aims at rendering help to its members in times of need, and improving their efficiency. Trade unions try to foster a spirit of co-operation and promote friendly industrial relations and diffuse education and culture among their members. They take up welfare measures for improving the morale of workers and generate self confidence among them. They also arrange for legal assistance to its members, if necessary. Besides these, they undertake many welfare measures for their members, e.g., school for the education of children, library, reading-rooms, in-door and out-door games, and other recreational facilities. Some trade unions even undertake publication of some magazine or journal. These activities, which may be called fraternal functions, depend on the availability of funds, which the unions raise by subscription from members and donations from outsiders, and also on their competent and enlightened leadership. Thus, the fraternal functions of trade unions can be summed up as:

(i) To take up welfare measures for improving the morale of workers;
(ii) To generate self confidence among workers;
(iii) To encourage sincerity and discipline among workers;
(iv) To provide opportunities for promotion and growth;
(v) To protect women workers against discrimination.

Theories

The growth and development of trade union movement depends on social, economic and political conditions of a country. The various theories of trade unions are as follows:

1. **Revolutionary Theory:** The Revolutionary Theory was propounded by **Marx**. According to Marx, trade union took the challenging role to streamline the forces of working classes to struggle against the capitalist. Trade unions took revolutionary programme in order to abolish the capitalist. This theory is also known as "the theory of class war and dialectical materialism".

2. **Evolutionary Theory:** This theory is also popular as "theory of industrial democracy". The theory was propounded by **Sydney and Beatrice Webbs**. According to Webbs, trade unionism is not an instrument to abolish the capitalism, but a means to establish the industrial democracy in the industry. Trade unions must raise their voice to overcome the managerial dictatorship.
3. **Rebellion Theory: Frank Rebellion** is the pioneer of this theory. According to him, trade unionism is the result of rapid mechanization. He believes that the use of machines leads to exploitation of workers. So, machine is the cause and trade unionism is the result. Therefore the basic objective of rebellion approach is to protect the interest of workers against mechanization.
4. **Gandhian Approach:** The Gandhian approach is based on "class collaboration rather than class conflict and struggle". Gandhi emphasized that the aim of trade unionism is eternal reform and also evolution of internal strength. According to Gandhi, self-consciousness among workers led to the emergence of trade unionism.
5. **Theory of Industrial Jurisprudence:** The profounder of this theory is **S.H. Slithers**. According to him, an individual worker is not able to protect his interest alone, and so they form trade unionism in order to protect their common interest through collective bargaining with employers. This system is known as "a system of industrial jurisprudence".

Structure of Trade Unions

The structure of trade unions in India varies from organization to organization. The structure can be classified into four types. These are: **(1)** Craft Union **(2)** General Union **(3)** Industrial union **(4)** Federations

1. **Craft Unions:** If the workers of the same craft or category of the job form into a union, that union is called craft union. These unions are called as horizontal unions. The basic logic behind the formation of such unions is that the workers belonging to the same craft do face similar problems. Mostly non managerial personnel form such unions. Examples of craft unions are Driver's Associations.
2. **General Unions:** If the workers of any industry, any region and of any job or occupation form into one union in order to protect the overall interests of the workers, such unions are called general unions. The Jamshedpur Labour Union is one example. In India there are several industry cum region unions due to concentration of some industries in particular regions.
3. **Industrial Unions:** An industrial union is organized upon an industry wise rather than a craft wise basis. Its members belong to different

crafts within the same industry. Ahmedabad Textile Labour Association, Giri Kamgar Union are examples of industrial unions in India. These unions are vertical in nature because they consist of all types of workers in an industry. Industrial unions are more powerful because they consist of both skilled and unskilled workers. It is easier for the employer to bargain with one union to cover all workers of a particular industry.

4. **Federations:** These are national level bodies to which plant level unions, craft unions, industrial unions and general unions are affiliated. Federations are the apex organizations of workers. They act as coordinating agencies. These are also called central trade unions e.g. INTUC, AITUC, CITU, BMS, HMS etc.

Trade Union Movement in India

The trade unionism in India developed quite slowly as compared to the western nations. Indian trade union movement can be divided into three phases:

1. The First Phase (1850 to 1900)

During this phase the inception of trade unions took place. During this period, the working and living conditions of the labour were poor and their working hours were long. Capitalists were only interested in their productivity and profitability. In addition, the wages were also low and general economic conditions were poor in industries. In order to regulate the working hours and other service conditions of the Indian textile workers, the Indian **Factories Act** was enacted in **1881**. As a result, employment of child labour was prohibited.

The growth of trade union movement was slow in this phase and later on the Indian Factories Act of 1881 was amended in 1891. Many strikes took place in the two decades following 1880 in all industrial cities. These strikes taught workers to understand the power of united action even though there was no union in real terms. Small associations like Bombay Mill-Hands Association came up by this time.

2. The Second Phase (1900 to 1946)

This phase was characterized by the development of organized trade unions and political movements of the working class. Between 1918 and 1923, many unions came into existence in the country. At Ahmedabad, under the guidance of Mahatma Gandhi, occupational unions like spinners' unions and weavers' unions were formed. A strike was launched by these unions under the leadership of Mahatma Gandhi who turned it into a satyagrah. These unions federated into industrial union known as Textile Labor Association in 1920.In 1920, the First National Trade Union Organization (The All India Trade Union Congress

(AITUC)) was established. Many of the leaders of this organization were leaders of the national movement. In 1926, trade union law came up with the efforts of Mr. N. N Joshi that became operative from 1927. During 1928, All India Trade Union Federation (AITUF) was formed.

3. The Third Phase (1946 onwards)

The third phase began with the emergence of Independent India (in 1947). The partition of country affected the trade union movement particularly Bengal and Punjab. By 1949, four central trade union organizations were functioning in the country:

1. The All India Trade Union Congress,
2. The Indian National Trade Union Congress,
3. The Hindu Mazdoor Sangh, and
4. The United Trade Union Congress

The working class movement was also politicized along the lines of political parties. For instance, Indian National Trade Union Congress (INTUC) is the trade union arm of the Congress Party. The AITUC is the trade union arm of the Communist Party of India. Besides workers, white-collar employees, supervisors and managers are also organized by the trade unions, as for example in the Banking, Insurance and petroleum industries.

Trade Unions in India

The Indian workforce consists of 430 million workers, growing 2% annually. The Indian labor markets consist of three sectors:

1. The rural workers, who constitute about 60 per cent of the workforce.
2. Organized sector, which employs 8 per cent of workforce, and
3. The urban informal sector (which includes the growing software industry and other services, not included in the formal sector) which constitutes the rest 32 per cent of the workforce.

At present there are twelve Central Trade Union Organizations in India:

All India Trade Union Congress (AITUC)-1920

Bharatiya Mazdoor Sangh (BMS) - 1955

Centre of Indian Trade Unions (CITU) - 1970

Hind Mazdoor Kisan Panchayat (HMKP)-1962

Hind Mazdoor Sabha (HMS) - 1948

Indian Federation of Free Trade Unions (IFFTU)

Indian National Trade Union Congress (INTUC) - 1947

National Front of Indian Trade Unions (NFITU) -1967

National Labor Organization (NLO)

Trade Unions Co-ordination Centre (TUCC)
United Trade Union Congress (UTUC) and
United Trade Union Congress - Lenin Sarani (UTUC - LS)

Classification Based on Agreement

Another basis on which labour agreements are sometimes distinguished is on basis of the type of agreement involved, based on the degree to which membership in the union is a condition of employment. These are:

(a) **Closed Shop:** Where management and union agree that the union would have sole responsibility and authority for the recruitment of workers, it is called a Closed Shop agreement. The worker joins the union to become an employee of the shop. The Taft-Hartley Act of 1947 bans closed shop agreements in the USA, although they still exist in the construction and printing trades. Sometimes, the closed shop is also called the '**Hiring Hall**.'

(b) **Union Shop:** Where there is an agreement that all new recruits must join the union within a fixed period after employment it is called a union shop. In the USA where some states are declared to be 'right-to-work'.

(c) **Preferential Shop:** When a Union member is given preference in filling a vacancy, such an agreement is called Preferential Shop.

(d) **Maintenance Shop:** In this type of arrangement no compulsory membership in the union before or after recruitment exists. However, if the employee chooses to become a member after recruitment, his membership remains compulsory right throughout his tenure of employment with that particular employer. This is called maintenance of membership shop or maintenance shop.

(e) **Agency Shop:** In terms of the agreement between management and the union a non union member has to pay the union a sum equivalent to a member's subscription in order to continue employment with the employer. This is called an agency shop.

(f) **Open Shop:** Membership in a union is in no way compulsory or obligatory either before or after recruitment. In such organizations, sometimes there is no union at all. This is least desirable form for unions. This is referred to as an open shop.

The above classifications are more usual in the west than on the Indian sub-continent.

Leadership

The trade union movement in India goes back to the year **1875** under, the **leadership of Sorabji Shaparji.**

Bombay Mills Hands Association in 1890 by **Mr. M.M. Lokhande**, a workman who organized a meeting of 10,000 workers as a result of which several demands were accepted by the mill owners in Bombay Textile Mills. He started a newspaper called **Dinabandhu** so as to educate the workmen.

In 1897, the **Amalgama Society of Railway Servants** of India was established and registered under the Companies Act, which is followed by the **Printers' Union Calcutta (1907)**, **Postal Union (1907)**, **Kamgar Hitwardhak Sabha (1909)** and the **Social Service League (1910)**. However, these organizations could not make the real start in the Labour Movement till World War I.

The first systematic attempt in this direction was made by **B.P Wadia** who established the **Madras Labour Union in 1918**. The **Madras Labor Union** was the first organized **Trade Union in India** followed by a large number of **trade unions** in the Indian industrial centers.

In 1947, the Indian national Trade Union Congress (INTUC) was formed as a labour wing of Indian national Congress.

In **1948**, Praja Socialist party started another trade union known as **Hind Mazdoor Panchayat**. Indian Federation of Labour and Hind Mazdoor Panchayat were **amalgamated** and formed **Hind Mazdoor Sabha** (H.M.S) in **1948**.

In 1949, I.T.U.C. was affiliated to the International Confederation of Free Trade Unions. The United Trade Union Congress was established in 1949 by some radicalists. In **1954**, another central trade union was formed in the name of **Bharatiya Mazdoor Sangh** (BMS). All these unions have been working for the betterment of workers.

In **1920**, the **All India Trade Union Congress** (AITUC) was set up. In 1926, the Trade Unions Act was passed which gave a legal status to the registered trade unions.

With independence and partition, the country was plunged into growing unemployment. A series of strikes occurred, in the country. The All India Trade Union Congress was split up as a result of which the Indian National Trade Union Congress (INTUC) was formed in 1947 under the control of congress party. The Hind Mazdoor Sabha (HMS) was formed by the socialist Party in 1948, and United Trade Union congress (UTUC) was formed in 1949. Recently, Centre of Indian Trade Unions (CITU) has been formed by the Communist Party (Marxists).

Finance

Small size of unions has its direct bearing on its financial health. Total income and total expenditure of 9,073 trade unions with a membership of

57.4 lakhs were Rs. 3,238 lakhs and Rs. 2,532 lakhs respectively in 1992. The per member income and expenditure, thus, come to Rs. 56.4 and Rs. 44.1 respectively". These are, by all means, very low. It is the small size of trade unions accompanied by small subscriptions; the trade unions cannot undertake welfare activities.

Sound financial position is an essential ingredient for the effective functioning of trade unions, because in the process of rendering services or fulfilling their goals, trade unions have to perform a variety of functions and organize programmes which require enormous financial commitments. Hence, it is imperative on the part of a trade union to strengthen its financial position.

But it is felt that the income and expenditure of trade unions in India over the years is such, with few exceptions, that the financial position of the union is generally weak, affecting their functioning. It is opined that, "trade unions could be more effective, if they paid more attention to strengthening their organizations and achieving higher attention of financial solvency."

The primary source of income to the unions is membership subscription. Their other sources of union finances are donations, sale of periodicals, etc. The items of expenditure include: allowances to office bearers, salaries to office, annual convention/meeting expenses, rents, stationery, printing, postage, telegrams, etc.

Most of the trade unions in India suffer from inadequate funds. This unsound financial position is mostly due to low membership and low rate of membership fee. Trade Union Act, 1926, prescribed the membership fee at **25 paisa per member per month**. But the National Commission on Labour recommended the increase of rate of membership subscription from 25 paisa to Re. 1 in the year 1990. But the Government did not accept this recommendation.

As the National Commission on Labour observes, "an important factor limiting the effective functioning of unions in our country has been their financial weakness.. In most unions, poor finances are the result of inadequate membership strength. This in turn, can be traced to the small size of units. In a majority of unions, the rate of contributions required of members is also small. With a relatively low rate of unionization, total funds collected are small. The general picture of finances of unions is disappointing."

Union Rivalry

The formal basis for Trade Union Organisation is provided by the Indian Trade Union Act, 1926. The relevant article reads as follows: "Any seven or more members of a trade union may be subscribing their name to the roles of the trade union and by otherwise complying with the provisions of this act with respect to the registration, apply for registration of the trade union under this Act."

This provision has led to the formation of multiple unions and resulted in interunion rivalry in different industries. But the inter-union rivalry breaks the very purpose of the trade unions by weakening the strength of collective bargaining. On the other hand, the existence of a single, strong union not only protects the employee interests more effectively but also halts the various unproductive activities of the unions and forces the leaders to concentrate on the strategic issues. Further, it helps to bring about congenial industrial relations by bringing about a system of orderliness in dealing with the employees and by facilitating expeditious settlement of disputes.

Inter and intra-union rivalries have been a potent cause of industrial disputes in the country. They are responsible for weak bargaining power of trade unions in collective bargaining. These rivalries are responsible for slow growth of trade union movement in the country.

Union Politics

Most popular trade unions in India are affiliated to certain political parties. These political parties are only keen on making every grievance of the working class a political issue to attain political gains. As a result the problem only gets wide publicity and remains unsolved.

Most unions today are run by rival political parties. These political parties have nothing constructive to offer, instead, use unions to spread their political agenda. Furthermore, decisions related to unions are made by politicians.

Dispute Resolution & Grievance Management

Dispute Resolution

1. Conciliation: Conciliation refers to the process by which representatives of employees and employers are brought together before a third party with a view to discuss, reconcile their differences and arrive at an agreement through mutual consent. The third party acts as a facilitator in this process. Conciliation is a type of state intervention in settling the Industrial Disputes. The Industrial Disputes Act empowers the Central & State Governments to appoint conciliation officers and a Board of Conciliation as and when the situation demands.

Conciliation Officer: The appropriate Government may, by notification in the official gazette, appoint such number of persons as it thinks fit to be the conciliation officer. The duties of a conciliation officer are:

(a) To hold conciliation proceedings with a view to arrive at amicable settlement between the parties concerned.

(b) To investigate the dispute in order to bring about the settlement between the parties concerned.

(c) To send a report and memorandum of settlement to the appropriate Government.

(d) To send a report to the Government stating forth the steps taken by him in case no settlement has been reached at.

The conciliation officer however has no power to force a settlement. He can only persuade and assist the parties to reach an agreement. The Industrial Disputes Act prohibits strikes and lockouts during that time when the conciliation proceedings are in progress.

2. Arbitration: A process in which a neutral third party listens to the disputing parties, gathers information about the dispute, and then takes a decision which is binding on both the parties. The conciliator simply assists the parties to come to a settlement, whereas the arbitrator listens to both the parties and then gives his judgement.

Advantages of Arbitration

(i) It is established by the parties themselves and therefore both parties have good faith in the arbitration process.

(ii) The process in informal and flexible in nature.

(iii) It is based on mutual consent of the parties and therefore helps in building healthy Industrial Relations.

Disadvantages

(i) Delay often occurs in settlement of disputes.

(ii) Arbitration is an expensive procedure and the expenses are to be shared by the labour and the management.

(iii) Judgment can become arbitrary when the arbitrator is incompetent or biased.

There are two types of arbitration:

(i) Voluntary Arbitration: In voluntary arbitration the arbitrator is appointed by both the parties through mutual consent and the arbitrator acts only when the dispute is referred to him.

(ii) Compulsory Arbitration: It implies that the parties are required to refer the dispute to the arbitrator whether they like him or not. Usually, when the parties fail to arrive at a settlement voluntarily, or when there is some other strong reason, the appropriate Government can force the parties to refer the dispute to an arbitrator.

3. Adjudication: Adjudication is the ultimate legal remedy for settlement of Industrial Dispute. Adjudication means intervention of a legal authority appointed by the Government to make a settlement which is binding on both the parties. In other words adjudication means a mandatory settlement of an Industrial dispute by a labour court or a tribunal. For the purpose of adjudication, the Industrial Disputes Act provides 3-tier machinery:

1. Labour Court
2. Industrial Tribunal
3. National Tribunal

(a) Labour Court: The appropriate Government may, by notification in the official gazette constitute one or more labour courts for adjudication of Industrial disputes relating to any matters specified in the second schedule of Industrial Disputes Act. They are:

(i) Dismissal or discharge or grant of relief to workmen wrongfully dismissed.

(ii) Illegality or otherwise of a strike or lockout.

(iii) Withdrawal of any customary concession or privileges.

Where an Industrial dispute has been referred to a labour court for adjudication, it shall hold its proceedings expeditiously and shall, within the period specified in the order referring such a dispute, submit its report to the appropriate Government.

(b) Industrial Tribunal: The appropriate Government may, by notification in the official gazette, constitute one or more Industrial Tribunals for the adjudication of Industrial disputes relating to the following matters:

(i) Wages
(ii) Compensatory and other allowances
(iii) Hours of work and rest intervals
(iv) Leave with wages and holidays
(v) Bonus, profit-sharing, PF etc.
(vi) Rules of discipline
(vii) Retrenchment of workmen
(viii) Working shifts other than in accordance with standing orders

It is the duty of the Industrial Tribunal to hold its proceedings expeditiously and to submit its report to the appropriate Government within the specified time.

(c) National Tribunal: The Central Government may, by notification in the official gazette, constitute one or more National Tribunals for the adjudication of Industrial Disputes in

1. Matters of National importance;

2. Matters which are of a nature such that industries in more than one state are likely to be interested in, or are affected by the outcome of the dispute.

It is the duty of the National Tribunal to hold its proceedings expeditiously and to submit its report to the Central Government within the stipulated time.

Grievance Management

Grievance

A grievance is a sign of employee's discontent with job and its nature. The employee has got certain aspirations and expectations which he thinks must be fulfilled by the organization where he is working. When the organization fails to satisfy the employee needs, he develops a feeling of discontent or dissatisfaction. Thus, grievance is caused due to the difference between the employee expectation and management practices.

Breach defines grievances as "any dissatisfaction or feeling of injustice in connection with one's employment situation that is brought to the notice of the management".

Methods to Know the Existence of Grievance

Grievances can be uncovered in a number of ways. Gossip and grapevine offer vital clues about employee grievances. Gripe boxes, open door policies, periodic interviews, exit surveys could also be undertaken to cover the mystery surrounding grievances. These methods are discussed below;

Observation: A manager/ supervisor can usually track the behaviours of people working under him. If a particular employee is not getting along with people, spoiling materials due to carelessness or recklessness, showing indifference to commands, reporting late for work or is remaining absent- the signals are fairly obvious. Since the supervisor is close to the scene of action, he can always spot such unusual behaviours and report promptly.

Grievance Procedure: A systematic grievance procedure is best means to highlight employee dissatisfaction at various levels. Management, to this end, must encourage employees to use it whenever they have anything to say. In the absence of such a procedure, grievances pile up and erupt in violent forms at a future date. By that time things might have taken an ugly shape, impairing cordial relations between labour and management. If management fails to induce employees to express their grievances, unions will take over and emerge as powerful bargaining representatives.

Gripe Boxes: A gripe box may be kept at prominent locations in the factory for lodging anonymous complaints pertaining to any aspect relating to work. Since the complainant need not reveal his identity, he can express his feelings of injustice or discontent frankly and without any fear of victimization.

Open Door Policy: This is a kind of walk-in-meeting with the manager when the employee can express his feelings openly about any work-related grievance. The Manager can cross-check the details of the complaint through various means at his disposal.

Exit Interview: Employees usually leave their current jobs due to dissatisfaction or better prospects outside. If the manager tries sincerely through an exit interview, he might be able to find out the real reasons why any employee is leaving the organization. To elicit valuable information, the manager must encourage the employees to give a correct picture so as to rectify the mistakes promptly. If the employee is not providing fearless answers, he may be given a questionnaire to fill up and post the same after all his dues are cleared from the organization where he is currently employed.

Opinion Surveys: Surveys may be conducted periodically to elicit the opinions of employees about the organization and its politics.

Model Grievance Procedure

The Model grievance procedure suggested by the National Commission of Labour involves six successive time bound steps each leading to the next, in case of dissatisfaction. The aggrieved worker in the first instance will approach the foreman and tell him of his grievances orally. The foreman has to redress his grievance and if the worker is not satisfied with this redressal, he can approach the supervisor. The Supervisor has to provide an answer within 48 hours. In the event of the supervisor not giving an answer or the answer not being acceptable to the worker, the worker goes to the next step. At this stage, the worker either alone or accompanied with his departmental representative approaches the Head of the Department who has to give an answer within three days. If the Department fails to give answer or if the worker is not satisfied with his answer, the worker may appeal to the Grievance Committee, consisting of the representatives of the employer and the employees. The recommendation of this Committee should be communicated to the Manager within seven days from the date of the grievance reaching it. Unanimous decisions, if any, of the Committee shall be implemented by the Management. If there is no unanimity, the views of the members of the Committee shall be placed before the Manager for decision. The Manager has to take a decision and the worker within three days.

The worker can make an appeal against the manager's decision and such an appeal has to be decided within a week. A Union official may accompany the worker to the manager for discussion and if no decision is arrived at this stage, both the union and management may refer the grievance to voluntary arbitration within a week of receipt of the management's decision. The worker in actual practice may not resort to all the above mentioned steps. For example, if the grievance is piqued because of his dismissal or discharge he can resort to the second step directly and he can make an appeal against dismissal or discharge.

Labour Welfare & Social Security Measures

Meaning of Labour Welfare

Welfare includes anything that is done for the comfort and improvement of employees and is provided over and above the wages. Welfare helps in keeping the morale and motivation of the employees high so as to retain the employees for longer duration. The welfare measures need not be in monetary terms only but in any kind/forms. Employee welfare includes monitoring of working conditions, creation of industrial harmony through infrastructure for health, industrial relations and insurance against disease, accident and unemployment for the workers and their families. Labour welfare entails all those activities of employer, which are directed towards providing the employees with certain facilities and services in addition to wages or salaries.

Definition

Labour Welfare means working out things for the well-being of the labours, knowing there wants and enabling them to fulfill their wants.

In the Report II of the ILO Asian Regional conference, it has been stated that worker's welfare may be understood to mean "such services, facilities and amenities, which may be established outside or in the vicinity of undertakings, to enable the persons employed therein to perform their work in healthy and congenial surroundings and to provide them with the amenities conducive to good health and high morale."

The Labour Investigation committee (1944-46) includes under labour welfare activities "anything done for the intellectual, physical, moral and economic betterment of the workers, whether by employers, by Government or by other agencies, over and above what is laid down by law or what is normally expected as per of the contractual benefits for which the workers may have bargained."

The Report of the Committee on Labour welfare (1969) includes under it "such services, facilities and amenities as adequate canteens, rest and recreation facilities, sanitary and medical facilities, arrangements for travel to and from work and for the accommodation of workers employed at a distance from their homes and such other services, amenities and facilities including social security measures as contribute to improve the conditions under which worker are employed."

Scope

The subject of labour welfare facilities is a very broad one covering a wide field of amenities and activities. In order to obtain a clearer understanding of its scope, we may examine the ways in which labour welfare is classified. Labour welfare work can be broadly divided into two categories: (a) statutory and non — statutory or voluntary and (b) intra-mural and extra-mural welfare facilities.

Theories of Labour Welfare

The form of labor welfare activities is flexible, elastic and differs from time to time, region to region, industry to industry and country to country depending upon the value system, level of education, social customs, degree of industrialization and general standard of the socio-economic development of the nation. Seven theories constituting the conceptual frame work of labour welfare activities are the following:-

1. The Police Theory: This is based on the contention that a minimum standard of welfare is necessary for labourers. Here the assumption is that without policing, that is, without compulsion, employers do not provide even the minimum facilities for workers. Apparently, this theory assumes that man is selfish and self centered and always tries to achieve his own ends, even at the cost of the welfare of others.

According to this theory, owners and managers of industrial undertakings get many opportunities for exploitation of labour. Hence, the state has to intervene to provide minimum standard of welfare to the working class.

2. The Religious Theory: This is based on the concept that man is essentially "a religious animal." Even today, many acts of man are related to religious sentiments and beliefs. These religious feelings sometimes prompt an employer to take up welfare activities in the expectation of future emancipation either in this life or after it.

3. The Philanthropic Theory: This theory is based on man's love for mankind. Philanthropy means **"Loving mankind."** Man is believed to have an instinctive urge by which he strives to remove the suffering of others and promote their well-being. In fact, the labour welfare movement began in the early years of the industrial revolution with the support of philanthropists.

4. The Trusteeship Theory: This is also called the Paternalistic Theory of Labour Welfare. According to this the industrialist or employer holds the total industrial estate, properties, and profits accruing from them in a trust. In other words, the employer should hold the industrial assets for himself, for the benefit of his workers, and also for society. The main emphasis of this theory is that employers should provide funds on an ongoing basis for the well-being of their employees.

5. The Placating Theory: This theory is based on the fact that the labour groups are becoming demanding and militant and are more conscious of their rights and privileges than ever before. Their demand for higher wages and better standards of living cannot be ignored. According to this theory, timely and periodical acts of labour welfare can appease the workers. They are some kind of pacifiers which come with a friendly gesture.

6. The Public Relation Theory: This theory provides the basis for an atmosphere of goodwill between labour and management, and also between management and the public. Labour welfare programmes under this theory, work as a sort of an advertisement and help an organization to project its good image and build up and promote good and healthy public relations.

7. The Functional Theory: This is also called the Efficiency Theory. Here, welfare work is used as a means to secure, preserve and develop the efficiency and productivity of labour, it is obvious that if an employer takes good care of his workers, they will tend to become more efficient and will thereby step up production. This theory is a reflection of contemporary support for labour welfare. It can work well if both the parties have an identical aim in view; that is, higher production through better welfare. And this will encourage labour's participation in welfare programmes.

Principles and Approaches

The success of welfare activities depends on the approach which has been taken into account in providing such activities to the employees. Welfare policy should be guided by idealistic morale and human value. Every effort should be made to give workers/ employees some voice in the choice of welfare activities so long as it does not amount to dictation from workers.

There are employers who consider all labour welfare activities as distasteful legal liability. There are workers who look upon welfare activities in terms of their inherent right. Both parties have to accept welfare as activities of mutual concern. Constructive and lasting progress in the matter of social justice can be achieved only if welfare activities are accepted as essential factors in the progress of the business organization.

Labour welfare is dependent on certain basic principles. The following are the principles on which successful implementation of welfare programmes depends:

1. Adequacy of Wages: Labour welfare measures cannot be a substitute for wages. Workers have a right to adequate wages. But high wage rates alone cannot create healthy atmosphere, nor bring about a sense of commitment on the part of workers. A combination of social welfare, emotional welfare and economic welfare together would achieve good results.

2. Social Liability of Industry: Industry, according to this principle, has an obligation or duty towards its employees to look after their welfare. The constitution of India also emphasizes this aspect of labour welfare.

3. Impact on Efficiency: This plays an important role in welfare services, and is based on the relationship between welfare and efficiency, though it is difficult to measure this relationship. Programmes for housing, education and training, the provision of balanced diet and family planning measures are some of the important programmes of labour welfare which increases the efficiency of the workers, especially in underdeveloped or developing countries.

4. Increase in Personality: The development of the human personality is given here as the goal of industrial welfare which, according to this principle, should counteract the baneful effects of the industrial system. Therefore, it is necessary to implement labour welfare services. Both inside and outside the factory, that is, provide intra-mural and extra-mural labour welfare services.

5. Totality of Welfare: This emphasizes that the concept of labour welfare must spread throughout the hierarchy of an organization. Employees at all levels must accept this total concept of labour welfare programme will never really get off the ground.

6. Co-ordination or Integration: This plays an important role in the success of welfare services. From this angle, a coordinated approach will promote a healthy development of the worker in his work, home and community. This is essential for the sake of harmony and continuity in labour welfare services.

7. Democratic Values: The co-operation of the worker is the basis of this principle. Consultation with, and the agreement of workers in, the formulation and implementation of labour welfare services are very necessary for their success. This principle is based on the assumption that the worker is "a mature and rational individual." Industrial democracy is the driving force. Workers also develop a sense of pride when they are made to feel that labour welfare programmes are created by them and for them.

8. Responsibility: This recognizes the fact that both employers and workers are responsible for labour welfare. Trade unions are also involved in these programmes in healthy manner. Labour welfare belongs to the domain of trade union activity. Further, when responsibility is shared by different groups, labour welfare work becomes simpler and easier.

9. Accountability: This may also be called the Principle of Evaluation. Here, one responsible person gives an assessment or evaluation of existing welfare services on a periodical basis to a higher authority. This is very necessary, for then one can judge and analyze the success of labour welfare programmes.

10. Timely: The timeliness of any service helps in its success. To identify the labour problem and to discover what kind of help is necessary to solve it and when to provide this help are all very necessary in planning labour welfare programmes. Timely action in the proper direction is essential in any kind of social work.

Approaches

Moreover the various approaches to labour welfare reflect the attitudes and beliefs of the agencies, which are engaged in welfare activities. The different approaches to labour welfare reflect the evolution of the concept of welfare. Researchers (Railkar, 1990; Kohli and Sharma, 1997) have noted the following approaches to labour welfare:

Paternalistic Approach

The Paternalistic Approach to labour welfare can be traced back to the beginning of the modern industrial system where there was hardly any difference between management and ownership. The owners could have first hand information of the living and working conditions of the workers. The employers felt that they were responsible for the moral and material well-being of persons employed by them. The underlying assumption of this approach is that it takes for granted that the workers belong to a different and inferior social category, in need of help and charity. This assumption colours the nature of welfare schemes. These schemes are imposed from above (managers being wiser than workers) and the attitude of the employer seems to be 'I have done so much for you, now you should respect me and be loyal to me'. It may work in the initial stages of the factory system where the workers come from the villages. But with the changes in the attitudes of the people in general and industrial workers in particular, this attitude is resented and welfare measures are not accepted as charity.

Atomistic Approach

This approach demanded that every individual should be left as free as possible. Every individual can attain his own best interest only under the conditions of maximum freedom. Therefore in the matters of labour welfare this view was completely opposed to any welfare promoting activities undertaken by the government or any social or public agency. According to this view the scope of labour welfare activities should be as little as possible. This hypothesis is based on three important principles, which are as follows:

Society in its natural form is made up of individuals. They are un-organized and un-coordinated. Under such a natural society every individual is self-centered.

Such an individual always acts in a calculated manner. An individual always need a secure life. He is engaged in the activities of self- preservation. He will therefore act in such a manner that his self or personal interest will always be maximized.

Every individual throughout the life will act in such a manner that helps to promote his self-interest. He is always in the pursuit of this objective. He fulfills it to the best of his ability.

Mechanistic Approach

With the beginning of the 20th century labour welfare and labour relations have been moving towards a more sympathetic approach. Efforts to increase efficiency of labour have become a matter of fundamental importance. It was observed that if labour administration is more scientifically managed then there is considerable scope for improving efficiency of labour. Such an approach to scientific management of the industry leads to the 'mechanistic' view about, labour welfare. It treats worker as 'labour' performed in some 'mechanical units' such as 'hours of work', 'man — days', 'man — hours'. Its emphasis is on the scientific and effective methods of production.

Such an approach is greatly favoured by the employers and management. However, it is strongly opposed to by the trade union organization. This approach is based on the 'stimulus and response' relationship. The essence of the scientific management and mechanistic approach is the '**carrot and stick**' method that it advocates. Under this approach welfare activities such as social security measures, better economic justice or healthy and hygienic atmosphere at the place of work are not found necessary in order to promote over all development of the personality of workers. Therefore this approach takes a highly restrictive view of labour welfare activities.

Humanistic Approach

The Australian sociologist **Elton Mayo** advocated this approach. Mayo finds that what is more important is to treat labour as a human element of production. Therefore it was necessary to take a fresh and more sympathetic view of labour welfare.

Humanistic approach is based on human relationships, which was missing in the earlier approaches to labour welfare. The human factor was particularly missing in the administration of the industry and Mayo discovered the importance of informal relations between groups of workers and stressed sociality of man. The approach considered human personality, attitudes and sentiments of workers, while promoting labour welfare. Therefore the humanistic approach to labour welfare takes an enlightened view about labour welfare.

Statutory & Non – Statutory Labour Welfare

Organizations provide welfare facilities to their employees to keep their motivation levels high. The employee welfare schemes can be classified into two categories viz. statutory and non-statutory welfare schemes. The statutory schemes are those schemes that are compulsory to provide by an organization as compliance to the laws governing employee health and safety. These include provisions provided in industrial acts like Factories Act, 1948, Dock Workers Act, (safety, health and welfare) 1986, Mines Act, 1962. The non statutory schemes differ from organization to organization and from industry to industry.

The Factories Act, 1948

The welfare facilities provided under this act are as follows:

1. Adequate, suitable and clean washing facilities separately for male and female workers.
2. Facilities for storing and drying clothes.
3. Canteens, if more than 250 workers are employed.
4. Shelter, rest rooms and lunch rooms if there are more than 150 workers.
5. Welfare officer, whenever more than 500 workers are employed.

The Plantation Labour Act, 1951

The welfare facilities provided under this act are as follows:

1. A canteen wherever 150 or more than workers are employed.
2. A crèche, if employing 50 or more women workers.
3. Recreational facilities for the workers and their children.
4. Educational arrangements.
5. Housing facilities for every worker and his family residing in the plantation.
6. Medical aid to workers and their families.
7. Sickness allowance and maternity allowance.
8. Appointment of welfare officer in plantations employing 300 or more.

The Mines Act, 1952

The mines owners are required to make provisions for:

1. Creches if 50 or more women are employed.
2. Shelters for taking food and rest, wherever 150 or more workers are employed.
3. First aid boxes for first aid room in mines employing more than 150 workers.
4. Pit head baths equipped with shower bath, sanitary and lockers etc.

The Motor Transport Workers Act, 1961

The welfare facilities provided under this act are as follows:

1. Canteens for prescribed standards.
2. Clean, ventilated, well lighted and comfortable rest rooms at every place where motor transport workers are required to halt at night.
3. Uniforms, raincoats to drivers, conductors and time checkers for protection against rain and cold.
4. Prescribed medical facilities.

The Contract Labour Act, 1970

The welfare facilities provided under this act are as follows:

1. A canteen in every establishment employing 100 or more workers.
2. Rest rooms or other suitable alternatives accommodation where the ontract labour is required.
3. Washing facilities.
4. First aid boxes.

Intra and Extra Mural Welfare

Labour welfare is of two types:

1. Intramural and

2. Extramural

1. Intramural: Intramural activities consist of such welfare schemes provided within the factories as provision for creches and canteens, supply of drinking water, washing and bathing facilities, sufficient lighting, first aid appliances, fire extinguishers etc.

2. Extramural: These services are provided outside the establishment. These consist of housing accommodation, transport, sports, fields, holiday homes, maternity benefits etc.

Agencies for Welfare Work

The following are the main welfare agencies. These are **1.**Central Government **2.** State Government **3.** Employers **4.** Trade unions and **5.** Other agencies. These are discussed below:

1. **Central Government:** The central government tries to extend its helping hand through various acts covering the safety, health and welfare of workers. These are mainly Factories Act, 1948, Mines Act, 1952, Shipping Act, 1948, Plantation Labour Act, 1951.
2. **State Government:** State Government in different states and unions territories offer welfare facilities to workers. In Assam, a statutory

welfare fund is created for offering medical, educational, and other facilities to plantation workers.

3. **Employers:** "The employers in general looked upon welfare work as fruitless and barren though some of them indeed had done pioneering work". Enlightened employers like HUL, Godrej, L&T, TISCO, Siemens, Voltas, Bajaj, Birla, Sandoz, Philips, HMT, LIC, BHEL, etc. have undertaken welfare activities in the interest of workers.
4. **Trade Unions:** The contribution of trade unions in India towards labour welfare activities is not significant. Poor finances, multiple unionisms, often significant come in the way of undertaking labour welfare work enthusiastically. There are certain exception to this-like the Ahmedabad Textile Labour Association, Mazdoor Sabha of Kanpur and the Indian Federation of Labour.
5. **Other Agencies:** In addition to the above agencies Bombay Social Service League, Seva Sadan Social Service League, Bombay Women's Societies, Assam Seva Samity, Y.M.C.A. etc. also provide services to the working class on a voluntary basis.

Social Security Measures

Some of the important social security measures are given below.

1. Workmen's Compensation Act 1923: The Act provides for the compensation to those workmen who sustain personal injuries by accidents arising out of and in the course of their employment. The Act applies to all permanent employees employed in railways, factories, mines, plantations, mechanically propelled vehicles, construction work and certain other hazardous occupations drawing a salary not exceeding Rs 1,000. The Act does not cover those employees who are in clerical or administrative capacity in armed forces, on casual work and to those who are getting a monthly salary exceeding Rs. 1,000/-. The State Governments are empowered to extend the application of the Act to other classes of persons or diseases also.

The employer is liable to pay, under this Act, the compensation in case of personnel injury caused by accident arising out of and in the course of employment. No compensation is, however, payable if the incapacity does not last for more than three days or is caused by the default of the worker, not resulting in death. Besides bodily injury, compensation is also payable in the case of certain occupational diseases as given in Schedule III. The State Governments are empowered to add any other disease to the list of diseases.

The amount of compensation payable depends on the nature of injury and the average monthly wages of the worker concerned. For this purpose, injury has been divided under three categories **(i)** causing death, **(ii)** total or partial permanent disablement, and **(iii)** temporary disablement. The rates of compensation are fixed for all types of injuries according to wage-ranges. No compensation is paid for first three days if the period of disablement does not exceed 28 days. The Act does not apply to those workers who are covered under the Employees State Insurance Scheme.

2. Employees State Insurance Act 1948: In order to provide sickness benefits to workers, the Employees State Insurance Act was passed in 1948. The Act applies to all non-seasonal factories run with power and employing 20 or more persons. It covers all types of employees — manual, clerical, supervisory and technical—not drawing a salary of more than Rs. 1,600 per month (the amount has been raised from Rs. 1000 to Rs. 1600 p.m. w.e.f. 27th January 1985). The scheme is compulsory and contributory. Compulsory in the sense that all workers covered under the act must be insured and contributory in the sense that it is financed by the contributions from employees and employers.

The administration of the scheme has been entrusted to an autonomous body called the Employees State Insurance Corporation.

The Corporation is managed by a governing body of 40 persons representing the Union and the State Governments, Parliament, employers and employees' organizations and the medical profession. This body elects a standing committee consisting of 13 members. A third body called Medical Benefit Council is constituted consisting of 26 members to advise the corporation on matters relating to medical benefits. State wise regional boards have also been constituted.

The scheme is financed by the Employees State Insurance Fund which consists of contributions from employers and employees, grants, donations and gifts from Central and State Governments, local authorities or any individual or body. The rate of contribution of employees depends upon its daily wages. The scheme provides six types of benefits to the insured workers and their dependents. These benefits are:

- **(i) Medical Benefit:** An insured person or (where medical benefit has been extended to his family) a member of his family who requires medical treatment is entitled to receive medical benefit free of charge. Such medical benefit may be given either in the form of outpatient treatment or as in patient treatment in a hospital which may be either run by the ESI Corporation or by any other agency.
- **(ii) Sickness Benefit:** An insured person, when he is sick, is also entitled to get sickness benefit at 62.5% of the average wage which he would have earned had he been well and at work.
- **(iii) Maternity Benefit:** An insured woman is entitled to receive maternity benefit (which is twice the sickness benefit rate) for all days on

which she does not work for remuneration, during a period of 12 weeks of which not more than 6 weeks shall precede the expected date of confinement.

(iv) Disablement Benefit: An insured person is entitled to receive disablement benefit for any injury -arising out of and in the course of his employment. If the disablement is temporary for not less than 3 days, excluding the day of accident, he is entitled to receive compensation according to the First Schedule to the Act. If the disablement is preeminent-whether total or partial -he is entitled to receive compensation according to the Second Schedule to the Act. Artificial limbs are also provided at the cost of Corporation to those who lose their limbs as a result of employment injury. Spectacles, dentures, pace-makers, etc., are also provided to insured person free of cost, depending upon the nature of the case.

(v) Dependent's Benefit: If an insured person meets with an accident in the course of his employment and dies as a result thereof, his dependent, i.e., his widow, legitimate (or adopted) sons and legitimate unmarried daughters get pension. The widow gets it throughout her life or till remarriage. The sons get it up to the age of 18 years or until they marry, whichever is earlier.

(vi) Funeral Benefit: The eldest surviving member of the family of an insured person who has died is entitled to receive payment for the expenditure incurred on funeral. However, this amount cannot exceed Rs. 100. The amount should be claimed within 3 months of the death of the insured person.

3. Maternity Benefits Act: Before Independence, many states passed the Maternity Benefits Acts but there was only one central Act in this respect-Mine's Maternity Benefits Act 1941. After independence two Central Acts-Employees State Insurance Act 1948 and Plantation Labour Act 1951-were also passed. With a view to achieve uniformity, Central Government passed in 1961 the Maternity Benefits Act. The Act applies to all mines, plantations and factories except those covered by the Employees State Insurance Scheme. The expectant mothers are entitled for 12 weeks leaves i.e., 6 weeks up to and including the day of delivery and 6 weeks immediately following that day, if they have put in 160 days service during twelve months preceding the date of expected delivery. A payment of Medical Bonus of Rs. 250/- by the employer if pre-natal and post-natal care is not provided free of charge.

4. Coalmines Provident Fund and Bonus Act 1948: The Coalmines Provident Fund and Bonus Act was passed in 1948 to make the old age provisions for all coalmine workers. The act was amended in 1950, 1951 and 1965. Under this Act, two different schemes, i.e., the Coalmines Provident

Fund Scheme and the Coalmines Bonus Scheme are in application and these schemes have been amended several times. Under the Provident Fund Scheme, the employers contribute 8% of their total emolument to the fund and an equal contribution is made by the employees. In June 1963, a provision was made in the scheme whereby the members are allowed to contribute voluntarily up to another 8% of their emoluments. The scheme is administrated by a Board of Trustees, consisting of equal members of representatives of the Government, employers and employees. A Special Reserve Fund was set up to make the payment to outgoing members. A Death Relief Fund has also been set up to ensure a guaranteed minimum payment of Rs. 750 to the dependents off the deceased whose accumulations in the fund are less than the amount at the time of death. The employees Family Pension Scheme 1971 also applies to coalmine workers.

5. Employees Provident Fund Act 1952: The Act was passed in 1952 covering factories employing 50 or more workers in 6 major industries, viz., iron and steel, textiles, engineering, cement, paper and cigarettes. By an amendment in 1960, the scheme was extended to all factories of five years standing and 20 or more workers. An exemption has been made for new undertakings, for a period of 3 years, Establishments employing between 20 and 50 persons are also exempted for 5 years. The scheme is contributory and compulsory. The employees and employers contribute 6 $^{1/4}$% of the total emoluments. The employees may, however, contribute 8 $^{1/3}$% of the total emoluments. The rate of contribution of employees has been raised to 8% in some notified industries. The scheme covers every employee drawing a salary of Rs. 1,000 or less and who has completed one year's continuous service and actually worked for 240 days in that period.

A Special Reserve Fund was made for making the payment to outgoing members. A Death Relief Fund has also been set up for affording financial assistance for the tune of Rs. 1000 to the nominees of the deceased whose pay does not exceed Rs. 500 p.m. at the time of death. The Provident Fund Act, 1952 was amended in 1971 to provide for the benefit of family pension to the members of the deceased in case of their death while in service. A family Pension-cum-life Insurance Scheme was introduced in 1971.

6. Family Pension Scheme 1971: This was launched for industrial workers covered by Provident Fund Schemes. Under this scheme, a financial assistance i.e., pension is provided to workers monthly after retirement till he survives and to his widow thereafter till she survives. The scheme is financed by the Central Government and the provident fund.

7. Payment of Gratuity Act 1972: Under this, employees in factories, mines, oil fields, plantation, ports, railways, etc. are entitled to gratuity after completing 5 years of service at the rate of 1/2 month's wages for each completed years of service subject to a maximum of 20 months wages.

8. Old-Age Pensions Scheme: Various State Governments - U.P, Kerala, Andhra Pradesh, Tamilnadu, etc. have introduced a scheme of old-age pension to persons of 60 years of age and are poor and destitute. It is open to all.

9. Compulsory Group Insurance: The scheme was introduced by the Central Government with the cooperation of the Life Insurance Corporation and applies to certain groups of workers. The employees contribute certain monthly amount towards the premium. If the member dies while in service, an amount of Rs. 10,000 is paid to the heir of the deceased. The U.P. Government has introduced the scheme for teachers, lawyers and police employees. The Government of Haryana has also taken certain steps.

10. Deposit-linked Insurance Scheme 1976: This scheme was launched on 1st August 1976 for the benefit of employees covered under Employees Provident Fund Scheme, and Coalmines Provident Fund Scheme. Under this scheme, a legal heir of the deceased or the nominee under provident fund schemes will get the average amount of balance in the provident fund account of the deceased in three years preceding death or Rs. 10,000 whichever is less. This scheme is financed by the Government and the employers.

11. Social Security Certificates: Social security certificates were introduced on 1st June 1982. These certificates can be purchased by any person who is between 18 and 45 years of age, maximum for an amount of not exceeding Rs. 5,000. The holder of the certificate will get three times of the amount invested after 10 years. There will not be any premature payment but in case where the holder of the certificate dies after two years from the date of purchase the legal heir can claim the maturity value of the certificate immediately.

Unit - III

Financial Management

Financial Management

Financial Management means planning, organizing, directing and controlling the financial activities such as procurement and utilization of funds of the enterprise. It means applying general management principles to financial resources of the enterprise. Financial management deals with three 'A' which are anticipation of fund, acquisition of fund and allocation of fund.

FM: Nature & Scope

Nature of Financial Management

The following are the main characteristics of the financial management:

1. **Analytical Thinking:** Under financial management financial problems are analyzed and considered. Study of trend of actual figures is made and ratio analysis is done.
2. **Continuous Process:** Previously financial management was required rarely but now the financial manager remains busy throughout the year.
3. **Basis of Managerial Decisions:** All managerial decisions relating to finance are taken after considering the report prepared by the finance manager. The financial management is the base of managerial decisions.
4. **Maintaining Balance between Risk and Profitability:** Larger the risk in the business, larger is the expectation of profits. Financial management maintains balance between the risk and profitability.

5. **Coordination between Processes:** There is always coordination between various processes of the business.
6. **Centralized Nature:** Financial management is of a centralized nature. Other activities can be decentralized but there is only one department for financial management.

Scope of Financial Management

Financial management is one of the important parts of overall management, which is directly related with various functional departments like personnel, marketing and production. Financial management covers wide area with multidimensional approaches. The following includes important scope of financial management.

1. Financial Management and Economics: Economic concepts like micro and macroeconomics are directly applied with the financial management approaches. Investment decisions, micro and macro environmental factors are closely associated with the functions of financial manager. Financial management also uses the economic equations like money value, discount factor, economic order quantity etc. Financial economics is one of the emerging areas, which provides immense opportunities to finance and economical areas.

2. Financial Management and Accounting: Accounting records includes the financial information of the business concern. Hence, we can easily understand the relationship between the financial management and accounting. In the olden periods, both financial management and accounting were treated as a same discipline and then it has been merged as Management Accounting because this part is very much helpful to finance manager to take decisions.

3. Financial Management and Mathematics: Modern approaches of the financial management apply large number of mathematical and statistical tools and techniques. They are also called as econometrics. Economic order quantity, discount factor, time value of money, present value of money, cost of capital, capital structure theories, dividend theories, ratio analysis and working capital analysis are used as mathematical and statistical tools and techniques in the field of financial management.

4. Financial Management and Production Management: Production management is the operational part of the business concern, which helps to multiply the money into profit. Profit of the concern depends upon the production performance. Production performance needs finance, because production department requires raw material, machinery, wages, operating expenses, etc.

5. Financial Management and Marketing: Produced goods are sold in the market with innovative and modern approaches. For this, the marketing department needs finance to meet their requirements. The financial manager or finance department is responsible to allocate the adequate finance to the marketing department.

6. Financial Management and Human Resource: Financial management is also related with human resource department, which provides manpower to all the functional areas of the management.

Valuation Concepts & Valuation of Securities

Concept of Time Value of Money

Time Value of Money (TVM) is an important concept in financial management. It can be used to compare investment alternatives and to solve a wide variety of financial calculations involving loans, mortgages, leases, savings and annuities.

Rupee received today is worth more than a Rupee received in the future. Three reasons may be attributed to individuals' time preference to money;

(i) Risk.

(ii) Preference of consumption.

(iii) Investment opportunity.

We know that Rs. 100 in hand today is more valuable than Rs. 100 receivable after a year. We will not part with Rs. 100 now if the same sum is repaid after a year. But we might part with Rs. 100 now if we are assured that Rs. 110 will be paid at the end of the first year. This "additional Compensation" required for parting Rs. 100 today, is called "interest" or "the time value of money". It is expressed in terms of percentage per annum.

Why should money have time value?

Money should have time value for the following reasons:

(a) Money can be employed productively to generate real returns;

(b) In an inflationary period, a rupee today has higher purchasing power than a rupee in the future;

(c) Due to uncertainties in the future, current consumption is preferred to future consumption.

Importance of Time Value of Money

The concept of time value of money helps in arriving at the comparable value of the different rupee amount arising at different points of time into equivalent values of a particular point of time (Present or future).

The cash flows arising at different periods of time can be made comparable by using any one of the following two ways.

(1) By compounding the present money to a future date i.e. by finding out the value of the present money.

(2) By discounting the future money to present date i.e. by finding out present value (PV) of future money.

Methods of Time Value of Money

(i) Compounding: We find the Future Values (FV) of all the cash flows at the end of the time period at a given rate of interest.

(ii) Discounting: We determine the Time Value of Money at Time "O" by comparing the initial outflow with the sum of the Present Values (PV) of the future inflows at a given rate of interest.

Time Value of Money

Compounding (Future Value)	**Discounting** (Present Value)
(a) Single Flow	(d) Single Flow
(b) Multiple Flows	(e) Uneven Multiple Flows
(c) Annuity	(f) Annuity
(g) Perpetuity	

(a) Future Value of a Single Flow

It is the process to determine the future value of a lump sum amount invested at one point of time.

$$FVn = PV\,(1+i)^n$$

Where,

FVn = Future value of initial cash outflow after n years

PV = Initial cash outflow

i = Rate of Interest p.a.

n = Life of the Investment

and $(1+i)^n$ = Future Value of Interest Factor (FVIF)

Illustration:

An amount of Rs. 15,000 invested today at a rate of 6% compound interest for 3 years will be compounded to:

$$\begin{aligned} FVn &= PV\,(1+i)^n \\ &= PV \times FVIF\,(6, 3) \\ &= PV \times (1.06)^3 \\ &= 15{,}000\,(1.191) \\ &= \text{Rs. } 17{,}865 \end{aligned}$$

Doubling Period: How long will it take for the amount invested to be doubled for a given rate of interest?

(i) By Applying "Rule of 72"

Doubling Period = 72/ Rate of Interest

For instance, if the rate is 5%, then the doubling period is = 72/5
= 14.4 years.

(ii) By Applying "Rule of 69"

Doubling Period = .35 + 69/ Rate of Interest

For instance, if the rate is 5%, then the doubling period is = .35 + 69/ 5
= .35 + 13.8
= 14.15 years

If compounding is done other than annual compounding:

$$\mathbf{FV_n = PV\ (1 + i/m)^{m \times n}}$$

PV = Initial Cash Outflow

i = Rate of interest p.a.

m = no. of times compounding is done per year

n = no. of years for which compounding is done.

Illustration: Calculate the Future value of Rs. 1000 invested in State Bank for 2 years @ 5.5% p.a., compounded semi-annually.

Solution:

$FV_n = PV\ (1 + i/m)^{mxn}$

$= 1000\ (1+ .055/2)^{2x2}$

$= 1000\ (1+1.0275)^4$

= 1000 x 1.11462

= Rs. 1114.62

(b) Future Value of Multiple Flows

So far we have considered only the future value of a single payment made at time zero. The transactions in real life are not limited to one. An investor investing money in installments may wish to know the value of his saving after n years.

Illustration: Mr. Rishi invests Rs. 500, Rs.1,000, Rs. 1,500, Rs. 2,000 and Rs. 2,500 at the end of each year. Calculate the Future value at the end of 5 years compounded annually when interest is charged at 5% p.a.

Solution:

Statement of the Future Value

End of Year (1)	*Amount Deposited (2)*	*Number of years Compounded (3)*	*Compounded Interest factor (4)*	*Future Value (2x4)*
1	500	4	1.216	608
2	1,000	3	1.158	1158
3	1,500	2	1.103	1654.50
4	2,000	1	1.050	2100
5	2,500	0	1.000	2500

Therefore the Future Value = (608 + 1158+1654.50+2100+2500) = Rs. 8020.50

(c) Future Value of Annuity

Annuity is a term used to describe a series of periodic flows of equal amounts. These flows can be inflows or outflows.

The future value of annuity is expressed as:

$FVA_n = A + ((1+i)^n - 1 / i)$

Where,

A = Amount of Annuity

i = rate of interest

n = time period

FVAn = compounded at the end of n years.

and $\mathbf{((1+i)^n - 1 / i)}$ is the Future Value of Interest Factor for Annuity (FVIFA)

Illustration:

Calculation the maturity value of a recurring deposit of Rs. 500 p.m. for 12 months @ 9% p.a. compounded quarterly.

Solution:

Effective rate of interest per annum = $(1+.09/4)^4 - 1 = 1.0931 - 1 = .0931$

Rate of interest per month = $(1+i)^{1/m} - 1 = (1+.0931)^{1/12} - 1 = 1.0074 - 1 = .0074 = 7.4\%$

Maturity Value can be calculated as follows:

$\mathbf{FVA_n = A + ((1+i)^n - 1 / i)}$ = $500 + ((1 + .0074)^{12} - 1/ .0074) = 500 \times 12.50$ = Rs. 6250/-

(d) Present Value of a Single Flow

$$PV = FV_n / (1+i)^n$$

Where,

PV = Present Value

FVn = Future Value receivable after n years

i = rate of interest

n = time period

Illustration:

Calculate the Present Value of Rs. 1000 receivable after 3 years. Cost of Capital is 10% p.a.

Solution:

P.V. of Re. 1 @ 10% p.a. receivable after 3 years. = 0.7513

P.V. of Rs. 1000 = Rs. 1000 × 0.7513 = Rs. 751.30

(e) Present Value of Uneven Multiple Flows

In a business situation, it is very natural that returns received by a firm are spread over a number of years. An investment made now may fetch returns for a period after some time. Every businessman will like to know whether it is worthwhile to invest or forego a certain sum now, in anticipation of returns he expects to earn over a number of years. In order to take this decision he will need to equate the total anticipated future returns to the present sum he is going to sacrifice. To estimate the present value of future series of returns, the present value of each expected inflow will be calculated.

The present value of series of cash flows can be represented by the following formula:

$$PV = C_1/(1+i)^1 + C_2/(1+i)^2 + \ldots\ldots + C_n/(1+i)^n$$

Illustration:

Year	*Cash Inflows*	*P.V. @ 10%*	*Discounted Cash Flows*
1.	50,000	0.9091	45,455
2.	90,000	0.8264	74,376
3.	1, 20,000	0.7513	90,156
	2, 60,000		2, 09,087

The present value of Rs. 2, 60,000 discounted @ 10% will be Rs. 2, 09,987.

Present Value of Even Cash Inflows

Calculate P.V. of Rs. 50,000 receivable for 3 years @ 10%

P.V. = Cash Flows × Annuity @ 10% for 3 years.

= 50,000 × 2.4868 = Rs. 1.24, 340/-

(f) Present Value of an Annuity

The present value of an annuity 'A' receivable at the end of every year for a period of n years at the rate of interest 'i' is equal to

$$PVAn = A\square \frac{(1+i)^n - 1}{i(1+i)^n}$$

Where, $\frac{(1+i)^n - 1}{i(1+i)^n}$

is called the PVIFA (Present Value of Interest Factor Annuity) and it represents the present value of Re. 1 for the given values of i and n.

Illustration:

Calculate the present value of Rs. 100 deposited per month for 12 months @ 12% p.a., compounded quarterly.

Solution:

Step (1) Calculate effective rate of interest per annum

$$r = (1+i/m)^m - 1 = (1+.12/4)^4 - 1 = 1.1255 - 1 = .1255 = 12.55\%$$

Where,

i = normal rate of interest p.a.

r = effective rate of interest p.a.

m = no. of terms compounded in a year.

Step (2) Calculate effective rate of interest per month.

$$= (1+r)\ 1^{/12} - 1$$
$$= (1+.1255)^{1/12} - 1$$
$$= 0.00990$$

Step (3) The present value of deposits

$$\mathbf{PVA_n} = A\square \frac{(1+i)^n - 1}{i(1+i)^n} = 100\ \frac{(1+.0090)^{12} - 1}{.0090\ (1+.0090)^{12}}$$

$$= \text{Rs.}1126$$

Capital Budgeting Decision- Risk analysis

Concept of Capital Budgeting

Capital Budgeting is the art of finding assets that are worth more than they cost to achieve a predetermined goal i.e., 'optimizing the wealth of a business enterprise'. Capital investment involves a cash outflow in the immediate future in anticipation of returns at a future date.

For making a rational decision regarding the capital investment proposals, the decision maker needs some techniques to convert the cash outflows and cash inflows of a project into meaningful yardsticks which can measure the economic worthiness of projects.

Definition

Capital budgeting is defined "as the firm's formal process for the acquisition and investment of capital. It involves firm's decisions to invest its current funds for addition, disposition, modification and replacement of fixed assets".

"Capital budgeting is long term planning for making and financing proposed capital outlays"- **Charles T Horngreen.**

"Capital budgeting consists in planning and development of available capital for the purpose of maximizing the long term profitability of the concern" – **Lynch**

Features of Capital Budgeting

The features of capital budgeting decision are as follows:

(a) Funds are invested in current period in order to obtain future benefits.

(b) Future benefits are obtained over a series of years and only in one year.

(c) Often there is relatively a long time lag between the initial outlay and getting the first return.

(d) A relatively higher degree of risk is involved in capital budgeting as many factors may change in future.

(e) Expenditure related to an investment and the benefits received from such investment should be measured in terms of cash flow and not in terms of accounting profits.

(f) Selection of a profitable investment satisfies objectives of shareholders' wealth maximization thereby maximizing the value of the term.

Importance of Capital Budgeting

Capital budgeting decisions are of paramount importance in financial decision. So it needs special care on account of the following reasons:

1. **Long-term Implications:** A capital budgeting decision has its effect over a long time span and inevitably affects the company's future

cost structure and growth. A wrong decision can prove disastrous for the long-term survival of firm. On the other hand, lack of investment in asset would influence the competitive position of the firm. So the capital budgeting decisions determine the future destiny of the company.

2. **Involvement of Large Amount of Funds:** Capital budgeting decisions need substantial amount of capital outlay. This underlines the need for thoughtful, wise and correct decisions as an incorrect decision would not only result in losses but also prevent the firm from earning profit from other investments which could not be undertaken.
3. **Irreversible Decisions:** Capital budgeting decisions in most of the cases are irreversible because it is difficult to find a market for such assets. The only way out will be scrap the capital assets so acquired and incur heavy losses.
4. **Risk and Uncertainty:** Capital budgeting decision is surrounded by great number of uncertainties. The future is uncertain and full of risks. Longer the period of project, greater may be the risk and uncertainty. The estimates about cost, revenues and profits may not come true.
5. **Difficult to Make:** Capital budgeting decision making is a difficult and complicated exercise for the management. These decisions require an overall assessment of future events which are uncertain. It is really a marathon job to estimate the future benefits and cost correctly in quantitative terms subject to the uncertainties caused by economic, political, social and technological factors.

Significance of Capital Budgeting

Capital budgeting is very important to a firm and there is need for capital budgeting for the following reasons:

Capital budgeting decision has long term significance. The effect of capital budgeting decision will persist in the long run. Hence any wrong decision is taken its burden will have to be borne for a long period of time. The future prospect of a firm depends mainly on its capital expenditure. The firm can earn huge profits if it can make appropriate capital expenditure at the appropriate time. Hence, the firm should have sufficient thinking and consideration before such decisions.

Capital expenditure decision generally involve large sum of money. Such investment give returns for a long period of time but to procure such assets, a firm has to invest large sum of money. So before making such investment, the firm has to take sufficient care and make arrangement for collecting large funds.

Capital budgeting decision is irreversible in most cases. If a machine on capital goods is once purchased, it is difficult to get back the money by reselling it because such capital goods have very limited market. Hence, in many cases the firm has no other alternative but to scrap the capital goods to sell it at throw away price.

Capital expenditure requires huge money. No firm has unlimited money. If the money is invested wrongly not only the firm losses, it will also be deprived of the profits it could have obtained from the alternative use of that money.

Capital budgeting is important because they are the most difficult decision to make. To make such decision one has to forecast future events and future income and expenditure. The future returns from an investment can't always be expressed in money terms.

Due to a particular capital budgeting decision the firms risk may increase. Suppose, due to an acceptance of an investment proposal, the firm income increased, but at the same time fluctuation in income also increased, in that case, both income and risk of the firm increased. The future cost structure of the firm is also related to the capital budgeting decisions.

Types of Capital Budgeting Decision

Generally the business firms are confronted with three types of capital budgeting decisions. **(i)** The accept-reject decisions; **(ii)** mutually exclusive decisions; and **(iii)** capital rationing decisions.

1. **Accept-Reject Decisions:** Business firm is confronted with alternative investment proposals. If the proposal is accepted, the firm incurs the investment and not otherwise. Broadly, all those investment proposals which yield a rate of return greater than cost of capital are accepted and the others are rejected. Under this criterion, all the independent proposals are accepted.
2. **Mutually Exclusive Decisions:** It includes all those projects which compete with each other in a way that acceptance of one precludes the acceptance of other or others. Thus, some technique has to be used for selecting the best among all and eliminates other alternatives.
3. **Capital Rationing Decisions:** Capital budgeting decision is a simple process in those firms where fund is not the constraint, but in majority of the cases, firms have fixed capital budget. So large amount of projects compete for these limited budgets. So the firm rations them in a manner so as to maximize the long run returns. Thus, capital rationing refers to the situations where the firm has more acceptable investment requiring greater amount of finance than is available with the firm. It is concerned with the selection of a

group of investment out of many investment proposals ranked in the descending order of the rate or return.

Capital Budgeting Process

Capital budgeting process involves the following:

1. **Project Generation:** Generating the proposals for investment is the first step. The investment proposal may fall into one of the following categories:
   (a) Proposals to add new product to the product line;
   (b) Proposals to expand production capacity in existing lines;
   (c) Proposals to reduce the costs of the output of the existing products without altering the scale of operation;
   (d) Sales campaigning, trade fairs people in the industry, R and D institutes, conferences and seminars will offer wide variety of innovations on capital assets for investment.
2. **Project Evaluation:** It involves two steps:
   (a) Estimation of Benefits and Costs: The benefits and costs are measured in terms of cash flows. The estimation of the cash inflows and cash outflows mainly depends on future uncertainties. The risk associated with each project must be carefully analysed and sufficient provision must be made for covering the different types of risks.
   (b) Selection of Appropriate Criteria to Judge the Desirability of the Project: It must be consistent with the firm's objective of maximizing its market value. The technique of time value of money may come as a handy tool in evaluating such proposals.
3. **Project Selection:** No standard administrative procedure can be laid down for approving the investment proposal. The screening and selection procedures are different from firm to firm.
4. **Project Execution:** Once the proposal for capital expenditure is finalized, it is the duty of the finance manager to explore the different alternatives available for acquiring the funds. He has to prepare capital budget. Sufficient care must be taken to reduce the average cost of funds. He has to prepare periodical reports and must seek prior permission from the top management. Systematic procedure should be developed to review the performance of projects during their lifetime and after completion.

The follow up, comparison of actual performance with original estimates not only ensures better forecasting but also helps in sharpening the techniques for improving future forecasts.

Methods of Capital Budgeting

Capital budgeting methods is of two types. One is traditional or non - discounting method and the second one is modern or discounting method of capital budgeting decision.

The modern or discounting method of capital budgeting decision must satisfy the following characteristics:

(i) It must consider time value of money.

(ii) A specific discounting factor is to be taken into consideration in order to compute the present value of cash flows.

(iii) All incremental costs and benefits are to be taken into consideration throughout the expected life of a project.

If any method does not fulfill the above stated conditions at a time then it will be treated as traditional or non - discounting method of capital budgeting decision.

Traditional methods of capital budgeting decision are mainly Payback period and Accounting Rate of Return (ARR).On the other hand, modern methods of capital budgeting decision are mainly Net Present Value (NPV), Internal Rate of Return (IRR) and Profitability Indices (PI) method.

1. Payback Period Method

It refers to the minimum period in which the project will generate the necessary cash to recover the initial investment.

Formula

(a) If the nature of cash inflows is uniform, the payback period will be computed by the following formula:

Payback period = Initial investment/ annual cash inflow

(b) If the nature of cash inflows is not uniform, the payback period will be computed with the cumulative cash flow table.

Accept or Reject Criterion

(i) If the computed payback period is less than standard payback period- Accept the project

(ii) If the computed payback period is more than standard payback period- Reject the project

(iii) If the computed payback period is equal to standard payback period- Accept or Reject the project depending upon the urgency of the project.

Advantages

(i) It does not take the effect of time value of money.

(ii) It emphasizes more on annual cash inflows, economic life of the project and original investment.

(iii) The selection of the project is based on the earning capacity of a project.

(iv) It involves simple calculation, selection or rejection of the project can be made easily, results obtained are more reliable, best method for evaluating high risk projects.

Disadvantages

(i) It is based on principle of rule of thumb.

(ii) It does not recognize importance of time value of money.

(iii) It does not consider profitability of economic life of project.

(iv) It does not recognize pattern of cash flows.

(v) It does not reflect all the relevant dimensions of profitability.

2. Accounting Rate of Return (ARR)

This method is based on conventional accounting concepts. The rate of return is expressed as percentage of the earnings of the investment in a particular project. This method has been introduced to overcome the disadvantage of payback period. The profits under this method are calculated as profit after depreciation and tax of the entire life of the project.

This method of ARR is not commonly accepted in assessing the profitability of capital expenditure. Because the method does to consider the heavy cash inflow during the project period as the earnings will be averaged.

Accept or Reject Criterion: Under the method, all project having Accounting Rate of Return higher than the minimum rate establishment by management will be considered and those having ARR less than the pre-determined rate will not be taken into consideration. This method ranks a Project as number one, if it has the highest ARR, and the lowest rank is assigned to the project with the lowest ARR.

Formula: ARR = Average Income x 100/ Average Investment

Here, Average Income = Total Income/ Number of years

Average Investment = Total Investment – Scrap value / 2

Accept or Reject Criterion

This method will accept all those projects whose accounting rate of return is higher than the minimum rate established by management. This will reject those projects whose accounting rate of return is lower than the minimum rate established by management.

Advantages

- **(i)** It is very simple to understand and use.
- **(ii)** This method takes into account saving over the entire economic life of the project. Therefore, it provides a better means of comparison of project than the payback period.
- **(iii)** It can readily be calculated by using the accounting data.

Disadvantages

- **(i)** It ignores the time value of money.
- **(ii)** It does not consider the length of life of the projects.
- **(iii)** It is not consistent with the firm's objective of maximizing the market value of shares.
- **(iv)** It ignores the fact that the profits earned can be reinvested.

Net Present Value Method

The NPV is the difference between the total present value of future cash inflows and the total present value of future cash outflows.

Formula: NPV = TPV – Total investment

Accept or Reject Criterion

- **(i)** If NPV is greater than zero - Accept the project
- **(ii)** If NPV is less than zero - Reject the project
- **(iii)** If NPV is equal to zero - Accept or Reject the project depending upon the urgency of the project.

Advantages

- **(i)** It recognizes the impact of time value of money. It is considered as the best method of evaluating the capital investment proposal.
- **(ii)** It is widely used in practice. The cash inflow to be received at different period of time will be discounted at a particular discount rate. The present values of the cash inflow are compared with the original investment. The difference between the two will be used for accept or reject criteria. If the different yields (+) positive value, the proposal is selected for investment. If the difference shows (-) negative values, it will be rejected.
- **(iii)** It recognizes the time value of money.
- **(iv)** It considers the cash inflow of the entire project.
- **(v)** It estimates the present value of cash inflows by using a discount rate equal to the cost of capital.
- **(vi)** It is consistent with the objective of maximizing the welfare of owners.

Disadvantages

(i) It is very difficult to find and understand the concept of cost of capital.

(ii) It may not give reliable answers when dealing with alternative projects under the conditions of unequal lives of project.

Internal Rate of Return

It is that rate at which the sum of discounted cash inflows equals the sum of discounted cash outflows. It is the rate at which the net present value of the investment is zero. It is the rate of discount which reduces the NPV of an investment to zero. It is called internal rate because it depends mainly on the outlay and proceeds associated with the project and not on any rate determined outside the investment.

Formula: IRR = A + (C – 0)/ (C-D) x (B-A)

Where:

A = Lower discounting factor

B = Higher discounting factor

C = TPV taking lower discounting factor

D = TPV taking higher discounting factor

0 = Initial investment

Accept or Reject Criterion

(i) If IRR is greater than cost of capital – accept the project

(ii) If IRR is lower than cost of capital –Reject the project

(iii) If IRR is equal to cost of capital –Accept or Reject the project depending upon the urgency of the project

Advantages

(i) It considers the time value of money.

(ii) Calculation of cost of capital is not a prerequisite for adopting IRR.

(iii) IRR attempts to find the maximum rate of interest at which funds invested in the project could be repaid out of the cash inflows arising from the project.

(iv) It is not in conflict with the concept of maximizing the welfare of the equity shareholders.

(v) It considers cash inflows throughout the life of the project.

Disadvantages

(i) Computation of IRR is tedious and difficult to understand.

(ii) Both NPV and IRR assume that the cash inflows can be reinvested at the discounting rate in the new projects. However, reinvestment of funds at the cut off rate is more appropriate than at the IRR.

(iii) It may give results inconsistent with NPV method. This is especially true in case of mutually exclusive project.

Profitability Indices (PI) Method

PI is the ratio of present value of future cash benefits at the required rate of return at the initial cash investment.

Formula: PI = PV of cash inflows/ Initial investment

Accept or Reject Criterion

(i) If PI value is greater than one – Accept the project

(ii) If PI value is less than one – Reject the project

(iii) If PI value is equal to one –Accept or Reject the project depending upon the urgency

NPV Vs IRR Comparison

Key differences between the most popular methods, the NPV (Net Present Value) Method and IRR (Internal Rate of Return) Method, include:

NPV is calculated in terms of currency while **IRR** is expressed in terms of the percentage return a firm expects the capital project to return;

Academic evidence suggests that the **NPV** method is preferred over other methods since it calculates additional wealth and the IRR Method does not;

The IRR method cannot be used to evaluate projects where there are changing cash flows (e.g., an initial outflow followed by in-flows and a later out-flow, such as may be required in the case of land reclamation by a mining firm);

However, the **IRR** method does have one significant advantage - managers tend to better understand the concept of returns stated in percentages and find it easy to compare to the required cost of capital; and, finally,

While both the NPV method and the IRR method are both DCF models and can even reach similar conclusions about a single project, the use of the IRR method can lead to the belief that a smaller project with a shorter life and earlier cash inflows is preferable to a larger project that will generate more cash.

Applying NPV using different discount rates will result in different recommendations. The IRR method always gives the same recommendation.

Capital Rationing

Capital rationing is a situation when a firm operates within a fixed budget. In this situation, a firm cannot accept all projects which are expected to increase the present value. The constraints which leads to capital rationing are market conditions and self– imposed factors. The question of capital rationing arises where there are several alternatives where investment is possible but the supply of fund is limited. Under the situation, a combination of profitable investment proposals is considered to maximize the net present values of the combined projects.

Capital rationing follows a process of selection of the projects in the following way:

1. **Making of the Ranks:** Ranking of the projects is made on the basis of NPV or PI of the projects. The ranking may be made by following any one of the discounted cash flow method.
2. **Selection of the proposals:** Selection of the projects is made in descending order of the profitability. The selection process is extended up to the available amount of the funds. If there is mutually exclusive projects, selection will be made on the basis of higher contribution or higher NPV of the projects.

Capital Structure & Cost of Capital

Concept of Capital Structure

The capital structure of a company is the particular combination of debt, equity and other sources of finance that it uses to fund its long term financing. The key division in capital structure is between debt and equity. The proportion of debt funding is measured by gearing.

Capital structure is the combination of long – term ownership capital and debt capital which indicates the proportion of debt and equity leading to the maximum value of the firm with minimum cost of capital.

According to Institute of Chartered Accountants of India, "Capital structure refers to the mix or proportion of sources from where long- term funds required in a business may be raised."

According to the Gerstenberg, "Capital structure refers to the types of securities to be issued and proportionate amount that mark-up the capitalisation."

According to Schwarty, "the Capital structure of business can be measured by the ratio of various kinds of permanent loan and equity capital to total capital".

Capital Structure vs. Financial Structure

Capital structure refers to the structure of long – term capital or long-term funds employed in the business enterprise. On the other hand, financial Structure refers to the structure of total funds including long – term and short –term sources of funds.

Capital structure does not include short-term funds or current liabilities but financial structure includes the short-term funds or current liabilities.

So, we can say that capital structure is a part of financial structure.

Importance of Capital structure

The importance of capital structure is stated as follows:

1. To Reduce the Overall Risk of Company: When we make capital structure before actual getting money from money supplier, we can do many adjustments for reducing our overall risk. Suppose, we have made capital structure in which we add three sources of fund, one is equity share, and other is debenture and last is pref. shares. Because we know that we have to pay debt at its maturity at any cost and its interest at fixed rate. So, we try to get minimum debt in new business because in new business our rate of return will be less than rate of interest and for getting more loan means taking high risk of return, more amount of interest even there is no profit.

2. To do Adjustment according to Business Environment: Company also adjusts different sources expected amount according to business environment. Suppose in future, if government of India cuts off his relation with China, from where our company is getting fund, it will definitely tough for us to get more money from China. But proper planning of capital structure of future sources will be helpful for us to enlarge our area for getting money. In finance, it is called **maneuverability.** It means to create mobility of sources of fund by including maximum alternatives in planned capital structure. Suppose, if RBI increases the interest rate, it means your cost for getting debt will be high, at that time, you can choose any other cheap source of fund.

3. Idea Generation of New Source of Fund: Good planning of capital structure will make **versatile** to finance manager for getting money from new sources. If you have studied Wikipedia's page of venture capital or private sources, you would precisely understand that how finance managers of company are generating new and new idea for getting money from public at **low risk**.

Factors Determining Capital structure

In planning the capital structure of a firm the following factors are to be taken into consideration:

Trading on Equity: The word 'equity' denotes the ownership of the company. Trading on equity means taking advantage of equity share capital to borrow funds on reasonable basis. It refers to additional profits that equity shareholders earn because of issuance of debentures and preference shares. It is based on the thought that if the rate of dividend on preference capital and the rate of interest on borrowed capital is lower than the general rate of company's earnings, equity shareholders are at advantage which means a company should go for a judicious blend of preference shares, equity shares as well as debentures. Trading on equity becomes more important when expectations of shareholders are high.

Degree of Control: In a company, it is the directors who are so called elected representatives of equity shareholders. These members have got maximum voting rights in a concern as compared to the preference shareholders and debenture holders. Preference shareholders have reasonably less voting rights while debenture holders have no voting rights. If the company's management policies are such that they want to retain their voting rights in their hands, the capital structure consists of debenture holders and loans rather than equity shares.

Flexibility of Financial Plan: In an enterprise, the capital structure should be such that there are both contractions as well as relaxation in plans. Debentures and loans can be refunded back as the time requires. While equity capital cannot be refunded at any point which provides rigidity to plans. Therefore, in order to make flexible capital structure, the company should go for issue of debentures and other loans.

Choice of Investors: The Company's policy generally is to have different categories of investors for securities. Therefore, a capital structure should give enough choice to all kind of investors to invest. Bold and adventurous investors generally go for equity shares and loans and debentures are generally raised keeping into mind conscious investors.

Capital Market Condition: In the lifetime of the company, the market price of the shares has got an important influence. During the depression period, the company's capital structure should generally consists of debentures and loans. While in period of boons and inflation, the company's capital should consist of share capital generally equity shares.

Period of Financing: When company wants to raise finance for short period, it goes for loans from banks and other institutions; while for long period, it goes for issue of shares and debentures.

Cost of Financing: In a capital structure, the company has to look to the factor of cost when securities are raised. It is seen that debentures at the time of profit earning of company prove to be a cheaper source of finance as compared to equity shares where equity shareholders demand an extra share in profits.

Stability of Sales: An established business which has a growing market and high sales turnover, the company is in position to meet fixed commitments. Interest on debentures has to be paid regardless of profit. Therefore, when sales are high, thereby the profits are high and company is in better position to meet such fixed commitments like interest on debentures and dividends on preference shares. If company is having unstable sales, then the company is not in position to meet fixed obligations. So, equity capital proves to be safe in such cases.

Sizes of Company: Small size business firm's capital structure generally consists of loans from banks and retained profits. While on the other hand, big companies having goodwill, stability and an established profit can easily go for issuance of shares and debentures as well as loans and borrowings from financial institutions. The bigger the size, the wider is total capitalization.

Theories of Capital Structure

There are mainly four theories of capital structure. The theories of capital structure are based on the following assumptions:

- There are only two kinds of funds used by a firm i.e. debt and equity.
- Taxes are not considered.
- The payout ratio is 100%.
- The firm's total financing remains constant.
- Business risk is constant over time.
- The firm has perpetual life.

Net Income Approach (NI-approach)

This approach has been suggested by Durand. According to this approach, a firm can increase its value or lower the overall cost of capital by increasing the proportion of debt in the capital structure. In other words, if the degree of financial leverage increases the weighted average cost of capital will decline with every increase in the debt content in total funds employed, while the value of firm will increase. Reverse will happen in a converse situation.

Net Income Approach is based on the following three assumptions:

(i) There are no corporate taxes

(ii) The cost of debt is less than cost of equity or equity capitalization rate.

(iii) The use of debt content does not change at risk perception of investors as a result both the k_d (debt capitalization rate) and k_c (equity-capitalization rate) remains constant.

The value of the firm on the basis of Net Income Approach can be ascertained as follows:

V = S + D

Where, V = Value of the firm

S = Market value of equity

D = Market value of debt

Market value of equity (S) = NI/K_c

Where, NI = Earnings available for equity shareholders

K_c = Equity Capitalization rate

Under, NI approach, the value of the firm will be maximum at a point where weighted average cost of capital is minimum. Thus, the theory suggests total or maximum possible debt financing for minimizing the cost of capital.

The overall cost of capital under this approach is:

Overall cost of capital = EBIT/ Value of the firm: According to this approach the average cost of capital (k_o) declines as gearing increases. The cost of shareholders funds (k_s) and the cost of debt (k_d) are independent. Since k_d is usually less than k_s as debt is less risky than equity from the investor's point of view, an increase in gearing should lead to a decrease in k_o.

Net Operating Income (NOI) Approach: This theory was propounded by 'David Durand' and is also known as 'Irrelevant Theory'. According to NOI approach the value of the firm and the weighted average cost of capital are independent of the firm's capital structure. Overall cost of capital is independent of degree of leverage. In the absence of taxes, an individual holding all the debt and equity securities will receive the same cash flows regardless of the capital structure and therefore, value of the company is the same.

Assumptions of NOI Theory

(i) The overall capitalization rate remains constant for all levels of financial leverage.

(ii) The cost of debt also remains constant for all levels of financial leverage.

(iii) The cost of equity increases linearly with financial leverage.

The formula to calculate the cost of capital is

$$K_o = K_d(B/(B+S)) + K_e(S/(B+S))$$

K_o and K_d are constant for all levels of leverage. Given this, the cost of equity can be expressed as follows:

$$Ke = Ko + (Ko - Kd)(B/S)$$

According to this approach, there is no optimal capital structure. The financing mix does not affect the average cost of capital of the company; and the total value of the firm remains unchanged with changes in the gearing i.e. k_o remains constant.

Traditional or Intermediate Approach

This approach is midway between the NI and the NOI approach. According to this theory, a firm can reduce the overall cost of capital or increase the total value of the firm by increasing the debt proportion in its capital structure to a certain limit. Because debt is a cheap source of raising funds as compared to equity capital.

The main propositions of this approach are:

(i) The cost of debt remains almost constant up to a certain degree of leverage but rises thereafter at an increasing rate.

(ii) The cost of equity remains more or less constant or rises gradually up to a certain degree of leverage and rises sharply thereafter.

(iii) The cost of capital due to the behaviour of the cost of debt and cost of equity decreases up to a certain point, remains more or less constant for moderate increases in leverage, thereafter rises beyond that level at an increasing rate.

MM Approach

This approach indicates that the capital structure is irrelevant because of the arbitrage process which will correct any imbalance i.e. expectations will change and a stage will be reached where further arbitrage is not possible.

Assumptions of MM Approach:

(i) Perfect Capital Market

(ii) No Transaction Cost

(iii) Homogeneous Risk Class: Expected EBIT of all the firms has identical risk characteristics.

(iv) Risk in terms of expected EBIT should also be identical for determination of market value of the shares

(v) Cent-Percent distribution of earnings to the shareholders

(vi) No Corporate Taxes: But later on in 1969 they removed this assumption.

MM Approach without Tax: Proposition I

MM's Proposition I, states that the firm's value is independent of its capital structure .The Total value of firm must be constant irrespective of the Degree of leverage (debt equity Ratio). With personal leverage, shareholders can receive exactly the same return, with the same risk, from a levered firm and an unlevered firm. Thus, they will sell shares of the over-priced firm and buy shares of the under-priced firm. This will continue till the market prices of identical firms become identical. This is called arbitrage.

MM Approach without Tax: Proposition II

The cost of equity for a levered firm equals the constant overall cost of capital plus a risk premium that equals the spread between the overall cost of capital and the cost of debt multiplied by the firm's debt-equity ratio. For financial leverage to be irrelevant, the overall cost of capital must remain constant, regardless of the amount of debt employed. This implies that the cost of equity must rise as financial risk increases.

MM Hypothesis with Corporate Tax

Under current laws in most countries, debt has an important advantage over equity: interest payments on debt are tax deductible, whereas dividend payments and retained earnings are not. Investors in a levered firm receive in the aggregate the unlevered cash flow plus an amount equal to the tax deduction on interest. Capitalizing the first component of cash flow at the all-equity rate and the second at the cost of debt shows that the value of the levered firm is equal to the value of the unlevered firm plus the interest tax shield which is tax rate times the debt (if the shield is fully usable).

It is assumed that the firm will borrow the same amount of debt in perpetuity and will always be able to use the tax shield. Also, it ignores bankruptcy and agency costs.

Arguments against the Modigliani – Miller Position

These are based on reasons why the arbitrage process may not work perfectly. These are as follows:

- **(i)** If there is a possibility of bankruptcy and if these costs are significant, a geared firm may be less attractive. In perfect markets if the firm is liquidated all assets are realized with zero costs.
- **(ii)** The perceived risks of personal and corporate gearing may be different because of limited liability on corporate debt.
- **(iii)** Personal borrowing costs are generally higher than corporate costs.
- **(iv)** Transaction costs restrict arbitrage.
- **(v)** Some institutional investors may be precluded from 'personal' borrowing by the articles or by law.
- **(vi)** Investors do not have access to perfect, cost-free information.

MM deny the importance of these criticisms by arguing that they are too general. They suggest that as long as there are enough market participants at the margin to behave in a manner consistent with 'homemade' gearing the total value of the firm cannot be altered through gearing. The MM approach is most vulnerable at extreme levels of gearing.

Extreme Gearing

When gearing reaches a certain level k_d will rise as debt investors expect the firm to pay a higher interest rate on debt. The greater the gearing, the lower the coverage of fixed charges and the riskier the loan.

Even if k_d rises, MM maintain the k_o will be constant because k_s will increase at a decreasing rate to offset the increase in k_d.

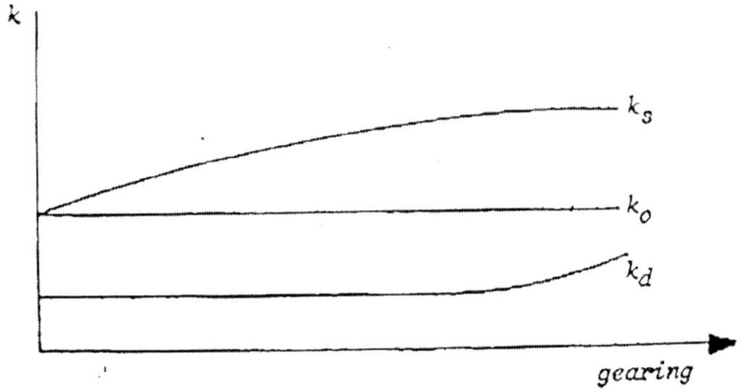

Many authorities object strongly to the contention that shareholders became relatively less risk-averse with extreme gearing.

Concept of Cost of Capital

The cost of capital of a company is the average rate of return required by investors who provide long term funds (equity, preference and long term debt). A central concept in financing decisions, the cost of capital is important for two reasons:

1. For evaluating capital investment proposals, an estimate of the cost of capital is required. As we have seen, the cost of capital is the discount rate in NPV calculation and also the financial benchmark against which the internal rate of return is compared.
2. To maximize the value of the firm, costs of all inputs must be minimized.

Types of Cost of Capital

There are two types of cost of capital. These are explicit cost of capital and implicit cost of capital. These are discussed below:

Explicit Cost of Capital

Explicit cost of capital is that cut off rate which equates present value of cash inflows to present value of cash outflows. In other words, it is nothing but internal rate of return. In capital budgeting decision, investor will see which investment provides high internal rate of return.

For Example: A company accepts loans by issuing new debentures of Rs. 5, 00,000. This company also promises to pay Rs. 50,000 per year, company's total inflow will be Rs. 5, 00,000 and total outflow of cash will be Rs.50, 000 per year and if there is nothing cost of capital, then this loan can be repaid within 10 years. But it is not possible that company would receive loan without giving interest. So, minimum value of interest which the company will pay on the condition that it will equal the present value of Rs. 5, 00,000 and Rs. 50,000 will be explicit cost of capital. This decision will be taken at the time when company gets loan. If company is giving high interest rate on loan, then its net explicit cost will be less because, interest is given out of net profit and company can save tax and if we adjust this tax rate, explicit cost will be less than actual interest on loan.

Implicit Cost of Capital

Implicit cost of capital is opportunity cost, if money is used for one of the best alternatives for effective use of resources. Suppose, I have Rs. 1, 00,000.I can deposit it in bank and earn Rs. 3,500 as bank interest but I did not invest it in saving bank account and invested in the shares of XYZ Company. So, my implicit cost of investment in shares will equal to the bank interest.

Significance of Cost of Capital

The concept of cost of capital is important in financial management in many ways. Especially, it is useful in deciding the capital structure of a company. It has great significance in the field of financial management. Recently, increasing attention is being paid to it by the academicians, as also by the newly appointed financial managers of the companies. In the past, the concept of cost of capital was neglected. Most of the economists took it for granted that cost of capital is not affected by the capital structure of a company. But at present, this concept plays an important role in the determination of capital structure and in capital budgeting decision. The significance of the concept of cost of capital will be clear from the following:

1. For Capital Budgeting Decisions: The concept of cost of capital helps in making financial decisions. Specially, in case of capital budgeting, it is used as a decision criterion in capital budgeting decision. If the present value of cash flows of the project is greater than the present value of investment in it, the project would be accepted. The rate of discount that is used to calculate the present value of future cash flows of the project is nothing but the cost of capital. Thus, cost of capital is the minimum rate of return required on investment project. It is the rate of discount which is used to evaluate the profitability of an investment project.

If the investment project is to be evaluated on the basis of an internal rate of return, the project will be acceptable when the internal rate of return exceeds the cost of capital.

2. Maintaining Market Value of Shares: An important decision in the field of financial planning is concerning maximization of the equity shareholder's wealth. For the maximization of equity shareholder's wealth, it is necessary that market value of shares is maintained at a high level. The cost of capital is in fact that minimum rate of return which maintains the market value of shares as its current level. If a company succeeds in raising its earnings, the market value of its shares would naturally move above this level. Thus, cost of capital serves as a criterion which helps in optimum utilization of company's financial resources.

3. Helps in Designing Capital Structure: A proper capital structure can be built with the help of the concept of cost of capital. The lower the cost of capital, the stronger can be the market value of the firm. Hence the capital structure should be planned in such a manner that cost of capital is minimized. This will raise the market value of the firm.

4. Issue of New Securities: If an investment scheme is found profitable, it may be necessary to issue new securities to raise money for this investment scheme. The concept of cost of capital provides guidance in deciding which type of securities should be used for this purpose. For taking such decisions the following must be taken into consideration: the nature of existing capital structure, the cost of capital of different sources of finance, the effect on aggregate cost of capital when money is raised through debts instead of equity shares etc. How to raise the required finance can be decided on the basis of the information about cost of existing capital and that of raising additional capital.

5. To Evaluate the Performance of Top Management: The concept of cost of capital is helpful also in evaluating the financial performance of the top management. For this purpose, actual profitability of the new scheme of investment is to be compared with the projected overall cost of capital, and actual cost incurred in raising required funds is also to be evaluated.

6. Financial Decisions: The concept of cost of capital is important in many other areas of financial decision making such as dividend decisions, working capital policy, etc. The decision about dividends to be taken on the basis of the amount of profit that is to be reserved in the company and the amount of reserves depends on the relation between its capital cost on the one hand and possible rate of return of it, invested in business.

Computation of Cost of Capital

Cost of capital is measured for different components or sources of capital structure of a company. Specific cost of capital includes cost of equity share capital, cost of preference share capital, cost of retained earnings, cost of debentures; cost of loan capital etc. The measurement of specific cost of capital of different components of capital structure is discussed below under different headings:

Cost of Equity Share Capital (Ke)

Different formula used for the purpose of cost of equity share capital is mentioned below:

1. **Earning Price Approach:** Under this approach the cost of capital is the ratio between the earnings (E) and the current market price (P) of the shares. Under this approach the cost of equity share capital is measured by using the following formula:

$$K_e = E/P$$

2. **Dividend Price Approach:** Under this approach the cost of capital is the ratio between the dividend paid (D) on the share and market price (P) of the share. This approach gives emphasis on the dividend declared not on the earnings of the company. Under this approach the cost of equity share capital is measured by using the following formula:

$$K_e = D/P$$

3. **Growth Model with Earning Approach:** This model considers growth rate of earnings. Under this approach the cost of equity share capital is measured by using the following formula:

$$\mathbf{K_e = E/P + g} \text{ (g = growth rate of earnings)}$$

4. **Growth Model with Dividend Approach:** This model considers growth rate in dividend. Under this approach the cost of equity share capital is measured by using the following formula:

$$\mathbf{K_e = D/P + g} \text{ (g = growth rate in dividend)}$$

5. **Calculation of Cost of Equity Share Capital:** Cost of equity share capital is calculated by using the following formula:

$$\mathbf{K_e = D_1 / r\text{-}g}$$

Where,

D_1 = expected dividend per share at the end of one year

r = investor's required rate of return

g = growth rate

6. **Capital Asset Pricing Model (CAPM):** CAPM is used as a method of estimating cost of capital of a company which is an alternative method of weighted average cost of capital. This method decomposes the risk of portfolio into systematic risk and specific risk. Systematic risk means the risk of holding the market portfolio. Specific risk means the risk which is unique to any individual portfolio. Under this approach the cost of equity share capital is measured by using the following formula:

$$K_e = R_f + b\,(Rm - R_f)$$

Where,

R_f = risk free rate of return

Rm = market rate of return

b = market risk

(a) $Kr = K_e$ **(External yield criteria)**

(b) $K_r = K_e (1- t)(1- c)$ **(Reinvestment criteria)**

Where,

t = marginal rate of tax

c = rate of floatation cost

Cost of Preference Share Capital (Kp)

(a) The cost of preference capital which has no specific maturity date is given by the following equation:

$$\mathbf{Kp = D/\ NP}$$

Where,

D = dividend outflow each year

NP= net proceeds from the issue

(b) Redeemable preference shares may be issued and redeemed at a premium, par and discount. In such a case the following formula can be used to find out cost of capital:

$$K_p = \frac{D + (RV - NP) / N}{(RV + NP) / 2}$$

Where,

D = dividend outflow each year

NP= net proceeds from the issue
RV = redeemable value
N = number of years for maturity

Cost of Debenture (K_d)

(a) When debentures are issued and redeemable at par:

$$K_d = r\,(1-t)$$

Where,

r = rate of normal interest
t = rate of tax

(b) When the debentures are issued at a premium or discount but redeemable at par:

$$K_d = \frac{I\,(1-t)}{NP}$$

Where,

I = fixed amount of interest
t = rate of tax
NP= net proceeds from the issue

(c) When the debentures are redeemable at a premium or discount and are redeemable after 'n' period:

$$K_d = \frac{I + (RV - NP)/N}{(RV + NP)/2} \times (1-t)$$

Where,

I = fixed amount of interest
NP= net proceeds from the issue
RV = redeemable value
N = number of years for maturity
t = rate of tax

Weighted Average Cost of Capital

After calculating the cost of each component, the average cost of capital is generally calculated on the basis of weighted average method. This is called as weighted average cost of capital (WACC).Weights are assigned to each source on the basis of its proportion in the capital structure.

Therefore, weighted average cost of capital is to be calculated by using the following formula:

$$K_o = K_e W_e + K_r W_r + K_p W_p + K_d W_d + K_l W_l$$

Where,

K_e = cost of equity share capital
W_e = weight of equity share capital in the total capital structure
K_r = cost of retained earnings
W_r = weight of retained earnings in the total capital structure
K_p = cost of preference capital
W_p = weight of preference capital in the total capital structure
K_d = cost of debenture
W_d = weight of debenture in the total capital structure
K_l = cost of loan capital
W_l = weight of loan in the total capital structure

Dividend Policy- Determinants

Concept of Dividend Policy

Dividend policies are the regulations and guidelines that companies develop and implement as the means of arranging to make dividend payments to shareholders. Dividend policy is an integral part of the firm's financing decision as it provides internal financing. Dividend policy is concerned with determining the proportion of firm's earnings to be distributed in the form of cash dividend and the portion of earnings to be retained. A firm has three alternatives regarding the payment of cash dividends:

1. It can distribute all of its earnings in the firm of cash dividends;
2. It can retain all of its earnings for reinvestment;
3. It can distribute a part of earnings as dividend and retain the rest for reinvestment purpose;

When dividends are paid to the shareholders the firm's cash is reduced. A firm may decrease its dividend payout and use the retained funds to expand its capacity, to pay off some of its debt or to increase investment. In this way, the firm's dividend policy is closely related with the firm's investment and financing decisions.

Determining the part of earnings to be distributed as dividends is a key decision that affects the value of firm's common stock in the market place. Similarly, the retained earnings are considered to be the most convenient internal source available for financing corporate growth. Thus, every corporate firm should establish and implement an effective dividend policy that leads the firm to shareholders wealth maximization.

It should be recognized that a firm's dividend payout ratio depends on many factors. For example, it may be affected by the volatility in firm's cash flows and changing investment needs over time. If the firm's cash flow is volatile, it may prefer to set a minimum level of regular cash dividends that can be maintained even at low profits. Similarly, if the firm has profitable investment opportunity it prefers to retain more amounts by reducing dividend payout ratio.

In many cases, companies choose to explicitly state the provisions within the dividend policy. This is definitely to the advantage of the shareholder, as a well defined policy makes it much easier to project the amount of payout profits generated for the period under consideration and thus be able to determine the size of the dividends that will be issued. When the dividend policy is well defined and documented, it is easy for the shareholder to obtain a written copy and thus be fully informed as to how the policy works.

However, there are cases where the dividend policy is not so well documented. When this is the case, investors sometimes base their assumptions on upcoming dividend payments on what has occurred in the past. While less systematic, it is still possible to project a more or less accurate estimate of what the dividend payout will actually be.

In cases where the dividend policy is not specifically defined, investors often look at the history to spot any trends that emerged in the past. If the dividend payments have been more or less constant for the last several years, and there has been no loss in business volume, it is reasonable to assume the payments will still be in the same general range as before. However, if the dividend history is more volatile, the shareholder may attempt to identify what factors led to the up and down movement of the dividends and determine if any of those factors are relevant to the current dividend period.

In both expressed and implied dividend policy procedures, it is less common for the dividends to be increased. Part of the reason for that is companies tend to look closely at retained earnings and want to make sure the increased level of earnings will be sustained over the long term. Once this upward trend is deemed to be more or less permanent, the company may choose to increase dividends.

Far more common is the practice of reducing dividends. This usually takes place because there is a decrease in the company's business volume that is not anticipated to be recaptured in the foreseeable future. At other times, the decrease may be due to the need to retain more cash on hand for capital expenses. In both these scenarios, companies tend to notify the shareholders in advance that these factors exist and a change in dividends will take place in order to meet the challenge to remain profitable.

Types of Dividend Policy

The following are various types of dividend policies:

1. Policy of No Immediate Dividend
2. Stable Dividend Policy
3. Regular Dividend plus Extra Dividend Policy
4. Irregular Dividend Policy
5. Regular Stock Dividend Policy
6. Regular Dividend plus Stock Dividend Policy
7. Liberal Dividend Policy.

We discuss these policies in detail:

1. **Policy of No Immediate Dividend:** Generally, management follows a policy of paying no immediate dividend in the beginning of its life, as it requires funds for growth and expansion. In case, when the outside funds are costlier or when the access to capital market is difficult for the company and shareholders are ready to wait for dividend for sometime, this policy is justified, provided the company is growing fast and it requires a good deal of amount for its expansion. But such a policy is not justified for a long time, as the shareholders are deprived of the dividend. It would be better if the period of dividend is followed by issue of bonus shares, so that later on rate of dividend is maintained at a reasonable level.
2. **Regular or Stable Dividend Policy:** When a company pays dividend regularly at a fixed rate, and maintains it for a considerably long time even though the profits may fluctuate, it is said to follow regular or stable dividend policy. Thus stable dividend policy means a policy of paying a minimum amount of dividend every year regularly. It raises the prestige of the company in the eyes of the investors. A firm paying stable dividend can satisfy its shareholders and can enhance its credit standing in the market. The benefits of stable dividend policy are **(i)** it helps in raising long-term finance. When the company tries to raise finance in future, the investors would examine the dividend record of the company. The investors would not hesitate to invest in company with stable dividend policy. **(ii)** As it will enhance the prestige of the company, the price of its shares would remain at a high level. **(iii)** The shareholders develop confidence in management. **(iv)** It makes long-term planning easier.
3. **Regular Dividend plus Extra Dividend Policy.** A firm paying regular dividends would continue with its payout ratio. But when the earnings exceed the normal level, the directors would pay extra dividend in addition to the regular dividend. But it would be named

'Extra dividend', as it should not give an impression that the company has enhanced rate of regular dividend. This would give an impression to shareholders that the company has given extra dividend because it has earned extra profits and would not be repeated when the business earnings become normal. Because of this policy, the company's prestige and its share values will not be adversely affected. Only when the earnings of the company have permanently increased, the extra dividend should be merged with regular normal dividend and thus rate of normal dividend should be raised.

4. **Irregular Dividend Policy:** When the firm does not pay out fixed dividend regularly then it is known as irregular dividend policy. It changes from year to year according to changes in earnings level. This policy is based on the management belief that dividend should be paid only when the earnings and liquid position of the firm warrant it. This policy is followed by firms having unstable earnings, particularly engaged in luxury goods.
5. **Regular Stock Dividend Policy:** When a firm pays dividend in the form of shares instead of cash regularly for some years continuously, it is said to follow this policy. We know stock dividend as bonus shares. When a company has deficit of cash or is facing liquidity crunch, because a large part of its earnings are blocked in high level of receivables or when the company is need of cash for its modernization and expansion program, it follows this policy. It is not advisable to follow this policy for a long time, as the number of shares will go on increasing, which would result in fall in earnings per share. This would adversely affect the credit standing of the firm and its share values will go down.
6. **Regular Dividend plus Stock Dividend Policy:** A firm may pay certain amount of dividend in cash and some dividend is paid in the form of shares. Thus, the dividend is split in to two parts. This policy is justified when **(i)** The company wants to maintain its policy of regular dividend; **(ii)** It wants to retain some part of its divisible profit with it for expansion; **(iii)** It wants to give benefit of its earnings to shareholders but has not enough liquidity to give full dividend in cash.
7. **Liberal Dividend Policy:** It is a policy of distributing a major part of its earnings to its shareholders as dividend and retains a minimum amount as retained earnings. Thus, the ratio of dividend distribution is very large as compared to retained earnings. The rate of dividend or the amount of dividend is not fixed. It varies according to earnings. The higher is the profit, the higher will be the rate of

dividend. In years of poor earnings, the rate of dividend will be lower. In fact, it is the policy of Irregular Dividend.

Forms of Dividend

Dividend may be of different types. It can be classified according to the mode of its distribution as follows:

1. **Regular Dividend:** By dividend we mean regular dividend paid annually, proposed by the board of directors and approved by the shareholders in general meeting. It is also known as final dividend because it is usually paid after the finalization of accounts. It is generally paid in cash as a percentage of paid up capital, say 10 % or 15 % of the capital. Sometimes, it is paid per share. No dividend is paid on calls in advance or calls in arrears. The company is, however, authorised to make provisions in the Articles prohibiting the payment of dividend on shares having calls in arrears.
2. **Interim Dividend:** If Articles so permit, the directors may decide to pay dividend at any time between the two Annual General Meetings before finalizing the accounts. It is generally declared and paid when company has earned heavy profits or abnormal profits during the year. Such payment of dividend in between the two Annual General Meetings before finalizing the accounts is called Interim Dividend. No Interim Dividend can be declared or paid unless depreciation for the full year has been provided for. It is, thus, an extra dividend paid during the year requiring no need of approval of the Annual General Meeting. It is paid in cash.
3. **Stock-Dividend:** Companies, not having good cash position, generally pay dividend in the form of shares by capitalizing the profits of current year and of past years. Such shares are issued instead of paying dividend in cash and called 'Bonus Shares'. Basically there is no change in the equity of shareholders.
4. **Scrip Dividend:** Scrip dividends are used when earnings justify a dividend, but the cash position of the company is not strong enough. So, shareholders are issued shares and debentures of other companies. Such payment of dividend is called Scrip Dividend. Such dividend was allowed before passing of the Companies (Amendment) Act 1960, but thereafter this practice was stopped.
5. **Bond Dividends:** In rare instances, dividends are paid in the form of debentures or bounds or notes for a long-term period. The effect of such dividend is the same as that of paying dividend in scripts. The shareholders become the secured creditors.
6. **Property Dividend.** Sometimes, dividend is paid in the form of asset instead of payment of dividend in cash. The distribution of

dividend is made whenever the asset is no longer required in the business such as investment or stock of finished goods.

But, it is, however, important to note that in India, distribution of dividend is permissible in the form of cash or bonus shares only. Distribution of dividend in any other form is not allowed.

Factors Affecting Dividend Policy

There is no definite answer to the question as to what should be the quantum of dividend every year. A number of factors affect it and the final figure of dividend is determined only after considering the following:

1. **Type of Business:** The type of business carried on by the company influences the dividend policy. If the company is in a business which has a stable demand and stable earnings, it can follow a stable dividend policy. While a company which deals in luxury items has irregular flow of income and cannot adopt a stable dividend policy.
2. **Current Year's Earnings:** A company has to determine the amount of dividend keeping in view the actual earnings of the current year only. Of course, the whole of earnings is not distributed by the company every year, but it is the base of dividend policy. Even the companies following stable dividend policy makes some changes within a certain limit on the basis of current year's profit. There is no definite proportion between dividend and profit but dividend is raised, if the current year's profit has increased considerably. As one author states, "The starting point of dividend policy is the earnings of the firm. The upper limit on dividends, practically speaking, is fixed by the earnings of the current period."
3. **Past Dividends:** The dividends declared during previous years must also be considered. Shareholders do expect that the company would pay not less than dividend paid in the past. Of course, if circumstances change, departure has to be made from the past trend of dividends. But generally directors are reluctant to reduce the dividend in comparison to the previous year and they would try to maintain the rate of dividend, withdrawing from the past accumulated profit.
4. **Estimate of Future Earnings:** A company cannot adopt a stable dividend policy without taking into account the estimates of future earnings. The current year's rate is rationally determined only when estimate of future earnings is considered. If the profit is likely to rise in future, then only the directors can think of raising current dividend. If the future is not so bright, the current dividend cannot be raised.
5. **Future Needs of Capital:** The current profit is divided into retained earnings and dividend. When the company is in need of additional

capital for future expansion of business, has to restrict its rate of dividend and keep a major part of its current earnings for meeting working capital needs and fixed capital requirements of expansion of business. Particularly small companies and newly established companies have no other source of raising finance and would therefore depend mainly on this source.

6. **Fluctuations in Business:** The alternative phases of depression and boom in business has a considerable impact on dividend policy. A wise management would adjust itself to the changes in business from time to time. During boom period, a company should build up a good amount of reserves, so that it can withstand the period of depression and can maintain a stable dividend policy.
7. **Present Amount of Reserves:** A company having sufficient amount of reserves would be able to face the times of low demand with confidence, the prudent management would therefore, try to build up, sufficient reserves during boom period by restricting the rate of dividend and thus try to strengthen its financial position. Of course, in India, it has been made compulsory by Companies Act that companies are required to transfer not more than 10% of their net profits to Reserve if the rate of dividend exceeds 10% on graded rates. No company is allowed to transfer less than this to the reserves before declaring dividend.
8. **Distribution of Shareholdings:** If the company is a closely-held, it is easy for the Board to postpone the dividend and transfer the entire profit to reserves. However, in case the shareholding is widely distributed, with a large number of shareholders, it would be difficult for the Board to take decision of reducing or suspending dividend. If shareholders are mostly from middle class group of society, they expect a higher and consistent rate of dividend and the directors cannot ignore the expectations of shareholders.
9. **Age of the Company:** The dividend policy is affected by the fact whether a company is an old and established one or is a new one. A new company cannot afford to declare a high rate of dividend from the beginning, as it has to fall back on retained earnings for its requirements of funds for expansion. However, an established company would have built up enough reserves and can afford to declare a high rate of dividend.
10. **Position of Liquidity:** Dividend is payable in cash as per provisions of Companies Act. Hence, the directors are required to take into account the liquid position before declaring dividend. A company may have good deal of profit but may not have enough cash. In that case, dividend has to be postponed or the lower rate of dividend

should be declared. Even if the present liquid position may be satisfactory, the company may require cash to buy assets for expansion of business. In that case too, management should postpone payment of dividend. There is thus a direct link between liquid position and payment of dividend. A company which maintains a satisfactory level of liquidity at all times may be able to maintain stable dividend policy in the long run.

11. **Government Policy:** The changes in Government fiscal policies, industrial and labour policies considerably affect the working of some or all of the business firms. Their profits are affected either favourably or adversely. Dividend policy has to be adjusted to such changes. In some cases, the Government may restrict the rate of dividend in certain industries or impose tax if the rate of dividend exceeds a particular limit. Dividend policy is thus affected by changes in Government policies.
12. **Taxation:** Due to high rates of taxes, the company's profits are reduced, leading to a lower rate of dividend. In case of closely-held companies, the shareholders who are mostly in the highest tax brackets would like to receive fewer dividends and opt for capital gains. Many companies would like to issue bonus shares frequently instead of paying high rates of dividend.
13. **Legal Restrictions:** The Companies Acts of various countries may put restrictions of payment of dividends. For example, according to Sec. 205 of Indian Companies Act, no dividend can be paid without providing depreciation on fixed assets, dividend has to be paid in cash, dividend warrants must be dispatched within 30 days of declaration of dividend etc. No dividend can be paid out of capital. It has to be paid out of earnings of the company. If the company declares a dividend in excess of 10%, it is required to transfer a particular percentage of profit to the reserve fund. It can make use of past accumulated profits for payment of dividend subject to certain rules issued by the Central Government. The objective of legal restrictions is to see that the paid up capital of the company is not reduced and the interest of creditors and shareholders is not adversely affected.
14. **Attitude of Management:** The attitude of management has considerable impact on dividend policy. The management with foresight and conservative attitude would declare lower dividend and major part of the profit would be kept in business to strengthen its financial position. The management with liberal attitude would be liberal in dividend policy. Prudent management would always adopt a bit conservative dividend policy.

Stable Dividend Policy

(1) Strict or Conservative dividend Policy which envisages the retention of profits on the cost of dividend pay-out. It helps in strengthening the financial position of the company; **(2)** Lenient Dividend Policy which views the payment of dividend at the maximum rate possible taking in view the current earring of the company. Under such policy company retains the minimum possible earnings; **(3)** Stable Dividend Policy suggests a mid-way of the above two views. Under this policy, stable or almost stable rate of dividend is maintained. Company maintains reserves in the years of prosperity and uses them in paying dividend in lean year. If company follows stable dividend policy, the market price of these shares shall be higher. There are various reasons why investors prefer stable dividend policy. Main reasons are:-

1. Confidence among Shareholders: A regular and stable dividend payment may serve to resolve uncertainty in the minds of shareholders. The company resorts not to cut the dividend rate even if its profits are lower. It maintains the rate of dividends by appropriating the funds from its reserves. Stable dividend presents a bright future of the company and thus gains the confidence of the shareholders and the goodwill of the company increases in the eyes of the general investors.

2. Income Conscious Investors: The second factor favouring stable dividend policy is that some investors are income conscious and favour a stable rate of dividend. They too, never favour an unstable rate of dividend. A Stable dividend policy may also satisfy such investors.

3. Stability in Market Price of Shares: Other things beings equal, the market price vary with the rate of dividend the company declares on its equity shares. The value of shares of a company having a stable dividend policy fluctuates not widely even if the earnings of the company turn down. Thus, this policy buffers the market price of the stock.

4. Encouragement to Institutional Investors: A stable dividend policy attracts investments from institutional investors. Such institutional investors generally prepare a list of securities, mainly incorporating the securities of the companies having stable dividend policy in which they invest their surpluses or their long term funds such as pensions or provident funds etc.

In this way, stability and regularity of dividends not only affects the market price of shares but also increases the general credit of the company that pays the company in the long run.

Walter Model

Prof. James E. Walter contends that the dividend is relevant. Dividend is an active variable that affects price of company's shares and value of firm, because that leads to wealth maximization. The optimum dividend will be determined by the relationship of internal rate of return (r) (which is the return on firm's investment) and the cost of capital (k). If the rate of return earned by firm in its business (r) is more than cost of capital (k) that is, the rate at which funds are available to the firm from outside sources, the firm should retain the earnings, as it could be invested more profitably in business. On the other hand, if the cost of capital (k) or the expected return is more than the return available on firm's investment (r), the firm should distribute its earnings as dividend, as in that case, the shareholders receive dividend, on which they can earn a higher return by investing it elsewhere.

Thus, Walter has related dividend policy with investment opportunity available to the firm. If the firm has adequate profitable opportunities of earning higher return (r) than what the shareholders expect (k), it should retain its earnings. Such firms are called Growth Firms. For growth firm, the optimum dividend policy would be zero dividend payout ratio. It means that it should retain the entire earnings to maximize owners' wealth. If the firm does not have profitable investment opportunities, that is, if its rate of return is less than its cost of capital ($r < k$), then the firm should distribute the earnings to the shareholders. This would enable the shareholders to invest it elsewhere and earn a higher return. Such firms are called Declining Firms. For them the optimum dividend policy would be to distribute the entire earnings as dividend to shareholders, which would maximize the value of the firm. The third case is that of the Normal Firms, where the rate of return is equal to cost of capital ($r = k$). For such firms, it is indifferent whether earnings are distributed as dividend or retained in the firm. There is no optimum dividend policy for such firms. They can distribute anything between zero percent to 100 per cent of earnings without affecting the value of the firm.

Assumptions: Walter's model is based on the following assumptions:

(1) The firm finances its investment exclusively by retained earnings. It does not resort to debt or new equity.

(2) Its rate of return (r) and its cost of capital (k) are constant. Even with additional investment, its risk does not change.

(3) All earnings of the firm are either distributed as dividend or retained and invested internally immediately.

(4) There is no change in the earnings per share and dividend per share.

(5) The firm has a perpetual life.

Formula: $$P = \frac{D + r/k\,(E-D)}{K}$$

Where,

P = Price of share,

r = Required rate of return,

K= Cost of capital,

D= Dividend per share,

E= Earnings per share

Conclusions of Walter's Model

1. When $r > k_e$, the value of shares is inversely related to the D/P ratio. As the D/P ratio increases, the market value of shares decline. Its value is the highest when D/P ratio is 0. So, if the firm retains its earnings entirely, it will maximize the market value of the shares. The optimum payout ratio is zero.
2. When $r < k_e$, the D/P ratio and the value of shares are positively correlated. As the D/P ratio increases, the market price of the shares also increases. The optimum payout ratio is 100%.
3. When $r = k_e$, the market value of shares is constant irrespective of the D/P ratio. In this case, there is no optimum D/P ratio.

Limitations of this Model

1. Walter's model assumes that the firm's investments are purely financed by retained earnings. So this model would be applicable only to all-equity firms.
2. The assumption of r as constant is not realistic.
3. The assumption of a constant k_e ignores the effect of risk on the value of the firm.

Gordon Model

Like Walters, Gordon also contended that dividend policy of the firm is relevant and affects the value of the firm. He says that investors always prefer dividend as current income and not the dividend to be obtained in future, because the investors are rational and are risk averse, that is, they do not like to take risk of uncertain future dividend. They put a positive premium on current dividend income and discounts uncertain future dividends as the current dividend received removes any possibility of risk.

If the firm retains the earnings and does not pay dividend, the investor would get it in future. But receipt of dividend in future is uncertain both in respect of time and amount. Hence, investors prefer current dividend. They place less emphasis on future dividends and so when the firm retains its earning, the value of shares is adversely affected. It goes down. The investors discount the future dividend more than the near dividend. In the Gordon's model it was also stated that the dividend policy of a normal firm where r = k is irrelevant where all the assumptions are held valid. But looking to reality, these assumptions have to be modified. He concluded that even in case of normal firm, where r = k, dividend policy does affect the value of the share. This is in sharp contrast to Walter's contention that investors are indifferent between dividends and retention in case where r = k.

A Bird in hand Argument: As we have seen that investors are rational and are risk-averse, meaning thereby that they do not like to take risk in respect of future dividend. Here risk means the possibility of not getting dividend. Hence, the value of shares of that firm which pay higher current dividend will be higher. The investors discount the distant dividend at a higher rate than the near dividend. This argument is described as 'a bird-in-the-hand' argument. Investors believe that a bird in hand is better than in the bush. It means that what is available today is more valuable than what may be available in futures. As Krishnan has said, "Of two stocks with identical earnings record and prospects, but the one paying a larger dividend than the other, the former will undoubtedly commands a higher price merely because stockholders prefer present to future values. Stockholders often act upon the principle that a bird in the hand is worth two in the bush and for this reason are willing to pay a premium for the stock with the higher dividend rate, just as they discount it with the lower rate."

This clearly emphasizes that an investor prefers current dividend than the future dividend, as future is uncertain. The more distant the future is more uncertain it becomes. Hence, when dividend is withheld and earnings are retained, it becomes uncertain whether the dividend would be received at all. Hence, the investors who are rational are prepared to pay a higher premium for shares on which current dividends are paid and would discount the value of shares of a firm which retains its earnings. The appropriate discount rate would increase with increase in retention ratio.

The assumptions that he has made are almost the same as those by Walters. They are as follows:

(1) The firm is an all-equity firm. It means its capital consists of only equity shares. There is no debt capital.
(2) The firm uses only retained earnings for financing its investment programmes. No external financing is used.
(3) The internal rate of return of the firm (r) is constant.
(4) The cost of capital or the appropriate discount rate (k) of the firm is constant.
(5) The firm has perpetual life and its earnings are also perpetual.
(6) There are no corporate taxes.
(7) The retention ratio (b), once decided upon is constant (retention ratio is the proportion of earnings retained in the business). Thus, the growth rate g = br is constant.

M.M Model

Miller and Modigliani Model assume that the dividends are irrelevant. Dividend irrelevance implies that the value of a firm is unaffected by the distribution of dividends and is determined solely by the earning power and risk of its assets. Under conditions of perfect capital markets, rational investors, absence of tax discrimination between dividend income and capital appreciation, have given the firm's investment policy. Its dividend policy may have no influence on the market price of the shares, according to this model.

Assumptions of MM Model

1. The capital market is perfect and all investors in it are rational. Information is available to all free of cost. There are no transactions costs. Securities are infinitely divisible. No investor is large enough to influence the market price of securities and there are no floatation costs.
2. There are no taxes. Alternatively, there are no differences in tax rates applicable to capital gains and dividends.
3. A firm has a given investment policy which does not change. It implies that the financing of new investments out of retained earnings will not change the business risk complexion of the firm and thus there would be no change in the required rate of return.
4. Investors know for certain future investments and profits of the firm (but this assumption has been dropped by MM later).

Argument of this Model

1. By the argument of arbitrage, MM Model asserts the irrelevance of dividends. Arbitrage implies the distribution of earnings to shareholders and raising an equal amount externally. The effect of dividend payment would be offset by the effect of raising additional funds.
2. MM model argues that when dividends are paid to the shareholders, the market price of the shares will decrease and thus whatever is gained by the investors as a result of increased dividends will be neutralized completely by the reduction in the market value of the shares.
3. The cost of capital is independent of leverage and the real cost of debt is the same as the real cost of equity.
4. That investors are indifferent between dividend and retained earnings imply that the dividend decision is irrelevant. With dividends being irrelevant, a firm's cost of capital would be independent of its dividend-payout ratio.

5. Arbitrage process will also ensure that under conditions of uncertainty the dividend policy would be irrelevant.

Limitations of MM Model

1. The assumption of perfect capital market is unrealistic. Practically, there are taxes, floatation costs and transaction costs.
2. Investors cannot be indifferent between dividend and retained earnings under conditions of uncertainty. This can be proved at least with the aspects of **(i)** near Vs distant dividends, **(ii)** informational content of dividends, **(iii)** preference for current income and **(iv)** sale of stock at uncertain price.

Long Term & Short Term Financing Instruments

Financing is a very important part of every business. Firms often need financing to pay for their assets, equipment, and other important items. Financing can be either long-term or short-term. Long-term financing is more expensive as compared to short-term financing.

There are different vehicles through which long-term and short-term financing is made available. The common sources of financing are capital that is generated by the firm itself and sometimes, it is capital from external funders, which is usually obtained after issuance of new debt and equity.

Long-Term Financing

Long-term financing is usually needed for acquiring new equipment, R&D, cash flow enhancement, and company expansion. Some of the major methods for long-term financing are discussed below:

Equity Financing

Equity financing includes preferred stocks and common stocks. This method is less risky in respect to cash flow commitments. However, equity financing often results in dissolution of share ownership and it also decreases earnings. The cost associated with equity is generally higher than the cost associated with debt, which is again a deductible expense. Therefore, equity financing can also result in an enhanced hurdle rate that may cancel any reduction in the cash flow risk.

Corporate Bond

A corporate bond is a special kind of bond issued by any corporation to collect money effectively in an aim to expand its business. This tern is usually used for long-term debt instruments that generally have a maturity date after one year after their issue date at the minimum. Some corporate bonds may have an associated call option that permits the issuer to redeem it before it reaches the maturity. All other types of bonds that are known as convertible bonds that offer investors the option to convert the bond to equity.

Capital Notes

Capital notes are a type of convertible security that are exercisable into shares. They are one type of equity vehicle. Capital notes resemble warrants, except the fact that they usually don't have the expiry date or an exercise price. That is why the entire consideration the company aims to receive, for the future issuance of the shares, is generally paid at the time of issuance of capital notes.

Short-Term Financing

Short-term financing with a time duration of up to one year is used to help corporations increase inventory orders, payrolls, and daily supplies. Short-term financing can be done using the following financial instruments:

Commercial Paper

Commercial Paper is an unsecured promissory note with a pre-noted maturity time of 1 to 364 days in the global money market. Originally, it is issued by large corporations to raise money to meet the short-term debt obligations.

It is backed by the bank that issues it or by the corporation that promises to pay the face value on maturity. Firms with excellent credit ratings can sell their commercial papers at a good price.

Asset-backed commercial paper (ABCP) is collateralized by other financial assets. ABCP is a very short-term instrument with 1 and 180 days' maturity from issuance. ABCP is typically issued by a bank or other financial institution.

Promissory Note

It is a negotiable instrument where the maker or issuer makes an issue-less promise in writing to pay back a pre-decided sum of money to the payee at a fixed maturity date or on demand of the payee, under specific terms.

Asset-based Loan

It is a type of loan, which is often short term, and is secured by a company's assets. Real estate, accounts receivable (A/R), inventory and equipment are the most common assets used to back the loan. The given loan is either backed by a single category of assets or by a combination of assets.

Repurchase Agreements

Repurchase agreements are extremely short-term loans. They usually have a maturity of less than two weeks and most frequently they have a maturity of just one day. Repurchase agreements are arranged by selling securities with an agreement to purchase them back at a fixed cost on a given date.

Letter of Credit

A financial institution or a similar party issues this document to a seller of goods or services. The seller provides that the issuer will definitely pay the seller for goods or services delivered to a third-party buyer.

The issuer then seeks reimbursement to be met by the buyer or by the buyer's bank. The document is in fact a guarantee offered to the seller that it will be paid on time by the issuer of the letter of credit, even if the buyer fails to pay.

Mergers & Acquisitions

A merger or acquisition is a combination of two companies where one corporation is completely absorbed by another corporation. The less important company loses its identity and becomes part of the more important corporation, which retains its identity. A merger extinguishes the merged corporation, and the surviving corporation assumes all the rights, privileges, and liabilities of the merged corporation. A merger is not the same as a consolidation, in which two corporations lose their separate identities and unite to form a completely new corporation.

Types of Mergers

Mergers appear in three forms, based on the competitive relationships between the merging parties. In a **horizontal merger**, one firm acquires another firm that produces and sells an identical or similar product in the same geographic area and thereby eliminates competition between the two firms. In a Vertical Merger, one firm acquires either a customer or a supplier. **Conglomerate mergers** encompass all other acquisitions, including pure conglomerate transactions where the merging parties have no evident relationship (e.g., when a shoe producer buys an appliance manufacturer), geographic extension mergers, where the buyer makes the same product as the target firm but does so in a different geographic market, and product-extension mergers, where a firm that produces one product buys a firm that makes a different product that requires the application of similar manufacturing or marketing techniques.

Unit - IV

Production Management

Role and Scope of Production Management

Production Management refers to the application of management principles to the production function in a factory. In other words, production management involves application of planning, organizing, directing and controlling the production process.

Role of Production Management

In short, the role of production management can be listed as follows:

(i) Specification and procurement of input resources namely management, material, and land, labour, equipment and capital.

(ii) Product design and development to determine the production process for transforming the input factors into output of goods and services.

(iii) Supervision and control of transformation process for efficient production of goods and services.

Scope of Production Management

The scope of production management is very vast. Commencing with the selection of location, production management covers such activities as acquisition of land, constructing building, procuring and installing machinery, purchasing and storing raw materials and converting them into saleable products. Apart from the above, quality management, maintenance management, production planning and control, methods improvement and work simplification and other related areas come under the ambit of production management.

Due to the dynamic change in the business environment, the scope of production and operation management has increased. Following are the activities which are included under production and operations management functions:

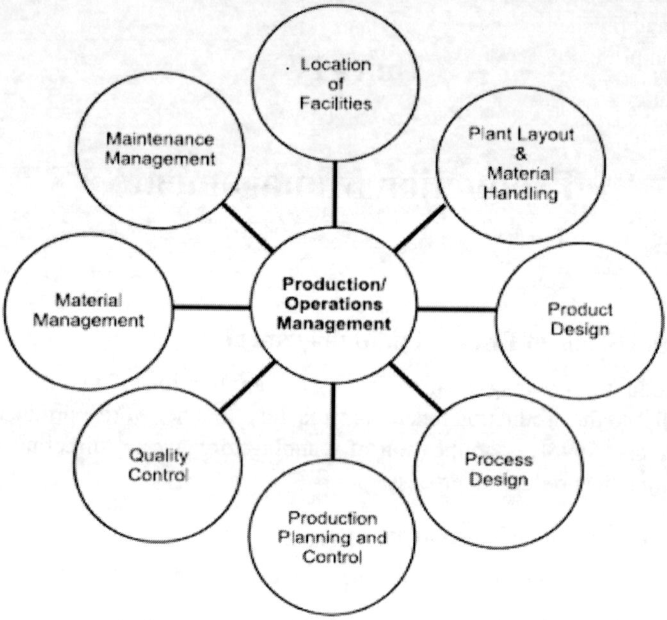

Scope of production and operations management

Facility Location: Selecting appropriate location for the production.

Plant Layouts and Material Handling: Deciding upon the machines, equipment and necessary devices which could lead to effectual and desired production in the most economic way. Preparation of plant layout for the establishment of machines in the required sequence. Storage of material and handling it in most effective way to avoid the wastage and delivery at the work centers as and when required.

Product Design: Designing the product and conceive the idea about its production.

Process Design: Determination of the production process which is most relevant and efficient in the given state of affairs.

Production and Planning Control: Planning the production and its various aspects how, when and where producing a particular product or its assembly will be done.

Quality Control: Controlling the production and ensuring the quality by setting the check points and taking the periodic measurements of the current performance.

Materials Management: Managing the inventories of raw material, semi-finished and finished goods in a way that neither excessive money may block in this non-productive operation nor the required material.

Maintenance Management: Analysis the deviations and formulating the corrective measures to stay in track with planned quality, time-schedule and predetermined cost schedules.

Facility Location

Facility Location is the right location for the manufacturing facility; it will have sufficient access to the customers, workers, transportation, etc.

Factors Influencing Facility Location

If the organization can configure the right location for the manufacturing facility, it will have sufficient access to the customers, workers, transportation, etc. For commercial success, and competitive advantage following are the critical factors:

Customer Proximity: Facility locations are selected closer to the customer as to reduce transportation cost and decrease time in reaching the customer.

Business Area: Presence of other similar manufacturing units around makes business area conducive for facility establishment.

Availability of Skill Labour: Education, experience and skill of available labour are another important factor which determines facility location.

Free Trade Zone/Agreement: Free-trade zones promote the establishment of manufacturing facility by providing incentives in custom duties and levies. On another hand, free trade agreement among countries providing an incentive to establish business in a particular country.

Suppliers: Continuous and quality supply of the raw materials is another critical factor in determining the location of manufacturing facility.

Environmental Policy: In current globalized world, pollution control is very important; therefore understanding of environmental policy for the facility location is another critical factor.

Market: It is a very important factor. If product is fragile and susceptible to spoilage, proximity of the facility to the market is critical. If the product is relatively cheap and transportation cost is high, a location close to the markets is desirable.

Community Attitude: Community attitude is difficult to evaluate. Normally communities provide the overwhelming support to new industries, because this generates significant employment opportunities to the local people. Moreover, infrastructure development of the city or town progresses very rapidly. In some cases, when there is a fear of generation of pollution, community attitude goes in the reverse.

Climate: Climate is another important factor to be considered for the facility location especially in industries where special constraints are needed, for example the textile industry requires a high humidity zone.

Site Size: The plot of land must be large enough to hold the facilities required by the proposed facility. Sometimes a good site may not have the required area.

Political Stability: **Companies that locate facilities in international locations might benefit from a cost perspective; however, an unstable local government that puts smooth operations at risk are a deterrent to choosing to locate there.**

Layout Planning & Analysis

Plant layout refers to the physical arrangement of production facilities. It is the configuration of departments, work centers and equipment in the conversion process. It is a floor plan of the physical facilities, which are used in production.

According to Moore "Plant layout is a plan of an optimum arrangement of facilities including personnel, operating equipment, storage space, material handling equipment and all other supporting services along with the design of best structure to contain all these facilities".

Objectives of Plant Layout

The primary goal of the plant layout is to maximize the profit by arrangement of all the plant facilities to the best advantage of total manufacturing of the product. The objectives of plant layout are as follows:

(i) Streamline the flow of materials through the plant. **(ii)** Facilitate the manufacturing process. **(iii)** Maintain high turnover of in-process in ventory. **(iv)** Minimize materials handling and cost. **(v)** Effective utilization of men, equipment and space. **(vi)** Make effective utilization of cubic space. **(vii)** Flexibility of manufacturing operations and arrangements. **viii)** Provide for employee convenience, safety and comfort. **(ix)** Minimize investment in equipment. **(x)** Minimize overall production time.

(xi) Maintain flexibility of arrangement and operation. **(xii)** Facilitate the organizational structure.

Principles of Plant Layout

Principle of Integration: A good layout is one that integrates men, materials, machines and supporting services and others in order to get the optimum utilization of resources and maximum effectiveness.

Principle of Minimum Distance: This principle is concerned with the minimum movement of man and materials. The facilities should be arranged such that, the total distance travelled by the men and materials should be minimum and as far as possible **straight line** movement should be preferred.

Principle of Cubic Space Utilization: The good layout is one that utilizes both horizontal and vertical space. It is not only enough if only the floor space is utilized optimally but the third dimension, i.e., the height is also to be utilized effectively.

Principle of Flow: A good layout is one that makes the materials to move in forward direction towards the completion stage, i.e., there should not be any backtracking.

Principle of Maximum Flexibility: The good layout is one that can be altered without much cost and time, i.e., future requirements should be taken into account while designing the present layout.

Principle of Safety, Security and Satisfaction: A good layout is one that gives due consideration to workers safety and satisfaction and safeguards the plant and machinery against fire, theft, etc.

Principle of Minimum Handling: A good layout is one that reduces the material handling to the minimum.

Production Planning & Control

Production Planning

Production planning is one part of production planning and control dealing with basic concepts of what to produce, when to produce, how much to produce, etc. It involves taking a long-term view at overall production planning. Therefore, objectives of production planning are as follows:

(i) To ensure right quantity and quality of raw material, equipment, etc. are available during times of production.

(ii) To ensure capacity utilization is in tune with forecast demand at all the time.

A well thought production planning ensures that overall production process is streamlined providing following benefits:

(i) Organization can deliver a product in a timely and regular manner.
(ii) Suppliers are informed in advance for the requirement of raw materials.
(iii) It reduces investment in inventory.
(iv) It reduces overall production cost by driving in efficiency.

Production planning takes care of two basic strategies' which are product planning and process planning. Production planning is done at three different time dependent levels i.e. long-range planning dealing with facility planning, capital investment, location planning, etc.; medium-range planning deals with demand forecast and capacity planning and lastly short term planning dealing with day to day operations.

Production Control

Production control looks to utilize different types of control techniques to achieve optimum performance out of the production system as to achieve overall production planning targets. Therefore, objectives of production control are as follows:

(i) Regulate inventory management
(ii) Organize the production schedules
(iii) Optimum utilization of resources and production process

The advantages of robust production control are as follows:

(i) Ensure a smooth flow of all production processes
(ii) Ensure production cost savings thereby improving the bottom line
(iii) Control wastage of resources
(iv) It maintains standard of quality through the production life cycle

Production control cannot be same across all the organization. Production control is dependent upon the following factors:

(i) Nature of production (job oriented, service oriented, etc.)
(ii) Nature of operation
(iii) Size of operation

Production planning and control are essential for customer delight and overall success of an organization.

Production Process Analysis

Process design is a macroscopic decision-making of an overall process route for converting the raw material into finished goods. These decisions encompass the selection of a process, choice of technology, process flow analysis and layout of the facilities. Hence, the important decisions in process design are to analyze the workflow for converting raw material into finished product and to select the workstation for each included in the workflow.

Demand Forecasting for Operations

There are two types of demand forecasting methods. These are as follows:

Qualitative Methods: These types of forecasting methods are based on judgments, opinions, intuition, emotions, or personal experiences and are subjective in nature. They do not rely on any rigorous mathematical computations.

Quantitative Methods: These types of forecasting methods are based on mathematical models, and are objective in nature. They rely heavily on mathematical computations.

Qualitative Methods: All qualitative methods under demand forecasting are described below:

(i) **Executive Opinion:** Approach in which a group of managers meet and collectively develop a forecast.

(ii) **Market Survey:** Approach that uses interviews and surveys to judge preferences of customer and to assess demand.

(iii) **Sales Force Composite:** Approach in which each salesperson estimates sales in his or her region.

(iv) **Delphi Method:** Approach in which **consensus agreement** is reached among a group of experts.

Quantitative Forecasting Methods

Time-Series Models: Time series models look at past patterns of data and attempt to predict the future based upon the underlying patterns contained within those data.

Model	*Description*
Naive	Uses last period's actual value as a forecast
Simple Mean (Average)	Uses an average of all past data as a forecast
Simple Moving Average	Uses an average of a specified number of the most recent observations, with each observation receiving the same emphasis (weight)
Weighted Moving Average	Uses an average of a specified number of the most recent observations, with each observation receiving a different emphasis (weight)
Exponential Smoothing	A weighted average procedure with weights declining exponentially as data become older
Trend Projection	Technique that uses the least squares method to fit a straight line to the data
Seasonal Indexes	A mechanism for adjusting the forecast to accommodate any seasonal patterns inherent in the data

Associative Models: Associative models assume that the variable being forecasted is related to other variables in the environment. They try to project based upon those associations.

Determinants of Product Mix

The **Product Mix** also called as **Product Assortment,** refers to the complete range of products that is offered for sale by the company. In other words, the number of **product lines** that a company has for its customers is called as **product mix**.

The Product Line refers to the list of all the related products manufactured or marketed by a single firm. The number of products within the product line are called as the **items**, and these might be similar in terms of technology used, channel employed, customer's needs and preferences or any other aspect. For example, the product lines of ITC are FMCG, Hotels, Paper Board and Packaging, Agribusiness.

The product mix has four dimensions: **Breadth**, **Length, Depth**, and **Consistency**. The **Breadth of a product mix** shows the different kinds of product lines that firm carries. Simply, it shows the number of items in the product line. This dimension of the product mix represents the extent to which the activities of the firm are diversified.

The **Length of a Product mix** refers to the number of items in the product mix. On adding all the items, we get the length of a product. The **Depth of a product mix** refers to the variants of each product in the product line.

The **Consistency of a product mix** shows the extent to which the product lines are closely related to each other in terms of their end-use, distribution requirements, production requirements, price ranges, advertising media, etc.

These terms in a product assortment help the firm to take a decision regarding the addition or removal of the product items in the product lines. Generally, the firms introduce a new product item into the existing product line as it is easy to gain the customer support for the new product due to the customer's familiarity with the existing product line.

Production Scheduling

Scheduling can be defined as "prescribing of when and where each operation necessary to manufacture the product is to be performed." It is also defined as "establishing of times at which to begin and complete each event or operation comprising a procedure". The principle aim of scheduling is to plan the **sequence of work** so that production can be systematically arranged towards the end of completion of all products by due date.

Types of Scheduling

Types of scheduling can be categorized as forward scheduling and backward scheduling.

Forward Scheduling

It is commonly used in job shops where customers place their orders on "**needed as soon as possible**" basis. Forward scheduling determines start and finish times of next priority job by assigning it the earliest available time slot and from that time, determines when the job will be finished in that work centre. Since the job and its components start as early as possible, they will typically be completed before they are due at the subsequent work centers in the routing. The forward method generates in the process inventory that are needed at subsequent work centers and higher inventory cost. Forward scheduling is simple to use and it gets jobs done in **shorter lead times**, compared to backward scheduling.

Backward Scheduling

It is often used in assembly type industries and commit in advance to specific delivery dates. Backward scheduling determines the start and finish times for waiting jobs by assigning them to the latest available time slot that will enable each job to be completed just when it is due. By assigning jobs as late as possible, backward scheduling minimizes inventories since a job is not completed until it must go directly to the next work centre on its routing.

Work Measurement

Work measurement is concerned with the determination of the amount of time required to perform a unit of work. Work measurement is very important for promoting productivity of an organization. Work measurement has been defined by British Standard Institution as, **"The application of techniques designed to establish the time for a qualified worker to carry out a specified job at a defined level of performance"**.

Objectives of Work Measurement

(i) To compare the times of performance by alternative methods.

(ii) To enable realistic schedule of work to be prepared.

(iii) To arrive at a realistic and fair incentive scheme.

(iv) To analyze the activities for doing a job with the view to reduce or eliminate unnecessary jobs.

(v) To minimize the human effort.

Time & Motion Study

Time Study

It was proposed by **Frederick Taylor** and later modified to include a performance rating (PR) adjustment. Once the method is established, the next objective is to set the standard time for the work. This aspect of work study is called Time study (or Work measurement).

Objectives of Time Study:

(i) To determine the standard time for various operations which helps in fixing wage rates and incentives.
(ii) To estimate the cost of product accurately.
(iii) To predict accurately the duration for a particular work and customer is promised accordingly.
(iv) To determine the number of machines an operator can run.
(v) To determine the optimum number of men and machine.
(vi) To provide information for planning and scheduling.
(vii) To balance the work of all workers working in a group.
(viii) To compare the work efficiency of different workers/operators.

Motion Study

It is defined as a systematic and critical study of existing method of doing a task with a view to evolve the most efficient and economic method of doing it. It is a method for setting up employee productivity standards in which a complex job is broken down into small or simple steps.

The sequence of movements taken by the employee in performing those steps is carefully observed to detect and eliminate wasteful motion. Precise time taken for each correct movement is measured. From these measurements, production and delivery times and prices are computed and incentive schemes are devised. Generally it is appropriate only for repetitive tasks.

Time and motion studies were pioneered by the US industrial engineer Frederick Winslow **Taylor** (1856-1915) and developed by the husband and wife team of **Frank Gilbreth** (1868-1924) and **Lillian Gilbreth** (1878-1972).

Objectives of Motion Study

(i) To improve the procedure of doing a work.
(ii) To improve the workplace layout.
(iii) To minimize the human motion for minimum fatigue of operators.
(iv) To maximize the utility of resources.
(v) To improve the overall working environment.

Statistical Quality Control

Quality Control (QC) may be defined as a system that is used to maintain a desired level of quality in a product or service. It is a systematic control of various factors that affect the quality of the product. It depends on materials, tools, machines, type of labour, working conditions, etc. QC is a broad term, it involves inspection at particular stage but mere inspection does not mean QC. As opposed to inspection, in quality control activity emphasis is placed on the quality future production. Quality control aims at prevention of defects at the source, relies on effective feedback system and corrective action procedure. Quality control uses inspection as a valuable tool.

According to **Juran** "Quality control is the regulatory process through which we measure actual quality performance, compare it with standards, and act on the difference".

Alford and Beatty define QC as "In the broad sense, quality control is the mechanism by which products are made to measure up to specifications determined from customers, demands and transformed into sales engineering and manufacturing requirements, it is concerned with making things right rather than discovering and rejecting those made wrong".

Important techniques of applying statistical quality control are: (A) Quality Control Charts and (B) Acceptance Sampling.

(A) Quality Control Charts: A quality control chart is a graphic presentation of the expected variations in quality. Certain presumptions are taken into consideration before drawing these charts e.g., inherent nature of certain variables in a product, tolerance limits and probability of chance in variations, etc.

Tolerance limits are clearly shown by these charts with regard to a particular product. Variations in quality beyond these limits clearly disclose that the production process is out of control and the quality of the product has not been achieved in accordance with the pre-determined standards. On the other hand, a process is said to be in control if the finished product remains within the tolerance limits.

Quality control charts are very helpful in spotting the causes responsible for variations from the set standards on the basis of information disclosed by these charts. Different types of quality control charts may be used for recording different types of analysis.

Some of the important quality control charts are chart of averages and that of range, etc. Information disclosed by these charts is very accurate and an authentic one.

(B) Acceptance Sampling: This is another technique of statistical quality control. This is also referred as 'Sampling Inspection Plan.' This method is usually followed after goods have been produced or are in the final stage of production. Thus, it can be said that it is a post mortem of the quality of the product that has already been produced.

Under this method, a sample of the product produced is selected at random to study in detail whether the product conforms to the pre-determined standards or not. A limited percentage of defective products are allowed.

But it has been observed that sometimes the sample selected turns out to be good, but the lot represented by the sample may be defective or sub-standard. In order to have more accurate and exact results, more than one sample of the product should be selected for carrying out the Sampling Inspection Plan.

The technique Acceptance Sampling undertakes two limiting levels of quality viz., **(i)** The Acceptable Quality Level (**AQL**) i.e. the least number or percentage of defective products that the buyer expects to purchase and the seller expects to sell and **(ii)** The Lot Percentage Tolerance Defective **(LPTD)** refers to that limit where the buyer wants to be certain about the rejection of the lot.

This technique can be greatly helpful for improving relations between vendor and the customer which may be adverse on account of disputes relating to quality. Both the parties may sit together and mutually decide the limits within which quality should be accepted.

Tools for Quality Control

To make rational decisions using data obtained on the product, or process, or from the consumer, organizations use certain graphical tools. These methods help us to learn about the characteristics of a process, its operating state of affairs and the kind of output we may expect from it. Graphical methods are easy to understand and provide comprehensive information; they are a viable tool for the analysis of product and process data. The seven quality control tools are as follows:

Pareto Charts

It helps prioritize by arranging them in decreasing order of importance. In an environment of limited resources these diagrams help companies to decide on the order in which they should address problems. The Pareto analysis can be used to identify the problem in a number of forms. These are: **(i)** Analysis of losses by material (number or past number). **(ii)** Analysis of losses by process i.e., classification of defects or lot rejections in terms of the process. **(iii)** Analysis of losses by product family. **(iv)** Analysis by supplier across the entire spectrum of purchases. **(v)** Analysis by cost of the parts. **(vi)** Analysis by failure mode.

Cause and Effect Diagram

It is sometimes called as **Fish-bone diagram**. It is first developed by **Kaorv Ishikawa** in 1943 and is sometimes called as **Ishikawa diagram**. The diameter helps the management trace customer complaints directly to the operations involved. The main quality problem is referred to Fish-head; the major categories of potential cause structural bones and the likely specific causes to ribs. It explores possible causes of problems, with the intention being to discover the root causes. This diagram helps identify possible reasons for a process to go out of control as well as possible effects on the process.

Scatter Diagram

It often indicates the relationship between two variables. They are often used as follow-ups to a cause and effect analysis to determine whether a stated cause truly does impact the quality characteristics.

Example: The plots advertising expenditure against company sales and indicates a strong positive relationship between the two variables. As the level of advertising expenditure increases sales tend to increase.

Histogram or Bar Charts

It displays the large amounts of data that are difficult to interpret in their raw form. A histogram summarizes data measured on a continuous scale showing the frequency distribution of some quality characteristics.

Often the mean of the data is indicated on the histogram. A bar chart is a series of bare representing the frequency of occurrence of data characteristics, the bar height indicates the number of times a particular quality characteristic was observed.

Flow Charts or Graphs

It shows the sequence of events in a process. They are used for manufacturing and service operations. Flow charts are often used to diagram operational procedures to simplify the system. They can identify bottlenecks, redundant steps and non-value added activities. A realistic flow chart can be constructed by using the knowledge of the person who are directly involved in the particular process. The flow chart can be identified where delays can occur.

Control Charts

It distinguishes special causes of variations from common causes of variation. They are used to monitor and control process on an ongoing basis.

A typical control chart plots a selected quality characteristic found from sub-group of observations as a function of sample number.

Characteristics such as sample average, sample range and sample proportion of non-conforming units are plotted. The centre line on a control chart represents the average value of characteristics being plotted. Two limits know as the upper control limit (UCL) and lower control limit (LCL) are also shown on control charts. These limits are constructed so that if the process is operating under a stable system of chance causes, the problem of an observation falling outside these limits is quite small. Control chart shows the performance of a process from two points of view. First, they show a snapshot of the process at the moment the data are collected. Second, they show the process trend as time progresses. Process trends are important because they help in identifying the out-of-control status if it actually exists.

Control charts can be used to monitor processes where output is measured as either variables or attributes. There are two types of control charts: Variable control chart and attribute control chart.

Variable Control Charts: It is one by which it is possible to measures the quality characteristics of a product. The variable control charts are **X-BAR** chart, **R-BAR** chart, **SIGMA** chart.

Attribute Control Chart: It is one in which it is not possible to measures the quality characteristics of a product, i.e., it is based on visual inspection only like good or bad, success or failure, accepted or rejected. The attribute control charts are **p-charts, np-charts, c-charts,** and **u-charts.** It requires only a count of observations on characteristics e.g., the number of nonconforming items in a sample.

Causes of Variation in Quality The variation in the quality of product in any manufacturing process is broadly classified as follows:

Chance Causes

The chance causes are those causes which are inherit in manufacturing process by virtue of operational and constructional features of the equipments involved in a manufacturing process. This is because of machine vibrations, voltage variations, composition variation of material, etc. They are difficult to trace and difficult to control, even under best condition of production. Even though, it is possible to trace out, it is not economical to eliminate. The chance causes results in only a minute amount of variation in process. Variation in chance causes is due to internal factors only the general pattern of variation under chance causes will follow a stable statistical distribution. Variation within the control limits means only random causes are present.

Assignable Causes

These are the causes which creates ordinary variation in the production quality. Assignable cause's variation can always be traced to a specific quality. They occur due to lack of skill in operation, wrong maintenance practice, new vendors, error in setting jigs and fixtures, raw material defects, etc.

Variation due to these causes can be controlled before the defective items are produced. Any one assignable cause can result in a large amount of variation in process. If the assignable causes are present, the system will not follow a stable statistical distribution. When the actual variation exceeds the control limits, it is a signal that assignable causes extend the process and process should be investigated.

Role & Scope of Operations Research

Role of OR

The Operations Research may be considered as a tool which is employed to enhance the efficiency of managerial decisions. Scientific method of OR is used to comprehend and explain the phenomena of operating system.

The role of OR in business and management decision making may be categorized as follows:

Better Control: The management of large concerns finds it much expensive to give continuous executive supervisions over routine decisions. An OR approach directs the executives to dedicate their concentration to more pressing matters. For instance, OR approach handles production scheduling and inventory control.

Better Coordination: Sometimes OR has been very helpful in preserving the law and order situation out of disorder. For instance, an OR based planning model turns out to be a vehicle for coordinating marketing decisions with the restrictions forced on manufacturing capabilities.

Better System: OR study is also initiated to examine a particular problem of decision making like setting up a new warehouse. Later OR approach can be more developed into a system to be employed frequently. As a result the cost of undertaking the first application may get better profits.

Better Decisions: OR models regularly give actions that do enhance an intuitive decision making. Sometimes a situation may be so complex that the human mind can never expect to assimilate all the significant factors without the aid of OR and computer analysis.

Scope of Operations Research

In recent years of organized development, OR has entered successfully in many different areas of research. It is useful in the following areas:

In Agriculture: With the sudden increase of population and resulting shortage of food, every country is facing the problem of

- Optimum allocation of land to a variety of crops as per the climatic conditions
- Optimum distribution of water from numerous sources like canal for irrigation purposes

Hence, there is a requirement of determining best policies under the given restrictions. Therefore a good quantity of work can be done in this direction.

In Finance: In these recent times of economic crisis, it has become very essential for every government to do a careful planning for the economic progress of the country. OR techniques can be productively applied

- To determine the profit plan for the company
- To maximize the per capita income with least amount of resources
- To decide on the best replacement policies, etc

In Industry: If the industry manager makes his policies simply on the basis of his past experience and a day approaches when he gets retirement, then a serious loss is encountered ahead of the industry. This heavy loss can be right away compensated through appointing a young specialist of OR techniques in business management. Thus, OR is helpful for the industry director in deciding optimum distribution of several limited resources like men, machines, material, etc to reach at the optimum decision.

In Marketing: With the assistance of OR techniques, a marketing administrator can decide upon

- Where to allocate the products for sale so that the total cost of transportation is set to be minimum
- The minimum per unit sale price
- The size of the stock to come across with the future demand
- How to choose the best advertising media with respect to cost, time etc?
- How, when and what to buy at the minimum likely cost?

In Personnel Management: A personnel manager can utilize OR techniques

- To appoint the highly suitable person on minimum salary
- To know the best age of retirement for the employees

- To find out the number of persons appointed in full time basis when the workload is seasonal

In Production Management: A production manager can utilize OR techniques

- To calculate the number and size of the items to be produced
- In scheduling and sequencing the production machines
- In computing the optimum product mix
- To choose, locate and design the sites for the production plans

In L.I.C: OR approach is also applicable to facilitate the L.I.C offices to decide

- What should be the premium rates for a range of policies?
- How well the profits could be allocated in the cases of with profit policies?

Methodologies from Operations Research are often applied in the following general application areas:

- Agriculture & Forestry
- Airline Crew Scheduling
- Bioinformatics
- Cutting & Packing Problems in the Production Industry
- Maritime Transportation and Logistics
- Materials Handling & Supply Chain Management
- Military, defense and Security Applications
- The Mining Industry
- Quality Control and Inspection
- Sustainability and the Environment
- Telecommunications and Information Technology
- Transportation of Materials
- Vehicle Routing Education
- Emergency Evacuation and Response
- The Energy Sector
- Finance, Investment Analysis, Insurance and Revenue Management
- Wildlife Management
- Health Care
- Inventory Management
- Layout and Structure of Manufacturing Plants
- Location of Facilities and Plants
- Production Scheduling and Control

- Public Transport
- Equipment Selection and Replacement
- Maintenance and Availability

Linear Programming

The technique of linear programming was formulated by a Russian mathematician L.V. **Kantorovich**. But the present version of simplex method was developed by Geoge B. **Dentzig** in 1947. Linear programming (LP) is an important technique of operations research developed for **optimum utilization of resources.**

Linear programming is often used in business to find maximum profit or minimum cost. The first step in solving linear programming problems is to set up a function that represents cost, profit, or some other quantity to be maximized or minimized subject to the constraints of the problem. Then define the constraints with a system of linear inequalities. The solution of these systems of inequalities is called the **feasible region**. Graph the inequalities to determine the coordinates of the vertices of the region. Evaluate the function at each vertex. The largest and smallest of those values are the maximum and minimum values of the function, respectively.

Let us define some terminologies used in Linear Programming using the above example.

Decision Variables: The decision variables are the variables which will decide the output. They represent the ultimate solution. To solve any problem, we first need to identify the decision variables.

Objective Function: It is defined as the objective of making decisions.

Constraints: The constraints are the restrictions or limitations on the decision variables. They usually limit the value of the decision variables.

Non-negativity Restriction: For all linear programs, the decision variables should always take non-negative values. This means the values for decision variables should be greater than or equal to 0.

Sensitivity Analysis

A sensitivity analysis is the hypothesis of what will happen if variables are changed. More specifically, it is analyzing what will happen if one variable is changed. In other words, if we change something about our business, how will it affect other aspects of our business or the overall operations?

Duality

The **Duality in linear programming** states that every linear programming problem has another linear programming problem related to it and thus can be derived from it. The original linear programming problem is called **"Primal,"** while the derived linear problem is called **"Dual."**

Before solving for the duality, the original linear programming problem is to be formulated in its standard form. Standard form means, all the variables in the problem should be non-negative and "e"," "d"" sign is used in the minimization case and the maximization case respectively.

The concept of Duality can be well understood through a problem given below:

Maximize $Z = 50x_1 + 30x_2$

Subject to:

$4x_1 + 3x_2$ d" 100

$3x_1 + 5x_2$ d" 150

$X_1, x_2 \geq 0$

The duality can be applied to the above original linear programming problem as:

Minimize $G = 100y_1 + 150y_2$

Subject to:

$4y_1 + 3y_1 \leq 50$

$3y_1 + 5y_2 \leq 30$

$y_1, y_2 \geq 0$

The following observations were made while forming the dual linear programming problem:

(i) The primal or original linear programming problem is of the maximization type while the dual problem is of minimization type.

(ii) The constraint values 100 and 150 of the primal problem have become the coefficient of dual variables y_1 and y_2 in the objective function of a dual problem and while the coefficient of the variables in the objective function of a primal problem has become the constraint value in the dual problem.

(iii) The first column in the constraint inequality of primal problem has become the first row in a dual problem and similarly the second column of constraint has become the second row in the dual problem.

(iv) The directions of inequalities have also changed, i.e. in the dual problem, the sign is the reverse of a primal problem. In the primal problem, the inequality sign was "$\leq$" but in the dual problem, the sign of inequality becomes "$\geq$".

Transportation Model

One of the most important and successful applications of quantitative analysis to solving business problems has been in the physical distribution of products, commonly referred to as transportation problems. Basically, the purpose is to **minimize the cost** of shipping goods from one location to another so that the needs of each arrival area are met and every shipping location operates within its capacity. However, quantitative analysis has been used for many problems other than the physical distribution of goods.

For example, it has been used to efficiently place employees at certain jobs within an organization. This application sometimes is called the assignment problem.

Inventory Control

Inventory control is a planned approach of determining what to order, when to order and how much to order and how much to stock so that costs associated with buying and storing are optimal without interrupting production and sales.

Objectives of Inventory Control

(i) To ensure adequate supply of products to customer and avoid shortages as far as possible.

(ii) To make sure that the financial investment in inventories is minimum.

(iii) Efficient purchasing, storing, consumption and accounting for materials are an important objective.

(iv) To maintain timely record of inventories of all the items and to maintain the stock within the desired limits.

(v) To ensure timely action for replenishment.

(vi) To provide a reserve stock for variations in lead times of delivery of materials.

(vii) To provide a scientific base for both short-term and long-term planning of materials.

Benefits or Advantages of Inventory Control

It is an established fact that through the practice of scientific inventory control, following are the benefits of inventory control:

(i) Improvement in customer's relationship because of the timely delivery of goods and service.

(ii) Smooth and uninterrupted production and, hence, no stock out.

(iii) Efficient utilization of working capital.

(iv) Helps in minimizing losses due to deterioration, obsolescence damage and pilferage.

(v) Economy in purchasing.

(vi) Eliminates the possibility of duplicate ordering.

Queuing Theory

It is a common phenomenon in everyday life to see a large number of persons waiting in front of a booking counter in a railway station or in a theatre or in a ration shop to have some service carried out. This formation of queue occurs whenever the present demand for a service exceeds the present capacity to provide the necessary government, industry, schools, hospitals, etc.

A decision regarding the amount of capacity to provide must be made frequently in industry and other places. It is difficult to predict about an arrival and the type of service required. If we provide too much service, it would involve unnecessary excessive costs. On the other hand, if we do not provide enough service capacity, this will result in a long waiting line, which proves costly. So, we are interested in reaching an economic balance between the cost of service and the cost associated with waiting for the service. Queuing theory or waiting line theory provides vital information required for such a decision. For describing a waiting line situation, queuing theory provides a number of alternative mathematical models.

The basic queuing system consists of two major components. Customers arriving at a queuing system wait in queue to get some service, or if the system is idle or empty, the arriving customer may be serviced immediately. Once the service is over the customer leaves the system.

Definition of Terms in Queueing Model

Customer: The arriving unit that requires some service to be provided is called the customer. The customer may represent people, machines, etc.

Server: A server is one who provides the arriving customer the necessary service. It may be persons in the counter or machines, etc.

Waiting Line or Queue: The queue represents the number of customers waiting to be served. Normally the queue does not include the customer being served.

Service Channel: This refers to the type of service provided. If we have one serving unit only, we have a single channel model or single server model. If service involves more than one server, we have a multi-channel server model. We use the symbol k to denote the number of service channels.

Arrival Rate: This is the rate at which customers arrive to be serviced. This arrival rate may not be constant. Hence it is treated as a random variable for which a certain probability distribution is to be assumed. The assumption regarding the distribution of this value has an effect upon the mathematical model. It is observed in general that in queuing theory, arrival rate is randomly distributed according to the Poisson distribution. The mean value of the arrival rate is denoted by ë (lambda); the unit is usually customers/time period.

Service Rate: This is the rate at which the service is offered to the customers. This can be done by a single server or sometimes by multiple servers, but this service rate refers to service offered by a single service channel. This rate is also a random variable as the service to one customer may be different from the other. Hence, it is also assumed to follow in general, the Poisson distribution. The mean value of the service rate is ì; the unit is customers/time period. The distribution of this rate plays a role in the mathematical model.

Infinite Queue: If the customers who arrive and form the queue are from a large population (e.g. people crowding at a cinema theatre, book in counter, etc.) then the queue is referred to as infinite queuing model. This assumption also has great influence in the mathematical formulation and its solution.

Finite Queue: If the customers arrive from a small number of population say less than 30, then this is treated as a finite queue. This value also has an effect in the mathematical model formulation and its solution.

Priority: This refers to the method of deciding which customer will be served next. The most common assumption is first come, first served (first in, first out). This assumption has also an effect in the derivation of formulae used for analysis.

Expected Number in Queue: This is the average or mean number of customers waiting to be serviced. This is denoted by Qu.

Expected Number in System: This is the average number of customers waiting in the line and/or being serviced, denoted by L.

Expected Time in Queue: This is the expected or mean time a customer waiting in line and/or being serviced, denoted by Wq.

Expected Number in Nonempty Queue: This is the average or expected number of customers waiting in the line excluding those times when the queue is empty. This figure can be arrived by counting and averaging only nonzero values. It would be equivalent to L. This expected number in the nonempty queue is denoted by Ln.

Expected Waiting Time For Nonempty Queue: This is the expected time a customer waits in line if he has to wait at all. This value is the average of waiting times for all customers entering the queue when the serving counter is filled. Customers entering the channel are empty needing not have to wait (zero waiting time) and these values are not taken into account in arriving at the average. Wn denotes this value.

System Utilization or Traffic Intensity: This is the ratio between arrival and service rate denoted by ρ given by (λ /μ).

Decision Theory

Decision theory is principle associated with decisions. Contemporary decision theory was developed in the mid of the 20th century with the support of several academic disciplines. Decision theory is typically followed by researchers who pinpoint themselves as economists, statisticians, psychologists, political and social scientists or philosophers. Decision theory provides a formal structure to make rational choices in the situation of **uncertainty**. Given a set of alternatives, a set of consequences, and a correspondence between those sets, decision theory offers conceptually simple procedures for choice. The origin of decision theory is derived from economics by using the utility function of payoffs. It proposes that decisions be made by computing the utility and probability, the ranges of options, and also lays down strategies for good decision.

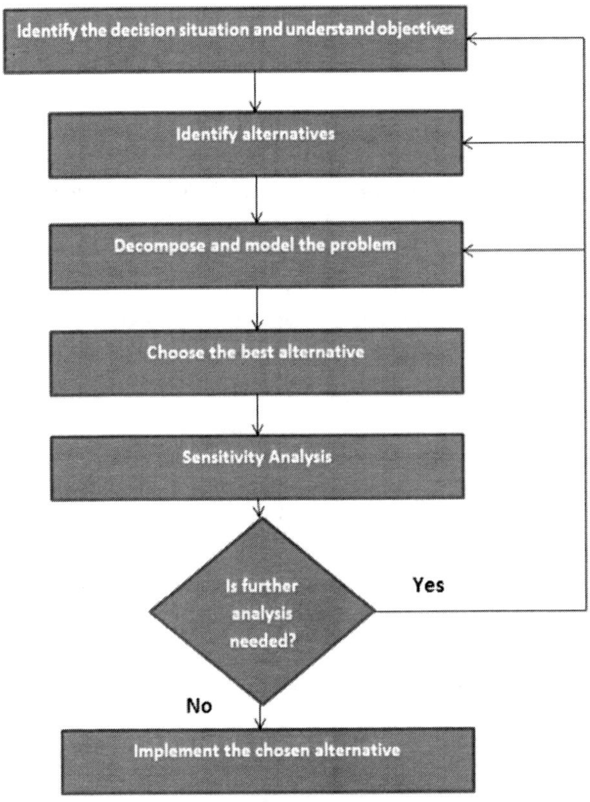

Decision theory is a set of concepts, principles, tools and techniques that help the decision maker in dealing with complex decision problems under uncertainty. More specifically, decision theory deals with methods for determining the optimal course of action when a number of alternatives are available and their consequences cannot be forecasted with certainty.

According to David Lewis (1974), "decision theory (at least if we omit the frills) is not an esoteric science, however unfamiliar it may seem to an outsider. Rather it is a systematic exposition of the consequences of certain well-chosen platitudes about belief, desire, preference and choice. It is the very core of our common-sense theory of persons, dissected out and elegantly systematized".

In theoretical literature, it is represented that decision theory signifies a generalized approach to decision making. It enables the decision maker to analyze a set of complex situations with many alternatives and many different possible consequences and to identify a course of action consistent with the basic economic and psychological desires of the decision maker.

Decision theory problems are categorized by the following:

1. A decision criterion
2. A list of alternatives
3. A list of possible future events
4. Payoffs associated with each combination of alternatives and events
5. The degree of certainty of possible future events

There are two categories of decisions theories that include normative or prescriptive decision theory to identify the best decision to take, assuming an ideal decision maker who is fully informed, able to compute with perfect accuracy, and fully rational. The practical application of this prescriptive approach is called decision analysis, and aimed at finding tools, methodologies and software to help people make better decisions. The most systematic and comprehensive software tools developed in this way are called **decision support systems**.

In contrast, positive or descriptive decision theory explains observed behaviours under the assumption that the decision-making agents are behaving under some consistent rules. These rules may, for instance, have a technical framework or an axiomatic framework, integration the Von Neumann-Morgenstern axioms with behavioural desecrations of the expected utility hypothesis, or they may explicitly give a functional form for time-inconsistent utility functions.

Solution to any decision problem include following steps:

1. Identify the problem
2. Specify objectives and the decision criteria for choosing a solution

3. Develop alternatives
4. Analyze and compare alternatives
5. Select the best alternative
6. Implement the chosen alternative
7. Verify that desired results are achieved

Decisions in Stages, Decision Trees

In many instances, the choice of the best act is not made in one stage, and the decision problem involves a sequence of acts and events. There may be a number of basic alternatives, each leading to one of a number of situations depending on the outcome of a certain random process. At each such situation, a number of other alternatives may be available which also lead to a new set of situations depending on another set of events and so on. Discrete decision theory problems can be represented pictorially using decision tress. It chronically portrays the sequence of actions and events as they unfold. In below figure, square symbol precedes the set of actions that can be taken by decision maker. The round node precedes the set of events or states of nature that could be encountered after decisions are made. The nodes are connected by branches.

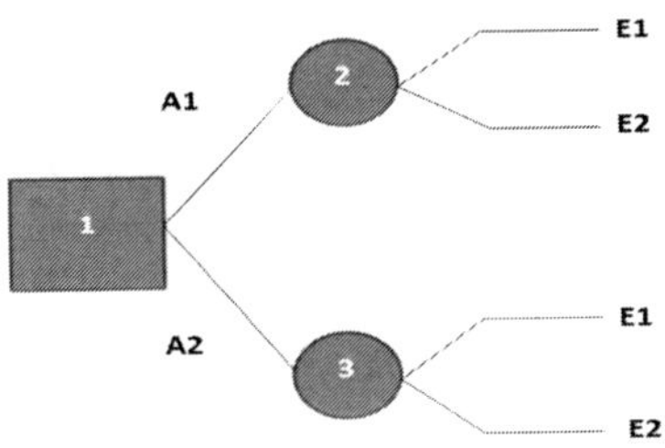

Analysis of Decision Trees

After the tree has been drawn, it is scrutinized from right to left. The aim of analysis is to determine the best strategy of the decision maker that means an optimal sequence of the decisions. To analyze a decision tree, managers must know a decision criterion, probabilities that are assigned to each event, and revenues and costs for the decision alternatives and the chance events that occur.

There are two possibilities to how to include revenues and costs in a decision tree. One possibility is to assign them only to terminating nodes where they are included in the conditional value of the decision criterion associated with the decisions and events along the path from the first part of the tree to the end. However, it can be appropriate to assign revenues and costs to branches. This reduces the required arithmetic for calculating the values of the decision criterion for terminating nodes and focuses attention on the parameters for sensitivity analysis.

When analyzing a decision tree, managers must start at the end of the tree and work backwards. They perform two kinds of calculations.

For chance event nodes managers calculate certainty equivalents related to the events emanating from these nodes. Under the assumption that the decision maker has a neutral attitude toward risk, certainty equivalent of uncertain outcomes can be replaced by their expected value. At decision nodes, the alternative with the best expected value of the decision criterion is selected.

Benefits of Decision Trees

They enable to obtain a visual portrayal of sequential decisions, i.e. they picture a series of chronological decisions. Decision tree are universal, they make more accurate the structure of the decision process and facilitate a communication among solvers of the decision problem. Decision tree force the decision maker to appreciate all consequences of his decisions. Construction and analysis of decision trees by means of computers makes possible to experiment with decision trees and quickly to establish the impact of changes in the input parameters of the tree on the choice of the best policy.

Limitations of Decision Trees:

(i) Only one decision criterion can be considered.

(ii) The decision tree is an abstraction and simplification of the real problem. Only the important decisions and events are included.

(iii) Managers cannot use decision trees if the chance event outcomes are continuous. Instead, they must redefine the outcomes so that there is a finite set of possibilities.

The significant result of the analysis of a decision tree is to choose the best alternative in the first stage of the decision process. After this stage, some changes in the decision situations can come, additional information can be obtained, and usually, it is essential to actualize the decision tree and to determine a new optimal strategy. This procedure is required before every further stage.

Theoretical studies have revealed that decision theory is a formal study of rational decision making formed largely by the joint efforts of mathematicians, philosophers, social scientists, economists, statisticians and management scientists (Jeffrey 1992). While decision theory has history of applications to real world problems in many disciplines, including economics, risk analysis, business management, and theoretical behavioural ecology. It has more recently gained acknowledgment as a beneficial approach to conservation in the last 20 years (Maguire 1986).

Markov Analysis

Markov analysis is a method of analyzing the current behaviour of some variable in an effort to predict the future behaviour of the same variable. This procedure was developed by the Russian mathematician, Andrei A. Markov early in this century. He first used it to describe and predict the behaviour of particles of gas in a closed container. As a management tool, Markov analysis has been successfully applied to a wide variety of decision situations.

Perhaps its widest use is in examining and predicting the behaviour of customers in terms of their brand loyalty and their switching from one brand to another. Markov processes are a special class of mathematical models which are often applicable to decision problems. In a Markov process, various states are defined. The probability of going to each of the states depends only on the present state and is independent of how we arrived at that state.

PERT & CPM

Project management can be understood as a systematic way of planning, scheduling, executing, monitoring, controlling the different aspects of the project, so as to attain the goal made at the time of project formulation. PERT and CPM are the two network based project management techniques, which exhibit the flow and sequence of the activities and events. **Program (Project) Management and Review Technique (PERT)** is appropriate for the projects where time needed to complete different activities are not known. On the other hand, **Critical Path Method** or **CPM** is appropriate for the projects which are recurring in nature.

The two scheduling methods, uses common approach for designing the network and for ascertaining its critical path. They are used in the successful completion of a project and hence used in conjunction with each other. Nevertheless, the truth is that CPM is different from PERT in a way that the former concentrates on time while the latter stresses on time-cost trade-off. In the same manner, there are many differences between PERT and CPM, which are as follows:

Basis for Comparison	***PERT***	***CPM***
Meaning	PERT is a project management technique used to manage uncertain activities of a project.	CPM is a statistical technique of project management that manages well defined activities of a project.
What is it?	A technique of planning and control of time.	A method to control cost and time.
Orientation	Event-oriented	Activity-oriented
Evolution	Evolved as Research & Development project	Evolved as Construction project

(Contd...)

Model	Probabilistic Model	Deterministic Model
Focus	Time	Time-cost trade-off
Estimates	Three time estimates	One time estimate
Appropriate	High precision time estimate	Reasonable time estimate
Management	Unpredictable Activities	Predictable Activities
Nature of Jobs	Non-repetitive nature	Repetitive nature
Critical and Non-critical Activities	No differentiation	Differentiated
Suitable	Research and Development Project	Non-research projects like civil construction, ship building etc.
Crashing Concept	Not Applicable	Applicable

Unit - V

Concept of Management

Concept, Types, Characteristics of Motivation

Concept of Motivation

The term motivation is derived from the word '**motive**'. The word 'motive' as a noun means an objective; as a verb this word means **moving into action**. Therefore, motives are forces which induce people to act in a way, so as to ensure the fulfillment of a particular human need at a time. Behind every human action, there is a motive. Therefore, management must provide motives to people to make them work for the organization.

Motivation is the **driving force** which helps us to achieve goals. Motivation is said to be intrinsic or extrinsic. The term is generally used for humans but, theoretically, it can also be used to describe the causes for animal behaviour as well. According to various theories, motivation may be rooted in a basic need to minimize physical pain and maximize pleasure, or it may include specific needs such as eating and resting, or a desired object, goal, state of being, ideal, or it may be attributed to less-apparent reasons such as altruism, selfishness, morality, or avoiding mortality. Conceptually, motivation should not be confused with either volition or optimism. Motivation is related to, but distinct from, emotion.

Motivation may be defined as a planned managerial process, which stimulates people to work to the best of their capabilities, by providing them with motives, which are based on their unfulfilled needs.

"Motivation means a **process of stimulating people** to action to accomplish desired goods." —WILLIAM G. SCOTT

"Motivation is the process of attempting to influence others to do your will through the possibility of gain or reward." — FLIPPO

Motivation is, in fact, pressing the right button to get the desired human behaviour.

Motivation is no doubt an essential ingredient of any Organisation. It is the psychological technique which really executes the plans and policies through the efforts of others.

Types of Motivation

There are many frameworks, models, and theories that focus on employee motivation. A few of the most common are quickly summarized below. While they are each based on good research and have some degree of universal applicability, none are the absolute doctrine on motivation. In fact, few motivation concepts are universal. However, one idea that is acknowledged by all frameworks that address motivation is that there are extrinsic and intrinsic motivational factors.

There are two types of motivation that exist: extrinsic motivation and intrinsic motivation. Extrinsic motivation is motivation that is inspired by outside forces, while intrinsic motivation is motivation that is inspired from within a person. Both types of motivation are essential to success. Below you will find different types of extrinsic and intrinsic motivational factors:

Extrinsic Motivation

Money

People around you

Good grades

Rewards

Intrinsic Motivation

Happiness

Personal goals, values, and morals

Willingness and eagerness to learn

Physiological, social, and self-esteem needs

Extrinsic factors are **external** to the subject. In our discussion, the subject is an employee. Factors, like money, vacation time, or awards, are all external to the individual. **Intrinsic factors** are **internal** to the individual, such as the drive to excel, fear of failure, or desire to be acknowledged.

Intrinsic motivation refers to motivation that is driven by an interest or enjoyment in the task itself, and exists within the individual rather than relying on any external pressure. Intrinsic motivation has been studied by social and educational psychologists since the early 1970s.

Extrinsic motivation comes from outside of the individual. Common extrinsic motivations are rewards like money and grades, coercion and threat of punishment. Competition is in general extrinsic because it encourages the performer to win and beat others, not to enjoy the intrinsic rewards of the activity.

Self-determination theory proposes that extrinsic motivation can be internalized by the individual if the task fits with their values and beliefs and therefore helps to fulfill their basic psychological needs.

Characteristics of Motivation

Following are the outstanding features of the concept of motivation:

1. Motivation is a personal and internal feeling. Motivation is a psychological phenomenon which generates within an individual.
2. Motivation is need based. If there are no needs of an individual, the process of motivation fails. It is a behavioural concept that directs human behaviour towards certain goals.
3. Motivation is a continuous process. As human wants are unlimited, therefore motivation is an ongoing process.
4. Motivation may be positive or negative. A positive motivation promotes incentives to people while a negative motivation threatens the enforcement of disincentives.
5. Motivation is a planned process. People differ in their approach, to respond to the process of motivation; as no two individuals could be motivated in an exactly similar manner. Accordingly, motivation is a psychological concept and a complex process.
6. Motivation is different from job satisfaction.

Competencies and Its Development

The term competency has a number of definitions which depend on the specific task to be performed by individuals under different conditions. These definitions differ on different counts.

Competency was first popularized by **Boyatzis** (1982), who performed a comprehensive study of over 2000 managers and he identified and assessed over a hundred potential competencies. He defined competency as, “A capacity that exists in a person that leads to behaviour that meets the job demands within the parameters of organizational environment, and that, in turn brings about desired results.”

The competency is considered to be an underlying characteristic that an individual brings to a job situation, which can result ineffective and/or superior performance in such job.

David McClelland claimed that competencies could be used for predicting job performances and further he held that competencies were not biased by race, gender or socio-economic factors. His study helped to identify performance aspects which are not attributable to a worker's intelligence or degree of knowledge and skill.

Spencer and Spencer (1993) defined "a competency as an underlying characteristic of an individual that is causally related to criterion referenced effective and/or superior performance in a job or situation."

Similarly, "A Competency is a set of skills, related knowledge and attributes that allow an individual to successfully perform a task or an activity within a specific function or job" (UNIDO, 2002).

Although theses definitions vary in different forms, however the following components are found commonly in all the definitions:

Competency is composed of **knowledge, skills, abilities** and other characteristics which underlie effective or successful job performance. These competency attributes are observable and measurable; and these attributes distinguish between superior and other performers.

In fact, the competency is a wider concept which includes the **knowledge, attitudes, behaviours and skills** which help a person capable of transforming his ideas in to realities with an excellence in its performance in a given context. It does not refer to those behaviours which do not demonstrate excellent performance. Therefore, they do not include knowledge, but do include "applied" knowledge or the behavioural application of knowledge that produces success. In addition, competencies do include skill, but only the manifestation of skills that produce success. Finally, competencies are not work motives, but do include observable behaviours related to motives.

Innovation and Entrepreneurship

Innovation

The word innovation recognizes a Latin origin. It is composed of "in" which means "**inward**" and "novare" = "**make new change**".

Innovation has a very wide application in economic and technological matters, as applies to bring to market new products, services, or apply new technologies that change the commercial stage and the consumption trends.

Something innovated is something new, which was reborn with different characteristics, either in its form, in its structure, in its appearance or its function. It is a concept opposite to the traditional and conservative.

An innovative entrepreneur is revolutionary in its field, risky, curious, and endowed with great creative ingenuity.

Technology changes or innovations produced are astonishing, which applies in all orders of life, it either daily, labour, time, and so on. The use of computers and Internet access has been huge innovations in the mode of study, work and communicate.

Among the different possibilities to innovate, those related to product or process innovations are known as technological innovations. Other types of innovations can relate to new markets, new business models, new processes and organizational methods.

Continuous improvements are not usually able to create competitive advantages of medium to long term, but they are able to maintain the competitiveness of the products in terms of cost.

Types of Innovation

The different forms of innovation can be classified in several ways.

Product Innovation

It consists of changes in product attributes with a change in how the product is noticed by consumers. Example: car with automatic transmission compared to "conventional" one.

Process Innovation

It consists of changes regarding the product or the service production process. It does not necessarily have an impact on the final product but produces benefits in the production process, generally increasing the productivity and reducing costs. Example: automobile produced by robots compared to that produced by human workers.

Entrepreneurship

Entrepreneurship involves decision making, innovation, implementation, forecasting of the future, independency, and success first and this is how entrepreneurship developed. Entrepreneurship is a discipline with a knowledge base theory. It is an outcome of complex socio-economic, psychological, technological, legal and other factors. It is a dynamic and risky process. It involves a fusion of capital, technology and human talent. Entrepreneurship is equally applicable to big and small businesses, to economic and non-economic activities. Different entrepreneurs might have some common traits but all of them will have some different and unique features. If we just concentrate on the entrepreneurs then there will be as many models as there are ventures and we will not be able to predict or plan, how and where, and when these entrepreneurs will start their ventures. Entrepreneurship is a process. It is not a combination of some stray incidents. It is the purposeful and organized search for change, conducted after systematic analysis of opportunities in the environment. Entrepreneurship is a philosophy. It is the way one thinks, one acts and therefore it can exist in any situation be it business or government or in the field of education, science and technology or poverty alleviation or any others. Entrepreneurship can be described as a process of action an entrepreneur undertakes to establish his enterprise. Entrepreneurship is a creative activity. It is the ability to create and build something from practically nothing. It is a knack of sensing opportunity where others see chaos, contradiction and confusion. Entrepreneurship is the attitude of mind to seek opportunities, take calculated risks and derive benefits by setting up a venture. It comprises of numerous activities involved in conception, creation and running an enterprise.

According to Peter Drucker, Entrepreneurship is defined as 'a systematic innovation, which consists in the purposeful and **organized search for changes**, and it is the systematic analysis of the opportunities such changes might offer for **economic and social innovation**.

Entrepreneurship is a dynamic process of vision, change, and creation. It requires an application of energy and passion towards the creation and **implementation of new ideas and creative solutions**. Essential ingredients include the willingness to take calculated risks in terms of time, equity, or career; the ability to formulate an effective venture team; the creative skill to marshal needed resources; the fundamental skills of building a solid business plan; and, finally, the vision to recognize opportunity where others see chaos, contradiction, and confusion.

Small Business: Concepts, Government Policy for Promotion of Small and Tiny Enterprise

Concept of Small Business

Small businesses are privately owned corporations, partnerships, or sole proprietorships that have fewer employees and/or less annual revenue than a regular-sized business or corporation. What businesses are defined as "small" in terms of being able to apply for government support and qualify for preferential tax policy varies depending on the country and industry. While small businesses can also be classified according to other methods, such as annual revenues, shipments, sales, assets, or by annual gross or net revenue or net profits, the number of employees is one of the most widely used measures.

Small businesses in many countries include service or retail operations such as convenience stores, small grocery stores, bakeries or delicatessens, hairdressers or trades people (e.g., carpenters, electricians), restaurants, guest houses, photographers, very small-scale manufacturing, and Internet-related businesses such as web design and computer programming. Some professionals operate as small businesses, such as lawyers, accountants, dentists and medical doctors (although these professionals can also work for large organizations or companies). Small businesses vary a great deal in terms of size, revenues and regulatory authorization, both within a country and from country to country. Some small businesses, such as a home accounting business, may only require a business license. On the other hand, other small businesses, such as day cares, retirement homes and restaurants serving liquor are more heavily regulated, and may require inspection and certification from various government authorities.

Small scale and cottage industrial sector has emerged as an engine of growth in several developing and developed economies of the world. In India, they have emerged as a vibrant and dynamic sector of Indian economy by virtue of their significant contribution to GDP, industrial production and export. However, the most vital contribution of this sector is headed for **employment generation** which is **next to agriculture**.

Government Policy for Promotion of Small and Tiny Enterprise

The growth of small scale industrial sector has been regarded as one of the most significant features of planned economic development. Keeping in view the importance of small scale and cottage industries, Government of India framed a policy package consisting of both promotional and protective instruments for fostering the growth of small scale and cottage industries, soon after independence. Government's attitude and intention towards industries in general and SSIs in particular are reflected in Industrial policy Resolutions.

(a) Industrial Policy Resolution of 1948: The Industrial Policy Resolution (IPR) of 1948 marked the beginning of "organized direction" for industrial development in India. The strategy of industrial planning aimed at diversifying the industrial base mainly through the development of basic, intermediate and capital goods industries. Nevertheless, it laid much emphasis on the indispensable role of small scale and cottage industrial sector for employment generation in the economic development of the country.

The IPR of 1948 stated that "Cottage and small scale industries have a very important role in the national economy. Offering as they do scope for individual, village or cooperative enterprise, and means for the rehabilitation of displaced persons. These industries are particularly suited for the better utilization of local resources and for the achievement of the local self-sufficiency in respect of certain types of essential consumer goods like food, cloth and agricultural implements". The IPR of 1948 reflected the emergence of a dualistic approach in government policy i.e. emphasis on both traditional and modern small scale sector. This approach has continued to form the basis of industrial policy towards the small scale sector ever since. **The industrial Development and Regulation Act, 1951** which was promulgated in order to provide the organizational support to IPR of 1948 provide scope for a coordinated development of cottage and small scale industries within the general framework of large scale development programmes.

(b) Industrial Policy Resolution of 1956: In 1955, Planning Commission setup a Committee on village and small scale industries popularly known as **Karve Committee**. The Committee recommended some important measures like: **(i)** Reservation of certain items only for village and small scale industries; **(ii)** Restriction of capacity expansion of large industry; **(iii)** Management of supply of raw materials; and **(iv)** A scheme of concessions and benefits to small producers.

(c) Industrial Policy Resolution of 1977: The IPR of 1977 was announced on 23rd December when Janata Party Government took initiatives for the development of small scale sector and asserted that "The main thrust of the new Industrial Policy will be on effective promotion of cottage and small industries widely dispersed in rural areas and small towns. It is the policy of the Government that whatever can be produced by small and cottage industries must only be so produced". The important features of the IPR were: **(i) 504 items** were reserved for exclusive production in the small-scale industries. **(ii)** The concept of **District Industries Centres** (DICs) was introduced so that in each district a single agency could meet all the requirements of SSIs under one roof. **(iii)** Technological up gradation was emphasized in traditional sector. **(iv)** Special marketing arrangements through the provision of services, such as, product standardization, quality control, market survey, were laid down.

(d) Industrial Policy Resolution of 1980: The Industrial Policy of 1980 marked a significant milestone in the policy of development of small scale industries in India. The IPR sought to harmonize the growth in small scale industries with the large and medium scale industries. Industrially backward districts were identified for faster growth of existing network of SSIs. Following measures were specified in the policy: **(i)** Investment limit was raised for **tiny, small, and ancillary units** to **Rs. 2 lakhs, Rs. 20 lakhs, and Rs. 25 lakhs** respectively. **(ii)** "Nucleus plants" in each industrially backward district replaced the "district industries centers." These were to concentrate on assembling the products of SSIs and to produce inputs needed by large number of small units. **(iii)** Reservation of items and marketing support for small industries was to continue. **(iv)** Availability of credit to growing SSI units was continued. **(v)** Buffer stocks of critical inputs were to continue. **(vi)** Agricultural base was to strengthen by providing preferential treatment to agro based industries. **(vii)** An early warning system was to establish to avoid sickness and take appropriate remedial measures.

(e) Industrial Policy Resolution of 1990: The Industrial Policy Resolution of 1990 emphasized on the need of modernization and technology up gradation to meet the **twin objectives** of employment generation and dispersal of industry in rural areas, and to enhance the contribution of small scale industries to exports. Main features of this Resolution are: **(i)** It raised the investment ceiling in plant and machinery for small scale industries to **Rs. 60 lakhs** and correspondingly, for ancillary units to **Rs. 75 lakhs**. **(ii)** It created central investment subsidy for this sector in rural and backward areas. Assistance was also granted to women entrepreneurs for widening the entrepreneurial base. **(iii)** Reservation of items to be produced by SSIs was increased to **836**. **(iv)** Small Industries Development Bank of India was established to ensure adequate flow of credit to SSIs. **(v)** Stress was reiterated to upgrade technology to improve competitiveness. **(vi)** Special emphasis was laid on training of women and youth under Entrepreneurial Development Programme. **(vii)** Activities of Kadhi and Village Industries Commission and Khadi and Village Industries Board were to expand.

(f) Industrial Policy Resolution of 1991: On July 24, 1991 the Government lunched '**Structural Adjustment Programme**' which has resulted in 1800 change in the policies governing the different aspects of Indian economy. In order to impart more vitality and growth to small scale sector, the Government of India announced a separate policy statement for small, tiny and village enterprises. The basic thrust of this resolution was to simplify regulations and procedures by delicensing, deregulating, and decontrolling. Its incredible features are: **(i)** SSIs were exempted from licensing for all articles of manufacture. **(ii)** The investment limit for tiny enterprises was raised to **Rs. 5 lakhs** irrespective of location. **(iii)** Equity participation by other industrial undertakings was permitted up to a limit of 24 percent of shareholding in SSIs. **(iv)** Factoring services were to launch to solve the problem of delayed payments to SSIs. **(v)** Priority was accorded to small and tiny units in allocation of indigenous and raw materials. **(vi)** Market promotion of products was emphasized through co-operatives, public institutions and other marketing agencies and corporations. On the whole, the Industrial Policy Resolution of 1991 outlined developmental, deregulatory and de-bureaucratic measures and underscored the need to shift from subsidized and cheap credit to a system which would ensure adequate flow of credit on timely and normative basis to the small scale industrial sector.

Recent Policy Measures for Small Scale and Cottage Industries

(A) Comprehensive Policy Package for small scale and tiny sector, 2000 The Government of India announced a comprehensive policy package for the development and promotion of small scale and tiny sector which aims to improve the competitiveness of the sector. The main focus of the policy package was: **(i)** The exemption for excise duty limit raised from **Rs.50 lakhs to Rs. 1 crore**. **(ii)** The limit of investment was increased in industry related service and business enterprises **from Rs. 5 lakhs to Rs. 10 lakhs**. **(iii)** The coverage of ongoing Integrated Infrastructure Development (IID) was enhanced to cover all areas in the country with 50 percent reservation for rural areas and 50 percent earmarking of plots for tiny sector. **(iv)** The family income eligibility limit of Rs. 24000 was enhanced to **Rs. 40000 per annum** under the Prime Minister Rozgar Yojana (PMRY). **(v)** The scheme of **granting Rs. 75000** to each small scale enterprise for obtaining ISO 9000 certification was continued till the end of 10th plan.

(B) Enactment of Micro, Small and Medium Enterprises Development Act, 2006. In May' 2006, the President has amended the Government of India (Allocation of Business) Rules, 1961; Ministry of Agro and Rural Industries and Ministry of Small Scale Industries have been merged into a single Ministry, namely, "Ministry of Micro, Small and Medium Enterprises. Consequently the Micro, Small and Medium enterprises Development (MSMED) Act was enacted, which provides the first ever legal framework for recognition of the concept 'enterprises' against 'industries' and integrating the three tiers of these enterprises viz. micro, small and medium and clearly fixed the investment limits for both manufacturing and service enterprises. It also provides for a statutory consultative mechanism at the national level with wide representation of all sections of stakeholders, particularly the three classes of enterprises. The Act also makes provisions for establishment of specific funds for the promotion, development and enhancement of competitiveness of these enterprises, progressive credit policies and practices, preference in Government procurements to products and services of the micro and small enterprises, more effective mechanism for mitigating the problems of delayed payments and simplification of the process of closure of business by all three categories of enterprises.

In a sense, opportunity identification and selection are akin to, what is termed in marketing terminology, 'new product development.' Thus, product or opportunity identification and selection process starts with the generation of ideas, or say, ideas about some opportunities or products are generated in the first instance.

The ideas about opportunities or products that the entrepreneur can consider for selecting the most promising one to be pursued by him/her as an enterprise, can be generated or discovered from various sources- both internal and external.

These may include:

(i) Knowledge of potential customer needs,
(ii) Watching emerging trends in demands for certain products,
(iii) Scope for producing substitute product,
(iv) Going through certain professional magazines catering to specific interests like electronics, computers, etc.,
(v) Success stories of known entrepreneurs or friends or relatives,
(vi) Making visits to trade fairs and exhibitions displaying new products and services,
(vii) Meeting with the Government agencies,
(viii) Ideas given by the knowledgeable persons,
(ix) Knowledge about the Government policy, concessions and incentives, list of items reserved for exclusive manufacture in small-scale sector,
(x) A new product introduced by the competitor, and
(xi) One's market insights through observation.

In nutshell, a prospective entrepreneur can get ideas for establishing his/her enterprise from various sources. These may include consumers, existing products and services presently on offer, distribution channels, the government officials, and research and development.

Process of Business Opportunity Identification, Detailed Business Plan Preparation

Process of Business Opportunity Identification

Identify Market Inefficiencies

When looking at a market, consider what inefficiencies are present in the market. Do you have an idea on how to correct these inefficiencies?

Remove Key Hassles

Take a look at some of the key hassles customers face when buying or using a product or a service.

You don't necessarily to have a new product or service. You can be innovative and improve a product, a service or a business process. Purchasing processes in some products categories are still a major source of irritation for customers. Think how you can improve and provide a superior alternative.

Customers Desire to Experience Something New

You may or may not have a new business idea or business process to serve a market and perhaps there are no market inefficiencies for you to exploit. But sometimes, gagging the customers' desire to experience something new can be a successful strategy.

Pick a Growing Sector/Industry

When considering a new business, it is important to look at whether or not your idea is in a growing sector or industry. For example, a lot of start-ups in the IT sector in India did very well because there was huge demand in that industry and the growth was outpacing other industries. Investing in a stagnant sector/industry may not best serve your interests, unless you identify a market inefficiency that you can exploit.

Product Differentiation

Creating superior products or services vs. alternatives is important for winning in the market place. What factors will set your product apart from the existing ones? If there is no such differentiating factor, your potential customers may just stick to the existing product rather than adopt yours.

Cash Flow Considerations

At the start-up stage, cash flow considerations are just as important as any other business function. If you run out of cash, despite holding inventory or other assets, your business will risk failure.

There are some types of businesses in which cash is typically held up for a long time. If you are in manufacturing for example, your cash flow can be held up for long periods of time, or money may be stuck in receivables. When picking the right business, you should consider one that provides fairly regular cash inflows and with slower outflows. It is imperative that you understand the need for constant cash flow in your business. Without cash flows, no matter how good your idea or business process is, you might be destined for failure.

Seasonal Business

When picking a new business, consider whether it is seasonal or the year round. If you do decide on a seasonal business, you will need to consider how to operate during off-season months. Managing the cash you make during the season will help you get through off-season. Financial planning will be of utmost importance.

Detailed Business Plan Preparation

Every business, whether a startup or a full-fledged, profitable organization, needs a business plan. To know where you are going, you have to know where you came from and what came before you.

1. Executive Summary: An executive summary is a summary of your entire business plan. It is often easiest to write your executive summary after you have finalized all the details within the plan itself.

2. Business Description: In your business description, you will need to include and define various aspects of your service offerings, the history of your field and any current happenings and your personal goals and objectives, elements that add to your success and the ownership of your company. This section is the backbone of your business plan and will set the stage for the information included in the rest of the plan.

3. Products and Services: Everyone has a product or service that they are offering to a prospective client. You should be able to describe what it is that you are selling as well as identify what makes your product or service unique.

4. Sales and Marketing: This section is very important. It gives you a window into your industry, the state of the market, general costs, how business is acquired and also affords you an opportunity to distinguish yourself from competitors.

5. Operations: The purpose of this section is to help you outline the more administrative side of your business, including how you operate, where your office is located, your staff or assistant if applicable, equipment, overhead and other expenses, legal relationships, your network of suppliers and credit policies.

6. Management Team: If you have a few advisers or people who help you to manage your business, this is where you acknowledge their involvement and the capacity by which they contribute to your overall success. if there is a hierarchy of positions within your company, you would detail that hierarchy and the relevancy of each relationship.

7. Development: This is wherc you can dream a bit. Not everything in this section is based upon pure fact like the information you would have provided in the other sections. Project into the future and think big. Development is a necessary part of business to remain competitive, so be sure to spend a significant amount of time when writing this part of your plan.

8. Financial Summary: You will need to provide a record of your financial dealings, investments, if any and how you came to the position you are in today. With some flexibility, you can project how your company will be operating and assess your financial status, including how things balance out at the end of each month, the overall financial health of your business and your cash flow.

Managing Small Enterprise, Planning for Growth

The managerial skills required for the management of small firms are not very much different from those necessary in large scale business. The managerial functions of planning, organisation, staffing, directing and controlling are common to both.

The owner-manager of a small scale firm requires all the qualities of a good manager. He must coordinate the functions of purchasing, production, marketing, financing, etc. however, the scale on which these functions are performed and the degree of complexity are lower. The organization structure of small scale units is simple due to a few employees and lack of specialization. The owner himself acts as the manger and can exercise personal control.

As the business grows, owner-manager finds it difficult to manage the firm efficiently. He has to employ expert mangers to carry out the diverse activities of the enterprise. "Even among small enterprises who have managed to succeed by their wit while their businesses were within the compass of one-man control, weaknesses in management have come to light and proved crucial when the business grew to a stature that required some recognition of departmental organization and discipline. In fact the lack of skilled personnel has been an important hurdle in the development of small business. Small scale firms cannot afford to train and develop specialized staff of their own. Therefore, arrangements must be made by the Government to ensure the supply trained and professional managers for the small scale sector.

In the course of their operations small units have to face a number of managerial problems which are described below:

1. Shortage of Materials and Power: There is acute shortage of basic raw materials required by small scale units. These units are under a handicap in obtaining raw materials of requisite quality at reasonable prices. They do not get the benefits of bulk buying. For instance, the hand loom industries facing shortage of yarn. Some bogus units secure the quota of scarce materials and sell them at inflated prices. Small scale industries also face shortage of power due to which they are unable to make full utilization of plant capacity. Majority of them cannot afford to install their own power generating plants to ensure uninterrupted operations.

2. Lack of Adequate Finance: All business firms require sufficient funds to meet their fixed capital and working capital requirements. Small scale units are often unable to procure adequate financial resources for the purchase of machinery, equipment and raw materials and for meeting day-to-day expenses. On account of their low goodwill and little fixed investment, they find it difficult to borrow at reasonable interest. Credit facilities for small scale firms are inadequate and they have to depend largely on internal resources. Sometimes, small firms have to close down or curtail their operations due to shortage of funds. There is very little scope for expansion and growth due to dearth of capital. As a result economies of scale are not available.

3. Outdated Technology: Majority of the small units use old techniques of production and outdated machinery and equipment. They cannot afford new machines and equipment and are, therefore not in a position to use the latest techniques of production. They do not find it possible to conduct research and development on a continuing basis. Therefore, the productivity and quality in small scale firms tends to be low while unit cost of production is generally high.

4. Inadequate Marketing Facilities: Small scale units have to face several difficulties in the marketing and distribution of their products. Most of them do not have their own marketing network. They find it difficult to sell their output at remunerative prices due to higher cost of production and non-standardised quality of products. Small Scale industries cannot afford to spend much on advertising, sales personnel, marketing research, etc. They have to sell their products at throwaway prices due to weak bargaining power and immediate need for money. They also face stiff completion from large firms.

5. Weak Organization and Management: Small scale firms are generally managed by the owner who very often does not possess the skills required for the efficient management of the enterprise. There is lack of proper division of work and the benefits of specialization are not available. Some owner-managers are reluctant to adopt modern methods of organisation and management. There is instability in business because the sickness and death of the owner manger directly affect the survival and growth of the small firm.

6. Lack of Trained Personnel: There is lack of trained and experienced employees because small firms cannot pay high salaries and cannot spend much on training of employees. Small scale firms find it difficult to recruit and motive skilled managerial and technical personnel as they look for better opportunities in the large scale industries. Therefore, they get the second rate talent or have to depend on family members who do not have diversified skills.

Planning for Growth

Here are five key elements to consider when drafting your business plan for growth.

1. **Define Your Goals and Priorities:** Create a list of long-term goals. Be sure to choose goals that are **SMART**: specific, measurable, achievable, realistic, and timed. These goals will guide you as you work through your business plan for growth, and will help to focus your efforts on doing what it will take to achieve these goals.

2. **Set up a Timeline:** A timeline with milestones should be established to mark your progress against reaching your goals. Include details in the timeline such as customers you hope to acquire, and additional employees you might need to hire. Elaborate on how these activities will contribute to achieving your goals for growth.
3. **Plan for Cash:** Growth strategies such as geographic or product expansion can initially generate negative cash flow. Increasing revenues doesn't necessarily mean increased profits, because at the outset, the cost to achieve growth can be high. Your financial plan, especially your cash flow projections, will be vital in determining how you'll sustain your company's growth.
4. **Profile Competitors:** Have new competitors emerged since you established your company? How have your existing competitors changed in response to your entrance into the market? Be aware of how your competition can affect your goals. Strategies to address competitive forces can include adjustments in:
   - Price
   - Speed
   - Quality
   - Niche markets
5. **Track Your Progress and Evaluate the Results:** To track your progress, establish company and industry benchmarks against which you can measure your performance. Conduct a gap analysis which compares "Where are we today?" with "Where do we want to be?"

Sickness in Small Enterprises

As per the RBI definition, a small-scale industrial unit is considered as sick when

(i) Any of borrowal accounts of a bank has become 'doubtful' advance i.e. principal or interest in respect of any of its borrowal accounts has remained **overdue** for a period **exceeding 2 ½ years** and

(ii) There is erosion in the net worth due to accumulated cash losses to the extent of **50 per cent or more** of its net worth during the **preceding two accounting years**. In respect of the tiny /decentralized sector also, a unit may be considered as sick if it satisfies the above definition. However, in such cases, if it is difficult to get financial particulars, a unit may be considered as sick provided it defaults continuously for a period of one year, in the payment of interest or installments of principal and there are persistent irregularities in the operations in its credit cash with the bank.

Causes of industrial sickness have to be viewed from the general background of an industrial economy which experience prosperity and depression over a period of time. At any point of time, the problems of industries are not uniform. However, factors generally responsible for the problems can be divided into external and internal. The **external factors** include changes in fiscal and monetary policies, prices and distribution, non-availability of inputs including power, transport, coal, etc., adverse changes in money market and capital market, adverse industrial relations, etc. **Internal factors** are those which are within the control of the management of the concern. These include faulty planning, implementation of the project, lack of inventory and cost control, wrong selection of the site, faulty management accounting, managerial deficiency, etc. Causes of sickness can vary from area to area, size to size of units and their product to product. Sickness can originate right from the stage of conception of the stage of crystallization of the concept and/or implementation of the project. In general, a unit becomes sick when it cannot generate adequate cash surplus from internal sources. **Internal cash generation** is the most important indicator of the unit and, therefore, this can be taken as a starting point of our analysis. Any decline in the internal cash generation is possible due to several reasons such as

1. Drop in production on account of: • problems of production • lack of orders • lack of raw material
2. Poor cash management
3. Increased cost of production
4. Delayed settlement of payments by customers
5. Diversion of funds for non-productive purposes

Thus, the causes of industrial sickness are numerous and varied. While studying causes, it could be seen that **liquidity constraint** is the root cause of sickness. With continuous cash losses, the unit fails to meet its obligations and in this process, the unit faces a major threat from the suppliers of materials. Loss in liquidity arises due to diversion of short-term funds for acquiring long-term assets. Due to deteriorating liquidity position the unit will have to operate at a lower capacity and lose its major customers. Thus, unit now is said to have lost viability and considered sick.

Rehabilitation of Sick Enterprises

If the project is found viable, it should be attempted to rehabilitate the sick unit. Every rehabilitation scheme involves certain relief and concessions. As per the recommendations the **Kohli Committee**, appointed by the RBI, certain guidelines are available on relief and concessions. Accordingly, relief/concessions are not to be given as a matter of routine in all cases. It is for the banks/financial institutions to decide on the nature and extent of concessions necessary/warranted within these parameters, depending upon the merits of each case. Further, in order to speed up the process of preparation and implementation of packages, the banks have been given freedom for extension of relief/concessions beyond the parameters in cases where it is absolutely necessary.

Process of Rehabilitation

In general, a sick SSI unit is defined in terms of its capacity to generate internal funds. A sick unit fails to generate internal surplus on a continuing basis and depends on its survival on frequent infusion of external funds.

Objectives of Rehabilitation Scheme:

(i) To enable the unit to operate at a profitable level.

(ii) To adjust the irregularity in the account, if any, according to a phased programme. Thus, the rehabilitation scheme involves two aspects i.e., (a) preparation of feasibility report before implementing the scheme and (b) careful monitoring of the performance of the unit during the nursing period.

Decision on Rehabilitation

Keeping in view all the possible outcomes, risk involved and the irregularity in the account, bank decision should aim at promoting the business activity and not the borrower as an individual. The decision should be based on likelihood of possible recovery. Finally, bank can support the borrower provided he has equal interest in coming out of the sickness. In other words, bank decision to rehabilitation a unit could be justified if it can:

- Generate adequate activity and employment
- Control the business activity effectively
- Commit additional funds, if necessary
- Elicit co-operation from workers, suppliers of materials, etc.

Intrapreneurship

Intrapreneurship is acting like an entrepreneur within a larger organization. Intrapreneurs are usually highly self-motivated, proactive and action-oriented people who are comfortable with taking the initiative, even within the boundaries of an organization, in pursuit of an innovative product or service. The intrapreneur has the comfort of knowing that failure does not have a personal cost as it does for an entrepreneur, since the organization absorbs losses arising from failure.

Difference between an Entrepreneur and an Intrapreneur

An entrepreneur takes substantial risk in being the owner and operator of a business with expectations of financial profit and other rewards that the business may generate. On the contrary, an intrapreneur is an individual employed by an organization for remuneration, which is based on the financial success of the unit he is responsible for. Intrapreneurs share the same traits as entrepreneurs such as conviction, zeal and insight. As the intrapreneur continues to expresses his ideas vigorously, it will reveal the gap between the philosophy of the organization and the employee. If the organization supports him in pursuing his ideas, he succeeds. If not, he is likely to leave the organization and set up his own business.

Features of Intrapreneurship

An entrepreneur will be able to look at things in novel ways. He will have the capacity to take calculated risk and to accept failure as a learning point. An intrapreneur thinks like an entrepreneur looking out for opportunities, which profit the organization. Intrapreneurship is a novel way of making organizations more profitable where imaginative employees entertain entrepreneurial thoughts. It is in the interest of an organization to encourage intrapreneurs. Intrapreneurship is a significant method for companies to reinvent themselves and improve performance.

Entrepreneurship appeals to people who possess natural traits that find start ups arousing their interest. Intrapreneurs appear to be those who generally would not like to get entangled in startups but are tempted to do so for a number of reasons. Managers would do well to take employees who do not appear entrepreneurial but can turn out to be good intrapreneurial choices.

Index

MANAGEMENT

FOR UGC - NET

(Paper II & III)

MANAGEMENT
FOR UGC - NET
(Paper II & III)

(VOLUME - II)

Debasish Biswas

First Edition, 2019

KALPAZ

First Published, 2019

Published by

Kalpaz Publications
C-30, Satyawati Nagar,
Delhi – 110052
Ph.: 011-47034999, 9811692060
www.kalpazpublications.com
E-mail: kalpaz@hotmail.com

Printed at: G. Print Process, Delhi

Cataloging in Publication Data—DK
Courtesy: D.K. Agencies (P) Ltd. <docinfo@dkagencies.com>

Biswas, Debasish, author.
Management for UGC-NET (paper II & III) / Debasish Biswas.
pages cm
ISBN 9789353240653 (Set)
9789353240677 (Vol. II) (HB)

1. Management—Examinations—Study guides. I. Title.

LCC HD30.413.B57 2018 | DDC 658.0076 23

In Memory of My Father

Whose Blessings are

My Fountain of Spirit and Inspiration

Contents

(Volume - II)

Preface

I feel great pleasure in placing the first edition of this book before my esteemed readers. It is the outcome of a great deal of encouragement from my colleagues and request from students.

This book is appropriate for management students for appearing NET and all other competitive examinations in the field of Management.

My sincere and deliberate efforts have been devoted to give the book comprehensive form.All units have been discussed in a very simple and lucid language so as to make the subject easily understandable to my beloved students.

I am grateful to the esteemed teachers who always provided me with their valuable suggestions from time to time. I am thankful to my students who always shown a keen interest in my publication. I offer my heartfelt congratulations to……Publications, New Delhifor quick publication of the book.

I welcome suggestions from esteemed teachers and my students for enrichment and improvement of the book in the future.

This book provides detailed information about the management related areas with simple language along with easy examples.

Dr. D. Biswas
M.Com, M.B.A, M.Phil, DLL, PGDHM,
PGDE, PGDMM, GDCA, PGDFM, Ph.D.
Assistant Professor&Head
Dept. of Business Administration
Vidyasagar University
Midnapore

Acknowledgements

First of all, I would like to express my sincere gratitude to Dr. Debabrata Mitra, Professor of Commerce, North Bengal University, who has been my motivator since the beginning of my write up. He provided me with many helpful suggestions, important advice and constant encouragement during the course of this work.

I am also grateful to Prof.Dr. Ajit Kumar Ghosh, Department of Commerce, Burdwan University for his valuable suggestions.

A special note of appreciation is due to Prof. Dr.Susanta Mitra, Professor of Commerce, Kaji Nazrul University, West Bengal for his valuable contributions towards enhancing the standard of the book.

I also thank to Mr. Nirmal Chandra Roy, Dr. Keya Das and Dr.Sudin Bag for extending their help in conducting the task. I am also indebted to all of my beloved students and colleagues for their whole hearted co-operation for this book.

I owe a deep gratitude to the authorities of Vidyasagar University, different librarians and all those who inspired and helped me in this work. I must thank Mr. Subhasish Khan for preparing a neat typed copy of the book.

Finally, my sincere thanks to my publisher,.....Publications, New Delhi, for their untiring effort and support in bringing out this book.

The responsibility for errors remains me alone.

Dr. D. Biswas

M.Com, M.B.A, M.Phil, DLL, PGDHM,
PGDE, PGDMM, GDCA, PGDFM, Ph.D.
Assistant Professor&Head
Dept. of Business Administration
Vidyasagar University

Acknowledgements

Unit - VI

Organizational Behaviour

Concept

In **1776, Adam Smith** advocated a new form of organizational structure based on the **division of labour**. One hundred years later, German Sociologist **Max Weber** introduced the concept about **rational organizations** and initiated the concept of charismatic leadership.

Though the origin to the study of Organizational Behaviour can trace its roots back to Max Weber and earlier organizational studies. It is generally considered to have begun as an academic discipline with the advent of scientific management in the **1890's**, with **Taylorism** representing the peak of the movement. Thus, it was Fredrick Winslow Taylor who introduced the systematic use of goal setting and rewards to motivate employees that could be considered as the **starting** of the academic discipline of Organizational Behaviour.

Proponents of scientific management held that rationalizing the organisation with precise sets of instructions and time-motion studies would lead to increased productivity. Studies of different compensation systems were also carried out to motivate workers.

In 1920's Elton Mayo an Australian born Harvard Professor and his colleagues conducted productivity studies at Western Electric's Hawthorne Plant. With this epoch making study, the focus of organizational studies shifted to analysis of how human factors and psychology affected organizations. This shift of focus in the study of organizations was called the Hawthorne Effect. The Human Relations Movement focused on teams, motivation, and the actualization of goals of individuals within organizations. Studies conducted by prominent scholars like Chester Barnard, Henri Fayol, Mary Parker Follett, Frederick Herzberg, Abraham Maslow, David Mc Cellan and Victor Vroom contributed to the growth of Organizational Behaviour as a discipline.

Organizational behaviour is the multidisciplinary approach which is an integration of different field of studies like psychology, sociology, social psychology, anthropology, and political science.

OB studies human behaviour at **individual level**, **group level** and **organizational level**. Basically, organizations are made up of people, therefore managers in the organisation must know how they behave in an organisation to make organisation productive.

Elements of Organizational Behaviour

1. **People:** People make up the internal social system of the organisation. They consist of individuals and groups. Groups may be formal or informal.
2. **Structure:** Structure defines the formal relationship between people in an organisation.
3. **Technology:** Technology consists of physical objects, activities and process, knowledge, etc through which people accomplish their tasks to achieve organizational objectives.
4. **Environment:** All organizations operate within an external environment. It is part of a larger system that contains thousand of other elements. This includes the suppliers, customers, competitors, governments' agencies, employees, unions, political parties, and economic, political, cultural, technological and social factors in which the organization embedded.

Keith Davis defined "Organizational Behaviour is the study and application of knowledge about how people as individual or as groups act within organizations."

Significance of O.B

OB is concerned with understanding, applying and controlling of behavioural and structural knowledge of an organisation for organization's effectiveness. Management function includes planning, organizing, leading and controlling where people are involved in different roles (interpersonal roles, informational roles, and decisional roles) and different capacities. Therefore, for an organisation to succeed, it is very important for it to understand its organization's culture, people by way of understanding their perception, attitudes, motivation, personality, key personality characteristics relevant to workplace, learning, job satisfaction, etc through theories of motivation, learning, and reinforcement and mould their dissatisfaction to satisfaction, motivate them to achieve desired results, provide them appropriate work culture, growth opportunities, punish their inappropriate behaviour, and infusing learning environment and leadership.

Skills and Roles in an Organization

Management Skills

1. **Technical Skills:** The ability to apply specialized or expertise.
2. **Human Skills:** The ability to work with, understands, and motivates other people, both individually and in groups.
3. **Conceptual Skills:** The mental ability to analyze and diagnose complex situations. This includes looking at relationships, attempting to attribute causes looking at relationships, conclusions on scientific evidence.

Management Roles

A. Interpersonal Roles:

1. **Leadership:** hiring, training, motivating, disciplining.
2. **Figurehead:** ceremonial and symbolic duties.
3. **Liaison:** contacting people for information.

B. Informational Roles:

1. **Monitor:** collecting information from environment.
2. **Disseminator:** transmitting information within organization.
3. **Spokesperson:** representing organization to outsiders.

C. Decisional Roles

1. **Entrepreneur:** initiating new projects to improve performance.
2. **Disturbance Handler:** correcting and solving problems.
3. **Resource Allocation:** human, physical and monetary.
4. **Negotiator:** bargaining to goal advantages.

Classical, Neo-Classical and Modern Theories of Organizational Structure

Organizational theories which explain the organization and its structure can be broadly classified as classical or modern.

Classical Organization Theory

1. Taylor's scientific management approach
2. Weber's bureaucratic approach
3. Administrative theory

Classical organization theories (Taylor, 1947; Weber, 1947; Fayol, 1949) deal with the formal organization and concepts to increase management efficiency. **Taylor** presented **scientific management** concepts, **Weber** gave the **bureaucratic approach**, and **Fayol** developed the **administrative theory** of the organization. They all contributed significantly to the development of classical organization theory.

1. Taylor's Scientific Management Approach

The scientific management approach developed by Taylor is based on the concept of planning of work to achieve efficiency, standardization, specialization and simplification. Acknowledging that the approach to increased productivity was through mutual trust between management and workers, Taylor suggested that, to increase this level of trust,

(i) The advantages of productivity improvement should go to workers,
(ii) Physical stress and anxiety should be eliminated as much as possible,
(iii) Capabilities of workers should be developed through training, and
(iv) The traditional 'boss' concept should be eliminated.

Taylor developed the following four principles of scientific management for improving productivity:

(i) Science, Not Rule of Thumb: Old rules of thumb should be supplanted by a scientific approach to each element of a person's work.

(ii) Scientific Selection of the Worker: Organizational members should be selected based on some analysis, and then trained, taught and developed.

(iii) Management and Labour Cooperation Rather Than Conflict: Management should collaborate with all organizational members so that all work can be done in conformity with the scientific principles developed.

(iv) Scientific Training of the Worker: Workers should be trained by experts, using scientific methods.

2. Weber's Bureaucratic Approach

Considering the organization as a segment of broader society, Weber (1947) based the concept of the formal organization on the following principles:

(i) Structure: In the organization, positions should be arranged in a hierarchy, each with a particular, established amount of responsibility and authority.

(ii) Specialization: Tasks should be distinguished on a functional basis, and then separated according to specialization, each having a separate chain of command.

(iii) **Predictability and Stability:** The organization should operate according to a system of procedures consisting of formal rules and regulations.

(iv) **Rationality:** Recruitment and selection of personnel should be impartial.

(v) **Democracy:** Responsibility and authority should be recognized by designations and not by persons.

3. Administrative Theory

The elements of administrative theory (Fayol, 1949) relate to accomplishment of tasks, and include principles of management, the concept of line and staff, committees and functions of management.

Division of Work or Specialization: This increases productivity in both technical and managerial work.

Authority and Responsibility: These are imperative for an organizational member to accomplish the organizational objectives.

Discipline: Members of the organization should honour the objectives of the organization. They should also comply with the rules and regulations of the organization.

Unity of Command: This means taking orders from and being responsible to only one superior.

Unity of Direction: Members of the organization should jointly work towards the same goals.

Subordination of Individual Interest to General Interest: The interest of the organization should not become subservient to individual interests or the interest of a group of employees.

Remuneration of Personnel: This can be based on diverse factors such as time, job, piece rates, bonuses, profit-sharing or non-financial rewards.

Centralization: Management should use an appropriate blend of both centralization and de-centralization of authority and decision making.

Scalar Chain: If two members who are on the same level of hierarchy have to work together to accomplish a project, they need not follow the hierarchy level, but can interact with each other on a 'gang plank' if acceptable to the higher officials.

Order: The organization has a place for everything and everyone who ought to be so engaged.

Equity: Fairness, justice and equity should prevail in the organization.

Stability of Tenure of Personnel: Job security improves performance. An employee requires some time to get used to new work and do it well.

Initiative: This should be encouraged and stimulated.

Esprit De Corps: Pride, allegiance and a sense of belonging are essential for good performance. Union is strength.

Neoclassical Theory

Neoclassical theorists recognized the importance of individual or group behaviour and emphasized human relations. Based on the Hawthorne experiments, the neoclassical approach emphasized social or human relationships among the operators, researchers and supervisors (Roethlisberger and Dickson, 1943). It was argued that these considerations were more consequential in determining productivity than mere changes in working conditions. Productivity increases were achieved as a result of **high morale**, which was influenced by the amount of individual, personal and intimate attention workers received.

Principles of the Neoclassical Approach

The classical approach stressed the formal organization. It was mechanistic and ignored major aspects of human nature. In contrast, the neoclassical approach introduced an **informal organization structure** and emphasized the following principles:

The Individual: An individual is not a mechanical tool but a distinct social being, with aspirations beyond mere fulfillment of a few economic and security works. Individuals differ from each other in pursuing these desires. Thus, an individual should be recognized as interacting with social and economic factors.

The Work Group: The neoclassical approach highlighted the social facets of work groups or informal organizations that operate within a formal organization. The concept of 'group' and its synergistic benefits were considered important.

Participative Management: Participative management or decision making permits workers to participate in the decision making process. This was a new form of management to ensure increases in productivity.

Note the difference between **Taylor's** scientific management which focuses on **work** and the **neoclassical** approach which focuses on **workers**.

Modern Theories

1. The Systems Approach
2. Socio-Technical Approach
3. The Contingency or Situational Approach

1. The Systems Approach

The systems approach views organization as a system composed of interconnected and thus mutually dependent sub-systems. These sub-systems can have their own sub-sub-systems. A system can be perceived as composed of some components, functions and processes (Albrecht, 1983). Thus, the organization consists of the following three basic elements (Bakke, 1959):

(i) Components: There are five basic, interdependent parts of the organizing system, namely:

(a) The individual,
(b) The formal and informal organization,
(c) Patterns of behaviour emerging from role demands of the organization,
(d) Role comprehension of the individual, and
(e) The physical environment in which individuals work.

(ii) Linking Processes: The different components of an organization are required to operate in an organized and correlated manner. The interaction between them is contingent upon the linking processes, which consist of communication, balance and decision making.

Communication is a means for eliciting action, exerting control and effecting coordination to link decision centres in the system in a composite form.

Balance is the equilibrium between different parts of the system so that they keep a harmoniously structured relationship with one another.

Decision analysis is also considered to be a linking process in the systems approach. Decisions may be to produce or participate in the system. Decision to produce depends upon the attitude of the individual and the demands of the organization. Decision to participate refers to the individual's decisions to engross them in the organization process. That depends on what they get and what they are expected to do in participative decision making.

(iii) Goals of Organization: The goals of an organization may be growth, stability and interaction. Interaction implies how best the members of an organization can interact with one another to their mutual advantage.

Socio-Technical Approach

It is not just job enlargement and enrichment which is important, but also transforming technology into a meaningful tool in the hands of the users. The socio-technical systems approach is based on the premise that every organization consists of the people, the technical system and the environment (Pasmore, 1988). People (the social system) use tools, techniques and knowledge (the technical system) to produce goods or services valued by consumers or users (who are part of the organization's external environment). Therefore, equilibrium among the social system, the technical system and the environment is necessary to make the organization more effective.

The Contingency or Situational Approach

The situational approach (Selznick, 1949; Burns and Stalker, 1961; Woodward, 1965; Lawrence and Lorsch, 1967) is based on the belief that there cannot be universal guidelines which are suitable for all situations. Organizational systems are inter-related with the environment. The contingency approach (Hellriegel and Slocum, 1973) suggests that different environments require different organizational relationships for optimum effectiveness, taking into consideration various social, legal, political, technical and economic factors.

Organizational Design

Many people equate organization design with an organization's structure: The words 'lean' and 'flat' are used to describe organization design as well as its structure. In fact, organizational design encompasses much more than simply the structure. Organization design is the process of aligning an organization's structure with its mission. This means looking at the complex relationship between tasks, workflow, responsibility and authority, and making sure these all support the objectives of the business.

Good organizational design helps communications, productivity, and innovation. It creates an environment where people can work effectively.

Many productivity and performance issues can be traced back to poor organization design. A company can have a great mission, great people, great leadership, etc. and still not perform well because of poor organizational design.

Types of Organization Structure

Most organizations are designed, or evolve, to have elements of both hierarchy and more flexible, organic structures within. (Organic structures are more informal, less complex and more 'ad-hoc' than hierarchical structures. They rely on people within the organization using their initiative to change the way they work as circumstances change.)

Before looking at some of the common types of organization structure, it's worth looking at what characterizes a hierarchical structure and how it contrasts with an organic structure. It's worth saying that one type of structure is not intrinsically better than another. Rather, it is important to make sure that the organization design is fit for organization's purpose and for the people within it and the section on making organization design decisions below discusses this in more detail.

Characteristic	Hierarchical Structure	Organic Structure
Complexity	High – with lots of horizontal separation into functions, departments and divisions	Usually lower – less differentiation or functional separation
Formality	High – lots of well defined lines of control and responsibility	Lower – no real hierarchy and less formal division of responsibilities
Participation	Low – employees lower down the organization have little involvement with decision making	Higher participation – lower level employees have more influence on decision makers
Communication	Downward – information starts at the top and trickles down to employees	Lateral, upward, and downward communication – information flows through the organization with fewer barriers

Functional structures and divisional structure are both examples of hierarchical organization structures.

In a **functional structure**, functions are quite separate; each led by a senior executive who reports to the CEO. The advantage can be efficiency and economies of scale where functional skills are paramount. The main disadvantage is that functional goals can end up overshadowing the overall goals of the organization.

In a **divisional structure**, the company is organized by office or customer location. Each division is autonomous and has a divisional manager who reports to the company CEO. Each business unit is typically structured along functional lines. The advantage here relates to local results, as each division is free to concentrate on its own performance. The disadvantage is that functions and effort may be duplicated. For example, each division may have a separate marketing function, and so risk being inefficient in its marketing efforts.

Understanding and Managing Individual Behaviour

Organizational behavior is the study of both group and individual performance and action within an enterprise. This field of study scans human behaviour in the working atmosphere.

It determines its effect on job structure, performance, communication, motivation, leadership, decision making abilities, etc. The way an individual behaves and behaviour as a group have two perspectives " internal and external.

Behaviour Analysis at Different Levels

Behaviour as an individual or in a group is always analyzed by everyone in the organization. It is analyzed at three different levels—

- Individual level of analysis

- Group level of analysis
- Organizational level of analysis

Individual Level of Analysis

Organizational behaviour, at this level of analysis massively draws upon psychology, engineering, and medicine. At the individual level of analysis, organizational behaviour includes the study of learning, perception, creativity, motivation, and personality.

In addition, it also includes the study of turnover, task performance and evaluation, coordinated behaviour, deviant work behaviour, ethics, and cognition.

Personality

Personality is a complex phenomenon and difficult to understand. There is no single universally acceptable definition. Personality refers to the personal characteristics that lead to consistent patterns of behaviour.

It represents the overall profile or combination of stable characteristics that capture the unique nature of a person. Personality combines a set of **physical and mental characteristics** that reflect how a person looks, thinks, acts and feels. It has both internal and external elements. External traits are observable behaviours on the basis of which we can understand one's personality. The internal factors are thoughts, values and genetic characteristics that are inferred from the observable behaviours. According to Hogan, personality refers to the relatively stable pattern of behaviours and consistent internal states that explain a person's behavioural tendencies.

We can understand from the above definition that people have some traits in common with others and some uncommon with them. Each employee in an organization is unique and he may or may not act similarly in a similar situation. Therefore, managers cannot use the same kind of rewards or motivation techniques to influence employee's behaviour.

The above definition does not mean that people do not ever change. It simply indicates that individuals do not change drastically overnight and their thoughts, feelings, values, and actions remain relatively stable over time. Personality changes in individuals occur slowly over an extended period of time. However, an understanding of personality dimensions would enable managers to predict the behaviour of employees and manage them effectively.

Determinants of Personality

Having understood the concept of personality, now we can move further to know how an individual's personality is determined? Is it inherited or is it formed after years of experience? There are no simple answers to these questions. In fact, several factors influence the shaping of our personality. Primarily, there are two sources contributing for personality differences. These are **i. Heredity** and **ii. Environment**. Environment has several factors within it like culture, family background, life experiences and the groups we interact with. These are discussed below:

(i) Heredity
(ii) Culture
(iii) Family background
(iv) Life experiences
(v) Groups we interact with

(i) Heredity

Our personality is partly inherited genetically from our parents. For example, whether we are fair or dark, tall or short, strong or weak are all characteristics that have something to do with heredity.

(ii) Culture

Culture refers to the distinctive ways in which people organize and live their lives. Hence people belonging to different societies will have different cultural orientations. Persons born into a particular society are exposed to family and societal values and to norms of acceptable behaviour in the culture of that society. People in the West and those in the East have cultural differences between themselves. In US culture, people are rewarded for being independent while in Japanese culture they are rewarded for being group oriented. These differences are primarily due to variations in cultural norms and expectations of acceptable behaviours in the respective societies. You may also note that though cultural values may have an impact on personality differences among people in different cultures, people born in the same culture may also differ from each other in many characteristics. Managers should keep this in mind when they are dealing with the employees.

(iii) Family Background

An important tool of socializing a person into a particular culture is the person's immediate family. Factors like the socio-economic status of the family, the number of children in the family and birth order, and education of the parents and extended members of the family such as cousins, uncles and aunts influence personality formation. In this regard, you may note that parents' influence on children's development is significant and it happens in three ways:

(a) Through their own behaviours they influence children's behaviours;
(b) They serve as role models; and
(c) They selectively reward and punish the behaviour of children.

(iv) Life Experiences

Perceptions, ego, temperaments, and self esteem, are all related to ones past experiences. A complex set of events and interactions with other people determine the level of self esteem of a person. Therefore, some personality traits get changed positively or negatively on the basis of the kind of experiences in one's life.

(v) Groups We Interact With

The first group of people, a person interacts with is the family. As they grow, people participate in various groups in the life time. The roles and experiences people have as members of different groups lead to personality differences. People influence each other and tend to associate with members who are similar to them in their attitudes and values.

Theories of Personality

Trait Theory

Many traits are common to most people. However, there are many other traits that are unique to a person. It may be remembered that traits are **reactions** and not what a person possesses. A person does not possess emotion but he acts emotionally in some circumstances. On the basis of the traits, people may be described as emotional, aggressive, loyal, creative, flexible, humorous, sentimental, and impulsive and so on. Traits are the basic elements of personality and can be used to summarize the behaviour of a person. However, determining basic traits is rather difficult because thousands of descriptive words are there.

Psychoanalytical Theory

The psychoanalytical theory of personality is based on the **Freudian concept** of unconscious nature of personality. On the basis of his clinical experience, Freud noted that his patient's behaviour could not always be consciously explained. This prompted him to believe that the personality structure is primarily founded on unconscious framework and that human behaviour and motivation are the outcomes of such conflicting psychoanalytic concepts as the **id**, the **ego** and the **super ego**.

Id is the foundation of the unconscious and is the basis of libido drives. It strives for sexual and other biological pleasures and has animal instincts of aggression, power and domination. Ego is conscious in nature and is a mechanism to relate our conscious urges to the outside real world. It keeps the id in check through the realities of the external environment. While id demands immediate pleasure, regardless of costs, ego controls it so that these pleasures are granted at an appropriate time and in an acceptable manner. Because of difficulty in keeping the id under control, ego is supported by super ego. The super ego is the higher level restraining force and can be described as the conscience of the person. The conscience creates standards of what is right and what is wrong and is generally subconsciously developed by the absorption of cultural and ethical values of the social environment. All these three Freudian elements are inter-related and each cannot exist in isolation from others. In order to create a "normal" personality, there must be a balance in the relationship among these three forces.

Social Learning Theory

The social learning theory differs from the psychoanalytical theory in two ways. First, it is believed that personality development is more a result of social variables than biological drives. Secondly, motives can be traced to known and conscious needs and wants rather than unconscious and latent desires. Thus, learning theory looks at personality as the sum total of all that a person has learned. The social learning theory focuses on behaviour patterns and cognitive activities in relation to the specific conditions that evoke maintain or modify them. The social learning theory uses "**reinforcement** and **punishment**" approach in understanding personality. For example, good behaviour is rewarded by management in terms of praise that further reinforces good behaviour. Thus, behaviour and external environment have mutual interaction. Behaviour partly creates the person's environment and the environment affects the behaviour as well.

Learning may also take place simply from observation rather than interaction with the environment. We watch the behaviour of other people, draw conclusions from it and come out with our own behaviour. Unlike trait theory or psychoanalytical theory, social learning theory considers **situation** as an important variable in determining human behaviour.

Individual Differences and Impact on Behaviour

The range of personality traits is quite bewildering. Personality trait means the basic components of personality. The important personality traits that influence employee behaviour at work place are need patterns, locus of control, introversion and extroversion, self-esteem and self-concept, risk taking, self monitoring, Type A or Type B personality, and goal orientation. These are briefly explained below.

Need Patterns

Primarily four personality needs can be identified that manifest them in the work setting. They are the needs for **achievement**, **affiliation**, **autonomy**, and **dominance**. Those with a high need to achieve engage themselves proactively in work behaviours in order to feel proud about their achievements and success. Those who are high in need for affiliation tend to work cooperatively with others. Those who are high in need for autonomy do well when not closely supervised. Those high in their need for dominance prove to be effective in situations where they can enforce their legitimate authority.

Locus of Control

Locus of control refers to a generalized belief that events are either within one's control (internal locus of control) or are determined by the fate or luck (external locus of control). People who have moderately strong internal locus of control are likely to perform better at work places. They are likely to be more successful than their external counterparts. Internals are more suitable for leadership positions and are likely to be more satisfied with the jobs. Internals typically have more control over their own behaviour than externals that leave everything to fate.

Introversion and Extroversion

Personality traits are commonly understood in terms of introversion and extroversion. Introversion is the tendency in individuals which directs them to turn inward and experience and process feelings, thoughts and ideas within themselves. Extroversion refers to the tendency in individuals to turn outward searching for external stimuli with which they can interact. While there is some element of introversion as well as extraversion in all of us, based on dominance, people are regarded as either introverts or extroverts. Extroverts are sociable, lively, gregarious, and seek outward stimuli or external interactions. Introverts are quiet, reflective, introspective, and intellectual people. They interact with a few intimate people. Introverts perform well when they are alone and when the environment is quiet. Since managers have to constantly interact with individuals both within and outside the organization and be able to influence them to achieve organization's goals, it is expected that extroverts prove to be better managers than introverts.

Risk – taking

Personality differences can be seen in the willingness of people to take risk. Some managers are prepared to take risk and act on little information. They prove to be as much effective as those other managers that are averse to take risk and make decision cautiously.

Self – Monitoring

It refers to a person's level of **sensitivity** and **ability to adapt** to situational cues. High self-monitors change their behaviour quite easily to suit the situation whereas low self monitors reveal their moods and personal characteristics to others who can easily predict their behaviour in a given situation. Self monitoring personality trait is important in carrying out organizational activities. Employees having this trait emerge as better performers, better leaders and are likely to grow faster in the organization.

Self – Esteem and Self-Concept

Self esteem is the result of a person's continuing self-evaluation. Self-esteem refers to the extent to which an individual consistently regards himself as capable, successful, important, and worthy. Self-esteem is an important personality factor that determines how managers perceive themselves and their role in the organization. It is important to self-concept, which refers to the way individuals define themselves as to who they are and derive their sense of identity. High self-esteem leads to a high sense of self-concept, which in turn, reinforces high self-esteem. The two are mutually reinforcing forces. As a trait, a person high in self-esteem is likely to take on more challenging assignments and be successful, thus enhancing their self-concept. That means they define themselves as highly valuable and valued individuals in the organization. The higher the self-concept and self-esteem of a person, the more he contributes to the goals of the organization.

Type A and Type B Personalities

Individuals can be grouped into two types of personalities – Type A and Type B. Type A persons feel a chronic sense of **time urgency**, are **highly achievement oriented**, exhibit a competitive drive, and are impatient when their work get slowed down for any reason. In contrast, Type B persons are easy going individuals who neither have sense of time urgency, nor the competitive drive. Type A individuals are more prone to heart attacks than Type B individuals. While helping the organization to move ahead in a relatively short period of time, Type A persons may suffer from health problems which are harmful to themselves apart from the organization.

Goal – Orientation

An important personality difference affecting behaviour at work is goal orientation. There are two orientations – learning goal orientation and performance goal orientation.

A person with learning orientation develops by acquiring new competencies whereas a person with performance orientation demonstrates competencies by seeking favorable judgments from others. As is well known, some individuals are highly work-oriented while others try to do the minimum that is necessary for not being fired on the job. The extremely work oriented person gets greatly involved in the job and lives up to being described as "living, eating, and breathing the job". Estrangement from immediate family members may occur. Though a high level of work orientation of members is good for the organization to achieve its goals, too much of it may lead to premature burnout and health problems.

Perception

Perception means perceiving, i.e., giving meaning to the environment around us. It can be defined as a process which involves seeing, receiving, selecting, organizing, interpreting and giving meaning to the environment.

Nature of Perception

(1) Perception is the intellectual process.

(2) Perception is the basic cognitive or psychological process.

(3) Perception becomes a subjective process and different people may perceive the same event differently.

Perception and Sensation

There is a distinction between sensation and perception. Sensation is the response of a physical sensory organ. The physical senses are vision, hearing, tough, smell and taste. These senses are bombarded by stimuli and reactions in particular sense organ take place because of these, e.g., of sensation may be reaction of eye to colour, ear to sound and so on. Sensation precedes perception. Perception is much more than sensation. Perception depends upon the sensory raw data. The perceptual process adds to or/and subtracts from the sensory world. Perception is determined by both physiological and psychological characteristics, of the organism. However, sensation only activates the organs of the body and is not affected by such psychological factors as learning and motives. Activation of eyes to see an object is sensation and the inference what is being seen is perception. For managerial action, it is the latter which is important.

Perceptual Process

Perception is a process of receiving, selecting, organizing, interpreting, checking and reacting to stimuli. This is like an input-through put-output process in which the stimuli can be considered as 'inputs' transformation of input through selection, organization and interpretation as 'through puts' and the ultimate behaviour/action as 'output'. The whole perceptional process can be presented as follows: These are explained one by one

1. **Receiving Stimuli:** The first process in the perception is the presence of stimuli. The stimuli are received from the various sources. It is a physiological aspect of perception process. Stimuli may be external to us (such as sound waves) and inside us (such as energy generation by muscles).

2. **Selection of Stimuli:** After receiving the stimuli or data, some are selected. Others are screened out. Two types of factors affect selection of stimuli for processing: external and internal factors. External factors relate to stimuli such as intensity of stimuli, its size, movement, repetition, etc. Internal factors, relate to the perceiver such as his/her age, learning, interest, etc. Normally, he will select the objects which interest him and will avoid that for which he is indifferent. This is also called 'selective perception'.
3. **Organization of Stimuli:** Organizing the bits of information into a meaningful whole is called 'organization'. There are three ways by which the selected data, i.e., inputs are organized. These are:**(i)** Grouping, **(ii)** Closure and **(iii)** Simplification.
   - **(i) Grouping:** In grouping, the perceiver groups the various stimuli on the basis of their similarity or proximity. For example, all the workers coming from the same place may be perceived as similar on the basis of proximity.
   - **(ii) Closure:** When faced with incomplete information, people fill up the gaps themselves to make the information meaningful. This may be done on the basis of past experience, past data, or hunches. For example, in many advertisements, alphabets are written by putting electric bulbs indicating the shape of the concerned alphabets but broken lines. In such cases, people tend to fill up the gap among different bulbs to get meaning out of these.
   - **(iii) Simplification:** People identify main stimulus features and assess how they are organized. He interprets a stimulus situation, the perceiver simples the information.

Factors Influencing Perceptual Set External Factors

1. **Size:** Bigger size attracts the attention of the perceiver.
2. **Intensity:** A loud sound, strong odor or bright light is noticed more as compared to a soft sound, weak odour or dim light.
3. **Repetition:** A repeated external stimulus is more attention getting than a single one. Advertisers use this principle.
4. **Novelty and Familiarity:** A novel or a familiar external situation can serve as attention getter.
5. **Contrast:** It is a kind of uniqueness which can be used for attention getting. Letters of bold types, persons dressed differently than others, etc., get more attention.
6. **Motion:** A moving object draws more attention as compared to a stationary object. Advertisers use this principle.

Internal Factors

Self-Concept: The way a person views the world depends a great deal on the concept or image he has about himself. The concept plays an internal role in perceptual selectivity.

Beliefs: A person's beliefs have profound influence on his perception. Thus, a fact is conceived not on what it is but what a person believes it to be.

Expectations: These affect what a person perceives. A technical manager may expect ignorance about the technical features of a product from non-technical people.

Inner Needs: The need is a feeling of tension or discomfort, when one thinks he is missing something. People with different needs experience different stimuli. According to Freud, wishful thinking is the means by which the Id attempts to achieve tension reduction.

Response Disposition: It refers to a person's tendency to perceive familiar stimuli rather than unfamiliar ones.

Response Salience: It is the set of disposition which are determined not by the familiarity of the stimulus situations, but by the person's own cognitive predispositions. Thus, a particular problem may be viewed as a marketing problem by marketing personnel, a control problem by accounting people and human relations problem by personnel people.

Perceptual Defence: It refers to the screening of those elements which create conflict and threatening situation in people.

1. Denying the existence or importance of conflicting information.
2. Distorting the new information to match the old one.
3. Acknowledging the new information but treating it as a non-representation exception. The factors that influence perception may be broadly divided into three categories:

1. Factors that reside in the 'Perceiver' (i.e., attitude, motives, interests, past experiences and personality, expectations)
2. Factors of the 'situation' and-factors connected with the 'Target'.
3. Factors that determine the preferred location of a brand on each of the relevant dimension in perceptive mapping.

Values

At the outset, let us examine a few definitions of values. According to Rokeach "values represent basic conviction that a specific mode of conduct or end state of existence is personally or socially preferable to an opposite or converse mode of conduct or end state of existence".

Chakravarti defines values as "the manner in which an individual tends to make judgments or choices, both about goals and means, at different stages of one's life, in different facets of it, as are deemed to lead to the well being and happiness of oneself and society".

From the above, we understand that values are learnt from the society and hence are acceptable to the society as preferred **'modes of conduct'** or **'end states'**. Values are stable and long-lasting beliefs about what is important in a variety of situations. They are evaluative standards that help us distinguish between right and wrong or good and bad in the world. Values do not represent what we need but they indicate what we ought to do to achieve the need in a socially desirable way. Some people value practicality while others value aesthetics. Some people value frugality while others value generosity. Values influence our priorities, preferences and our actions. Value systems represent prioritizing of individual values in relation to their relative importance. We all have a set of values that form a **value system**. This system is identified by the relative importance assigned to such values as pleasure, self-respect, honesty, freedom, equality, and so on. Consequently, values of an individual influence his attitudes and also his behaviour.

Importance of Values

In the organisational context, values are important because they influence **employee conduct** and **behaviour**. They play a vital role in behavioural disposition and the decision making behaviour of an individual. Now-a-days, employees resent the traditional command-and-control supervision and expect a lot of autonomy and operational freedom.

Organizational ethics is becoming important in view of the manipulations and malpractices indulged in at various levels in the organization. It has something to do with the values of that organization.

Values influence behaviour of an employee in several ways. If an employee feels that payment of wages on the basis of performance is right, he / she cannot accept payment of wages on the basis of seniority, he becomes indifferent to such a system followed in the organization. Therefore, the values of individuals need to be studied, so that employees' values could be matched with that of the organization.

Sources of Values

Values are learnt right from the childhood. They are taught by mother when she guides the child in several ways like "you go to bed early", "you should wear clean clothes", "you should achieve first rank" and things like that. Early ideas of what is right and wrong were probably formulated from the views expressed by the parents. As one grows, there is a likelihood of getting exposed to other value systems and be induced by them. We derive the values from the people we love or respect like our parents, teachers, friends, and other famous celebrities in movies, sports, business, and politics. Out of our admiration for them, we are likely to emulate them by imbibing their values also.

You may remember that in our culture itself, certain values have been developed over time and they are continuously reinforced. Peace, cooperation, harmony, equity, and democracy are the desirable societal values nurtured in our culture.

It is interesting to know that values are relatively **stable** and **enduring**. This is because of the way in which they are originally learned. In childhood, you are told that certain behaviour is always desirable or always undesirable. You are told, for example, that you should be honest and truthful. It is this absolute learning of values which ensures their stability and endurance. You may also note that values of an individual do change, but change very slowly. The process of questioning our values may lead to change in the existing values system.

Types of Values

You may note that values do not operate in isolation. Several values interact with each other to form value system in a society. According to Rikeach, value systems are composed of rank-ordered sets of values that fall into two general categories namely **terminal** values and **instrumental** values. Terminal values reflect the desired end states of existence whereas instrumental values are related to the choice of behaviour in reaching those end states. Terminal values are desired states of existence that we try to achieve. Preferences like duty, equality and wisdom and a compatible life are some of the terminal values. On the other hand, instrumental values are desirable modes of behaviour that help us to reach terminal values. Being polite, courageous, logical, self controlled, ambitious, etc., are some of the instrumental values.

Values can be categorized on the basis of the level at which they operate. These may be: **(i)** Personal values which are formed from past experience and interaction with others; **(ii)** Cultural values which are the dominant beliefs held collectively in society; **(iii)** Organizational values which are at the heart of organizational culture in terms of shared assumptions, values and beliefs; and **(iv)** Professional values which are held by the members of an occupational group.

Values may also be classified as the espoused values and enacted values. **Espoused** values represent the values that we want other to belief we avoid by. Values are socially desirable and so people create a positive public image by claiming to believe in values that others expect them to hold. Contrary to this, **enacted values** represent the values actually practiced. These values, in fact, guide our decisions and behaviours.

It may be recognized that values are functions of preferences. The most important early work in categorizing values was done by Allport and his associates. They identified six types of values. They are:

1. Theoretical-places high importance on the discovery of truth through a critical and rational approach.
2. Economic-emphasizes the usefulness and practicability.
3. Aesthetic-places the highest value on form and harmony.
4. Social-the highest value is given to the love of people.
5. Political-places emphasis on acquisition of power and influence.
6. Religious-concerned with the unity of experience and understanding of the cosmos as a whole.

Values at Workplace

The values at work place may be defined as the perception of what is preferable from among the alternative modes of conduct or end states with respect to one's work. Work values are expected to be an integral part a nation's cultural system and hence we notice differences between the work values of American organizations and Japanese organizations.

They represent the values internalized by members of the society through the process of socialization. In global organizations, now-a-days, it is becoming difficult to achieve congruence between the diverse values of employees and those of the organization. While defining managerial values, Indian executives mentioned work ethics, commitment, self-motivation, integrity, hard work, character, etc. It is reported in a study that the most important goals of an ethical Indian manager are customer satisfaction, achievement of organizational goals within scheduled time, employee motivation and career progress.

According to Upadhyay, Indian managers are status and power oriented and considers decision making as their prerogative and consultation as a means of eroding their authority. They tend to take credit for work done by them rather than share it with individual members of the team. It may be noted that while values are stable and enduring, they are not rigid.

Therefore, new generations of employees may bring into the organizations new set of values. In some of the studies, **age** has been found to be a major factor in differentiating employee values. Young employees give importance to more autonomy at work place, instant gratification, quick growth, individualism, and openness compared to older employees.

As a result, young employees bring a different set of values to the work place. Hence, management should understand those new values and accordingly deal with them for good performance. Managers have to study values because they are the foundations for understanding a person's attitudes, perceptions, motivation and behaviour in the organization.

Attitudes

Having understood the values, let us try to understand the attitudes and their formation. You should recognize that attitudes are **evaluative statements**- favourable or unfavourable- concerning objects, people, or events. They indicate how one feels about something. When you say "I like my job," or "I hate telling lies" they represent your attitudes.

Attitudes are different from values. Values could be a little broader in concept while attitudes are more specific. Values indicate the rightness or desirability of something. For example, a statement like "gender discrimination is bad" reflects the values one stands for. On the other hand, a statement "I prefer women to be given an equal place with men in recruitment" represents the attitude of a person. Attitudes are learned predispositions towards various aspects of our environment. While, attitudes and values are different, there are also some similarities. Both are powerful instruments influencing cognitive process and behaviour of people. Both are learned and acquired from the same sources – people and objects. Both are relatively permanent and resistant to change. Both values and attitudes influence each other and are used interchangeably.

Sources of Attitudes

As already explained, attitudes, like values, are acquired from the environment - parents, teachers, friends, and colleagues. It may be noted that they are **only acquired** but not inherited. We begin modeling our attitudes after those we admire and respect. We observe the way family members and friends behave and we shape our attitudes and behaviour to align with theirs. You tend to imitate the attitudes of famous persons or those you admire and respect. Attitudes may also be developed from a personally rewarding or punishing experience with an object or event. If employees are rewarded for being regular in an organization, you are likely to believe that you will also be rewarded if you are regular.

In contrast to values, attitudes are less stable. That is why advertising messages attempt to change your attitudes toward a certain product or service. If Maruti Company is able to create a favorable opinion towards their car, that attitude may lead to a desirable behaviour i.e., the purchase of Maruti car.

Therefore, sound understanding of attitudes is important for managers because they affect job behaviour. Manager's knowledge can serve two purposes. Firstly, it helps him in understanding and predicting how a person is likely to behave. Secondly, it helps him in changing unfavourable attitudes into favourable attitudes.

Types of Attitudes

A person may have a multitude of attitudes, but for the purpose of our study let us know about the job-related attitudes. These job-related attitudes are positive or negative evaluations held by employees about various aspects of their work environment. Essentially, there are three important attitudes concerned with job: **job satisfaction**, **job involvement**, and **organizational commitment**.

Job Satisfaction

One of the tasks of a manager is to provide job satisfaction to the employees. Job satisfaction refers to an individual's general attitude toward his or her job. A person with a high level of job satisfaction holds positive attitudes toward the job, while a person with low job satisfaction holds negative attitudes towards the job. When we talk about **employee attitudes**, mostly we mean job satisfaction. As a matter of fact, the two are closely related.

Job Involvement

The term "job involvement" is relatively a recent concept in the literature. There is no complete agreement over what the term means. Generally, it refers to the degree to which a person identifies with his job, actively participates in it, and considers his performance important to his self-worth. Individuals who express high involvement in their jobs are likely to be more productive, have higher satisfaction, and are less likely to resign than employees with low involvement.

Organizational Commitment

Commitment reflects an individual's orientation towards the organization by tapping his or her loyalty to, identification with, and involvement in the organization. Individuals who are highly committed see their identity as closely attached to that of the organization. Like job involvement, highly committed employees will be better performers and have lower turnover than those with low levels of commitment to the organization.

It may be understood that when people talk about job attitudes and their impact on behaviour, obviously they are referring to the positive or negative appraisals that people make about their job or organization. Job satisfaction is the most popular attitude measured in organizations, but more recently there has been increased attention given to job involvement and organizational commitment. All these attitudes are measured with a view to predict employee behaviours like performance, productivity, absenteeism, turnover and unionization.

Implications of Attitudes

Attitudes and Productivity

The attitude-productivity relationship is not very clear. Bradfield and Crockett in 1955 made an extensive study of this relationship and concluded that there was minimal or no relationship between attitudes and performance. However, two years later, Herzberg and his associates concluded from the review of studies that there was generally a positive relationship between attitudes and productivity. However, they noted that in many cases the correlations, although positive were low. Similarly, a review in 1964 of twenty-three separate studies revealed that, except in three cases, there was a low but positive relationship between satisfaction and performance. It is clear that the studies on the relationship between attitudes and productivity give rise to mixed findings.

Attitudes and Withdrawal Behaviours

It was found in earlier studies that employee satisfaction is inversely related to absenteeism and turnover. The higher the job satisfaction on the part of an employee, the lower is the scope for employee's withdrawal behaviour. Bradfield and Crockett found a significant but complex relationship between attitudes and both absenteeism and turnover. Vroom found a consistent negative relationship between job satisfaction and turnover, but a less consistent negative relationship between satisfaction and absenteeism. A few studies have also found that satisfaction has a consistent impact on absenteeism, but an even more profound and consistent relationship on turnover.

Attitudes and Satisfaction

Attitudes towards job and job satisfaction are closely related. In many research studies, these terms are used interchangeably. In studies of job attitudes, it is generally thought that the result is some measure of job satisfaction or dissatisfaction. Job satisfaction, however, is not behaviour but rather a general feeling of contentment with the job. As a result, if attitudes are positive, job satisfaction tends to be positive. On the other hand, if the attitudes are negative, satisfaction tend to be low.

Therefore, if a manager wants to have employees satisfied with their jobs, he should strive to create in them positive attitudes towards their job and the organization.

Learning

Now, let us understand the term 'learning' and the various processes of learning. Learning is any relatively **permanent change** in behaviour that occurs as a result of experience. There are two important elements in learning:

(i) Change must be relatively permanent. It means after 'learning' the behaviour of a person must be different from the previous behaviour. If a person learns car driving, it will last for a long time indicating the changed behaviour. Temporary changes may be only reflexive and fail to represent any learning. Therefore, this requirement rules out behavioural changes caused by fatigue or other temporary adaptations.

(ii) The second element is that the change of behaviour should take place as a result of some kind of experience. Learning must be because of some interaction with the environment and some feedback from such environment that affects behaviour. The experience may be direct or indirect. Sometimes we learn to change our behaviour when our colleagues are punished for that kind of behaviour. You may note that learning itself cannot be observed. The behavioural changes consequent upon learning only can be seen. This kind of change in behaviour should be differentiated from change in behaviour caused by other factors. For example, aging may cause behavioural changes.

Learning Theories

In an organization, employees have to learn and practice productive work behaviours. The manager's task is to provide sufficient learning experiences to employees in an environment that will facilitate learning process and promote desired behaviours. Training prepares employees to meet the challenges of the job, for which incentives are to be provided to learn and practice right behaviours. The following are the important theories of learning.

Classical Conditioning

Classical conditioning is the process by which individuals learn to link the information from a neutral stimulus to a stimulus that causes a response. This response may not be under an individual's conscious control. **Pavlov**, in his experiments, hanged some meat in front of dogs. This meat is **unconditioned stimulus** or unlearned stimulus. The dogs responded to this stimulus by salivating. This kind of response was instinctive or unconditioned. Afterwards Pavlov started to ring a bell at the same time when meat was offered. Ringing the bell without offer of meat was not connected to any responses. However, by ringing the bell every time when meat was offered, Pavlov established a relationship between the two stimuli that is the bell and the meat. With the continuation of the process, the ringing of the bell alone acted like a stimulus to evoke the response of salivating even without presentation of meat. As a result, the bell became a **conditioned stimulus** leading to conditioned response.

Operant Conditioning

B.F. Skinner coined the term operant conditioning to refer to a process by which individuals learn **voluntary behaviour**. Voluntary behaviours are called operant because they operate or have some influence on the environment. Learning occurs from the consequences of behaviour, and many employee work behaviours are operant behaviours. As a matter of fact, most behaviours in everyday life are forms of operant behaviour. Managers are interested in operant behaviours because they can influence the results of such behaviours. On the basis of the direct relationship between the consequences and behaviour, the management can identify the relationship and try to modify the behaviour. That is how the behaviour can be controlled by manipulating its consequences. Two principles guide this relationship.-The behaviour that results in positive rewards is likely to be repeated and behaviour with negative consequences is likely to be extinguished. Based on such consequences, the behaviour can be predicted and controlled. Therefore, some consequences can be used to increase the recurrence of desired behaviour and some other consequences can be used to decrease the recurrence of undesired behaviour.

Principle of Reinforcement

We understand that some behaviours are strengthened by the process of reinforcement. Reinforcer may be any stimulus that prompts a behaviour to be repeated or stopped. Managements expect that the employee should behave in a desirable manner in the organization and avoid undesirable behaviour. By the appropriate use of reinforcement, the organizations are able to maintain or increase the probability of behaviours like quality oriented performance, wise decision making, regular attendance and punctuality and so on. Some reinforcers work by their application to a situation whereas other reinforcers work by their removal from this situation.

Positive Reinforcement

Positive reinforcement is provided by offering **rewards** for desired behaviours. Such rewards should be powerful and durable so as to increase the probability of occurrence of desirable behaviour. Money, as you understand, is the most powerful reinforcement for positive behaviour since money can be used for a number of other purposes. Some other positive reinforcers are recognition for good performance, challenging task, participation in decision making and so on. As individuals have different motivations of performance, positive reinforcers should be individually tailored with a view to facilitate the repetition of desired behaviour. That means reinforcer must be valued by the employee. For example, money would be a less reinforcer who values praise for his performance more. The reward must be directly linked with behaviour so that the higher the performance of an employee, the grater would be the reward.

Negative Reinforcement

In negative reinforcement, an unpleasant event that precedes the employee behaviour is removed when the desired behaviour occurs. This procedure increases the likelihood of the desired behaviour to follow. Negative reinforcement is sometimes confused with punishment because both use unpleasant events to influence behaviour. However, **negative reinforcement** is used to increase the frequency of a desired behaviour, whereas **punishment** is used to decrease the frequency of an undesired behaviour. Managers frequently use negative reinforcement when an employee hasn't done something that is desired.

Omission

Omission is the removal of all reinforcing events. While reinforcement increases the frequency of a desirable behaviour, omission decreases the frequency and eventually extinguishes an undesirable behaviour. Managers use omission to reduce undesirable employee behaviours that obstruct achievement of organizational goals. The omission procedure consists of three steps.

(i) Identifying the behaviour to be reduced or eliminated,

(ii) Identifying the reinforcer that maintains the behaviour, and

(iii) Stopping the reinforcer.

Punishment

Punishment is an unpleasant event that follows a behaviour and decreases its frequency. As in positive reinforcement, a punishment may include a specific antecedent that cues the employee that a consequence will follow a specific behaviour. While a positive consequence of reinforcement encourages the frequency of a desired behaviour, a consequence of punishment decreases the frequency of an undesired behaviour.

Organizations typically use several types of unpleasant events to punish individuals. They may be a wage cut, a suspension without pay, a demotion, or a transfer. The severe punishment is the dismissing an employee for failure to perform. In general, organizations use punishments of unpleasant nature sparingly for cases of serious behavioural problems.

Motivation

Motivation Theories

Some of the most important theories of motivation are as follows:

1. Maslow's Need Hierarchy Theory 2. Herzberg's Motivation Hygiene Theory 3. McClelland's Need Theory 4. McGregor's Participation Theory 5. Urwick's Theory Z 6. Argyris's Theory 7. Vroom's Expectancy Theory 8. Porter and Lawler's Expectancy Theory 9. ERG Theory 10. Skinner's Theory of Motivation.

From the very beginning, when the human organizations were established, various thinkers have tried to find out the answer to what motivates people to work. Different approaches applied by them have resulted in a number of theories concerning motivation.

These are discussed in brief in that order.

1. Maslow's Need Hierarchy Theory

It is probably safe to say that the most well-known theory of motivation is Maslow's need hierarchy theory. Maslow's theory is based on the human needs. He classified all human needs into a hierarchical manner from the lower to the higher order.

In essence, he believed that once a given level of need is satisfied, it no longer serves to motivate man. Then, the next higher level of need has to be activated in order to motivate the man. Maslow identified five levels in his need hierarchy.

These are now discussed one by one:

(i) Physiological Needs: These needs are basic to human life and, hence, include food, clothing, shelter, air, water and necessities of life. These needs relate to the survival and maintenance of human life. They exert tremendous influence on human behaviour. These needs are to be met first at least partly before higher level needs emerge. Once physiological needs are satisfied, they no longer motivate the man.

(ii) Safety Needs: After satisfying the physiological needs, the next needs felt are called safety and security needs. These needs find expression in such desires as economic security and protection from physical dangers. Meeting these needs requires more money and, hence, the individual is prompted to work more. Like physiological needs, these become inactive once they are satisfied.

(iii) Social Needs: Man is a social being. He is, therefore, interested in social interaction, companionship, belongingness, etc. It is this socialising and belongingness why individuals prefer to work in groups and especially older people go to work.

(iv) Esteem Needs: These needs refer to self-esteem and self-respect. They include such needs which indicate self-confidence, achievement, competence, knowledge and independence. The fulfillment of esteem needs leads to self-confidence, strength and capability of being useful in the organisation. However, inability to fulfill these needs results in feeling like inferiority, weakness and helplessness.

(v) Self-Actualization Needs: This level represents the culmination of all the lower, intermediate, and higher needs of human beings. In other words, the final step under the need hierarchy model is the need for self-actualization. This refers to fulfillment.

The term self-actualization was coined by **Kurt Goldstein** and means to become actualized in what one is potentially good at. In effect, self-actualization is the person's motivation to transform perception of self into reality.

According to Maslow, the human needs follow a definite sequence of domination. The second need does not arise until the first is reasonably satisfied, and the third need does not emerge until the first two needs have been reasonably satisfied and it goes on. The other side of the need hierarchy is that human needs are unlimited. However, Maslow's need hierarchy-theory is not without its detractors.

The main criticisms of the theory include the following:

(a) The needs may or may not follow a definite hierarchical order. So, there may be overlapping in need hierarchy. For example, even if safety need is not satisfied, the social need may emerge.

(b) The need priority model may not apply at all times in all places.

(c) Researches show that man's behaviour at any time is mostly guided by multiplicity of behaviour. Hence, Maslow's preposition that one need is satisfied at one time is also of doubtful validity.

(d) In case of some people, the level of motivation may be permanently lower. For example, a person suffering from chronic unemployment may remain satisfied for the rest of his life if only he/she can get enough food.

Notwithstanding, Maslow's need hierarchy theory has received wide recognition, particularly among practicing managers. This can be attributed to the theory's intuitive logic and easy to understand.

2. Herzberg's Motivation Hygiene Theory

The psychologist Frederick Herzberg extended the work of Maslow and proposed a new motivation theory popularly known as Herzberg's Motivation Hygiene **(Two-Factor)** Theory. Herzberg conducted a widely reported motivational study on **200 accountants and engineers** employed by firms in and around Western Pennsylvania.

He asked these people to describe two important incidents at their jobs:

(1) When did you feel particularly good about your job, and

(2) When did you feel exceptionally bad about your job?

The responses when analysed were found quite interesting and fairly consistent. The replies respondents gave when they felt good about their jobs were significantly different from the replies given when they felt bad. Reported good feelings were generally associated with job satisfaction, whereas bad feeling with job dissatisfaction. Herzberg labeled the job satisfiers as motivators, and he called job dissatisfiers as hygiene or maintenance factors.

Herzberg's motivational and hygiene factors have been shown below:

Motivating Factors	***Hygiene Factors***
Achievement	Company policy & administration
Recognition	Supervision
Work itself	Interpersonal relations
Responsibility	Working conditions
Advancement	Salary
Growth	Status
	Security

According to Herzberg, the opposite of satisfaction is not dissatisfaction. The underlying reason, he says, is that removal of dissatisfying characteristics from a job does not necessarily make the job satisfying. According to Herzberg, today's motivators are tomorrow's hygiene because the latter stop influencing the behaviour of persons when they get them. Accordingly, one's hygiene may be the motivator of another.

However, Herzberg's model is labeled with the following criticism also:

(a) People generally tend to take credit themselves when things go well. They blame failure on the external environment.

(b) The theory basically explains job satisfaction, not motivation.

(c) Even job satisfaction is not measured on an overall basis. It is not unlikely that a person may dislike part of his/ her job, still thinks the job acceptable.

(d) This theory neglects situational variable to motivate an individual.

3. McClelland's Need Theory

Another well-known need-based theory of motivation, as opposed to hierarchy of needs of satisfaction-dissatisfaction, is the theory developed by McClelland and his associates'. McClelland developed his theory based on Henry Murray's developed long list of motives and manifest needs used in his early studies of personality. He found that people who acquire a particular need behave differently from those who do not have. His theory focuses on Murray's three needs; achievement, power and affiliation. In the literature, these three needs are abbreviated "n Ach", "n Pow", and "n Aff" respectively'.

They are defined as follows:

Need for Achievement

This is the drive to excel, to achieve in relation to a set of standard, and to strive to succeed. In other words, need for achievement is a behaviour directed toward competition with a standard of excellence. McClelland found that people with a high need for achievement perform better than those with a moderate or low need for achievement.

Need for Power

The need for power is concerned with making an impact on others, the desire to influence others, the urge to change people, and the desire to make a difference in life. People with a high need for power are people who like to be in control of people and events. This results in ultimate satisfaction to man.

Need for Affiliation

The need for affiliation is defined as a desire to establish and maintain friendly and warm relations with other people.

4. McGregor's Participation Theory

Douglas McGregor formulated two distinct views of human being based on participation of workers. The first basically **negative, labeled Theory X**, and the other basically **positive, labeled Theory Y**.

Theory X is based on the following assumptions:

1. People are by nature indolent. They like to work as little as possible.
2. People lack ambition, dislike responsibility, and prefer to be directed by others.
3. People are inherently self-centered and indifferent to organizational needs and goals.
4. People are generally gullible and not very sharp and bright.

On the contrary, Theory Y assumes that:

1. People are not by nature passive or resistant to organizational goals.
2. They want to assume responsibility.
3. They want their organisation to succeed.
4. People are capable of directing their own behaviour.
5. They have need for achievement.

What McGregor tried to dramatise through his theory X and Y is to outline the extremes to draw the fencing within which the organizational man is usually seen to behave. The fact remains that no organizational man would actually belong either to theory X or theory Y. In reality, he/she shares the traits of both. What actually happens is that man swings from one set or properties to the other with changes in his mood and motives.

5. Urwick's Theory Z

Much after the propositions of theories X and Y by McGregor, the three theorists **Urwick, Rangnekar, and Ouchi** propounded the third theory labeled as Z theory.

The two propositions in Urwick's theory are that:

(i) Each individual should know the organizational goals precisely and the amount of contribution through his efforts towards these goals.

(ii) Each individual should also know that the relation of organizational goals is going to satisfy his/her needs positively.

In Urwick's view, the above two make people ready to behave positively to accomplish both organizational and individual goals.

However, Ouchi's Theory Z has attracted the lot of attention of management practitioners as well as researchers.

Theory Z is based on the following four postulates:

1. Strong Bond between Organisation and Employees
2. Employee Participation and Involvement
3. No Formal Organisation Structure
4. Human Resource Development

Ouchi's Theory Z represents the adoption of Japanese management practices (group decision making, social cohesion, job security, holistic concern for employees, etc.) by the American companies. In India, Maruti-Suzuki, Hero-Honda, etc., apply the postulates of theory Z.

6. Argyris's Theory

Argyris has developed his motivation theory based on proposition how management practices affect the individual behaviour and growth. In his view, the seven changes taking place in an individual personality make him/her a mature one.

Immaturity	***Maturity***
Passivity	Activity
Dependence	Independence
Capable of behaving in a few ways	Capable of behaving in many ways
Shallow interest	Deep interest
Short-term perspective	Long-term perspective
Subordinate position	Superordinate position
Lack of self-awareness	Self-awareness and control

Argyris views that immaturity exists in individuals mainly because of organizational setting and management practices such as task specialization, chain of command, unity of direction, and span of management. In order to make individuals grow mature, he proposes gradual shift from the existing pyramidal organisation structure to humanistic system; from existing management system to the more flexible and participative management.

He states that such situation will satisfy not only their physiological and safety needs, but also will motivate them to make ready to make more use of their physiological and safety needs. It will motivate them to make ready to make more use of their potential in accomplishing organizational goals.

7. Vroom's Expectancy Theory

One of the most widely accepted explanations of motivation is offered by Victor Vroom in his Expectancy Theory. It is a **cognitive process theory** of motivation. The theory is founded on the basic notions that people will be motivated to exert a high level of effort when they believe there are relationships between the effort they put forth, the performance they achieve, and the outcomes/ rewards they receive.

The relationships between notions of effort, performance, and reward are depicted below:

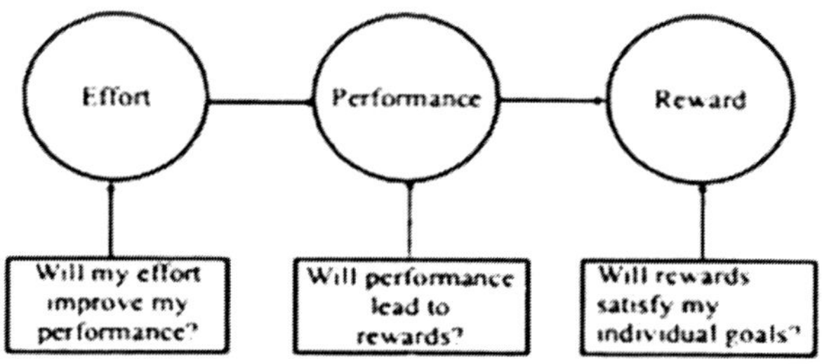

Vroom's Expectancy Model of Motivation

Thus, the key constructs in the expectancy theory of motivation are:

1. Valence: **It means the** value or strength **one places on a particular outcome or reward.**
2. Expectancy: **It relates** efforts to performance.
3. Instrumentality: **It means the belief that** performance is related to rewards.

Thus, Vroom's motivation can also be expressed in the form of an equation as follows:

Motivation = Valence x Expectancy x Instrumentality

Being the model multiplicative in nature, all the three variables must have high positive values to imply motivated performance choice. If any one of the variables approaches to zero level, the possibility of the so motivated performance also touches zero level.

8. Porter and Lawler's Expectancy Theory

In fact, Porter and Lawler's theory is an improvement over Vroom's expectancy theory. They proposed a multivariate model to explain the complex relationship that exists between **satisfaction and performance**.

There are three main elements in this model. Let us briefly discuss these one by one.

Effort: **Effort refers to the amount of energy an employee exerts on a given task. How much effort an employee will put in a task is determined by two factors-**

(i) Value of reward and

(ii) Perception of effort-reward probability.

Performance: One's effort leads to his/her performance. Both may be equal or may not be. However the amount of performance is determined by the amount of labour and the ability and role perception of the employee. Thus, if an employee possesses less ability and/or makes wrong role perception, his/her performance may be low in spite of his putting in great efforts.

Satisfaction: **Performance leads to satisfaction. The level of satisfaction depends upon the amount of rewards one achieves. If the amount of actual rewards meet or exceed perceived equitable rewards, the employee will feel satisfied. On the contrary, if actual rewards fall short of perceived ones, he/she will be dissatisfied.**

9. ERG Theory

Clayton P. **Alderfer's** ERG theory from 1969 condenses Maslow's five human needs into three categories: **Existence**, **Relatedness** and **Growth**.

Existence Needs

It includes all **material and physiological desires** (e.g., food, water, air, clothing, safety, physical love and affection).

Relatedness Needs

It encompasses social and external esteem; relationships with family, friends, co-workers and employers. This also means to be recognized and feel secure as part of a group or family.

Growth Needs

It impels a person to make creative or productive effects on himself and the environment (e.g., to progress toward one's ideal self). This includes desires to be creative and productive, and to complete meaningful tasks.

There are three relationships among the different categories in Alderfer's ERG theory:

Satisfaction-Progression: It means moving up to higher-level needs based on satisfied needs. Individuals move up the need hierarchy as a result of satisfying lower order needs.

Frustration-Regression: If a higher level need remains unfulfilled, a person may regress to lower level needs that appear easier to satisfy. Frustration-Regression suggests that an already satisfied need can become active when a higher need cannot be satisfied.

Satisfaction-Strengthening: Satisfaction-Strengthening indicates that an already satisfied need can maintain satisfaction or strengthen lower level needs iteratively when it fails to gratify high-level needs.

10. Skinner's Theory of Motivation

This theory is linked with reinforcement theory of motivation. Skinner's work is built on the assumption that behaviour is influenced by its consequences. These consequences are referred to as '**operants**', and so this theory uses the term "operant conditioning." Behaviour modification is used to describe the learning by reinforcement of an individual.

Understanding and Managing Group Behaviour

Group Level of Analysis

Organizational behaviour, at this level of analysis, draws upon the sociological and socio-psychological discipline. At the group level of analysis, organizational behaviour includes the study of group gesture, intra-group and intergroup dispute and attachment.

It is further extended to the study of leadership, power, norms, interpersonal communication, networks, and roles.

Organizational Level of Analysis

Organizational behaviour, at this level of analysis draws upon sociology and political science. At this level of analysis, organizational behaviour includes the study of organizational culture, structure, cultural diversity, inter-organizational cooperation and coordination.

It further includes the study of dispute, change, technology, and external environmental forces. Some other fields of study that adds to the interest of organizational behaviour are ergonomics, statistics, and psychometrics.

Processes- Interpersonal and Group Dynamics

Group Dynamics

Kurt Lewin had an impact on a generation of researchers and thinkers concerned with group dynamics. In particular, two key ideas which emerged out of field theory, it is argued are crucial to an appreciation of group processes; they are **interdependence of fate and task interdependence.**

According to **Tuckman's theory**, there are five stages of group development: **forming, storming, norming, performing, and adjourning**. During these stages group members must address several issues and the way in which these issues are resolved determines whether the group will succeed in accomplishing its tasks.

Stages of Group Development

Group Development is a dynamic process. How do groups evolve? There is a process of five stages through which groups pass through. The process includes the five stages: forming, storming, forming, performing, and adjourning.

Forming: The first stage in the life of a group is concerned with forming a group. This stage is characterized by members seeking either a work assignment (in a formal group) or other benefit, like status, affiliation, power, etc. (in an informal group). Members at this stage either engage in busy type of activity or show apathy.

Storming: The next stage in this group is marked by the formation of dyads and triads. Members seek out familiar or similar individuals and begin a deeper sharing of self. Continued attention to the subgroup creates a differentiation in the group and tensions across the dyads / triads may appear. Pairing is a common phenomenon. There will be conflict about controlling the group.

Norming: The third stage of group development is marked by a more serious concern about task performance. The dyads/triads begin to open up and seek out other members in the group. Efforts are made to establish various norms for task performance. Members begin to take greater responsibility for their own group and relationship while the authority figure becomes relaxed. Once this stage is complete, a clear picture will emerge about hierarchy of leadership. The norming stage is over with the solidification of the group structure and a sense of group identity and camaraderie.

Performing: This is a stage of a fully functional group where members see themselves as a group and get involved in the task. Each person makes a contribution and the authority figure is also seen as a part of the group. Group norms are followed and collective pressure is exerted to ensure the Process of Group effectiveness of the group. The group may redefine its goals Development in the light of information from the outside environment and show an autonomous will to pursue those goals. The long-term viability of the group is established and nurtured.

Adjourning: In the case of temporary groups, like project team, task force, or any other such group, which have a limited task at hand, also have a fifth stage, This is known as adjourning. The group decides to disband. Some members may feel happy over the performance, and some may be unhappy over the stoppage of meeting with group members. Adjourning may also be referred to as mourning, i.e. mourning the adjournment of the group.

Types of Groups

There are two types of groups. These are formal groups and informal groups.

A formal group is a collection of persons, who come together for achieving a specified goal. They are always created with intent to fulfill some official requirement. Formation of the group is done by the management. It possesses a systematic structure, in hierarchical form.

In general, the employees of the organization are divided into groups and a task is hand over to each group. In this way, the task of the group is accomplished along with the fulfillment of organizational goals. The given are the types of formal groups:

1. **Command groups**: The groups that consist of managers and their subordinates.
2. **Committees**: The group of people who are appointed by an organization, to resolve the matters, referred to them are known as Committee. For example Advisory Committee, Standing Committee, etc.

3. **Task Forces**: The group form to carry out a particular task is known as Task Forces.

The various kinds of informal groups are:

1. **Friendship Groups:** Friendship groups are associations of people who like each other and who like to be together. Such groups are formed because members have one or more common characteristics, such as age or ethnic heritage, political beliefs, religious values and other bonds of attraction.
2. **Interest Groups:** Interest groups are composed of individuals who may not be members of the same organization (command or task groups), but they are united by their interest in a common issue. Example of interest groups may include a group of University Professors. They organize a seminar on Law and Order Problems in the State of West Bengal.
3. **Reference Group:** A reference group is a special type of informal group that people use to evaluate themselves. A reference group may not be an actual one that meets together; it can be an imaginary group.
4. **Cliques: It** consists of colleagues and associates closely intimated to each other. Cliques may be of three types:
   (i) **Vertical cliques** consist of members working in the same department irrespective of their rank.
   (ii) Horizontal cliques consist of people of similar rank working more or less in the same area.
   (iii) Mixed cliques consist of both vertical and horizontal cliques.
5. **Sub-cliques:** It consists of member of a clique along with outsiders.
6. **Isolates:** Who are not members of any group?

Another classification of informal groups by **Sayles** from the standpoint of **pressure tactics** is divided into four groups:

(i) **The Apathetic Group:** Not sincere to their demand and members do not actively engage in union activity.

(ii) **The Erratic Group:** Very sensitive to their demand. Easily inflamed and easily pacified. Engage in union activity.

(iii) **The Strategic Group:** These groups have a well planned strategy for fighting with the management for their grievances. They build continuous pressure.

(iv) **Conservative Group:** Consists of members having critical or scarce skills. Though they have strong position yet are least engaged in union activity.

Theories of Group Formation

1. Propinquity Theory

The most basic theory explaining affiliation is propinquity. This interesting word simply means that individuals affiliate with one another because of **spatial or geographical proximity**. In an organisation employees who work in the same area of the plant or office or managers with offices close to one another would more probably form into groups than would those who are not physically located together. There is some research evidence to support the propinquity theory and on the surface, it has a great deal of merit for explaining group formation. The drawback of this theory is that it is not analytical and does not begin to explain some of the complexities of group formation. Some more theoretical and practical reasons need to be explored.

2. Homan's Theory

According to George C. Homans, "The more activities persons share, the more numerous will be there interactions and the stronger will be their shared activities and sentiments, and the more sentiments people have for one another, the more will be their shared activities and interactions."

It is a very comprehensive theory and based on activities, interactions and Homan's theory is based on sentiments. These three elements are directly related to each other. The members' activities interactions and of a group share activities and interact with one another not just because of physical proximity but also to accomplish group goals.

The key element is interaction because of which they develop common sentiments for one another. These sentiments gradually get expressed through the formation of informal groups. If any disturbance is caused to any of the three-**activities, interactions and sentiments**, it is likely to disturb all the others.

Their relationships are shown in the following figure:

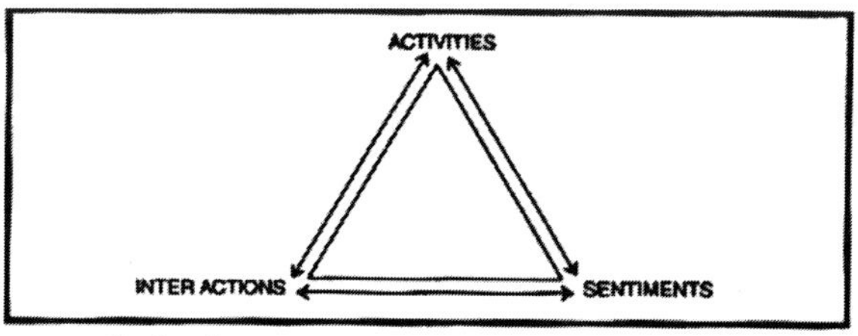

(The Inter-Dependence of Activities, Interaction and Sentiments)

3. Balance Theory

Another very comprehensive theory is a Balance Theory of group formation. This theory as proposed by **Theodore Newcomb** states that "Persons are attracted to one another on the basis of similar attitudes towards commonly relevant objects and goals. Once a relationship is formed, it strives to maintain a symmetrical balance between the attraction and the common attitudes. If an imbalance occurs, attempts are made to restore the balance. If the balance cannot be restored, the relationship dissolves."

Thus, the balance theory is additive in nature in the sense, that it introduces the factor of balance to the propinquity and interaction factors. There must be a balance in the relationship between the group members for the group to be formed and for its survival. The following figure shows the balance theory.

Individual (A) will interact and form a relationship/group with individual (B) because of common attitudes and values (C). Once this relationship is formed, the participants strive to maintain a symmetrical balance between the **attraction and the common attitudes**. If an imbalance occurs, an attempt is made to restore the balance. If the balance cannot be restored, the relationship dissolves.

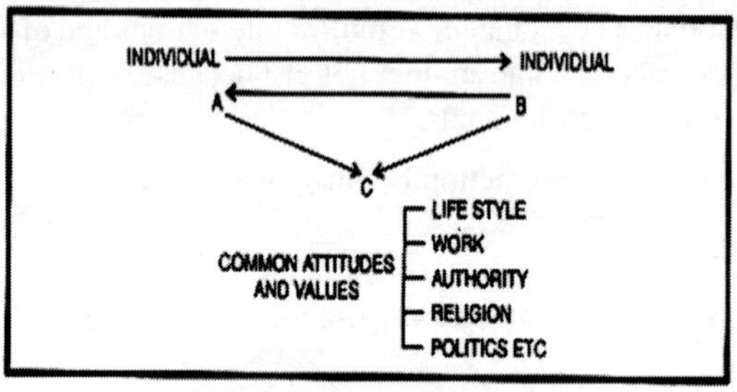

(A Balance Theory of Group Formation)

4. Exchange Theory

This theory is based on **reward-cost** outcomes of interactions. To be attracted towards a group, a person thinks in terms of what he will get in exchange of interaction with group members. A minimum positive level (rewards greater than costs) of an outcome must exist in order for attraction or affiliation to take place. Rewards from interactions gratify needs while costs incur anxiety, frustrations, embarrassment or fatigue. **Propinquity, interaction and common attitudes all have roles in the exchange theory**.

Group Decision Making Process

(i) Brainstorming: This technique involves a group of people, usually between five and ten, sitting around a table, generating ideas in the form of free association. The primary focus is on **generation of ideas** rather than on evaluation of ideas.

If a large number of ideas can be generated, then it is likely that there will be a unique and creative idea among them. All these ideas are written on the black board with a piece of chalk so that everybody can see every idea and try to improve upon such ideas.

Brainstorming technique is very effective when the problem is comparatively specific and can be simply defined. A complex problem can be broken up into parts and each part can be taken separately at a time.

(ii) Nominal Group Technique (NGT): Nominal group technique is similar to brainstorming except that the approach is more structured. Members form the group in name only and operate independently, generating ideas for solving the problem on their own, in silence and in writing. Members do not **interact with each other** so that strong personality domination is avoided. It encourages individual creativity.

The group coordinator either collects these written ideas or writes then on a large black board for everyone to see or he asks each member to speak out and then he writes it on the black board as he receives it.

These ideas are then discussed one by one in turn and each participant is encouraged to comment on these ideas for the purpose of clarification and improvement. After all ideas are discussed, they are evaluated for their merits and drawbacks and each participating member is required to vote on each idea and assign it a rank on the basis of priority of each alternative solution. The idea with the highest aggregate ranking is selected as the final solution to the problem.

(iii) Delphi Technique: This technique is the modification of the nominal group technique, except that it involves obtaining the opinions of experts **physically separated from each other and unknown to each other**. This insulates group members from the undue influence of others. Generally, the types of problems handled by this technique are not specific in nature or related to a particular situation at a given time. For example, the technique could be used to understand the problems that could be created in the event of a war. The steps in the Delphi technique are:

1. The problem is identified and a sample of experts is selected. These experts are asked to provide potential solutions through a series of carefully designed questionnaires.
2. Each expert completes and returns the initial questionnaire.
3. The results of the questionnaire are compiled at a central location and the central coordinator prepares a second questionnaire based on the previous answers.

4. Each member receives a copy of the results along with the second questionnaire.
5. Members are asked to review the results and respond to the second questionnaire. The results typically trigger new solutions or cause changes in the original position.
6. The process is repeated until a consensus is reached.

The process is very time consuming and is primarily useful in illuminating broad range, long term complex issues such as future effects of energy shortages that might occur.

(iv) Didactic Interaction: This technique is applicable only in certain situations, but is an excellent method when such a situation exists. The type of problem should be such that it results in a yes-no solution. For example, the decision may be to buy or not to buy, to merge or not to merge, to expand or not to expand and so on. Such a decision requires an extensive and exhaustive discussion and investigation since a wrong decision can have serious consequences.

Since, in such a situation, there must be advantages as well as disadvantages of either of the two alternatives, the group required to make the decision is split into two sub-groups, **one favouring the "go" decision and the other favouring the "no go" decision**.

The first group lists all the "pros" of the problem solution and the second group lists all the "cons". These groups meet and discuss their findings and their reasons. After the exhaustive discussions, the groups switch sides and try to find weaknesses in their own original viewpoints. This interchange of ideas and understanding of opposing viewpoints results in mutual acceptance of the facts as they exist so that a solution can be built around these facts and opinions relating to these facts and thus a final decision is reached.

Communication

The term 'communication' is derived from the Latin word '**communis**' which means common. The term communication is used to signify the act of transferring ideas or receiving it by any means-word of mouth, the telephone, telegram, letter, message, etc. In an organisation, managers have to communicate constantly. If we observe the activities of any manager, we will find that he is busy writing a letter or receiving one, meeting a worker or a group of workers or his superior attending a conference or addressing one, telephoning or discussing a project with an expert, negotiating terms and so on. Managerial functions are discharged through communication. Direction, guidance, delegation of authority, assignment of duties, etc., are done through communication. Thus, communication is not a one way process.

The term "communication" is freely used by everyone. It is one of the most frequently discussed subjects in the field of organisational behaviour. According to Louis Allen, Communication is the sum of all things, a person does when he wants to create an understanding in the mind of another. It involves a systematic and continuous process of telling, listening and understanding.

According to Keith Davis, "It is the process of passing information and understanding from one person to another. It is essentially a bridge of meaning between people. By using this bridge of meaning, a person can safely cross the river of misunderstanding that separates all people".

Thus, in reality communication is the sum total of direct or indirect, consciously or unconsciously transmitted words, attitudes, feelings, actions, gestures and tones. Even **silence** is an effective form of communication.

Characteristics of Communication

The following are the characteristics of communication.

(i) Communication is a two-way process because orders, instructions, directions, guidelines, etc., are directed or communicated downwards while suggestions, complaints, grievances, etc., are communicated upwards. This not only involves giving ideas but also receiving them.

(ii) No business organisation can exist without communication because it is necessary to have a congenial relationship among the different employees working at different levels and that is why it is a continuous process.

(iii) The communication process continues to the extent that ideas and messages are communicated and received.

(iv) It may be formal or informal and it may be in different mediums.

The Communication Process

Communication process contains the following elements:

(i) **Communicator:** The Communication commences with the communicator. He is the sender of the message. He realizes the need for conveying something to someone else. A communicator or the sender is the source of communication. He has a purpose of communicating some information to one or more persons.

(ii) **Encoding:** Encoding means putting message into code. A message is initiated by encoding a thought. The communicator encodes the information to be transmitted. It is done by translating into a series of symbols or gestures. Encoding is essential because information can be conveyed only through representations or symbols. The sender of the message should establish mutuality of meaning with the receiver. Coded messages may be oral or written words or gestures.

(iii) The Message: A message is the output of encoding process. It is the physical form of the encoded message. The message may be in any form- oral, written or gesture. But it must be unambiguously understood by the receiver. Speech may be heard. Written words may be read. Gestures may be seen or felt. Message must be clear and precise.

(iv) The Medium: The communicator can communicate the message through a medium. The medium is the carrier of communication. The communication channel is the mode of transmission. Air is the medium for oral message. The medium is inseparable from the message. It links the sender with the receiver. The message may be conveyed through a memorandum, letter, telegram, the telephone, a computer or T.V., but the channel or the medium must be appropriate for the message.

(v) Decoding: Decoding refers to the finding of the meaning of something conveyed in code. It is the process by which the receiver **interprets** the message. It means translating the message that is significant and meaningful to the receiver. The recipient has to be ready for the message. Then only the message can be decoded into thought. In decoding, the receiver converts the message into thoughts. Decoding is affected by several factors such as the recipient's knowledge, past experience, personal interpretations of the symbols and gestures used expectations and mutuality of meaning. Thus, decoding is very important for understanding the message.

(vi) The Receiver: Communication requires at least a couple of people, the sender and the receiver. One "encodes" and the other "decodes" the message. It will be complete only when the receiver perceives the message intact. The receiver must decode the message without distortion. If the message does not reach a receiver, communication cannot be said to have taken place.

(vii) Feed Back: Feedback refers to the **reaction** of the receiver. It is a reversal of the communication process. Feedback enables the communicator to know whether his message is received and interpreted correctly or not. Further, Feedback enables the communicator to know the reaction of the receiver so that future communication can be modified, if necessary. The importance of Feedback is incalculable. It helps to check the effectiveness of communication. It makes communication a two-way process.

(viii) Noise: "Noise" is the enemy of Feedback. It refers to any factor that interferes with communication. Interference may occur in all the above stages of the communication process. It hinders or blocks communication.

Importance of Communication

Over the years, the importance of communication has increased tremendously to the advent of various modern devices. The following points bring out the importance of communication in management.

(i) **Smooth Running of the Enterprise:** Effective communication ensures the smooth running of an enterprise. Communication plays a vital role in all kinds of organizations. In the case of complex organizations, effective communication solves lot of problems. The work of the subordinates depends to a large extent upon the communication they receive from their superiors. Similarly, successful completion of the task by the superior depends upon the nature and flow of communication from the subordinates to the superiors.

(ii) **Quick Decisions and Implementation:** Communication greatly facilitates decision making. However intelligent the personnel may be, it would be of no use, if the top management cannot effectively communicate policies and decisions to them. Effective implementation of decisions depends upon the nature of communication. It is said that communication acts as a lubricant and keeps all the individuals working in line with the expectations of top management.

(iii) **Planning and Co-ordination:** Communication greatly helps in planning and co-ordination. Participation in planning is essential in order to successfully execute it and this is secured by communication. Similarly, co-ordination between various individuals and activities is brought out by communication.

(iv) **Maximum Productivity:** Maximum output with minimum input is the aim of all managers. This can be achieved by effective communication. Communication helps in minimizing costs and friction and maximizing production.

(v) **Morale Building and Democratic Management:** When there is an effective system of communication, employees will have the opportunity to present their ideas, suggestions and complaints. If the grievances are not set right at the early stage, they will ultimately result in industrial unrest. It is pointed out that many conflicts arise because of lack of communication or misunderstood motives. Democratic management is possible only when there is an effective communication system.

Types of Communication

We spend a great deal of our time in communication. No one can afford to waste time be indulging in unnecessary communication. It is often very difficult to determine which communication is necessary and which is not necessary. Again it is difficult to determine the extent of information to be passed on. The method of presentation is also to be decided - narrative, statistical or graphical form. The following are some of the types of communication.

Verbal or Oral Communication

In this method of communication, the two parties exchange their ideas or the message with the help of word of mouth. The message, instruction, order, directive, etc., is conveyed through spoken words. Examples of verbal communications are – telephone talk, oral orders, face to face talks, counseling, etc. Some of the advantages of verbal communication are as follows:

(i) It saves time and money.

(ii) No other device is so short, simple and quick.

(iii) Because of the face contact or personal touch, it is effective.

(iv) Oral communication is easily understood. Even when there are doubts they can be cleared on the spot.

(v) The effect of the communication or response to the communication can be easily measured.

(vi) Suitable changes can also be done immediately.

(vii) During periods of emergency, oral communication is the best method.

However, oral communication is not suitable in the following cases:

(i) When the communicator and the recipient are far off, oral communication will not serve the purpose.

(ii) If the message to be transmitted is lengthy and requires a thorough clarification, oral communication will not be suitable.

(iii) Oral communication does not serve as a record or as evidence. It cannot be made use of in future.

(iv) There are chances of misunderstanding and misinterpreting the communication.

Written Communication

A written communication is conveyed through a letter, report, circular notes, memoranda, notice and communiqué. It is a very common form of communication in most of the organizations and is suitable for many situations. The usual forms of written communication are:

Orders – given by the superiors to the subordinates. These can be of three types.

(a) General

(b) Specific

(c) Definite

General orders are given by the top management, specific orders by the middle level management to lower level managers and definite orders by the supervisor to workers.

Written communications have the following advantages.

(i) They serve as permanent record and as a source or reference.

(ii) More care is taken in drafting written communication and this saves the subsequent loss of time and money.

(iii) When the communicator and recipient are far off, written communication is the best method.

(iv) The recipient can ponder over the communication and request for changes, if necessary.

The disadvantages are listed below:

(i) As everything is to be translated into black and white, it consumes a lot of time and money.

(ii) People do not care at all to pass the appropriate message. Consequently, poor messages are to be followed by clarifications and explanations.

(iii) Sometimes it may not be possible to reduce everything into writing. Any omission will call for additional communication.

(iv) Written communication is subject to delay and red tapism.

(v) It is very difficult to keep some communications up to date.

Formal and Informal Communication

The formal organisation chart describes the formal lines of authority, power, responsibility and accountability of the organizational members. All these relationships involve communication. For instance, the delegation of authority involves the flow information from a superior to his subordinate.

On the other hand, informal communication is free from all the formalities of formal communication. Informal communication is based on the informal relationship among the organisation members. It is conveyed by a simple gesture, glance, nod, smile or mere silence. For instance, when the worker approaches the manager and informs about the completion of the job entrusted to him, and if the manger simply nods his head or gives an approving smile, then it amounts to informal communication.

The informal communication which supplements the formal organizational relationship is referred to as the "**Grapevine**". Though this relationship is structure less, it comes into existence when formal organizational members who know each other pass on information relating to the enterprise. It thrives on information not openly available to the entire work group. This may be due to the fact that information is regarded as confidential. The Grapevine may flourish, if formal lines of communication are inadequate. The Grape vine is inevitable and valuable, because all forms of informal organisation serve essential human communication needs. It is very effective for quick communication.

Downward, Upward or Horizontal Communication

Communications are classified as downward, upward or horizontal. Communication is said to be downward when it flows from the top to the bottom, it is upward when it flows from the sub-ordinates to the top management. It is horizontal when it flows between **individuals at the same level** (e.g. between two departmental or section heads). All these three kinds of communications may be either oral or written.

Barriers to Communication

It is not possible that every time an order, instruction, guideline, direction, programme, information, etc, transmitted by the superior is properly understood and assimilated by those for whom it is intended.

Similarly suggestions, reports, advice, recommendations, complaints, etc., transmitted by the sub-ordinates to their superiors may be misunderstood or misinterpreted.

As such, the process of communication is not always smooth. It is obstructed by many obstacles. These are referred to as barriers of communication. The important barriers to effective communication are as follows:

(i) Ineffective Expression: The first and the most common barrier in the process of communication is bad expression. This means that the messages suffer from omissions, uncertainty, inaccuracies, verbosity, repetitions, ambiguity, lack of clarity and precision. In order to remove this, the staff should be trained to draft various kinds of effective communication. This will save time because otherwise much time has to be devoted in giving subsequent clarifications.

(ii) Inaccurate Translation: Decisions are generally conveyed from the top to the lower level. The superiors are known for their specialized knowledge. They generally draft messages in a technical language which may not be clearly understood by those who have to implement the decisions. Even if they are able to understand, they may not be able to convey it further down the line in simple words.

In many such cases, it becomes necessary to translate the subject matter or the message into a simpler language, i.e., the language which the Communicatee can understand easily. But the translation may be done inaccurately. Sometimes the translator is not in a position to find out the equivalent of many terms. With the result, the translation leads to further confusion. It becomes necessary that competent persons are appointed for the job and are provided the necessary equipment for the execution of the entrusted tasks.

(iii) Inattention: Inattention is a very common and chronic human failing. This barrier generally arises in case of oral communication. It can be illustrated with the help of the following example: a superior is giving a message on the telephone. The subordinate is busy in reading a magazine or looking through the window or his mind is occupied with some family problem. Superiors have to face this problem of inattention quite frequently. The communicator should choose the appropriate time for communicating. Thus, for example, communicating at lunch hour or while at rest will not invite due attention. Holding a meeting at an odd time or calling the worker for a talk on a holiday are some other examples.

(iv) Loss in Transmission: Loss in transmission is another barrier of communication which arises in oral communication. When messages are conveyed from the higher to the lower level step by step, much of it is likely to be lost in transit. This problem may arise in case of written communication as well. At every level, the superior will interpret the message which is likely to be distorted.

Further, the meaning will change if some words are dropped, changed or miss pelt. Harold Koontz and Cyril O'Donnell estimate that about 30% of the information is lost in each transmission. Written communications too are subject to loss in transmission. It is no wonder that enterprises often operate in a cloud of ignorance.

(v) Vague and Unclarified Assumptions: The object of a communication is to distinctly tell the Communicatee what is desired of him. If the message is not clear in meaning, assumptions are not clear to the personnel; communication will lose its purpose. If the personnel are not able to know what they are supposed to do even after receiving the message, the communication will be no more than a waste paper.

(vi) Inadequate Adjustment Period: Certain messages affect a large number of people in their personal life. For example, a notice is issued informing change in the timings of the shift in a factory. This requires sufficient lead time for the workers to make an adjustment. In case sufficient time is not granted there will be a communication barrier. Similarly communications regarding changes in the rules about bonus, over time should allow an adjustment period. Sufficient time should be allowed to the employees to adjust their schedule or get them mentally prepared.

(vii) Distrust: It arises if the superior is known for making frequent changes in the communication, quite often even reversing the original message. It is due to ill conceived adjustment, improper technology, etc. Repeated experience of this type will damage employee's interest in the communication.

(viii) Fear: This indicates anxiety, awe, alarm or apprehension. This arises in upward communication and creates a barrier in communication. It may be illustrated as below. A subordinate is not sure if the information conveyed by him to the superior will be useful or not. He thinks if it is not liked, boss will be annoyed and might take action against him. He requests another sub-ordinate to transmit the information on his behalf.

(ix) Noise, Distance and Time: The world will not be worth living in, if it is quiet everywhere. But at the same time noise is a big menace. In modern factories the constant rattling of the machines and tools, the squeaking of the wheels constantly create a lot of noise. It is a very common experience that noise proves a big hindering factor if two persons are talking. If somehow the noise is not controlled, it may not be possible for Communicatee to listen anything or make out the sense. He will properly feel strained.

(x) Impression: Sometimes in an effort to impress others, the communicator starts talking in a confused manner or speaks with a changed pronunciation. These actions hinder communication. It leads to wastage of time, resources and energy and causes misunderstanding.

How can Communication be more Effective

The following aspects, if taken care of, will make communication effective.

Clarity of Thoughts

The idea to be transmitted must be absolutely clear in the mind of the communicator. Just as it is not possible to have a clear print from a blurred negative, similarly one can never make his views intelligible to others, if he himself is confusing at certain points. Hence the process of communication to be complete must spring out from a clear head. Further, the academic level of the workers, their power of grasping things, etc., should also be taken into account. Even when the language spoken by the workers, superiors and the management is the same, words often mean different things to people with a different experimental background.

Attach Importance to Actions Rather Than Words

In all communications, actions are more significant than words. A manger who invariably says that he trusts subordinates and then proceeds to make too many checks on the sub ordinate's work, usually fails to make him understood. A boss who is not punctual cannot succeed in enforcing the timing-rules on the subordinates.

Participation

The next most important essential point is that both the parties (communicator and the recipient) should participate in the communication process. It is a common complaint of the workers that proper and patient hearing is not given to their voice. Listening plays a very fundamental part in oral communication because it is listening only which leads to sharing, participation and understanding in oral communication. But this listening is not merely passive hearing. It is an art which is to be perfected with practice based on sound knowledge of the principles of human nature.

Transmission

The communicator must plan carefully what to communicate, whom to communicate and how to communicate. Further, delegation of authority without responsibility breaks down the spirit of communication.

Keep the Channel Always Alive

The channel of communication should be kept open and alive. It is only by honest attempts that good communication relations can be developed.

Cordial Superior-Subordinate Relationship

Effective communication requires good quality of relationship between people immediately connected with each other. It requires sound industrial relations, policies and practices, an all round atmosphere of friendly co-operation and a feeling of trust and confidence throughout the organization right from the top management down to the humblest worker. Under such conditions only, the meaning of communication is grasped quickly and correctly. On the other hand, if the relations are not satisfactory, much of the information may be suppressed or misunderstood.

Leadership

Theory of Leadership

1. Great Man Theory

The 'great man' theory was originally proposed by **Thomas Carlyle**.

Assumptions

Leaders are born and not made.

Great leaders will arise when there is a great need.

Description

Early research on leadership was based on the study of people who were already great leaders. These people were often from the aristocracy, as few from lower classes had the opportunity to lead. This contributed to the notion that leadership had something to do with breeding.

2. Trait Theory

Assumptions

People are born with inherited traits.

Some traits are particularly suited to leadership.

People who make good leaders have the right combination of traits.

Stogdill (1974) identified the following traits and skills as critical to leaders.

Traits	*Skills*
• Adaptable to situations • Alert to social environment • Ambitious and achievement-orientated • Assertive • Cooperative • Decisive • Dependable • Dominant (desire to influence others) • Energetic (high activity level) • Persistent • Self-confident • Tolerant of stress • Willing to assume responsibility	• Clever (intelligent) • Conceptually skilled • Creative • Diplomatic and tactful • Fluent in speaking • Knowledgeable about group task • Organized (administrative ability) • Persuasive • Socially skilled

McCall and Lombardo (1983) researched both success and failure identified four primary traits by which leaders could succeed or derail:

- **Emotional Stability and Composure:** Calm, confident and predictable, particularly when under stress.
- **Admitting Error:** Owning up to mistakes, rather than putting energy into covering up.
- **Good Interpersonal Skills:** Able to communicate and persuade others without resort to negative or coercive tactics.
- **Intellectual Breadth:** Able to understand a wide range of areas, rather than having a narrow area of expertise.

3. Behavioural Theory of Leadership

There are two important Behavioural studies. These are discussed below:

(a) Ohio State University (1940s)

As leadership studies that were aimed at identifying the appropriate traits didn't yield any conclusive results, a group of people from Ohio State University developed a list of **150 statements** from their generated responses that included 1,800 hundred statements. The list was designed to measure **nine** different behavioural leadership dimensions. The resulting questionnaire is now well-known as the LBDQ or the **Leaders Behaviour Description Questionnaire**.

As part of the study, the LBDQ was administered to various groups of individuals ranging from college students and their administrators, private companies including military personnel. One of the primary purposes of the study was to identify common leadership behaviours. After compiling and analyzing the results, the study led to the conclusion that there were two groups of behaviours that were strongly correlated. These were defined as **Consideration** (People Oriented behavioural Leaders) and **Initiating Structure** (Task Oriented Leaders).

Task Oriented Leaders

The task concerned leaders are focusing their behaviours on the organizational structure, the operating procedures and they like to keep control. They will favour behaviours that are in line with:

- Initiating
- Organizing
- Clarifying
- Information Gathering

People Oriented Leaders

The people oriented leaders are focusing their behaviours on ensuring that the inner needs of the people are satisfied. Thus they will seek to motivate their staff through emphasizing the human relation. People oriented leaders still focus on the task and the results; they just achieve them through different means. They will favour behaviours that are in line with:

- Encouraging
- Observing
- Listening
- Coaching and Mentoring

(b) University of Michigan (1950s)

Dr. Rensis Likert, the leadership studies at the University of Michigan identified three characteristics of effective leadership; two of which were previously observed in studies that had been conducted at Ohio State University. The study showed that task and relationship-oriented behaviours were not of major significance within the world of organizational psychology. However it was the third observation that introduced a new concept, one of **participative leadership**.

Blake and Mouton's Managerial Grid

The treatment of task orientation and people orientation as two independent dimensions was a major step in leadership studies. Many of the leadership studies conducted in the 1950s at the University of Michigan and the Ohio State University focused on these two dimensions.

Building on the work of the researchers at these Universities, **Robert Blake and Jane Mouton** (1960s) proposed a graphic portrayal of leadership styles through a **managerial grid**. The grid depicted two dimensions of leader behaviour, **concern for people** on y-axis and **concern for production** on x-axis, with each dimension ranging from low (1) to high (9), thus creating **81** different positions in which the leader's style may fall.

The five resulting leadership styles are as follows:

Impoverished Management (1, 1): Managers with this approach are **low on both the dimensions** and exercise minimum effort to get the work done from subordinates. The leader has low concern for employee satisfaction and work deadlines and as a result disharmony and disorganization prevail within the organization. The leaders are termed ineffective wherein their action is merely aimed at preserving job and seniority.

Task Management (9, 1): Here leaders are more **concerned about production** and have **less concern for people**. The employees' needs are not taken care of and they are simply a means to an end. The leader believes that efficiency can result only through proper organization of work systems and through elimination of people wherever possible. Such a style can definitely increase the output of organization in short run but due to the strict policies and procedures, high labour turnover is inevitable.

Middle-of-the-Road (5, 5): This is basically a **compromising style** wherein the leader tries to maintain a balance between goals of company and the needs of people. The leader does not push the boundaries of achievement resulting in average performance for organization. Here neither employee nor production needs are fully met.

Country Club (1, 9): This is a **collegial style** characterized by **low task and high people orientation** where the leader gives thoughtful attention to the needs of people thus providing them with a friendly and comfortable environment. The leader feels that such a treatment with employees will lead to self-motivation and will find people working hard on their own. However, a low focus on tasks can hamper production and lead to questionable results.

Team Management (9, 9): Characterized by **high people and task focus**, the style is based on the theory Y of McGregor and has been termed as most effective style according to Blake and Mouton. The leader feels that empowerment, commitment, trust, and respect are the key elements in creating a team atmosphere which will automatically result in high employee satisfaction and production.

House's Path Goal Theory

The theory was developed by **Robert House** and has its roots in the expectancy theory of motivation. The theory is based on the premise that an employee's perception of expectancies between his effort and performance is greatly affected by a leader's behaviour. The leaders help group members in attaining rewards by clarifying the paths to goals and removing obstacles to performance. They do so by providing the information, support, and other resources which are required by employees to complete the task.

House's theory advocates **servant leadership**. As per servant leadership theory, leadership is not viewed as a position of power. Rather, leaders act as coaches and facilitators to their subordinates. According to House's path-goal theory, a leader's effectiveness depends on several employee and environmental contingent factors and certain leadership styles.

Leadership Styles

The four leadership styles are:

Directive: Here the leader provides guidelines, lets subordinates know what is expected of them, sets performance standards for them, and controls behaviour when performance standards are not met. He makes judicious use of rewards and disciplinary action.

Supportive: The leader is friendly towards subordinates and displays personal concern for their needs, welfare, and well-being.

Participative: The leader believes in group decision-making and shares information with subordinates. He consults his subordinates on important decisions related to work, task goals, and paths to resolve goals.

Achievement-oriented: The leader sets challenging goals and encourages employees to reach their peak performance. The leader believes that employees are responsible enough to accomplish challenging goals.

According to the theory, these leadership styles are not mutually exclusive and leaders are capable of selecting more than one kind of a style suited for a particular situation.

Hersey Blanchard Model

According to this model, the leader has to match the leadership style according to the readiness of subordinates which moves in stage and has a cycle. Therefore, this theory is also known as the **life-cycle theory** of leadership.

The theory, developed by Paul Hersey and Kenneth Blanchard, is based on the '**readiness**' level of the people the leader is attempting to influence. Readiness is the extent to which followers have the ability and willingness to accomplish a specific task. Ability is the knowledge, experience, and skill that an individual possesses to do the job and is called job readiness. Willingness is the motivation and commitment required to accomplish a given task. The style of leadership depends on the level of readiness of the followers.

The readiness (R) is divided into a continuum of four levels which are:

R1 - **Low Follower Readiness** - refers to **low ability and low willingness of followers** i.e. those who are unable and insecure.
R2- Low to Moderate Follower Readiness - refers to **low ability and high willingness of followers** i.e. those who are unable but confident.
R3 - **Moderate to High Follower Readiness** - refers to **high ability and low willingness of followers** i.e. those who are able but insecure.
R4 - **High Follower Readiness** - refers to **high ability and high willingness of followers** i.e. those who are both able and confident.

The direction is provided by the leader at the lower levels of readiness. Therefore, the decisions are leader directed. On the other hand, the direction is provided by the followers at the higher levels of readiness. Therefore, the decisions in this case are follower directed. When the followers move from low levels to high levels of readiness, the combinations of task and relationship behaviours appropriate to the situation begin to change.

For each of the four levels of readiness, the leadership style used may be a combination of task and relationship behaviour.

By combining the task and the relationship behavior, we arrive at the following four different styles of leadership which correspond with the different levels of readiness as shown below.

S1 - Telling: This style is most appropriate for low follower readiness (R1). It emphasizes high task behaviour and limited relationship behaviour.
S2 - Selling: This style is most appropriate for low to moderate follower readiness (R2). It emphasizes high amounts of both task and relationship behaviour.
S3 - Participating: This style is most appropriate for moderate to high follower readiness (R3). It emphasizes high amount of relationship behaviour but low amount of task behaviour.
S4 - Delegating: This style is most appropriate for high follower readiness (R4). It emphasizes low levels of both task and relationship behaviour.

Fiedler's Contingency Model

Fred E. Fiedler's contingency theory of leadership effectiveness was based on studies of a wide range of group effectiveness, and concentrated on the relationship between leadership and organizational performance. This is one of the earliest situation-contingent leadership theories given by Fiedler. According to him, if an organization attempts to achieve group effectiveness through leadership, then there is a need to assess the leader according to an underlying trait, assess the situation faced by the leader, and construct a proper match between the two.

Leader's trait

In order to assess the attitudes of the leader, Fiedler developed the '**least preferred co-worker**' (LPC) scale in which the leaders are asked about the person with whom they least like to work. The scale is a questionnaire consisting of 16 items used to reflect a leader's underlying disposition toward others. The items in the LPC scale are pleasant / unpleasant, friendly / unfriendly, rejecting / accepting, unenthusiastic / enthusiastic, tense / relaxed, cold / warm, helpful / frustrating, cooperative / uncooperative, supportive / hostile, quarrelsome / harmonious, efficient / inefficient, gloomy / cheerful, distant / close, boring / interesting, self-assured / hesitant, open / guarded. Each item in the scale is given a single ranking of between one and eight points, with eight points indicating the most favourable rating.

Friendly	8	7	6	5	4	3	2	1	Unfriendly

Fiedler states that leaders with **high LPC scores are relationship-oriented and the ones with low scores are task-oriented**. The high LPC score leaders derived most satisfaction from interpersonal relationships and therefore evaluate their least preferred co-workers in fairly favourable terms. These leaders think about the task accomplishment only after the relationship need is well satisfied. On the other hand, the low LPC score leaders derived satisfaction from performance of the task and attainment of objectives and only after tasks have been accomplished, these leaders work on establishing good social and interpersonal relationships.

Situational Factor

According to Fiedler, a leader's behaviour is dependent upon the favourability of the leadership situation. Three factors work together to determine how favourable a situation is to a leader. These are:

Leader-Member Relations- The degree to which the leaders is trusted and liked by the group members, and the willingness of the group members to follow the leader's guidance.

Task Structure- The degree to which the group's task has been described as structured or unstructured has been clearly defined and the extent to which it can be carried out by detailed instructions.

Position Power - The power of the leader by virtue of the organizational position and the degree to which the leader can exercise authority on group members in order to comply with and accept his direction and leadership

With the help of these three variables, eight combinations of group-task situations were constructed by Fiedler. These combinations were used to identify the style of the leader.

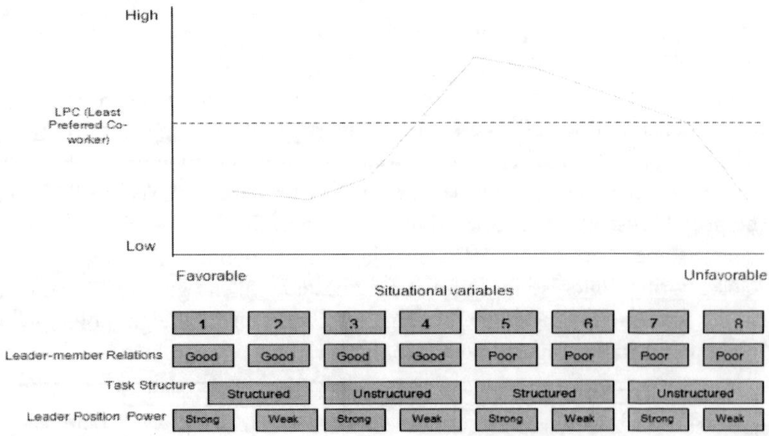

Leader's LPC Scores and Group Effectiveness

Leadership Effectiveness

The leader's effectiveness is determined by the interaction of the leader's style of behaviour and the favourableness of the situational characteristics. The most favourable situation is when leader-member relations are good, the task is highly structured, and the leader has a strong position power.

Research on the contingency model has shown that task-oriented leaders are more effective in highly favorable (1, 2, 3) and highly unfavorable situation (7, 8), whereas relationship-oriented leaders are more effective in situations of intermediate favourableness (4, 5, 6).

Continuum of Leadership Behaviour

The leadership continuum was originally written in 1958 by **Tannenbaum and Schmidt** and was later updated in the year 1973. Their work suggests a continuum of possible leadership behaviour available to a manager and along which many leadership styles may be placed. The continuum presents a range of action related to the degree of authority used by the manager and to the area of freedom available to non-managers in arriving at decisions. A broad range of leadership styles have been depicted on the continuum between two extremes of autocratic and free rein. The left side shows a style where control is maintained by a manager and the right side shows the release of control. However, neither extreme is absolute and authority and freedom are never without their limitations.

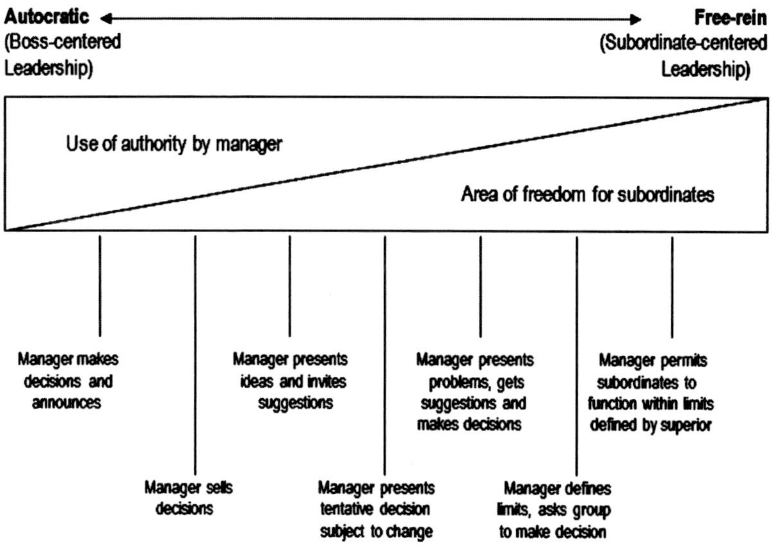

Continuum Leadership Behaviour

The Tannenbaum and Schmidt continuum can be related to McGregor's supposition of Theory X and Theory Y. Boss-centered leadership is towards theory X and subordinate-centered leadership is towards theory Y.

A manager is characterized according to degree of control that is maintained by him. According to this approach, four main styles of leadership have been identified:

Tells: The manager identifies a problem, chooses a decision, and announces this to subordinates. The subordinates are not a party to the decision making process and the manager expects them to implement his decisions as soon as possible.

Sells: The decision is chosen by the manager only but he understands that there will be some amount of resistance from those faced with the decision and therefore makes efforts to persuade them to accept it.

Consults: Though the problem is identified by the manager, he does not take a final decision. The problem is presented to the subordinates and the solutions are suggested by the subordinates.

Joins: The manager defines the limits within which the decision can be taken by the subordinates and then makes the final decision along with the subordinates.

According to Tannenbaum and Schmidt, successful leaders know which behaviour is the most appropriate at a particular time. They shape their behaviour after a careful analysis of self, their subordinates, organization, and environmental factors.

Transactional Leadership Theory

The transactional style of leadership was first described by **Max Weber in 1947** and then by **Bernard Bass** in 1981. This style is most often used by the managers. It focuses on the basic management process of controlling, organizing, and short-term planning. The famous examples of leaders who have used transactional technique include McCarthy and de Gaulle.

Transactional leadership involves motivating and directing followers primarily through appealing to their own self-interest. The power of transactional leaders comes from their **formal authority and responsibility** in the organization. The main goal of the follower is to obey the instructions of the leader. The style can also be mentioned as a 'telling style'.

The leader believes in motivating through a system of **rewards and punishment**. If a subordinate does what is desired, a reward will follow, and if he does not go as per the wishes of the leader, a punishment will follow. Here, the exchange between leader and follower takes place to achieve routine performance goals.

Leadership-Member Exchange (LMX) Theory

Informal observation of leadership behaviour suggests that leader's action is not the same towards all subordinates. The importance of potential differences in this respect is brought into sharp focus by **Graen's leader-member exchange model**, also known as the **vertical dyad linkage theory**. The theory views leadership as consisting of a number of dyadic relationships linking the leader with a follower. The quality of the relationship is reflected by the degree of mutual trust, loyalty, support, respect, and obligation.

According to the theory, leaders form different kinds of relationships with various groups of subordinates. One group, referred to as the **in-group**, is favored by the leader. Members of in-group receive considerably more attention from the leader and have more access to the organizational resources. By contrast, other subordinates fall into the **out-group**. These individuals are disfavoured by the leader. As such, they receive fewer valued resources from their leaders.

Leaders distinguish between the in-group and out-group members on the basis of the perceived similarity with respect to personal characteristics, such as age, gender, or personality. A follower may also be granted an in-group status if the leader believes that person to be especially competent at performing his or her job. The relationship between leaders and followers follows two stages:

Role Taking: When a new member joins the organization, the leader assesses the talent and abilities of the member and offers them opportunities to demonstrate their capabilities.

Role Making: An informal and unstructured negotiation on work-related factors takes place between the leader and the member. A member who is similar to the leader is more likely to succeed. A betrayal by the member at this stage may result in him being relegated to the out-group.

The **LMX 7 scale** assesses the degree to which leaders and followers have mutual respect for each other's capabilities, feel a deepening sense of mutual trust, and have a sense of strong obligation to one another. Taken together, these dimensions determine the extent to which followers will be part of the leader's in-group or out-group.

Transformational Leadership Theory

Creating high-performance workforce has become increasingly important and to do so business leaders must be able to inspire organizational members to go beyond their task requirements. As a result, new concepts of leadership have emerged - transformational leadership being one of them.

Transformational leadership may be found at all levels of the organization: teams, departments, divisions, and organization as a whole. Such leaders are visionary, inspiring, daring, risk-takers, and thoughtful thinkers. They have a charismatic appeal. But charisma alone is insufficient for changing the way an organization operates. For bringing major changes, transformational leaders must exhibit the following four factors:

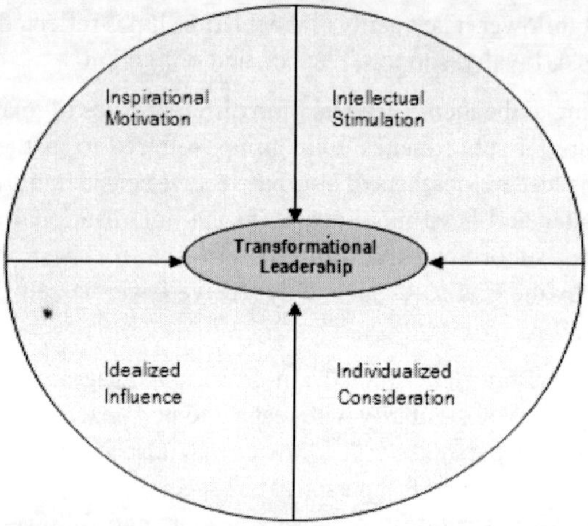

Model of Transformational Leadership

Inspirational Motivation: The foundation of transformational leadership is the promotion of consistent vision, mission, and a set of values to the members. Their vision is so compelling that they know what they want from every interaction. Transformational leaders guide followers by providing them with a sense of meaning and challenge. They work enthusiastically and optimistically to foster the spirit of teamwork and commitment.

Intellectual Stimulation: Such leaders encourage their followers to be innovative and creative. They encourage new ideas from their followers and never criticize them publicly for the mistakes committed by them. The leaders focus on the "what" in problems and do not focus on the blaming part of it. They have no hesitation in discarding an old practice set by them if it is found ineffective.

Idealized Influence: They believe in the philosophy that a leader can influence followers only when he practices what he preaches. The leaders act as role models that followers seek to emulate. Such leaders always win the trust and respect of their followers through their action. They typically place their followers needs over their own, sacrifice their personal gains for them, and demonstrate high standards of ethical conduct. The use of power by such leaders is aimed at influencing them to strive for the common goals of the organization.

Individualized Consideration: Leaders act as mentors to their followers and reward them for creativity and innovation. The followers are treated differently according to their talents and knowledge. They are empowered to make decisions and are always provided with the needed support to implement their decisions.

Likert's Management System

Rensis Likert and his associates studied the patterns and styles of managers for three decades at the University of Michigan, USA, and identified a four-fold model of management systems. The model was developed on the basis of a questionnaire administered to managers in over 200 organizations and research into the performance characteristics of different types of organizations. The four systems of management system or the four leadership styles identified by Likert are:

System 1 - Exploitative Authoritative: Responsibility lies in the hands of the people at the upper echelons of the hierarchy. The superior has no trust and confidence in subordinates. The decisions are imposed on subordinates and they do not feel free at all to discuss things about the job with their superior. The teamwork or communication is very little and the motivation is based on threats.

System 2 - Benevolent Authoritative: The responsibility lies at the managerial levels but not at the lower levels of the organizational hierarchy. The superior has condescending confidence and trust in subordinates. Here again, the subordinates do not feel free to discuss things about the job with their superior. The teamwork or communication is very little and motivation is based on a system of rewards.

System 3 - Consultative: Responsibility is spread widely through the organizational hierarchy. The superior has substantial but not complete confidence in subordinates. Some amount of discussion about job related things takes place between the superior and subordinates. There is a fair amount of teamwork, and communication takes place vertically and horizontally. The motivation is based on rewards and involvement in the job.

System 4 - Participative: Responsibility for achieving the organizational goals is widespread throughout the organizational hierarchy. There is a high level of confidence that the superior has in his subordinates. There is a high level of teamwork, communication, and participation.

Managing Change

1. Be intentional about the changes you make. If you initiate change just for the sake of change, it will be challenging for you to get support from your leaders, employees, and clients. Have a good reason for each change and be able to explain those reasons clearly to your organization.

- Keep your whole organization in mind. It is easy to think about making a change in one department without realizing the effects it will have on all the others. Explore all the potential consequences of organizational change before announcing it.
- Get feedback from leaders in the organization, as well as from others outside of the company. Different perspectives will help you make a well-informed decision.
- Make role changes for a specific purpose. Organizational change often leads to an adjustment in roles and responsibilities. People are moved from one department to another or from one location to another. Do your best to handle these changes sensitively and intentionally.

2. Get the support of those in your organization. This is vital to helping your organization transition and move forward with the changes you would like to implement. The more you can engage and include those in your organization, the better.

- Explain the reasoning behind organizational changes instead of just announcing the change itself. People are more likely to support you if they understand why you made a particular decision.
- Start with the senior leadership team. If your leaders do not support you, it will be difficult to get the support from the rest of the organization.
- Include all employees. Everyone on staff needs to be committed to the new vision, mission, or whatever the change might be. Work to earn their support and dedication. Invite employees to help formulate the wording of the new vision statement.

3. Communicate openly as much as possible. Inform employees of changes before they hear it from somewhere else. Utilize company email, all-staff meetings, newsletters, or whatever form of communication is most beneficial for the news you are sharing.

- Share major changes face to face and then follow up with an email. This makes your announcement more personal. It also gives employees a chance to ask questions or clear up any confusion.
- Communicate early and often. Keep employees informed throughout all aspects of your organizational change so they can be on your side when the change actually takes place.

- Encourage feedback. Give employees the opportunity to ask questions or provide suggestions as your organization moves towards change.

4. Acknowledge the process of change. Change takes place in several stages. There are also different emotions attached to the idea of organizational change.

- Some workers will immediately accept announced changes, while others may deny the need for it, prolong the change itself, or actively resist it. As your company encounters change, keep an eye on how employees are responding.
- Do not expect behaviour to change all at once. It will take time for your employees to get used to doing things differently. Do what you can to support them during the transition.

5. Model a positive response to the organizational change. Employees often take the lead from their supervisors. Set the example by displaying a positive attitude about upcoming changes, supporting your own leaders, and helping your team make changes. If you have any disagreements about potential changes, keep that within the leadership team.

Managing Conflicts

Here are five conflict styles that a manager will follow according to Kenneth W. Thomas and Ralph H. Kilmann:

An **accommodating** manager is one who cooperates to a high degree. This may be at the manager's own expense and actually work against that manager's own goals, objectives, and desired outcomes. This approach is effective when the other person is the expert or has a better solution.

Avoiding an issue is one way a manager might attempt to resolve conflict. This type of conflict style does not help the other staff members reach their goals and does not help the manager who is avoiding the issue and cannot assertively pursue his or her own goals. However, this works well when the issue is trivial or when the manager has no chance of winning.

Collaborating managers become partners or pair up with each other to achieve both of their goals in this style. This is how managers break free of the win-lose paradigm and seek the win-win. This can be effective for complex scenarios where managers need to find a novel solution.

Competing: This is the **win-lose** approach. A manager is acting in a very assertive way to achieve his or her own goals without seeking to cooperate with other employees, and it may be at the expense of those other employees. This approach may be appropriate for emergencies when time is of the essence.

Compromising: This is the **lose-lose** scenario where neither person nor manager really achieves what they want. This requires a moderate level of assertiveness and cooperation. It may be appropriate for scenarios where you need a temporary solution or where both sides have equally important goals.

Organization Development

Business development is defined as "a planned organization-wide effort to increase an organization's effectiveness and viability," according to Noetic Outcomes Consulting. One of the most widely known means of implementing organization development is enterprise master planning. This process allows an organization to choose the best business solution out of a multitude of alternatives or options. Enterprise master planning involves a thorough analysis of existing business processes and a good understanding of opportunities available for improving those processes. Documentations and resources are used to determine the most appropriate business options, and to qualify and justify the master plan.

The methods used for organizational development will vary, and the steps taken to implement organizational change is contingent on the scale of the project and the sort of results being sought. The timeline for the plan development and integration will therefore depend on the complexity of the enterprise and its starting point in the development stage.

Lewin's Model of OD

Lewin's model is based on premise that before introducing a change, organization needs to be prepared for change motivated to change and established and integrated the change into behaviours of organization. A brief description of this model is mentioned below:

Unfreezing: This necessitates unlearning of old things in order to learn new things. It involves encouraging individuals to discard old behaviours by shaking up the equilibrium that maintains status quo. Thus, unfreezing motivates people for change and minimizing resistance to change.

Changing: Efforts are made to inject new attitudes, values and behaviours to experimentation with new behaviour. This implies transition from old behaviour to new one.

Refreezing: In this final step, new attitudes, values and behaviours are established. This implies stabilizing and integrating the change by reinforcing the new behaviours and integrating them into formal and interpersonal relationships and in one's personality.

Unit - VII

Marketing Environment

Marketing Environment & Environment Scanning

Marketing Environment

The Marketing Environment includes the internal factors (employees, customers, shareholders, retailers & distributors, etc.) and the external factors (political, legal, social, technological, economic) that surround the business and influence its marketing operations.

Some of these factors are controllable while some are uncontrollable and require business operations to change accordingly. Firms must be well aware of its marketing environment in which it is operating to overcome the negative impact the environment factors are imposing on firm's marketing activities.

The marketing environment can be broadly classified into three parts:

1. **Internal Environment:** The Internal Marketing Environment includes all the factors that are within the organization and affects the overall business operations. These factors include labour, inventory, company policy, logistics, budget, capital assets, etc. which are a part of the organization and affects the marketing decision and its relationship with the customers. These factors can be controlled by the firm.
2. **Microenvironment:** The Micro Marketing Environment includes all those factors that are closely associated with the operations of the business and influences its functioning. The microenvironment factors include customers, employees, suppliers, retailers &

distributors, shareholders, competitors, government and general Public. These factors are controllable to some extent.

(i) **Customers:** Every business revolves around fulfilling the customer's needs and wants. Thus, each marketing strategy is customer oriented that focuses on understanding the need of the customers and offering the best product that fulfills their needs.

(ii) **Employees:** Employees are the main component of a business who contributes significantly to its success. The quality of employees depends on the training and motivation sessions given to them. Thus, Training & Development is crucial to impart marketing skills in an individual.

(iii) **Suppliers:** Suppliers are the persons from whom the material is purchased to make a finished good and hence are very important for the organization. It is crucial to identify the suppliers existing in the market and choose the best that fulfills the firm's requirement.

(iv) **Retailers & Distributors:** The channel partners play an imperative role in determining the success of marketing operations. Being in direct touch with customers they can give suggestions about customer's desires regarding a product and its services.

(v) **Competitors:** Keeping a close watch on competitors enables a company to design its marketing strategy according to the trend prevailing in the market.

(vi) **Shareholders:** Shareholders are the owners of the company, and every firm has an objective of maximizing its shareholder's wealth. Thus, marketing activities should be undertaken keeping in mind the returns to shareholders.

(vii) **Government:** The Government departments make several policies viz. pricing policy, credit policy, education policy, housing policy, etc. that do have an influence on the marketing strategies. A company has to keep track on these policies and make the marketing programs accordingly.

(viii) **General Public:** The business has some social responsibility towards the society in which it is operating. Thus, all the marketing activities should be designed that result in increased welfare of the society as a whole.

3. Macro Environment: The Macro Marketing Environment includes all those factors that exist outside the organization and cannot be controlled. These factors majorly include Social, Economic, Technological Forces, Political and Legal Influences. These are also called as **PESTLE** framework.

(i) **Political & Legal Factors:** With the change in political parties, several changes are seen in the market in terms of trade, taxes, and duties, codes and practices, market regulations, etc. So the firm has to comply with all these changes and the violation of which could penalize its business operations.

(ii) **Economic Factors:** Every business operates in the economy and is affected by the different phases it is undergoing. In the case of recession, the marketing practices should be different as what are followed during the inflation period.

(iii) **Social Factors:** Since business operates in a society and has some responsibility towards it must follow the marketing practices that do not harm the sentiments of people. The companies are also required to invest in the welfare of general people by constructing public conveniences, parks, sponsoring education, etc.

(iv) **Technological Factors:** As technology is advancing day by day, the firms have to keep themselves updated so that customers needs can be met with more precision.

Therefore, marketing environment plays a crucial role in the operations of a business and must be reviewed on a regular basis to avoid any difficulty.

(v) **Legal Factors:** Legal factors influence the company's operation, its costs, and the demand for its products. Factors include:

- Consumer law
- Antitrust law
- Employment law
- Discrimination law
- Health and safety law

(vi) **Environmental Factors:** It refers to ecological and environmental aspects such as weather, climate, and climate change. Climate change is a hot topic these days and organizations are restructuring their operations thus giving space to innovation and concept of Green Business.

Environment Scanning

Organizational environment consists of both external and internal factors. Environment must be scanned so as to determine development and forecasts of factors that will influence organizational success. Environmental scanning refers to possession and utilization of information about occasions, patterns, trends, and relationships within an organization's internal and external environment. It helps the managers to decide the future path of the organization. Scanning must identify the threats and opportunities existing in the environment. While strategy formulation, an organization must take advantage of the opportunities and minimize the threats. A threat for one organization may be an opportunity for another.

Internal analysis of the environment is the first step of environment scanning. Organizations should observe the internal organizational environment. This includes employee interaction with other employees, employee interaction with management, managers' interaction with other managers, and management interaction with shareholders, access to natural resources, brand awareness, organizational structure, main staff, operational potential, etc. Discussions, interviews, and surveys can be also used to assess the internal environment. Analysis of internal environment helps in identifying strengths and weaknesses of an organization.

As business becomes more competitive, and there are rapid changes in the external environment, information from external environment adds crucial elements to the effectiveness of long-term plans. As environment is dynamic, it becomes essential to identify competitors' moves and actions. Organizations have also to update the core competencies and internal environment as per external environment. Environmental factors are infinite, hence, organization should be agile and vigil to accept and adjust to the environmental changes. For instance - Monitoring might indicate that an original forecast of the prices of the raw materials that are involved in the product are no more credible, which could imply the requirement for more focused scanning, forecasting and analysis to create a more trustworthy prediction about the input costs. In a similar manner, there can be changes in factors such as competitor's activities, technology, market tastes and preferences.

While in external analysis, three correlated environment should be studied and analyzed —

- immediate / industry environment
- national environment
- broader socio-economic environment / macro-environment

Examining the industry environment needs an appraisal of the competitive structure of the organization's industry, including the competitive position of a particular organization and its main rivals. An assessment of the nature, stage, dynamics and history of the industry is also essential. It also implies evaluating the effect of globalization on competition within the industry. Analyzing the national environment needs an appraisal of whether the national framework helps in achieving competitive advantage in the globalized environment. Analysis of macro-environment includes exploring macro-economic, social, government, legal, technological and international factors that may influence the environment. The analysis of organization's external environment reveals opportunities and threats for an organization.

Strategic managers must not only recognize the present state of the environment and their industry but also be able to predict its future positions.

Marketing Information System

Marketing information system is a system that meets the information needs of an organization in sales, distribution, advertising, market analysis, market intelligence, product research, service management, customer profile and other marketing functions.

Marketing information system generally includes all activities relating to promotion and sales of products or services. The transactions are sales orders, promotion orders, etc. The operational control activities include the selection and training of the sales force, the day-to-day scheduling of sales and promotion efforts, and periodic analysis of sales by region, territory, product, customer, etc. Managerial control concerns comparative analysis of performance against marketing plan, data on customers, competitors and their products, sales force requirements, etc. Strategic planning for the marketing function includes consideration of new market and new marketing strategies. The information requirements for strategic planning include customer analyses, competitor analyses, income and demographic projections, technology projections, etc.

Philip Kotler has identified three types of marketing information.

(a) **Marketing Intelligence:** Information that flows into the firm from the environment.

(b) **Internal Marketing Information:** Information collected within the firm.

(c) **Marketing Communications:** Information that flows from the firm outward to the environment.

Inputs to Marketing Information Systems: The information used for marketing is as follows:

(a) **Transaction Processing Data:** Transaction processing data show the sales that result from specific mixes of the four P's. Thus, they provide feedback on the effectiveness of past marketing strategies.

(b) **Marketing Research Data:** It is done for gathering consumer related data that can be used to support marketing decisions, for example, personal interviews, phone interviews and mail surveys.

(c) **Marketing Intelligence Data:** Marketing intelligence refers to the information about the strategies of competitors.

(d) **External Environment Data:** In marketing, success is largely attributable to what will happen in the future external environment. For example, when a new car is introduced, the firm never knows exactly how consumers will react to it.

(e) **Strategic Plan:** The strategic plan is really the starting point of all marketing decisions. It contains the types of products that the firm plans to supply to the consumer marketplace. These broad guidelines define the direction of the marketing effort. The tactical marketing plan addresses what, how, when and where questions, those are appropriate to the implementation of the strategic plan.

Outputs of Marketing Information Systems: Each output subsystem provides information about its part of the marketing mix and are as follows:

(a) **Product Planning:** Product planning is often completed, unstructured decision. A number of factors contribute to a product's success or failure. A number of techniques have been developed to provide the manager with the information needed for making product oriented decisions.

(b) **Place Planning:** It refers to the channels of distribution that a firm uses to get its products to the consumer. The resources flowing through a channel includes a supplier, manufacturer, wholesaler, retailer and consumer. The material flow originates with the suppliers and ends with the consumer. Information that flows in the direction opposite to the material flow is called feedback information and the flow of information toward the consumer is called feed forward information.

(c) **Promotion:** It is composed of two principal areas which are personal selling and advertising. Technology is vital to the selling effort in several ways:

 (i) Increasing selling time;

 (ii) Increasing effectiveness of the client site;

 (iii) Identifying selling opportunities and;

 (iv) Making salespeople more efficient.

(d) **Price:** Some firms engage in cost - based pricing by determining their cost and then adding a desired mark-up. A less cautious pricing policy compatible with the value that the consumer places correctly estimating demand. This requires a good understanding of the consumer and also of the market, including the state of the economy and competition.

Marketing Research

Marketing Research has two words, viz., marketing and research.

1. Marketing means buying and selling activities.
2. Research means a systematic and complete study of a problem. It is done by experts. It uses scientific methods.

Thus, we can say, "Marketing Research is a systematic method of collecting, recording and analyzing of data, which is used to solve marketing problems."

A company faces many marketing problems. It faces problems about consumers, product, market competition, sales promotion, etc. Marketing research helps to solve these problems.

Marketing research is a systematic process. It first collects data about the marketing problem. Secondly, it records this data. Then it analyses this data and draws conclusions about it. After that, it gives suggestions for solving the marketing-problem.

So, marketing research helps to solve the marketing problems quickly, correctly and systematically.

Marketing research collects full information about consumers. It finds out the needs and expectations of the consumers. So, the company produces the goods according to the needs and expectations of the consumers.

Marketing research helps the company to make its production and marketing policies. It helps the company to introduce new products in the market. It helps to identify new markets.

Marketing research also collects full information about the competitors. The company uses this information to fight competition. It also helps the marketing manager to take decisions.

Marketing research is a special branch and soul of 'Marketing Management'. It is of recent origin and widely used by manufacturers, exporters, distributors and service organizations.

Marketing research is very systematic, scientific, objective and organized. It has a wide scope. It includes product research, consumer research, packaging research, pricing research, etc.

Marketing research is a continuous process. It has a few limitations. However, a company cannot survive and succeed without it.

Definition of Marketing Research

There are many definitions of marketing research. Some important ones are:

1. According to **American Marketing Association** (AMA), "Marketing Research is the systematic gathering, recording and analyzing of data about problems relating to the marketing of goods and services."
2. According to **Philip Kotler**, "Marketing research is a systematic problem analysis, model building and fact finding for the purpose of

improved decision-making and control in the marketing of goods and services."

3. According to **Paul Green** and **Donald Tull**, "Marketing research is the systematic and objective search for, and analysis of, information relevant to the identification and solution of any problem in the field of marketing."
4. According to **David Luck**, **Donald Taylor** and **Hugh Wales**, "Marketing Research is the application of scientific methods in the solution of marketing problems."

Features of Marketing Research

The salient features of marketing research are as follows:

(i) **Wide and Comprehensive Scope:** Marketing research has a very wide scope. It includes product research, packaging research, pricing research, market research, sales research, etc. It is used to solve marketing problems and to take marketing decisions. It is used to make marketing policies. It is also used to introduce new products in the market and to identify new markets. Marketing research is used to select channels of distribution, in advertising strategy, for sales promotion measures, etc.

(ii) **Systematic and Scientific:** Marketing research is conducted in a step-by-step manner. It is conducted in an orderly fashion. Therefore, it is systematic. Marketing research uses scientific methods. Thus, it is also scientific.

(iii) **Science and Art:** A Science collects knowledge while an Art uses this knowledge for solving problems. Marketing research first collects data. It then uses this data for solving marketing problems. Therefore, it is both, a Science and an Art.

(iv) **Collects and Analyzes Data:** Marketing research gathers data accurately and objectively. It first collects reliable data and then analyses it systematically and critically.

(v) **Continuous and Dynamic Process:** The company faces marketing problems throughout the year. So, marketing research is conducted continuously. It continuously collects up-to-date data for solving the marketing problems. Large companies have their own marketing research departments. They conduct marketing research continuously throughout the year. Therefore, marketing research is a continuous process. It is a dynamic process because it goes on changing. It does not remain static. It uses new methods and techniques for collecting, recording and analyzing the data.

(vi) **Tool for Decision-Making:** The marketing manager has to take many decisions. For this, he requires a lot of data. Marketing research provides correct and up-to-date data to the marketing manager. This helps him to take quick and correct decisions. Therefore, marketing research is an important tool for decision-making.

(vii) **Benefits Company and Consumers:** Marketing research is useful to the company in many ways. It increases the sales and profits of the company. It helps the company to fight competition and boost its goodwill in the market. It reduces the marketing risks. In short, marketing research brings success to the company. It also brings the company closer to the consumers. It gives convenience and satisfaction to the consumers.

(viii) **Similar to Military Intelligence:** Marketing research is a commercial intelligence-gathering activity. It works similar to military intelligence. Marketing intelligence first makes a systematic study and only then takes a business action. Marketing research collects reliable data about the consumers, the competitors, the market, etc. This data is then organized and used for planning, decision-making and problem solving. This data is also further used for introducing new products and services in the market.

(ix) **Applied Research:** Applied research is used for solving problems. Marketing research is used for solving marketing problems. Therefore, we can say that, marketing research is also an applied research. It has a practical value because it is used for solving present and future problems.

(x) **Connected with MIS:** Marketing research is a component of Marketing Information System (MIS). Marketing research and MIS are interrelated. Both are used to solve marketing problems and to take marketing decisions.

(xi) **Reduces Gap between Producers and Consumers:** Marketing research informs producers about the needs and wants of the consumers. The producers produce goods according to the needs and demands of the consumers. This brings satisfaction to the consumers and in return producers make good profits. So, marketing research reduces the gap between the producers and the consumers.

(xii) **Uses Different Methods:** Marketing research uses three methods for collecting data, viz., Survey Method, Experiment Method and Observation Method. All three methods are scientific. The researcher has to use a suitable method for collecting a reliable data.

(xiii) **Few Limitations:** Marketing research has few limitations too. It is not an exact science. So, it does not give accurate results. It provides suggestions and not solutions. It is also a costly and time-consuming process.

(xiv) Accurate Data Collection and Critical Analysis: Marketing research gives much importance to accurate data collection and its critical analysis. Thus, in a marketing research, the data must be first collected accurately. That is, collected data or gathered information must be accurate, reliable and relevant. Later, this information must be systematically and critically examined before making any decisions.

Marketing Research V/S Market Research

Marketing research is a broader term including market research. Marketing research is concerned with all the major functions of marketing. Market research is primarily concerned with knowing the capacity of the market to absorb a particular product. Marketing research is not only concerned with the jurisdiction of the market but also covers nature of the market, product analysis, sales analysis, time, place and media of advertising, personal selling and marketing intermediaries and their relationships, etc.

Understanding Consumer & Industrial Markets

Market is the place where we find buyers and sellers.

Consumer Market

In this market, the goods and services produced by the industrial products will be consumed by the consumers. In economics, this is also called as **product markets**.

Economic activity is the cycle how goods and services are produced and consumed. Industries and companies employ labour to produce goods and services, these goods and services are in turn consumed by the labour employed and other public making profits to industries and companies. Now companies pay wages to labour employed. So, this is a continuous process and called as economic activity.

Industrial Market

This is the market where you find buyers and sellers of goods of industrial inputs like, labour, machinery, land, capital and more. In economics this is also called as **factor markets.**

Demand Measurement & Forecasting

Broadly speaking, there are two approaches to demand forecasting– one is to obtain information about the likely purchase behaviour of the buyer through collecting expert's opinion or by conducting interviews with consumers, the other is to use past experience as a guide through a set of statistical techniques. Both these techniques of demand forecasting rely on varying degrees of judgment. The first method is usually found suitable for short-term forecasting, the latter for long-term forecasting. There are specific techniques which fall under each of these broad methods.

Judgmental Approaches to Forecasting

By their nature, judgment-based forecasts use subjective and qualitative data to forecast future outcomes. They inherently rely on expert opinion, experience, judgment, intuition, conjecture, and other "soft" data. Such techniques are often used when historical data are not available, as is the case with the introduction of a new product or service, and in forecasting the impact of fundamental changes such as new technologies, environmental changes, cultural changes, legal changes, and so forth. Some of the more common procedures include the following.

1. Simple Survey Methods: For forecasting the demand for existing product, such survey methods are often employed. In this set of methods, we may undertake the following exercise.

(a) **Consumers Survey – Complete Enumeration Method:** Under this method, the forecaster undertakes a complete survey of all consumers whose demand he intends to forecast. Once this information is collected, the sales forecasts are obtained by simply adding the probable demands of all consumers. The principle merit of this method is that the forecaster does not introduce any bias or value judgment of his own. He simply records the data and aggregates. But it is a very tedious and cumbersome process; it is not feasible where a large number of consumers are involved. Moreover, if the data are wrongly recorded, this method will be totally useless.

(b) **Consumer Survey – Sample Survey Method:** Under this method, the forecaster selects a few consuming units out of the relevant population and then collects data on their probable demands for the product during the forecast period. The total demand of sample units is finally blown up to generate the total demand forecast. Compared to the former survey, this method is less tedious and less costly, and subject to less data error; but the choice of sample is very critical. If the sample is properly chosen, then it will yield dependable results; otherwise there may be sampling error. The sampling error can decrease with every increase in sample size.

(c) **End-user Method of Consumers Survey:** Under this method, the sales of a product are projected through a survey of its end-users. A product is used for final consumption or as an intermediate product in the production of other goods in the domestic market, or it may be exported as well as imported. The demands for final consumption and exports net of imports are estimated through some other forecasting method, and its demand for intermediate use is estimated through a survey of its user industries.

2. Consensus Methods: As an alternative to the "bottom-up" survey approaches, consensus methods use a small group of individuals to develop general forecasts.

(a) **Experts Opinion Poll:** In this method, the experts on the particular product whose demand is under study are requested to give their 'opinion' or 'feel' about the product. These experts, dealing in the same or similar product, are able to predict the likely sales of a given product in future periods under different conditions based on their experience. If the number of such experts is large and their experience-based reactions are different, then an average-simple or weighted –is found to lead to unique forecasts. Sometimes, this method is also called the 'hunch method' but it replaces analysis by opinions and it can thus turn out to be highly subjective in nature.

(b) **Reasoned Opinion – Delphi Technique:** This is a variant of the opinion poll method. Here is an attempt to arrive at a consensus in an uncertain area by questioning a group of experts repeatedly until the responses appear to converge along a single line. The participants are supplied with responses to previous questions. Such feedback may result in an expert revising his earlier opinion. This may lead to a narrowing down of the divergent views of the experts expressed earlier. The Delphi Techniques, followed by the Greeks earlier, thus generates "reasoned opinion" in place of "unstructured opinion"; but this is still a poor proxy for market behaviour of economic variables.

Judgmental techniques of demand forecasting are important in that they are often used to determine an enterprise's strategy. They are also used in more mundane decisions, such as determining the quality of a potential vendor by asking for references, and there are many other reasonable applications. It is true that judgment based techniques are an inadequate basis for a demand forecasting system, but this should not be construed to mean that judgment has no role to play in logistics forecasting or that salespeople have no knowledge to bring to the problem. In fact, it is often the case that sales and marketing people have valuable information about sales promotions, new products, competitor activity, and so forth, which should be incorporated into the forecast somehow. Many organizations treat such data as additional information that is used to modify the existing forecast rather than as the baseline data used to create the forecast in the first place.

Experimental Approaches to Forecasting

In the early stages of new product development it is important to get some estimate of the level of potential demand for the product. A variety of market research techniques are used to this end.

1. **Customer Surveys** are sometimes conducted over the telephone or on street corners, at shopping malls, and so forth. The new product is displayed or described, and potential customers are asked whether they would be interested in purchasing the item. While this approach can help to isolate attractive or unattractive product features, experience has shown that "intent to purchase" as measured in this way is difficult to translate into a meaningful demand forecast. This falls short of being a true "demand experiment".
2. **Consumer Panels** are also used in the early phases of product development. Here a small group of potential customers are brought together in a room where they can use the product and discuss it among themselves. Panel members are often paid a nominal amount for their participation. Like surveys, these procedures are more useful for analyzing product attributes than for estimating demand, and they do not constitute true "demand experiments" because no purchases take place.
3. **Test Marketing** is often employed after new product development but prior to a full-scale national launch of a new brand or product. The idea is to choose a relatively small, reasonably isolated, yet somehow demographically "typical" market area. The total marketing plan for the item, including advertising, promotions, and distribution tactics, is "rolled out" and implemented in the test market, and measurements of product awareness, market penetration, and market share are made. While these data are used to estimate potential sales to a larger national market, the emphasis here is usually on "fine-tuning" the total marketing plan and insuring that no problems or potential embarrassments have been overlooked. For example, Proctor and Gamble extensively test-marketed its Pringles potato chip product made with the fat substitute Olestra to assure that the product would be broadly acceptable to the market.
4. **Scanner Panel Data** procedures have recently been developed that permit demand experimentation on existing brands and products. In these procedures, a large set of household customers agrees to participate in an ongoing study of their grocery buying habits. Panel members agree to submit information about the number of individuals in the household, their ages, household income, and so forth. Whenever they buy groceries at a supermarket participating in the research, their household identity is captured along with the identity and price of every item they purchased. This is straightforward due to the use of UPC codes and optical scanners at checkout. This

procedure results in a rich database of observed customer buying behaviour. The analyst is in a position to see each purchase in light of the full set of alternatives to the chosen brand that were available in the store at the time of purchase, including all other brands, prices, sizes, discounts, deals, coupon offers, and so on. Statistical models such as discrete choice models can be used to analyze the relationships in the data. The manufacturer and merchandiser are now in a position to test a price promotion and estimate its probable effect on brand loyalty and brand switching behaviour among customers in general. This approach can develop valuable insight into demand behaviour at the customer level, but once again it can be difficult to extend this insight directly into demand forecasts in the logistics system.

Complex Statistical Methods

We shall now move from simple to complex set of methods of demand forecasting. Such methods are taken usually from statistics. As such, you may be quite familiar with some the statistical tools and techniques, as a part of quantitative methods for business decisions.

1. Time Series Analysis or Trend Method: Under this method, the time series data on the under forecast are used to fit a trend line or curve either graphically or through statistical method of Least Squares. The trend line is worked out by fitting a trend equation to time series data with the aid of an estimation method. The trend equation could take either a linear or any kind of non-linear form. The trend method outlined above often yields a dependable forecast. The advantage in this method is that it does not require the formal knowledge of economic theory and the market; it only needs the time series data. The only limitation in this method is that it assumes that the past is repeated in future. It is an appropriate method for long-run forecasts, but inappropriate for short-run forecasts. Sometimes the time series analysis may not reveal a significant trend of any kind. In that case, the moving average method or exponentially weighted moving average method is used to smoothen the series.

2. Barometric Techniques or Lead-Lag Indicators Method: This consists in discovering a set of series of some variables which exhibit a close association in their movement over a period of time.

For example, it shows the movement of agricultural income (AY series) and the sale of tractors (ST series). The movement of AY is similar to that of ST, but the movement in ST takes place after a year's time lag compared to the movement in AY. Thus, if one knows the direction of the movement in agriculture income (AY), one can predict the direction of movement of tractors' sale (ST) for the next year. Thus agricultural income (AY) may be used as a barometer to help the short-term forecast for the sale of tractors.

Generally, this barometric method has been used in some of the developed countries for predicting business cycles situation. For this purpose, some countries construct what are known as 'diffusion indices' by combining the movement of a number of leading series in the economy so that turning points in business activity could be discovered well in advance. Some of the limitations of this method may be noted however. The leading indicator method does not tell you anything about the magnitude of the change that can be expected in the lagging series, but only the direction of change. The lead period itself may change overtime. Through our estimation we may find out the best-fitted lag period on the past data, but the same may not be true for the future. Finally, it may not be always possible to find out the leading, lagging or coincident indicators of the variable for which a demand forecast is being attempted.

3. Correlation and Regression: These involve the use of econometric methods to determine the nature and degree of association between/among a set of variables. Econometrics, you may recall, is the use of economic theory, statistical analysis and mathematical functions to determine the relationship between a dependent variable (say, sales) and one or more independent variables (like price, income, advertisement, etc.). The relationship may be expressed in the form of a demand function. Such relationships, based on past data can be used for forecasting. The analysis can be carried with varying degrees of complexity. Here, we shall not get into the methods of finding out 'correlation coefficient' or 'regression equation'; you must have covered those statistical techniques as a part of quantitative methods. Similarly, we shall not go into the question of economic theory. We shall concentrate simply on the use of these econometric techniques in forecasting.

We are on the realm of multiple regressions and multiple correlation. The form of the equation may be:

$$D_X = a + b_1 A + b_2 P_X + b_3 P_y$$

You know that the regression coefficients b_1, b_2, b_3 and b_4 are the components of relevant elasticity of demand. For example, b_1 is a component of price elasticity of demand. This reflects the direction as well as proportion of change in demand for x as a result of a change in any of its explanatory variables. For example, $b_2 < 0$ suggest that D_X and P_X are inversely related; $b_4 > 0$ suggest that x and y are substitutes; $b_3 > 0$ suggest that x is a normal commodity with commodity with positive income-effect.

Given the estimated value of and b_i, you may forecast the expected sales (D_X), if you know the future values of explanatory variables like own price (P_X), related price (P_y), income (B) and advertisement (A). Lastly, you may also recall that the statistics R2 (Co-efficient of determination) gives the measure of goodness of fit. The closer it is to unity, the better is the fit, and that way you get a more reliable forecast.

The principle advantage of this method is that it is prescriptive as well descriptive. That is, besides generating demand forecast, it explains why the demand is? What it is? In other words, this technique has got both explanatory and predictive value. The regression method is neither mechanistic like the trend method nor subjective like the opinion poll method. In this method of forecasting, you may use not only time-series data but also cross section data. The only precaution you need to take is that data analysis should be based on the logic of economic theory.

4. Simultaneous Equations Method: Here is a very sophisticated method of forecasting. It is also known as the 'complete system approach' or 'econometric model building'. In your earlier units, we have made reference to such econometric models. Presently we do not intend to get into the details of this method because it is a subject by itself. Moreover, this method is normally used in macro-level forecasting for the economy as a whole; in this course, our focus is limited to micro elements only. Of course, you, as corporate managers, should know the basic elements in such an approach.

The method is indeed very complicated. However, in the days of computer, when package programmes are available, this method can be used easily to derive meaningful forecasts. The principle advantage in this method is that the forecaster needs to estimate the future values of only the exogenous variables unlike the regression method where he has to predict the future values of all, endogenous and exogenous variables affecting the variable under forecast. The values of exogenous variables are easier to predict than those of the endogenous variables. However, such econometric models have limitations, similar to that of regression method.

Market Segmentation

A market refers to a set up where two or more parties are involved in transaction of goods and services in exchange of money. The two parties here are known as sellers and buyers.

It is the responsibility of the marketers to create awareness of their products amongst the consumers. It is essential for the individuals to be aware of the brand's existence. The USPs of the brands must be communicated well to the end-users.

An organization can't afford to have similar strategies for product promotion amongst all individuals. Not every individual has the same requirement and demand.

The marketers thus came with the concept of **STP**.

STP stands for:

S – Segmentation

T – Targeting

P - Positioning

The first step in the process of product promotion is **Segmentation**

The division of a broad market into small segments comprising of individuals who think on the same lines and show inclination towards similar products and brands is called Market Segmentation.

Market Segmentation refers to the process of creation of small groups (segments) within a large market to bring together consumers who have similar requirements, needs and interests.

The individuals in a particular segment respond to similar market fluctuations and require identical products.

In simpler words market segmentation can also be called as **Grouping**.

Kids form one segment; males can be part of a similar segment while females form another segment. Students belong to a particular segment whereas professionals and office goers can be kept in one segment.

Basis of Market Segmentation

Gender

The marketers divide the market into smaller segments based on gender. Both men and women have different interests and preferences, and thus the need for segmentation. Organizations need to have different marketing strategies for men which would obviously not work in case of females. A woman would not purchase a product meant for males and vice versa. The segmentation of the market as per the gender is important in many industries like cosmetics, footwear, jewellery and apparel industries.

Age Group

Division on the basis of age group of the target audience is also one of the ways of market segmentation.

The products and marketing strategies for teenagers would obviously be different than kids.

Age group (0 - 10 years) - Toys, Nappies, Baby Food, Prams

Age Group (10 - 20 years) - Toys, Apparels, Books, School Bags

Age group (20 years and above) - Cosmetics, Anti-Ageing Products, Magazines, Apparels and so on

Income

Marketers divide the consumers into small segments as per their income. Individuals are classified into segments according to their monthly earnings.

The three categories are:

High Income Group

Mid Income Group

Low Income Group

Stores catering to the higher income group would have different range of products and strategies as compared to stores which target the lower income group.

Pantaloon, Carrefour, Shopper's stop target the high income group as compared to Vishal Retail, Reliance Retail or Big Bazaar who cater to the individuals belonging to the lower income segment.

Marital Status

Market segmentation can also be as per the marital status of the individuals. Travel agencies would not have similar holiday packages for bachelors and married couples.

Occupation

Office goers would have different needs as compared to school / college students. A beach house shirt or a funky T Shirt would have no takers in a Zodiac Store as it caters specifically to the professionals.

Types of Market Segmentation

Psychographic Segmentation

The basis of such segmentation is the **lifestyle** of the individuals. The individual's attitude, interest, value help the marketers to classify them into small groups.

Behaviouralistic Segmentation

The **loyalties** of the customers towards a particular brand help the marketers to classify them into smaller groups, each group comprising of individuals loyal towards a particular brand.

Geographic Segmentation

Geographic segmentation refers to the classification of market into various **geographical areas**. A marketer can't have similar strategies for individuals living at different places.

Nestle promotes Nescafe all through the year in cold states of the country as compared to places which have well defined summer and winter season.

McDonald's in India does not sell beef products as it is strictly against the religious beliefs of the countrymen, whereas McDonald's in US freely sells and promotes beef products.

Targeting & Positioning

Targeting

Once the marketer creates different segments within the market, he then devises various marketing strategies and promotional schemes according to the tastes of the individuals of particular segment. This process is called targeting. Once market segments are created, organization then targets them.

Targeting is the **second stage** and is done once the markets have been segmented. Organizations with the help of various marketing plans and schemes target their products amongst the various segments.

Nokia offers handsets for almost all the segments. They understand their target audience well and each of their handsets fulfils the needs and expectations of the target market.

Tata Motors launched Tata Nano especially for the lower income group.

Positioning

Positioning is the last stage in the Segmentation Targeting Positioning Cycle. Once the organization decides on its target market, it strives hard to create an **image of its product** in the **minds** of the consumers. The marketers create a first impression of the product in the minds of consumers through positioning.

Positioning helps organizations to create a perception of the products in the minds of target audience. Ray Ban and Police Sunglasses cater to the premium segment while Vintage or Fastrack sunglasses target the middle income group. Ray Ban sunglasses have no takers amongst the lower income group.

Garnier offers wide range of merchandise for both men and women.

Each of their brands has been targeted well amongst the specific market segments. (Men, women, teenagers as well as older generation)

Men - Sunscreen lotions, Deodorant

Women - Daily skin care products, hair care products

Teenagers - Hair colour products, Garnier Light (Fairness cream)

Older Generation - Cream to fight signs of ageing, wrinkles

A female would never purchase a sunscreen lotion meant for men and vice versa. That's brand positioning.

Product Decisions

Product decisions need to be made after researching the target market and with the needs of that market in mind. Questions like, "What does the customer want and need?" and "How will the customer use it?" are examples of the answers required to make good product decisions. "What does it look like?" and "How will it be unique?" are some other great questions. The Product – market manager is going to have to make decisions about things like: quality, design, sizes, warranties, returns, brand name, features, functionality, colour, safety, repairs, support, styling, accessories and much more.

These are not static decisions because every product is subject to the product life cycle that includes introduction, growth, maturity and decline stages that will require modifications to the product decisions to remain competitive and optimize profitability at each stage.

It is also possible that if the product is being sold into multiple markets that it may be beneficial to have a custom offering for each market.

Classification of Products

Marketers are required to plan marketing activities for all type of products. To design marketing plan efficiently and effectively it is necessary to understand the product belongs to different categories and each category requires different plan. There can be three bases for the classification of product.

(i) Durability

(ii) Users

(iii) Visibility

(i) Durability

On the basis of durability, product can be further classified into two categories:

- Durable Goods
- Non-durable Goods

Goods that can be used **for a longer period of time** and can survive many uses are called durable goods for example, T.V., refrigerator, clothes, etc.

Goods that can be used **for shorter span of time** or are of perishable nature and can survive few uses are called non-durable goods for example, bread, butter, etc.

(ii) Visibility

On the basis of tangibility, a product can be classified into two categories:

- Tangible Goods
- Intangible Goods

Products that can be seen, felt are called tangible good for example, mobiles, computers, etc.

Products that can't be seen and can only be felt are called intangible products for example, banking services, insurance, etc.

(iii) Users

On the basis of users, a product can be classified into following categories:

- Consumer Goods
- Industrial Goods

Consumer goods are the goods consumed by final consumer to satisfy his/her needs. Industrial goods are basically intermediate goods used for the production of consumer goods.

As the name describes consumer goods are used by consumers and industrial goods are used by industries.

Consumer Goods can be further classified into following categories:

- Convenience Goods
- Shopping Goods
- Specialty Goods
- Unsought

Convenience goods are those goods that are **purchased with minimum efforts**, frequently and for immediate consumption. e. g. soaps, shampoos, toothpaste, matchstick, etc.

Goods for which consumer will make certain efforts and **spend time** in comparing price, quality, features, style, uniqueness, etc. are called **shopping goods**. e. g. clothes, watch, purse, mobile, etc.

Goods which are associated with a **brand name** and provide some unique benefits are called **specialty goods.** Specialty goods are associated with brand loyal consumers. For specialty goods consumer makes special efforts for buying them. For these goods, consumer don't mind spending extra time, or travelling long distances.

There are many goods about which consumers are not aware and don't think of buying those goods in normal course are called **unsought goods.** Unsought goods exist in the market but consumers are either **not aware** of them or may have some misconceptions about them or their usage or their effectiveness. e. g. smoke detectors, dishwashers, etc.

Industrial goods can also be classified into following categories:

- Material and Parts
    - o Raw material

- o Fabricated material and parts
- o Capital Items
    - Installations
    - Equipment
    - Supplies and Business Services
    - Supplies
    - Maintenance and repair items
    - Operating supplies
- Business services
    - o Maintenance services
    - o Business advisory services

Product Mix

Product mix, also known as product **assortment**, refers to the **total number of product lines** that a company offers to its customers. For example, a small company may sell multiple lines of products. Sometimes, these product lines are fairly similar, such as dish washing liquid and bar soap, which are used for cleaning and use similar technologies. Other times, the product lines are vastly different, such as diapers and razors. The four dimensions to a company's product mix include **width, length, depth and consistency**.

Width

The width of a company's product mix pertains to the **number of product lines** that a company sells. For example, if a company has two product lines, its product mix width is two. Small and upstart businesses will usually not have a wide product mix. It is more practical to start with some basic products and build market share. Later on, a company's technology may allow the company to diversify into other industries and build the width of the product mix.

Length

Product mix length pertains to the **number of total products** or items in a company's product mix, according to Philip Kotler's textbook "Marketing Management: Analysis, Planning, Implementation and Control." For example, ABC Company may have two product lines, and five brands within each product line. Thus, ABC's product mix length would be 10. Companies that have multiple product lines will sometimes keep track of their average length per product line. In the above case, the average length of an ABC Company's product line is five.

Depth

Depth of a product mix pertains to the **total number of variations for each product**. Variations can include size, flavour and any other distinguishing characteristic. For example, if a company sells three sizes and two flavours of toothpaste, that particular brand of toothpaste has a depth of six. Just like length, companies sometimes report the average depth of their product lines; or the depth of a specific product line.

Consistency

Product mix consistency pertains to how closely related product lines are to one another in terms of use, production and distribution. A company's product mix may be consistent in distribution but vastly different in use. For example, a small company may sell its health bars and health magazine in retail stores. However, one product is edible and the other is not. The production consistency of these products would vary as well.

Product Mix Example

Coca Cola has product brands like minute maid, sprite, Fanta, thumps up, etc. under its name. These constitute the **width of the product mix**. There are a total of 3500 products handled by the Coca Cola brand. These constitute the **length**. Minute maid juice has different variants like apple juice, mixed fruit, etc. They constitute the **depth of the product line** 'Minute Maid'. Coca Cola deals majorly with drinking beverage products and hence has more **product mix consistency**.

Let us take an example of P&G as a company and understand product mix. This will not be a precise example and all products of P&G might not be taken into consideration. But the example will help you understand product mix within an organization.

Detergents – Arial, Arial oxyblue, Ariel bar, Tide, Tide naturals, Tide bleach, Tide plus.

Shampoos – Head and shoulders, Head and shoulders anti dandruff, Pantene, Pantene damage repair, Pantene pro-v

In the above example the following can be learned about the product mix of P&G

Product mix Length – **12**

Product mix Width – **2**

Product mix Depth – **7** in detergents and **5** in shampoos

Product mix Consistency – **High** as both are bathroom products.

Product Life Cycle

As consumers, we buy millions of products every year. These products have a life cycle. Older, long-established products eventually become less popular, while in contrast, the demand for new, more modern goods usually increases quite rapidly after they are launched.

Because most companies understand the different product life cycle stages, and that the products they sell all have a limited lifespan, the majority of them will invest heavily in new product development in order to make sure that their businesses continue to grow.

Product Life Cycle Stages

The product life cycle has 4 very clearly defined stages, each with its own characteristics that mean different things for business that are trying to manage the life cycle of their particular products.

Introduction Stage: This stage of the cycle could be the most expensive for a company launching a new product. The size of the market for the product is small, which means sales are low, although they will be increasing. On the other hand, the cost of things likes research and development, consumer testing, and the marketing needed to launch the product can be very high, especially if it is a competitive sector.

Growth Stage: The growth stage is typically characterized by a strong growth in sales and profits, and because the company can start to benefit from economies of scale in production, the profit margins, as well as the overall amount of profit, will increase. This makes it possible for businesses to invest more money in the promotional activity to maximize the potential of this growth stage.

Maturity Stage: During the maturity stage, the product is established and the aim for the manufacturer is now to maintain the market share they have built up. This is probably the most competitive time for most products and businesses need to invest wisely in any marketing they undertake. They also need to consider any product modifications or improvements to the production process which might give them a competitive advantage.

Decline Stage: Eventually, the market for a product will start to shrink, and this is what's known as the decline stage. This shrinkage could be due to the market becoming saturated (i.e. all the customers who will buy the product have already purchased it), or because the consumers are switching to a different type of product. While this decline may be inevitable, it may still be possible for companies to make some profit by switching to less-expensive production methods and cheaper markets.

New Product Development

Improving and updating products is an ongoing task as consumer 'needs and wants' continuously change. A failure to develop products could result in a reduction in sales if consumers decide to buy competitor products. Learn more about the reasons why firms should develop new products. The eight stages of new product development are captured in the diagram below.

Stage 1: Idea Generation

New product ideas have to come from somewhere. But where do organizations get their ideas for NPD? Sources include:

- Market Research
- Employees
- Consultants
- Competitors
- Customers
- Distributors and Suppliers

Stage 2: Idea Screening

This process involves shifting through the ideas generated above and selecting ones which are feasible and practical to develop. Pursing impractical ideas is expensive and a waste of resources.

Stage 3: Concept Development and Testing

The organisation may have come across what they believe to be a feasible idea; however, the idea needs to be taken to the target audience. What do they think about the idea? Will it offer the benefit that the organisation hopes it will? or have they overlooked certain issues? Will there be a demand for the product? Note the idea taken to the target audience is not a working prototype at this stage, it is just a concept.

Stage 4: Marketing Strategy and Development

How will the product/service idea be launched within the market? A proposed marketing strategy will be written laying out the marketing mix strategy of the product, the segmentation, targeting and positioning strategy and expected sales and profits.

Stage 5: Business Analysis

The company has a great idea, the marketing strategy seems feasible, but will the product be financially worthwhile in the long run? The business analysis stage looks more deeply into the Cash flow the product could generate, what the cost will be, likely market share and the expected life of the product.

Stage 6: Product Development

At this stage, the prototype is produced. The prototype will undergo serious tests, and will be presented to a selection of people made up of the target market segment to see if changes need to be made.

Stage 7: Test Marketing

Test marketing means testing the product within a specific geographic area. The product will be launched within a particular region so the marketing mix strategy can be monitored and if needed modified before national launch.

Stage 8: Commercialization

If test marketing is successful, the product is ready for national launch. The following decisions regarding the launch need to be made

- Timing of the launch
- How the product will be launched?
- Where the product will be launched?
- Will there be a national roll out or will it be region by region?

Branding & Packaging

Branding

Branding is a process of creating a unique name and image for a product in the mind of consumer, mainly through advertising campaigns. A brand is a **name**, **term**, **symbol**, **design** or combination of these elements, used to identify a product, a family of products, or all products of an organisation.

Branding is an important component of product planning process and an important and powerful tool for marketing and selling products.

According to **American Marketing Association** - Brand is "A name, term, design, symbol, or any other feature that identifies one seller's good or service as distinct from those of other sellers. The legal term for brand is trademark. A brand may identify one item, a family of items, or all items of that seller. If used for the firm as a whole, the preferred term is trade name."

According to **Philip Kotler** - "**Brand** is a name, term, sign, symbol, design, or a combination of them, intended to identify the goods or services of one seller or group of sellers and to differentiate them from those of competitors"

Branding is "a seller's promise to deliver a specific set of features, benefits and services consistent to the buyers."

Elements of Branding

Brand includes various elements like - brand names, trade names, brand marks, trademarks, and trade characters. The combinations of these elements form a firm's corporate symbol or name.

Brand Name: It is also called Product Brand. It can be a word, a group of words, letters, or numbers to represent a product or service. For example - Pepsi, iPhone 5, and etc.

Trade Name: It is also called Corporate Brand. It identifies and promotes a company or a division of a particular corporation. For example - Dell, Nike, Google, and etc.

Brand Mark: It is a unique symbol, colouring, lettering, or other design element. It is visually recognizable, not necessary to be pronounced. For example – Apple's apple, or Coca-Cola's cursive typeface.

Trade Mark: It is a word, name, symbol, or combination of these elements. Trade mark is **legally protected** by government. For example - NBC colourful peacock, or McDonald's golden arches. No other organisation can use these symbols.

Trade Characters: Animal, people, animated characters, objects, and the like that are used to advertise a product or service, that come to be associated with that product or service. For example - Keebler Elves for Keebler cookies

Branding Strategies

There are various branding strategies on which marketing organizations rely to meet sales and marketing objectives. Some of these strategies are as follows:

(i) **Brand Extension:** According to this strategy, an existing brand name is used to promote a new or an improved product in an organization's product line. Marketing organizations uses this strategy to minimize the cost of launching a new product and the risk of failure of new product. There is risk of brand diluting if a product line is over extended.

(ii) **Brand Licensing:** According to this strategy, some organizations allow other organizations to use their brand name, trade name, or trade character. Such authorization is a legal licensing agreement for which the licensing organisation receives royalty in return for the authorization. Organizations' follow this strategy to increase revenue sources, enhance organisation image, and sell more of their core products.

(iii) **Mixed Branding:** This strategy is used by some manufacturers and retailers to sell products. A manufacturer of a national brand can make a product for sale under another company's brand. Like this a business can maintain brand loyalty through its national brand and increase its product mix through private brands. It can increase its profits by selling private brands without affecting the reputation and sales of its national brand.

(iv) Co-Branding: According to this strategy, one or more brands are combined in the manufacture of a product or in the delivery of a service to capitalize on other companies' products and services to reach new customers and increase sales for both companies' brands.

Packaging

Packaging refers to all those activities related to designing, evaluating and producing the container for a product. Simply, the box-like container, wherein the product is stored to protect it from any physical damage and at the same time attracting the customer through its appeal is called as packaging.

The product might have three layers of packaging, such as, a toothpaste come in the **plastic tube** (primary package), then it is packed in a **cardboard box** (secondary package) and then finally is packed in a **corrugated box** (shipping or third package). Nowadays, the packaging is not limited to the protection of a product alone, but it has been used as a marketing tool for building the brand equity and boosting sales.

In today's scenario, most of the companies use packaging as an important marketing tool because of the following factors:

(i) The packaging enables the **self-service**; as in the case of purchases done in the supermarkets and retail mart the customers select the products on their own without any assistance from the retailers. Thus, the company must design its product package in such a way, that it is capable enough to draw customer's attention towards it.

(ii) It helps in increasing the **consumer affluence**, which means the customers are willing to pay even more for the convenience, appearance, dependability of the better packages.

(iii) The packages help in increasing the **brand recognition** among the customers. As soon as the customers see the package, they can instantly relate it to the company or brand. For example, the Brooke Bond's Taj Mahal Tea comes in the blue pack with an image of a Taj Mahal on its box; this gives an identity to the brand.

(iv) The **innovative packaging** also helps in bringing huge profits and benefits for the firm. Here, the company gives a unique design to its product package with the intent to grab customer's attention. For example, the calcium Sandoz bottles targeted at children and women have been designed to make them attractive to the target segment (A dog shaped bottle for kids, while a lady-shaped bottle for women).

Thus, the packaging is capable of influencing a buyer to initiate sales since the buyer comes in contact with the package first and then after with the product.

Basic Functions of Packaging in Marketing a Product

Packaging performs five basic functions: (1) Protection (2) Containment (3) Information (4) Utility of Use (5) Promotion

(1) Protection: One of the major functions of packaging is to provide for the ravages of time and environment for the natural and manufactured products. The protection function can be divided into some classes viz.

- **A. Natural Deterioration:** It is caused by the interaction of products with water, gases and fumes, microbiologic organisms like bacteria, yeasts and moulds, heat, cold, desiccation (dry environment in deserts and high-altitude areas), contaminants and insects and rodents.
- **B. Physical Protection:** The packaging is also used for physical protection, which include improving shock protection, internal product protection and reducing shock damage caused from vibration, snagging, friction and impact.
- **C. Safety:** A special kind of protective packaging is required for products that are deemed hazardous to those who transport them or use them. These product include highly inflammable gas and liquid, radioactive elements, toxic materials, etc. The packaging should also be done so that children could not easily use or dispose them.
- **D. Waste Reduction:** Packaging also serves to reduce the amount of waste especially in case of food distribution

(2) Containment: This involves consolidation of unit loads for shipping. It starts with spots of adhesives on the individual shippers that stick them together, straps of steel and plastic, entire shrouds of shrinkable or stretchable plastic films and paper or corrugated wraps that surround an entire pallet of product.

There are some special bulk boxes or pallet bins made from unusually strong corrugated board or fabricated form plastics or metal, the method of which depends on the type and weight of product and its protective needs. The cargo containers made of aluminum used to hold many pallet loads of goods can be transferred to or from ships, trains and flatbed trucks by giant cranes.

(3) Information: The packaging conveys necessary information to the consumers. The common information that packaging provides include general features of the product, ingredients, net weight of the contents, name and address of the manufacturers, maximum retail price (MRP).

Packaging of medicine and some food products is required to provide information on methods of preparations, recipes and serving ideas, nutritional benefits, and date of manufacturing, date of expiry, warning messages and cautionary information. Sometimes, the colour of the packaging itself provides some information. For example, orange colour of the bottle of Mirinda or Fanta conveys the information that these brands are of orange coloured soft drinks.

(4) Utility of Use: The convenience packaging has been devised for foods, household chemicals, drugs, adhesives, paints, cosmetics, paper goods and a host of other products. This type of packaging includes dispensing devices, prepackaged hot metals, disposable medical packaging.

(5) Promotion: Companies use attractive colours, logos, symbols and captions to promote the product that can influence customer purchase decision.

Pricing Methods & Strategies

Pricing methods or pricing strategies in marketing

There are different pricing methods or strategies which are used by the marketer to attract the customer.

1. **Cost Based Pricing:** This type of pricing strategies uses break even concept which means the point where the total cost = total revenue. Profit will be zero at breakeven point. At level where the total revenue > total cost, there is profit and where total revenue< total cost, there is loss.
2. **Demand Based Pricing:** It is of two types;
   (A) **Skimming Pricing:** It means skim the market initially with **high price** and high profit, later settle down for the lower price. It means skim the cream initially from the market.
   (B) **Penetration Pricing:** It seeks to achieve high sale with **low price**. It is generally used when there are non luxury goods.
3. **Competition Oriented Pricing:** In a competitive market, the companies generally opt for this.pricing strategy. It has three types.
   (A) **Premium Pricing:** It means price above the competitor's price.
   (B) **Discount Pricing:** It means price below the competitor's price.
   (C) **Parity Pricing:** It means price equals to the competitor's price.
4. **Value Pricing:** This method is used when the objective is not to recover the cost of the product but to judge the value of the product in the eyes of the customer.
5. **Product Line Pricing:** In this case, the company need not fix the price for each product rather they fix the price for the entire product line which results in optimal sales through optimal profit.

6. **Sealed Bid or Tender Pricing:** This is suitable for those companies where institutional customers call the tenders from the companies. The best and lowest price tender is accepted.
7. **Affordable or Social Welfare Pricing:** The pricing is done in such a way that all the segments of the market afford to buy and consume the product as per their need. Like government subsidy help each segment of the consumer to buy the product at an affordable pricing.
8. **Differentiated Pricing:** In this case, different price is charged by the company from the different segment. Like charging low price from the whole sellers and high price from the retailers.
9. **Psychological Pricing:** Many sellers use this technique of selling the product. Like 99 store.
10. **Target Pricing:** Here the price is fixed at **full cost + mark up**.
11. **Loss Leader:** Sometimes firm sell multiple products, charge relatively low price on some popular product with the hope that customer who will buy this product will also buy the other product of the firm.
12. **Cyclical Pricing:** In depression, firm reduce the price of the product while in boom increases the price.
13. **Suggested Pricing:** In this case, the manufacturer or whole seller suggests the retailer to charge this price from the customers.

All the above discussed are the general pricing strategies used by the marketer.

Promotion Decisions

In the context of the marketing mix, promotion represents the various aspects of marketing communication, that is, the **communication of information** about the product with the goal of generating a positive customer response.

Promotion decisions include:

(i) Promotional Strategy (push, pull, etc)

(ii) Advertising

(iii) Personal Selling & Sales Force

(iv) Sales Promotions

(v) Public Relations & Publicity

(vi) Marketing Communications Budget

Promotion Mix

The **Promotion Mix** refers to the blend of several promotional tools used by the business to create, maintain and increase the demand for goods and services.

The fourth element of the 4 P's of Marketing Mix is the promotion; that focuses on creating the awareness and persuading the customers to initiate the purchase. The several tools that facilitate the promotion objective of a firm are collectively known as the Promotion Mix.

The Promotion Mix is the integration of Advertising, Personal Selling, Sales Promotion, Public Relations, Direct Marketing and Publicity. The marketers need to view the following questions in order to have a balanced blend of these promotional tools.

- What is the most effective way to inform the customers?
- Which marketing methods to be used?
- To whom the promotion efforts to be directed?
- What is the marketing budget? How is it to be allocated to the promotional tools?

Elements of Promotion Mix

(i) Advertising: The advertising is any **paid form of non-personal presentation** and promotion of goods and services by the identified sponsor in the exchange of a fee. Through advertising, the marketer tries to build a pull strategy; wherein the customer is instigated to try the product at least once. The complete information along with the attractive graphics of the product or service can be shown to the customers that grab their attention and influences the purchase decision.

(ii) Personal Selling: This is one of the traditional forms of promotional tool wherein the salesman interacts with the customer directly by visiting them. It is a face to face interaction between the company representative and the customer with the objective to influence the customer to purchase the product or services.

(iii) Sales Promotion: The sales promotion is the short term incentives given to the customers to have an increased sale for a given period. Generally, the sales promotion schemes are floated in the market at the time of festivals or the end of the season. Discounts, Coupons, Payback Offers, Freebies, etc. are some of the sales promotion schemes. With the sales promotion, the company focuses on the increased short term profits, by attracting both the existing and the new customers.

(iv) Public Relations: The marketers try to build a favourable image in the market by creating relations with the general public. The companies carry out several public relations campaigns with the objective to have a support of all the people associated with it either directly or indirectly. The public comprises of the customers, employees, suppliers, distributors, shareholders, government and the society as a whole. The publicity is one of the forms of public relations that company may use with the intention to bring newsworthy information to the public. E.g. Large Corporates such as Dabur, L&T, Tata Consultancy, Bharti Enterprises, Sęrvices, Unitech and PSU's such as Indian Oil, GAIL, and NTPC have joined hands with Government to clean up their surroundings, build toilets and support the swachh Bharat Mission.

(v) Direct Marketing: With the intent of technology, companies reach customers directly without any intermediaries or any paid medium. The e-mails, text messages, Fax, are some of the tools of direct marketing. The companies can send the emails and messages to the customers if they need to be informed about the new offerings or the sales promotion schemes. E.g. The Shopperstop sends SMS to its members informing about the season end sales and extra benefits to the golden card holders.

(vi) Publicity: Publicity is also a way of mass communication. It is not a paid form of mass communication that involves getting favourable response of buyers by placing commercially significant news in mass media. William J. Stanton defines: "Publicity is any promotional communication regarding an organisation and/or its products where the message is not paid for by the organisation benefiting from it."

It is the traditional form of public relations. Publicity is not paid for by the organisation. Publicity comes from reporters, columnists, and journalists. It can be considered as a part of public relations. Publicity involves giving public speeches, giving interviews, conducting seminars, charitable donations, inauguration by film actor, cricketer, politician or popular personalities, stage show, etc., that attract mass media to publish the news about them.

Thus, the companies can use any tool of the promotion mix depending on the nature of a product as well as the overall objective of the firm.

Advertising

Advertising can be defined as the act of drawing the attention of the target audience, towards a product or service. It is an impersonal, paid message, delivered to the general public with the sole aim of creating demand for the product and thus increasing sales. It has a great role to play in marketing, to make people aware of the product.

The sponsors of the advertisement have full control over it. The advertising message is aired through various channels like radio, television, magazines, newspapers, posters, billboards, websites, blogs, apps, text messages, social networks, e-mail, etc.

Advertising aims at creating such an image in the minds of the audience, that they are instigated to purchase that product. The greatest advantage of advertising is its range, i.e. it reaches a large number of people in one go.

Types of Advertising Media Available to an Advertiser

Nine types of advertising media available to an advertiser are: (1) direct mail (2) newspapers and magazines (3) radio advertising (4) television advertising (5) film advertising (6) outdoor advertising (7) window display (8) fairs and exhibition and (9) specially advertising

(1) Direct Mail: This is one of the oldest types of advertising media. Under this method, message is sent to the prospective buyers by post. A mailing list is prepared for this purpose. Circular letters, folders, calendars, booklets and catalogues are sent under this type of advertising. In the sales letter, an appeal is made to the buyers separately.

It contains detailed information with regard to the product. The main aim of these letters is to create the reader's interest in the product. The letter should be attractive, interesting and convincing. Booklets and catalogues contain information regarding detailed description and prices of different varieties of products.

This method is very effective as it establishes direct contact with the consumer and also maintains secrecy in advertising. Detailed information with regard to the product can be sent to the buyers. The letters and circulars contain personal appeals which are greatly helpful in arousing their interest in the products. This method can be effectively undertaken in case the manufacturers are selling directly to the consumers.

Direct mail advertising suffers from certain drawbacks also. It has limited access i.e. a small number of buyers can be covered. There are practical difficulties in preparing and maintaining up-to-date mailing list. This is also not suitable for every type of product.

(2) Newspapers and Magazines: These are the important forms of press advertising, newspapers are the most effective and powerful medium of advertising. Newspapers contain valuable information with regard to different current events. It may be referred to as 'a store house of information'. There are daily, bi-weekly and weekly newspapers. Newspapers have widest circulation and read by many people. The newspapers may be local, provincial or national.

There is a separate advertisement department in every newspaper which classifies and designs different advertisements in the paper. Before selecting a newspaper, the advertiser should take into consideration various factors viz., coverage of the newspaper, the class of customers and the cost of advertising, etc.

The newspapers offer widest circulation and have universal appeal. The cost of advertising is lesser as compared to other media. The newspapers have more repetitive value and are very helpful in introducing a new product. These are suitable for all types of goods having **wider markets**.

A high degree of flexibility is ensured by newspapers i.e., the advertisement campaign can be undertaken and stopped quickly. Advertisements are the main source of revenue to the publishers. The most important benefit derived from the newspapers is that the advertiser's message can be conveyed to the readers quickly.

Besides newspapers suffer from certain drawbacks also. They have shorter life and are not suitable for illiterate people. Most of the people read the papers casually especially in the morning hours when they are in a hurry to join their respective jobs.

Secrecy cannot be maintained in this type of advertising. Another drawback of newspaper advertising is that they are in black and white prints. Coloured advertisements are not covered, which are more appealing and attractive.

Magazines

Magazines or periodicals are other important media of communication. Magazines may be released weekly, monthly, quarterly, bi-annual or annual. These are read with more interest by the readers as compared to newspapers. Advertisements given in magazines are more descriptive and attractive. They are usually in coloured form which depicts the product nicely and gives lasting impression to the reader.

There are magazines or journals meant for general public and special class of people. There are exclusive magazines relating to industry, trade, finance and economics, etc. There are also special magazines for men, women and children. The magazines have longer life and are very suitable for advertising specific goods.

Magazines have lesser flexibility as compared to newspapers. Last minute changes cannot be introduced in the advertisement as they are sent to the press many days before the publication. There is lesser repetitive value and no secrecy can be maintained.

Cost of advertising is higher as compared to newspapers. Their circulations are small and are suitable for educated readers only. In the introduction of a new product, magazines are not much suitable on account of lesser continuity.

(3) Radio Advertising: Radio advertising is very popular these days. The advertisements are broadcasted from different stations of All India Radio. Radio advertising can be explained as "word of mouth advertising on a wholesale scale". The advertising messages can be in different regional languages.

The most important advantage derived from radio advertising is that it covers every type of listener whether illiterate or educated. It is a very effective medium for popularizing on mass scale various consumer articles. The coverage of this medium is wider extending to a large number of listeners. It ensures quicker repetition.

Radio advertising suffers from shorter life, limited memory and short messages. Cost of advertising is higher. The message may not be listened properly by the listener. There is no secrecy. This is useful for those who possess radio sets. There is lesser flexibility and lack of personal touch.

(4) Television Advertising: This is the latest and the fast developing medium of advertising and is getting increased popularity these days. It is more effective as compared to radio as it has the advantages of sound and sight. On account of pictorial presentation, it is more effective and impressive and leaves ever lasting impression on the mind of the viewer.

It is a very costly medium which can be employed by big concerns only; it has a shorter life span and limited coverage. Back reference to the advertisement cannot be made after its presentation. The duration of the advertisement is very limited.

Despite of the above mentioned drawbacks, this method of advertising is gaining rapid coverage and immense popularity among the masses.

(5) Film Advertising: This is also known as cinema advertising. This also provides sight and hearing facilities like television. Short advertisement films are not prepared by big business houses which are sent to different cinema houses to be shown to the audience before the regular shows or during the intermission. It has more repetitive value but not to the same viewers. Its coverage is limited which benefits the local population only.

It is a very costly medium involving higher distribution and film making costs. Only big organizations can afford to produce advertisement films. It ensures more flexibility at larger costs. Its effectiveness cannot be measured properly. Film making is a time consuming process.

(6) Outdoor Advertising: This type of advertising include different media like posters, placards, electric displays or neon signs, sandwich men, sky writing, bus, train and tram advertising. This is also known as '**Mural Advertising**'. The main aim of outdoor advertising is to catch the attention of passerby within twinkling of an eye.

This is the most effective medium of advertising. This is very suitable in the case of consumable and household articles like soaps, medicines, fans, shoes and pens, etc.

Posters and placards are usually fixed on the walls near the road sides, railway station and bus stands. These posters are made of thick paper or metal plate or wood and carry the advertising message which can be easily read and seen from a distance.

The posters also pasted on the back of buses, trains and trams which are greatly helpful in carrying the message throughout and outside the city. Painted displays are prepared by expert painters which carry attractive multi-coloured pictures also to impress upon the people.

Electric displays or neon signs are also used in order to impress the passerby. These carry a very short message. This is a very costly device.

Sandwich-men move from street to street carrying the posters and peculiarly. They shout and sing praising the concern and the product. Sky writing is also known as air advertising.

The pilots of the aero planes through whom this is carried write the advertiser's message in the form of smoke or illumination. The message is quite visible even from a long distance. Balloons fitted with the message and pictures of the product are also flown in the sky.

This type of advertising has a wider coverage and leaves effective impression on the people. It is very suitable for making the product popular and creating proper brand image. It has greater flexibility and can be designed by keeping in view the peculiarities of a particular locality. It requires lesser time and effort on the part of the advertiser to undertake this medium. This is more durable and economical form of advertising medium.

It has been referred as reminder or residuary publicity which is used by the advertiser after all the other advertising media.

Sticking of bills and posters destroys the walls of different building and adversely affects the cleanliness and beautification of a particular area.

Various media like skywriting, sandwich men, balloons and electric displays are very costly. They are beyond the means of a small trader.

(7) Window Display: It is a common method which is usually undertaken by retailers who display their products in the shop windows in order to attract the customers. This is also known as exterior display.

It is the most effective and direct method of influencing the people. Window display has direct appeal to the onlookers. It is instrumental in arousing the desire to purchase in the prospective customers. It acts as a silent salesman.

In order to operate this method successfully, goods should be arranged properly and systematically in the show windows. The articles in the windows should be regularly- changed. The advertiser should not forget that the window is the index of his shop. Utmost care should be undertaken to display the products in windows.

(8) Fairs and Exhibition: A trade exhibition or a fair is organized on extensive scale which is attended by different manufacturers and traders along with their products to be sold to the large number of people who visit the exhibition. The exhibition may be either organized on local, provincial or international basis. The examples of some of the international exhibitions are EXPO 70 of JAPAN, ASIA 72 and recent trade fair at Delhi every year.

Different stalls or pavilions are allotted to various traders who display their goods in these pavilions. The manufacturers also distribute the sales literature and sometimes free samples of goods to the people. Facilities of practical demonstration are also provided to the customers. The customers clearly understand the method of operation and use of the product.

In the case of international exhibitions, traders of different countries assemble at one place; they can conveniently share the experiences of their respective countries with each other which are really informative and useful for all of them. It provides ample opportunity for learning. The huge gathering of people in the exhibition provides a larger market for sale.

(9) Specially Advertising: Most of the business houses in order to increase their sales, advertise their products, give free gifts like diaries, purses, paper weights and calendars to the customers. The name of the firm or the dealer is inscribed on the articles presented.

Personal Selling

Personal selling, as the name signifies, is a promotional tool, where companies use sales force, to increase sales of product and services.

Under personal selling, there is a face to face meeting between the clients or customers and the sales representative, wherein the representatives visit customers personally, so as to transact a sale, by offering and inducing them to make a purchase. Personal selling involves developing a strong relationship with customers, discovering their needs and providing them such products, which satisfy their needs.

The process requires huge workforce to cover the entire market. Moreover, proper training is also an important requirement of this process, to deal with different types of customers and instigating them to buy the product.

Comparison Chart

Basis for Comparison	***Advertising***	***Personal Selling***
Meaning	Advertising is a means of communication, which calls customer's attention towards the product or service, through mass media	Personal selling refers to a form of promotion, wherein the sales representative sells the product to customers, by directly visiting them
Communication	One-way communication	Two-way communication
Form	Impersonal form of communication	Personal form of communication
Strategy	Pull strategy	Push strategy
Message	Standardised	Customized
Channel	Mass media	Sales personnel
Time	Conveys message to end number of individual in less time	Conveys message to a few customers only in relatively high time
Feedback	Lacks direct feedback	Facilitates direct and instant feedback

Channel Management

The term Channel Management is widely used in sales marketing parlance. It is defined as a process where the company develops various marketing techniques as well as sales strategies to reach the widest possible customer base. The channels are nothing but ways or outlets to market and sell products. The ultimate aim of any organization is to develop a **better relationship** between the customer and the product.

Channel management helps in developing a program for selling and servicing customers within a specific channel. The aim is to streamline communication between a business and the customer. To do this, you need to segment your channels according to the characteristics of your customers: their needs, buying patterns, success factors, etc. and then customize a program that includes goals, policies, products, sales, and marketing program (1) The goal of channel management is to establish direct communication with customers in each channel. If the company is able to effectively achieve this goal, the management will have a better idea which marketing channel best suits that particular customer base. The techniques used in each channel could be different, but the overall strategy must always brand the business consistently throughout the communication (2) A business must determine what it wants out of each channel and also clearly define the framework for each of those channels to produce desired results. Identifying the segment of the population linked to each channel also helps to determine the best products to pitch to those channels.

Vertical Marketing Systems

A Vertical Marketing system (VMS) comprises of the main distribution channel partners- the producer, the wholesaler and the retailer who work together as a **unified group** to serve the customer needs.

In conventional marketing system, the producer, wholesaler and the retailer worked separately with the intention to maximize their profits even at the expense of one another. This led to the unending conflicts between the channel partners resulting in less profit for the business as a whole.

In order to overcome these conflicts, several firms have started using a vertical marketing system wherein producers, wholesalers and retailers have joined hands with each other and are working in unison towards the accomplishment of the business objective as a whole. This has led to the increased profits for each involved in the channel of distribution.

Vertical Marketing System is further divided into three parts which are explained below:

(i) **Corporate Vertical Marketing System:** In Corporate VMS, one member of the distribution channel be it a producer, a wholesaler or a retailer owns all the other members of the channel, thereby having all the elements of production and distribution channel under a single ownership. For example, Amway is an American cosmetic company, which manufactures its own product range and sells these products only through its authorized Amway stores. Here the ownership of production and distribution is with the company itself.

(ii) **Contractual Vertical Marketing System:** In Contractual VMS, every member in the distribution channel works independently and integrates their activities on a contractual basis to earn more profits that are earned when working in isolation. The most common form of Contractual VMS is **franchising**. In franchising, the producer authorizes the distributor to sell its product under the producer's name against some annual license fee. For example, Mc-Donalds, Dominos, Pizza Hut, etc. are all forms of the franchise which are working on a contractual basis.

(iii) **Administered Vertical Marketing System:** Under Administered VMS, there is no contract between the members of production & distribution channel but their activities do get influenced by the Size and Power of any one of the member. In simple words, any powerful and influential members of the channel dominate the activities of other channel members. For example, big brands like HUL, ITC, Procter & Gamble, etc. command a high level of cooperation from the retailers in terms of display, shelf space, pricing policies, and promotional schemes.

Thus, through a vertical marketing system, the channel partners establishes a close contact with each other and work in unison towards the accomplishment of common objectives thereby enjoying more profits which they would have been earning when working alone.

Evaluation & Control of Marketing Effort

Techniques used after the marketing plan period to analyze success in achieving individual marketing objectives and to more broadly assess the entire organization's marketing efforts.

Marketing Evaluation Techniques

(a) Sales analysis
(b) Market-share analysis
(c) Marketing cost and profitability analysis
(d) Efficiency ratios
(e) Marketing-effectiveness rating review
(f) Marketing audit

Marketing Control

Steps that an organization takes to ensure that its marketing plans are successful.

Control Process for the Marketing Plan

(a) Setting standards based on plans
(b) Measuring performance against standards
(c) Correcting deviations from standards and plans

Marketing of Services

Service marketing is marketing based on relationship and value. It may be used to market a service or a product. With the increasing prominence of services in the global economy, service marketing has become a subject that needs to be studied separately. Marketing services is different from marketing goods because of the unique characteristics of services namely, intangibility, heterogeneity, perishability and inseparability.

In most countries, services add more economic value than agriculture, raw materials and manufacturing combined. In developed economies, employment is dominated by service jobs and most new job growth comes from services.

Jobs range from high-paid professionals and technicians to minimum wage positions. Service organizations can be of any size from huge global corporations to local small businesses. Most activities by the government agencies and non-profit organizations involve services.

The American Marketing Association defines services as activities, benefits, or satisfactions that are offered for sale or provided with sale of goods to the customer, that is, pre-sale and after-sales services. Berry states, 'while a product is an object, devise or physical thing, a service is a deed, performance, or an effort'.

Features of Services

1. Intangibility: A physical product is visible and concrete. Services are intangible. The service cannot be touched or viewed, so it is difficult for clients to tell in advance what they will be getting. For example, banks promote the sale of credit cards by emphasizing the conveniences and advantages derived from possessing a credit card.

2. Inseparability: Personal services cannot be separated from the individual. Services are created and consumed simultaneously. The service is being produced at the same time that the client is receiving it; for example, during an online search or a legal consultation. Dentist, musicians, dancers, etc. create and offer services at the same time.

3. Heterogeneity: Services involve people, and people are all different. There is a strong possibility that the same enquiry would be answered slightly differently by different people (or even by the same person at different times). It is important to minimize the differences in performance (through training, standard setting and quality assurance). The quality of services offered by firms can never be standardized.

4. Perishability: Services have a high degree of perishability. Unused capacity cannot be stored for future use. If services are not used today, it is lost forever. For example, spare seats in an aero plane cannot be transferred to the next flight. Similarly, empty rooms in five-star hotels and credits not utilized are examples of services leading to economic losses. As services are activities performed for simultaneous consumption, they perish unless consumed.

5. Changing Demand: The demand for services has wide fluctuations and may be seasonal. Demand for tourism is seasonal, other services such as demand for public transport, cricket field and golf courses have fluctuations in demand.

6. Pricing of Services: Quality of services cannot be standardized. The pricing of services are usually determined on the basis of demand and competition. For example, room rents in tourist spots fluctuate as per demand and season and many of the service providers give off-season discounts.

7. Direct Channel: Usually, services are directly provided to the customer. The customer goes directly to the service provider to get services such as bank, hotel, doctor, and so on. A wider market is reached through franchising such as McDonald's and Monginis.

Problems in Marketing Services

1. A service cannot be demonstrated.
2. Sale, production and consumption of services takes place simultaneously.
3. A service cannot be stored. It cannot be produced in anticipation of demand.
4. Services cannot be protected through patents.
5. Services cannot be separated from the service provider.
6. Services are not standardized and are inconsistent.
7. Service providers appointing franchisees may face problems of quality of services.
8. The customer perception of service quality is more directly linked to the morale, motivation and skill of the frontline staff of any service organization.

Customer Relation Management

In an organization, sales representatives have the responsibility of creating brand awareness and making products popular among the end users. They are the ones who interact with the customers, understand their requirements and fulfill their needs and expectations.

The art of managing the organization's relationship with the customers and prospective clients refer to customer relationship management.

Customer relationship management includes various strategies and techniques to maintain healthy relationship with the organization's existing as well as potential customers. Organizations must ensure customers are satisfied with their products and services for higher customer retention. Remember one satisfied customer brings ten new customers with him where as one dissatisfied customer takes away ten customers along with him.

In simpler words, customer relationship management refers to the study of needs and expectations of the customers and providing them the right solution.

Need for Customer Relationship Management:

(i) Customer relationship management leads to satisfied customers and eventually higher business every time.

(ii) Customer relationship management goes a long way in retaining existing customers.

(iii) Customer relationship management ensures customers return back home with a smile.

(iv) Customer relationship management improves the relationship between the organization and customers. Such activities strengthen the bond between the sales representatives and customers.

Steps to Customer Relationship Management:

(i) It is essential for the sales representatives to understand the needs, interest as well as budget of the customers. Don't suggest anything which would burn a hole in their pockets.

(ii) Never tell lies to the customers. Convey them only what your product offers. Don't cook fake stories or ever try to fool them.

(iii) It is a sin to make customers waiting. Sales professionals should reach meetings on or before time. Make sure you are there at the venue before the customer reaches.

(iv) A sales professional should think from the customer's perspective. Don't only think about your own targets and incentives. Suggest only what is right for the customer. Don't sell an expensive mobile to a customer who earns rupees five thousand per month. He would never come back to you and your organization would lose one of its esteemed customers.

(v) Don't oversell. Being pushy does not work in sales. If a customer needs something; he would definitely purchase the same. Never irritate the customer or make his life hell. Don't call him more than twice in a single day.

(vi) An individual needs time to develop trust in you and your product. Give him time to think and decide.

(vii) Never be rude to customers. Handle the customers with patience and care. One should never ever get hyper with the customers.

(viii) Attend sales meeting with a cool mind. Greet the customers with a smile and try to solve their queries at the earliest.

(ix) Keep in touch with the customers even after the deal. Devise customer loyalty programs for them to return to your organization. Give them bonus points or gifts on every second purchase.

(x) The sales manger must provide necessary training to the sales team to teach them how to interact with the customers. Remember customers are the assets of every business and it is important to keep them happy and satisfied for successful functioning of organization.

Uses of Internet as a Marketing Medium

Now a day's internet has become an integral part of most of our lifestyle. "Achieving organizational or individual goals by satisfying target market's needs and wants effectively by using internet as a medium is called internet marketing."

Internet Marketing includes SEO and additional online marketing tools one can use to gain the attention of potential customers. Different kind of internet marketing techniques listed below work to reach more and more people on internet and drive interested people to the website and allow to compete more effectively.

Email Marketing

It is the easy, effective and affordable way to keep customers attract and coming back to one site. This is a form of direct permission based relationship marketing, which uses e-mail as a means of communicating messages to the target audience. An email marketing campaign allows businesses to promote a new product, send information about an upcoming corporate event or share important news about their business, products and services using attractive email newsletter to stay in regular touch with them and build strong customer relationships. It is best way to keep in touch. It is easy to start and quick to see the result with real time reports

Interactive Advertising

Use of banner ads, Flash presentations and other interactive media to elicit active participation from recipients. They promote products and services and educate prospects. If well crafted, interactive advertising allows engaging consumers in direct and personal ways and they enable a sophisticated dialogue between organization and prospects which may affect buying decisions.

Blog Marketing

A blog is a regularly updated collection of content like blogger.com, wordpress.com, indianbloggers.com and blogs.hindustantimes.com. From a business marketing view, blogs offer many benefits. Blogs provide an easy way to introduce fresh, relevant content to the website on a regular basis.

It also provides real time genuine information to the information seekers. Fresh content attracts more attention from the search engines.

Social Media Marketing

Social Media such as Facebook, Twitter, LinkedIn, Google+, etc are emerging as big markets. There are sponsored pages on facebook of different companies, groups and individuals. Facebook flash their ads on individual member's profile according to their demography when the user click or like these pages, facebook is paid and the individual's information is accessible to the sponsor. Sponsors also run many contests and activities to gain attention or clicks.

Search Engine Optimization

It is the process of bringing business name on the first page of search engines like Google, Yahoo, Bing, etc. All of the Internet users use search engines as that is the primary method to find information/product or services online. Statistics Says: More than 8 out of 10 internet users look on search engines to find product or services they want to buy and 80% of searchers clicks on first page result on Google. So, Search Engine Optimization is definitely worth the effort for all the websites those are serious about their business because customers are now looking online for service.

Pay Per Click (PPC) Advertising

With this the keywords one believes prospects would type in the search bar when looking for similar products or services. For example, if one sells sofas, he would bid on the keyword 'sofa', hoping a user would type those words in the search engine, see his ad, click it and buy. These ads are called sponsored links or sponsored ads and typically appear next to the natural (also known as "organic") results on a search page. Money is paid for the ad only when the user clicks on it. Google AdWords and Yahoo Search Marketing are currently the largest PPC providers.

Here are some reasons that give an insight about why most of the businesses are using internet as a medium of marketing:

1. **More Visibility:** Digital marketing makes it quick and easy for prospective and existing customers to find business, product or services.
2. **Brand Growth:** With the rise in social media, customers can now connect with a brand on a personal level.
3. **Less Turnaround Time to Implement:** As compared to the other marketing techniques, internet marketing can be implemented in less turnaround time.
4. **Highly Monitored and Measurable Results:** The success of a web campaign can be easily monitored or measured by the traffic generation, number of clicks, etc.
5. **Focus on Target Consumers:** Digital Marketers can design their online marketing techniques targeted towards their potential consumers.

6. **Cost Effective:** Digital marketing is most cost effective media to market product, services or brand online.

Branding

Branding is a process that is used by the businesses to utilize marketing strategies to enhance their product or service image so that it is more readily recollected by the customer. Branding helps the product or service to make a favourable impact on the target customer while the branding concepts help in outlining the guidelines that should be followed during the branding process.

Branding of any product and service should follow some constants that help in establishing a brand in the long run. The internet branding strategies should have the following constants in your branding formula.

Branding Should be Simple

The most popular brands in the world have very simple, easy to remember logos. The reason behind this concept is, we tend to remember and associate ourselves with simple things and choose to ignore or forget complex ideas.

Branding Should be Different

Your brand should have individuality, should be different. The brand should stand out from other similar product or service; otherwise the whole idea of branding is lost. Only an individualistic brand makes a mark on the psyche of the target customer and he remembers it when he makes a buying decision. This is why most of the MNCs take strict action on trademark violations.

Branding Should be Safe

Play safe and do your research if you are catering to international audience. If you are using symbols in your logo make sure they do not offend the target market in any way or you can chances of shutting your shop before making any sales. Therefore keep the regional and cultural sensibilities in mind during the branding process.

The three most important branding concepts that are the basis of all branding processes are **brand promise, brand attributes and brand personality**.

A brand promise is a promise or commitment the company makes to its customers. The promise should be clearly stated and tells about the most important benefit of the product or customer.

Brand attributes are the features that describe the customer's experience like quality, innovation or customer service. The attributes help the company to deliver the brand promise.

Brand personality is the characteristic the customer experiences when they experience the brand. Thus the essence of the brand is a symbiosis of all three.

Market Development

Market development is a business strategy whereby a business attempts to find new groups of buyers as potential customers for its existing products and services. In other words, the goal of market development is to expand into untapped markets. These potential customer groups may already be served by competitors or may not be currently marketed to by anyone for the product.

The Process of Market Development

Market development is a two-step process. It starts with market research. You need to engage in segmentation analysis to determine which market segments are worth pursuing. A segment is simply a small slice of an overall market. You can segment a market along demographic, geographic, psychographic (based on values and lifestyles), and product-benefit lines.

Once you have determined which market segments are worth pursuing, the second step of market development involves creating a promotional strategy to penetrate the new market. For example, you may decide to engage in an aggressive television and direct mail campaign. You will also have to consider the pricing of your product. If there are competitors in the market, then you may opt for penetration pricing, where you aggressively price your product lower than the competition in order to quickly obtain a large share of the market and customer loyalty.

Advertising & Retailing on the Net

Online advertising is a marketing strategy that involves the use of the Internet as a medium to obtain website traffic and target and deliver marketing messages to the right customers. Online advertising is geared toward defining markets through unique and useful applications.

Since the early 1990s there has been an exponential increase in the growth of online advertising, which has evolved into a standard for small and large organizations. Online advertising is also known as Internet advertising.

A major advantage of online advertising is the quick promotion of product information without geographical boundary limits. A major challenge is the evolving field of interactive advertising, which poses new challenges for online advertisers.

Online advertisements are purchased through one of the following common vehicles:

(i) Cost Per Thousand (CPT): Advertisers pay when their messages are exposed to specific audiences.

(ii) Cost Per Click (CPC): Advertisers pay every time a user clicks on their ads.

(iii) Cost Per Action (CPA): Advertisers only pay when a specific action (generally a purchase) is performed.

Examples of online advertising include banner ads, search engine results pages, social networking ads, email spam, online classified ads, pop-ups, contextual ads and spyware.

The **Electronic Retailing** also called as *e-tailing or internet retailing*, is the process of selling the goods and services through electronic media, particularly the internet. Simply, the sale of retail goods and services online is called as electronic retailing. It follows the **B2C business model** wherein the business interacts directly with the customers without the involvement of any intermediaries.

The e-retailers can be of two types:

(i) Pure Play E-Retailers such as **Amazon**, that emerged as the online bookseller. It is present only online and do not have any physical outlet for the customers.

(ii) Brick and Click E-Retailers such as **Dell**, that sells computers through the internet as well as has the physical store front for the customers.

Advantages of Electronic Retailing

(i) Through electronic retailing, customers can save both the efforts and time.

(ii) The wide range of products is available online, so the comparison can be made easily before the purchase.

(iii) The customer can shop anytime and from anywhere, the facility is available 24*7

(iv) The huge discounts can be availed while shopping online.

(v) The detailed information about the product is available online; that helps the customer to make the purchase decision.

(vi) The electronic retailing offers the easy payment terms such as payment on delivery that instigate the customer to shop online.

Disadvantages of Electronic Retailing

(i) The customers may not be sure of the quality of the products offered online.

(ii) It is the tendency of every individual to bargain before making the final purchase, but this quotient is missing in electronic retailing.

(iii) The customers may not trust on the payment gateways and fear the misuse of credit cards or any other mode of payment.

(iv) Every customer wants to see and feel the product that he purchases, but it is not possible in case of electronic retailing where the customer makes the decision just by looking at the image.

(v) The product is not readily available; the customer has to wait for some time to get the product in his hands.

(vi) The customer misses the emotional attachment with the seller that leads to less faith on the offerings.

New Issues in Marketing

We are experiencing change in our daily life and at marketplace too. Customer needs, wants, expectations are changing more rapidly. Customers are increasingly demanding better quality and reliability in products and services. New products and services are coming to market more quickly. Competition is getting intense and global rather than just domestic. Technology is changing rapidly; and e-commerce and Internet is having a great impact on marketing practices.

In such a rapidly changing marketing environment, it is really difficult for business organizations to make quick and sound decisions, and facing various marketing challenges.

Marketing Challenges the Business Organizations Facing Today

(i) Rapidly Changing Customer Needs, Wants, and Expectations: Today, the needs, wants, and expectations of customer are changing rapidly. It is a great challenge not only for small marketers but also for big players. It requires extensive study of market trends and consumer behaviour while developing new product or updating existing product.

(ii) Increasing Global and Domestic Competition: Competition today is global rather than just domestic. Marketers have to compete not only with domestic players but with global players too. The intense and global competition is a great challenge for marketers to deal with.

(iii) Increasing Popularity of Internet: With the increase in popularity of Internet, a new spectrum of marketing channel is emerged. The worldwide increase in number of Internet users brought a shift from traditional print-based media to new online platforms. It presents a new set of marketing challenges - challenge of deciding how much to allocate to digital v/s print-based media; challenge of using social media marketing largely because of regulatory issues and concerns over its measurability; and challenge of doing more with less money as the rise of Internet made communication cheaper and efficient.

(iv) **Challenge of Selecting Among Too Many Options:** The greatest challenge the marketers facing today is simply too many options. There are too many potential customer segments, product or service options and many communication tools. It is really difficult and challenging for marketers to choose among too many options. The marketers today don't suffer from lack of opportunities or options. The picture is totally opposite today. Now they suffer from too many opportunities or options.

Ways to Overcome These Challenges

For the success of any business, overall performance is required to be taken care of. Marketing performance includes sales volume, market share, and customer satisfaction. Various marketing challenges make it difficult for marketing managers to achieve the targeted marketing performance. But, there are ways to overcome such challenges. Some of the important ways are stated below:

(i) **Create a Learning Organization:** Business organizations must include **learning** as a key to improvement in their organizational values. Proper training must be given to marketing employees and it should be considered as an investment rather than as a cost. Marketing managers are required to continually question their own views of the market place. Learning is not a onetime activity. It's a continuous process; ability to learn can be a key competitive advantage for any business.

(ii) **Market Research:** Marketing organizations must invest in market research and they are required to make extensive use of it. Organizations are required to be good at using information about markets, customers, and competitors. Market research must be focused on understanding customer needs, wants, and expectations.

(iii) **Reevaluate the Old Mix - Four Ps to Four Cs:** With the increasing globalization, competition, and popularity of Internet, the old marketing mix is facing many new challenges; and to tackle these challenges marketing management must reevaluate the old marketing mix to new mix by converting four Ps to four **Cs**.

Unit - VIII

Probability Theory

Probability Theory

The probability is the chance that a particular event will occur. The theory of probability provides a quantitative measure of uncertainty of occurrence of different events resulting from a random experiment in terms of quantitative measure ranging from 0 to 1.

Probability of any event A can be denoted by P (A) then $0 \geq P(A) \leq 1$

For certain event the probability is 1.

For absurd event probability is 0.

Basic formula of probability:

P (A) = Favorable number of events/Total number of events

Random Experiment

A random experiment is a process which produces more than one outcome. For example, if we toss a coin we may obtain a head or a tail. Tossing a coin is an experiment which can produce two outcomes- head and tail.

Event

An event is defined as the outcome of an experiment. For example, for the experiment of tossing a coin an event can be obtaining a tail or for an experiment of rolling a dice, an event can be defined as obtaining a multiple of 2.

Sample Space

The set of all possible outcomes of an experiment is called sample space. A sample space can be finite or infinite, and discrete or continuous.

Example: Discrete, Finite Sample Space

Experiment: Tossing a coin once.

Sample space: {H, T}.

Event: Let us define an event A of obtaining a head

Total number of events = 2 {Head and Tail}

Favourable number of events = 1 {Head}

Probability (A) = 1/2

Example: Discrete, Infinite Sample Space

Experiment: Eating potato chips:

Sample space: {0, 1, 2, 3, 4, 5, 6, 7, 8, 9, 10, 11, ...}

This sample space is **discrete**; as it has one to one correspondence with whole numbers. This sample space is **infinite**, however, since there are an infinite number of possibilities.

Example: Continuous Sample Space

Experiment: Burning a light bulb until it burns out. Suppose there is a theoretical maximum number of an hour that a bulb can burn and that is 10,000 hours.

Sample Space: The set of all real numbers between 0 & 10,000.

This sample space is continuous. It is also infinite, since there are an infinite number of possibilities. All continuous sample spaces are infinite.

Compound Event

The joint occurrence of two or more simple events is known as a compound event.

Example: A bag contains 3 red and 4 white balls

Experiment: Two balls are drawn from the bag randomly.

Event: Let us define the event A as obtaining one red and one white balls. This is a compound event as there is a joint occurrence of two simple events of (1) drawing a red ball and (2) drawing a white ball.

Sample Space: {3 red balls, 4 white balls}

Probability of having one red ball

Total number of events: = 3+4 = 7

Favourable number of events = 3

Probability of having one red ball = 3/7 1

Probability of having one white ball

Total number of events: = 3+4 = 7

Favourable number of events = 4

Probability of having one white ball = 4/7 2

Probability of having one red and one white balls = 3/7 X 4/7 = 12/49

Independent Event

Two events are said to be independent if the result of the second event is not affected by the result of the first event. If A and B are independent events, the probability of both events occurring is the product of the probabilities of the individual events.

If A and B are independent events then probability of occurring A and B would be

P (A and B) = P (A) • P (B)

Example: A drawer contains 3 red paperclips, 4 green paperclips, and 5 blue paperclips. One paperclip is taken from the drawer and then replaced. Another paperclip is taken from the drawer. What is the probability that the first paperclip is red and the second paperclip is blue?

Solution: Sample space: {3 red paperclips, 4 green paperclips, 5 blue paperclips}

Event A: Drawing the first paperclip

The probability that the paperclip is red

Total number of events: 3 + 4 + 5 = 12

Favourable number of events = 3

P (A) = 3/12 = 1/4

Event B: Drawing the second paperclip after the first being replaced.

The probability that the paperclip is blue

Total number of events: 3 + 4 + 5 = 12 (since the first paperclip is replaced so total number of events remain the same)

Favourable number of events = 5

P (B) = 5/12

Probability that the first is red and the second is blue

P (A and B) = P (A) • P (B)

P (A and B) = 1/4 X 5/12 = 5/48

Dependent Event

Two events are said to be dependent if the occurrence of one event influences the occurrence of the other.

If A and B are **dependent** events, and A occurs first,

P (A and B) = P (A) • P (B, once A has occurred)

P (A and B) = P (A) • P (B|A)

Example: A drawer contains 3 red paperclips, 4 green paperclips, and 5 blue paper clips. One paperclip is taken from the drawer and is not replaced. Another paperclip is taken from the drawer. What is the probability that the first paperclip is red and the second paperclip is blue?

Solution: Sample space: {3 red paperclips, 4 green paperclips, 5 blue paperclips}

Event A: Drawing the first paperclip

The probability that the paperclip is red

Total number of events: 3 + 4 + 5 = 12

Favourable number of events = 3

P (A) = 3/12 = 1/4

Event B: Drawing the second paperclip after the first not being replaced

The probability that the paperclip is blue

Total number of events: 2 + 4 + 5 = 11 (since the first paperclip (red one) is not being replaced so total number of events will reduced by one)

Favourable number of events = 5

P (B) = 5/11

Probability that the first is red and the second is blue

P (A and B) = P (A) • P (B|A)

P (A and B) = 1/4 X 5/11 = 5/44

Mutually Exclusive Events

Two or more events are said to be mutually exclusive if the occurrence of one implies that the other cannot occur. In other words, if the occurrence of one event rules out the occurrence of the other, the events are called mutually exclusive.

Example: A pair of dice is rolled. The events of rolling a sum of 9 and of rolling a double have NO outcomes in common. These two events are **mutually exclusive.**

Sample space: {(1,1) (1,2) (1,3) (1,4) (1,5) (1,6) (2,1) (2,2) (2,3) (2,4) (2,5) (2,6) (3,1 (3,2) (3,3) (3,4) (3,5) (3,6) (4,1) (4,2) (4,3) (4,4) (4,5) (4,6) (5,1) (5,2) (5,3) (5,4) (5,5) (5,6) (6,1) (6,2) (6,3) (6,4) (6,5) (6,6)}

Event A: Rolling a sum of 9

Total number of events = 36 = (6 faces of the dice x 6), each face has the probability of turning up as many as 6 times.

Favourable number of events = 4 ((3, 6) (4, 5) (5, 4) (6, 3)); (see the pairs underlined in the **Sample space)**

P (A) = 4/36 = 1/9

Event B: Rolling a double

Total number of events = 36

Favourable number of events = 6 ((1, 1) (2, 2) (3, 3) (4, 4) (5, 5) (6, 6))

P (B) = 6/36 = 1/6

Since there is no common outcome, the events A and B are mutually exclusive.

Example: A pair of dice is rolled. The events of rolling a sum of 6 and of rolling a double have the outcome (3, 3) in common. These two events are not mutually exclusive.

Sample space: {(1,1) (1,2) (1,3) (1,4) (1,5) (1,6) (2,1) (2,2) (2,3) (2,4) (2,5) (2,6) (3,1 (3,2) (3,3) (3,4) (3,5) (3,6) (4,1) (4,2) (4,3) (4,4) (4,5) (4,6) (5,1) (5,2) (5,3) (5,4) (5,5) (5,6) (6,1) (6,2) (6,3) (6,4) (6,5) (6,6)}

Event A: Rolling a sum of 6

Total number of events = 36

Favourable number of events = 5 ((1, 5) (2, 4) (3, 3) (4, 2) (5, 1))

P (A) = 5/36 = 5/36

Event B: Rolling a double

Total number of events = 36

Favourable number of events = 6 ((1, 1) (2, 2) (3, 3) (4, 4) (5, 5) (6, 6))

P (B) = 6/36 = 1/6

Since there is one common outcome which is (3, 3), the events A and B are not mutually exclusive.

Mutually Exhaustive Events

A set of event is said to be mutually exhaustive if they include all the possible outcomes of a random experiment.

Example: In the experiment of rolling a die, let A be the event “getting a prime number”, B be the event “getting an even number” and C be the event “getting a number less than 3”.

Sample space: {1, 2, 3, 4, 5, 6}

Event A: Getting a prime number A = {2, 3, 5}

Event B: Getting an even number B = {2, 4, 6}

Event C: Getting a number less than 3 C = {1, 2}

Events A, B and C include all the possible outcomes of the experiment so these are mutually exclusive events.

The Addition Theorem in the Probability

Addition theorem of probability determines the probability that either event ‘A’ or event ‘B’ occurs or both occur. The addition is denoted as ‘U’ and pronounced as Union.

Statement: If A and B are two events then

P (A U B) = P (A) + P (B) – P (A)” B),
Where,

P (A) = probability of occurrence of event ‘A’

P (B) = probability of occurrence of event ‘B’

P (A U B) = probability of occurrence of event ‘A’ OR event ‘B’.

P (A)” B) = probability of occurrence of event ‘A’ AND event ‘B’.

Conditional Probability

Let A be an event with P (A) > 0. The probability that the event B occurs subject to the condition that A has already occurred is known as conditional probability of B given that A has already occurred. It is denoted by the symbol P (B|A) and read as Probability of B given A.

If A and B are dependent events then

P (A|B) = P (A)”B)/P (B)

P (B|A) = P (A)”B)/P (A)

If A and B are independent

P (A|B) = P (A)

P (B|A) = P (B)

Multiplication Theorem on Probabilities for Independent Events

If two events A and B are independent, the probability that both of them occur is equal to the product of their individual probabilities. i.e. **P (A and B) = P (A) • P (B)**

Example: The probability that a teacher will take a surprise test during any class meeting is 1/5. If a student is absent on two days, what is the probability that he misses at least one test?

Solution: Probability of conducting a surprise test = 1/5

Probability of not conducting a surprise test = 1- 1/5 = 4/5

The student will miss one test if there is test on first day and there is no test on second day or there is no test on first day and there is test on second day

Probability that there is test on first day and there is no test on second day
= 1/5 X 4/5 = 4/25

Probability that there is no test on first day and there is test on second day
= 4/5 X 1/5 = 4/25

Probability that the student will miss one test = 4/25 + 4/25 = 8/25

The student will miss both the tests if there are tests at both the days.

Probability that there is test on first day and test on second day
= 1/5 X 1/5 = 1/25

Probability that the student misses at least one test = probability that he misses one test or he misses both the tests

Required probability = 8/25 + 1/25 = 9/25

Multiplication Theorem for Dependent Events

When the events are not independent, i.e., they are dependent events, then the multiplication theorem has to be modified. The modified multiplication theorem states that if A and B are two dependent events, then the probability of their simultaneous occurrence is equal to the probability of one event multiplied by the conditional probability of the other.

P (AB) = P (A) • P (B/A)

OR

P (AB) = P (B) • P (A/B)

Where,

P (B/A) = Conditional Probability of B given A;

P (A/B) = Conditional Probability of A given B.

Bayes' Theorem

Bayes' theorem gives the relationship between the probabilities of A and B, P(A) and P(B), and the conditional probabilities of A given B and B given A, P(A|B) and P(B|A).

$$P(A|B) = \{P(B|A \cdot P(A)\} / \{P(B)\}$$

Probability Distribution- Binomial, Poisson, Normal & Exponential

Probability Distribution

A probability distribution is a graph, table, or formula that gives the probability for each value of the random variable. Probability distribution can be considered as a theoretical frequency distribution. Probability distribution describes how outcomes are expected to vary. Frequency distribution is a listing of the observed frequencies of all the outcomes of an experiment whereas a probability distribution is a listing of probabilities of all the possible outcomes that could result if the experiment were done.

Types of probability distribution: There are basically two types of probability distributions.

1. Discrete Probability Distribution: It can take on only a limited number of values, which can be listed.

Example: Probability that you were born in a given month.

There are only 12 possible values. All the values are equally likely.

So, in this case, the distribution would be

Month	Jan	Feb	March	April	May	June
Probability	0.08	0.08	0.08	0.08	0.08	0.08

Month	July	Aug	Sep	Oct	Nov	Dec
Probability	0.08	0.08	0.08	0.08	0.08	0.08

2. Continuous Probability Distribution: In continuous distribution, the variable under consideration is allowed to take on any value within a given range. So, we cannot list all the possible values.

Example: Let us define a variable x denoting "Volume poured into a 100cc cup from a coffee machine." The variable X can take any value between 0 to 100cc so the distribution will be a continuous one.

Binomial Distribution

Definition: A Bernoulli trial is a random experiment in which there are only two possible outcomes - success and failure.

For example:

If you are tossing a coin and considering heads as success and tails as failure.

If you are checking items from a production line: success = not defective, failure = defective.

Binomial Experiment: Consider the following type of random experiment:

- The experiment consists of n repeated Bernoulli trials – each trial has only two possible outcomes labeled as success and failure;
- The trials are independent - the outcome of any trial has no effect on the probability of the others;
- The probability of success in each trial is constant which we denote by p.

Definition of Binomial Distribution: The random variable X that counts the number of successes, 'r', in the 'n' trials is said to have a binomial distribution with parameters n and p, written bin(r; n; p).The probability mass function of a binomial random variable X with parameters n and p is

$f(r) = P(X = r) = {}^{n}Cr\ P^{r}\ (1-P)^{n-r}$

For $r = 0, 1, 2, 3 \ldots\ldots n$

Characteristics of Binomial Distribution

1. Each outcome must be classified as a success (p) or a failure (q).
2. The probability distribution is discrete.
3. Each trial is independent and therefore, the probability of success and the probability of failure is the same for each trial.
4. Mean of a binomial distribution with n number of trials and probability of success p is given by Mean = np
5. Variance of a binomial distribution with n number of trials and probability of success p and probability of failure q (= 1-p) is given by Variance = npq

Example: A quality control engineer is in charge of testing whether or not 90% of the DVD players produced by his company conform to specifications. To do this, the engineer randomly selects a batch of 12 DVD players from each day's production. The day's production is acceptable provided no more than 1 DVD player fails to meet specifications. Otherwise, the entire day's production has to be tested.

(i) What is the probability that the engineer incorrectly passes a day's production as acceptable if only 80% of the day's DVD players actually conform to specification?

(ii) What is the probability that the engineer unnecessarily requires the entire day's production to be tested if in fact 90% of the DVD players conform to specifications?

Solution: Let X denote the number of DVD players in the sample that fail to meet specifications

(i) We want P(X <= 1) with binomial parameters n = 12, p = 0.2.

$$P(X <= 1) = P(X = 0) + P(X = 1)$$
$$= 12C_0 (0.2)^0 (0.8)^{12} + 12C_1 (0.2) (0.8)^{11}$$
$$= 0.069 + 0.206 = 0.275$$

(ii) We now want P(X > 1) with parameters n = 12, p = 0:1.

$$P(X <= 1) = P(X = 0) + P(X = 1)$$
$$= 12C_0 (0.1)^0 (0.9)^{12} + 12C_1 (0.1) (0.9)^{11}$$
$$= 0.659$$
$$P(X>1) = 1\text{-}0.659 = 0.341$$

Poisson Distribution

The Poisson distribution is named after the famous French mathematician Simeon Denis Poisson. Poisson distribution focuses on the number of discrete occurrences over an interval. For example, the number of arrivals at an automobile service station in 10 hours, the number of accidents at a road intersection in a month, the number of patients arriving at a health center every day, the number of defects per unit length of an electrical wire, etc. Poison distribution is a widely used distribution in the field of managerial decision making. Poisson formulae are widely used in queuing models which are based on the assumption that the Poisson distribution is the proper distribution to describe random arrival rates over a period of time.

Properties of Poisson Distribution:

1. Each occurrence of an event is independent of the occurrence of the other event.
2. The probability of an occurrence is the same for any two intervals of equal length.
3. Poisson distribution describes discrete occurrences over a specific time interval.
4. The expected number of occurrences must hold constant for all the time intervals of the same size.
5. In each interval, occurrences can range from zero to infinity.

The mean number of events per interval is denoted by l. The probability of observing x events in a given interval is given by

$P(X = x) = e^{-\lambda}\lambda^{x}/x!$

$x = 0, 1, 2, 3$............

e is a mathematical constant i.e ~ 2.718282.

Example: In a certain factory, blades are manufactures in packets of 10.There is a 0.2% probability for any blade to be defective. Using Poisson distribution, calculate approximately the number of packets containing two defective blades in a consignment of 20,000 packets (Given that e-.02 = .9802).

Solution: Mean = λ = 0.2% of 10 = 0.02

$P(X=2) = e^{-0.02}\, 0.02^2/2!$

$P(X=2) = 0.9802 \times 0.0004/2$

$P(X=2) = 0.0001961$

Expected number of packets containing two defective blades in a consignment of 20000 packets = $0.0001961 \times 20000 = 3.922$

Normal Distribution

The normal distribution is the most widely known and used of all distributions. Because the normal distribution approximates many natural phenomena so well, it has developed into a standard of reference for many probability problems.

Properties of Normal Distribution:

1. Symmetric, bell shaped
2. Continuous for all values of X between $-\infty$ and ∞ so that each conceivable interval of real numbers has a probability other than zero. $-\infty \leq X \leq \infty$
3. Two parameters, μ and σ. Note that the normal distribution is actually a family of distributions, since μ and σ determine the shape of the distribution.
4. The highest point occurs at $x=\mu$.
5. It is symmetric about the mean, μ. One half of the curve is a mirror image of the other half, i.e., the area under the curve to the right of μ is equal to the area under the curve to the left of μ.
6. The curve is asymptotic to the horizontal axis at the extremes.
7. The total area under the curve equals one.

Standardized Variable: A variable is said to be standardized if it has been adjusted (or transformed) such that its mean equals 0 and its standard deviation equals 1. Standardization can be accomplished using the formula for a z-score:

$$\mathbf{Z = (x\text{-}\mu)/\sigma)}$$

The z-score represents the number of standard deviations that a data value is away from the mean.

Example 13: A placement company has conducted a written test to recruit people in a software company. Assume that the test marks are normally distributed with mean 120 and standard deviation 50. Calculate the following:

(a) Probability of randomly obtaining scores greater than 200 in the test.

(b) Probability of randomly obtaining a score that is 180 or less.

Solution: Given: Mean = 120, Standard deviation = 50

(a) Z = (200-120)/50 = 1.6

Area under Z score = 1.6 = 0.4452

Required Probability = 0.5-0.4452 = 0.0548

(b) Z = (180-120)/5 = 6/5 = 1.2

Probability for this Z score = 0.3849

Required probability = 0.5+0.3849 = 0.8849

Exponential Distribution

The exponential distribution describes the arrival time of a randomly recurring independent event sequence. If ì is the mean waiting time for the next event recurrence, its probability density function is:

$$f(x) = \begin{cases} \frac{1}{\mu}e^{-x/\mu} & when\ x \geq 0 \\ 0 & when\ x < 0 \end{cases}$$

Here is a graph of the exponential distribution with $\mu = 1$.

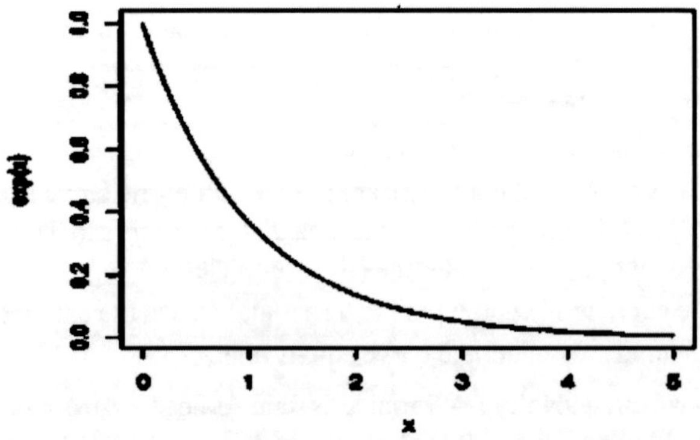

Problem

Suppose the mean checkout time of a supermarket cashier is three minutes. Find the probability of a customer checkout being completed by the cashier in less than two minutes.

Solution

The checkout processing rate is equals to one divided by the mean checkout completion time. Hence the processing rate is 1/3 checkouts per minute. We then apply the function pexp of the exponential distribution with rate=1/3.

> Pexp (2, rate=1/3)

0.48658

Answer

The probability of finishing a checkout under two minutes by the cashier is 48.7%

Correlation and Regression Analysis

Correlation

Correlation is a measure of association between two variables. The variables are not designated as dependent or independent.

The two most popular correlation coefficients are: Spearman's correlation coefficient and Pearson's product-moment correlation coefficient. When calculating a correlation coefficient for ordinal data, select Spearman's technique. For interval or ratio-type data, use Pearson's technique.

The value of a correlation coefficient can vary from minus one to plus one. A minus one indicates a perfect negative correlation, while a plus one indicates a perfect positive correlation. A correlation of zero means there is no relationship between the two variables. When there is a negative correlation between two variables, as the value of one variable increases, the value of the other variable decreases, and vice versa.

A Scatter Diagram is a graphical technique used to analyze the relationship between two variables. It shows whether the variables are related to each other or not. Two sets of data are plotted on a graph, with the y-axis being used for the variable to be predicted and the x-axis being used for the variable to make the prediction. The graph will show possible relationships.

Characteristics of Correlation Coefficient:

1. Correlation coefficient can only be calculated for quantitative data.
2. Positive value of 'r' indicates positive association between the variables, that is, the variables move in the same direction, negative

value of 'r' indicates negative association between the variables, that is, the variables move in the opposite direction.

3. The correlation coefficient (r) is always a number lying between -1 and +1.
4. The correlation coefficient (r) is a pure number without units. r is not affected by interchanging the two variables $r_{xy} = r_{yx}$
5. Because r uses the standardized values of the observations, r does not change when we change units of measurement (inches vs. centimeters, pounds vs. kilograms, miles vs. meters). r is "scale invariant".
6. The correlation coefficient measures clustering about a line, but only relative to the SD's.
7. The correlation can be misleading in the presence of outliers or nonlinear association. r does not describe curved relationships. r is affected by outliers.
8. Correlation measures association. But association does not necessarily show causation. Both variables may be influenced simultaneously by some third variable.
9. Correlation Coefficient is independent of the change of origin and scale.

The standard error of a correlation coefficient is used to determine the confidence intervals around a true correlation of zero. If your correlation coefficient falls outside of this range, then it is significantly different from zero. The standard error can be calculated for interval or ratio-type data (i.e., only for Pearson's product-moment correlation).

The significance (probability) of the correlation coefficient is determined from the t-statistic. The probability of the t-statistic indicates whether the observed correlation coefficient occurred by chance if the true correlation is zero. In other words, it asks if the correlation is significantly different than zero. When the t-statistic is calculated for Spearman's rank-difference correlation coefficient, there must be at least 30 cases before the t-distribution can be used to determine the probability. If there are fewer than 30 cases, you must refer to a special table to find the probability of the correlation coefficient.

Regression

Simple regression is used to examine the relationship between one dependent and one independent variable. After performing an analysis, the regression statistics can be used to predict the dependent variable when the independent variable is known.

The regression line (known as the least squares line) is a plot of the expected value of the dependent variable for all values of the independent variable. Technically, it is the line that "minimizes the squared residuals". The regression line is the one that best fits the data on a scatter plot.

Using the regression equation, the dependent variable may be predicted from the independent variable. The slope of the regression line (b) is defined as the rise divided by the run. The y intercept (a) is the point on the y axis where the regression line would intercept the y axis. The slope and y intercept are incorporated into the regression equation. The intercept is usually called the constant, and the slope is referred to as the coefficient. Since the regression model is usually not a perfect predictor, there is also an error term in the equation.

In the regression equation, y is always the dependent variable and x is always the independent variable. Here is a way to mathematically describe a linear regression model:

$$y = a + bx + e$$

The significance of the slope of the regression line is determined from the t-statistic. It is the probability that the observed correlation coefficient occurred by chance if the true correlation is zero.

Some researchers prefer to report the F-ratio instead of the t-statistic. The F-ratio is equal to the t-statistic squared. The t-statistic is equal to the estimated coefficient divided by its standard error.

The t-statistic for the significance of the slope is essentially a test to determine if the regression model (equation) is usable. If the slope is significantly different than zero, then we can use the regression model to predict the dependent variable for any value of the independent variable.

On the other hand, take an example where the slope is zero. It has no prediction ability because for every value of the independent variable, the prediction for the dependent variable would be the same. Knowing the value of the independent variable would not improve our ability to predict the dependent variable.

Thus, if the slope is not significantly different than zero, don't use the model to make predictions. The coefficient of determination (r-squared) is the square of the correlation coefficient. Its value may vary from zero to one. It has the advantage over the correlation coefficient in that it may be interpreted directly as the proportion of variance in the dependent variable that can be accounted for by the regression equation. For example, an r-squared value of 0.49 means that 49% of the variance in the dependent variable can be explained by the regression equation. The other 51% is unexplained.

The standard error of the estimate for regression measures the amount of variability in the points around the regression line. It is the standard deviation of the data points as they are distributed around the regression line. The standard error of the estimate can be used to develop confidence intervals around a prediction.

Properties of Regression Coefficients

Followings are the properties of the regression coefficients:

1. Correlation coefficient is the geometric mean of the regression coefficients. If b_{yx} be the regression coefficient of the line Y on X, and b_{xy} be the regression coefficient of the line X on Y and r be the correlation coefficient between X and Y then $r^2 = b_{yx} \times b_{xy}$
2. If one of the regression coefficients is greater than unity, the other must be less than unity.
3. Arithmetic mean of the regression coefficients is greater than the correlation coefficient r, provided $r > 0$.
4. Regression coefficients are independent of the changes of origin but not of scale.

Sampling Theory

Sampling theory is the field of statistics that is involved with the collection, analysis and interpretation of data gathered from random samples of a population under study. The application of sampling theory is concerned not only with the proper selection of observations from the population that will constitute the random sample; it also involves the use of probability theory, along with prior knowledge about the population parameters, to analyze the data from the random sample and develop conclusions from the analysis. The normal distribution, along with related probability distributions, is most heavily utilized in developing the theoretical background for sampling theory.

Type of Sampling	*When to Use It*	*Advantages*	*Disadvantages*
Probability Strategies			
Simple Random Sampling	When the population members are similar to one another on important variables	Ensures a high degree of representativeness	Time consuming and tedious
Systematic Sampling	When the population members are similar to one another on important variables	Ensures a high degree of representativeness, and no need to use a table of random numbers	Less random than simple random sampling
Stratified Random Sampling	When the population is heterogeneous and contains several different groups, some of which are related to the topic of the study	Ensures a high degree of representativeness of all the strata or layers in the population	Time consuming and tedious

(Contd...)

Cluster Sampling	When the population consists of units rather than individuals	Easy and convenient	Possibly, members of units are different from one another, decreasing the techniques effectiveness
Non-Probability Sampling			
Convenience Sampling	When the members of the population are convenient to sample	Convenience and inexpensive	Degree of generalizability is questionable
Quota Sampling	When strata are present and stratified sampling is not possible	Insures some degree of representativeness of all the strata in the population	Degree of generalizability is questionable
Type of Sampling	**When to Use It**	**Advantages**	**Disadvantages**

Sampling Distributions

Sample statistics are random variables because they vary from sample to sample. As a result, sample statistics also have a distribution called the **sampling distribution**. These sampling distributions, similar to distributions discussed previously, have a mean and standard deviation. We refer to the standard deviation of a sampling distribution as the **standard error**. Thus, the standard error is simply the standard deviation of a sampling distribution. Often, statisticians will interchange these two terms.

Consider taking two random samples, each sample consisting of 5 students, from a class and calculating the mean height in each sample. Would you expect both sample means to be exactly the same?

No, the two sample means would be different because of random sampling error. If you were to repeatedly pull samples of 5 students from the population of all students and compute the mean of each sample, you could construct a distribution of sample means. That distribution of sample means (i.e., **sampling distribution**) would have a mean that is equal to the population mean (ì) and a standard deviation that is known as the **standard error** (SE (x¯).

Tests of Hypothesis

A statistical hypothesis is an assumption about a population parameter. This assumption may or may not be true. Hypothesis testing refers to the formal procedures used by statisticians to accept or reject statistical hypotheses.

Statistical Hypotheses

The best way to determine whether a statistical hypothesis is true would be to examine the entire population. Since that is often impractical, researchers typically examine a random sample from the population. If sample data are not consistent with the statistical hypothesis, the hypothesis is rejected. There are two types of statistical hypotheses. These are stated below:

Null Hypothesis: The null hypothesis, denoted by H_0, is usually the hypothesis that sample observations result purely from chance.

Alternative Hypothesis: The alternative hypothesis, denoted by H_1 or Ha, is the hypothesis that sample observations are influenced by some non-random cause.

For example, suppose we wanted to determine whether a coin was fair and balanced. A null hypothesis might be that half the flips would result in Heads and half in Tails. The alternative hypothesis might be that the number of Heads and Tails would be very different. Symbolically, these hypotheses would be expressed as

H_0: P = 0.5

Ha: P $\neq$ 0.5

Suppose we flipped the coin 50 times, resulting in 40 Heads and 10 Tails. Given this result, we would be inclined to reject the null hypothesis. We would conclude, based on the evidence, that the coin was probably not fair and balanced.

Hypothesis Tests

Statisticians follow a formal process to determine whether to reject a null hypothesis based on sample data. This process, called hypothesis testing, consists of four steps.

State the Hypotheses: This involves stating the null and alternative hypotheses. The hypotheses are stated in such a way that they are mutually exclusive. That is, if one is true, the other must be false.

Formulate an Analysis Plan: The analysis plan describes how to use sample data to evaluate the null hypothesis. The evaluation often focuses around a single test statistic.

Analyze Sample Data: Find the value of the test statistic (mean score, proportion, t statistic, z-score, etc.) described in the analysis plan.

Interpret Results: Apply the decision rule described in the analysis plan. If the value of the test statistic is unlikely, based on the null hypothesis, reject the null hypothesis.

Decision Errors

Two types of errors can result from a hypothesis test.

Type I Error: A Type I error occurs when the researcher rejects a null hypothesis when it is true. The probability of committing a Type I error is called the significance level. This probability is also called alpha, and is often denoted by α.

Type II Error: A Type II error occurs when the researcher fails to reject a null hypothesis that is false. The probability of committing a Type II error is called Beta, and is often denoted by β. The probability of not committing a Type II error is called the **Power of the test.**

Decision Rules

The analysis plan includes decision rules for rejecting the null hypothesis. In practice, statisticians describe these decision rules in two ways - with reference to a P-value or with reference to a region of acceptance.

P-Value: The strength of evidence in support of a null hypothesis is measured by the P-value. Suppose the test statistic is equal to S. The P-value is the probability of observing a test statistic as extreme as S, assuming the null hypothesis is true. If the P-value is less than the significance level, we reject the null hypothesis.

Region of Acceptance: The region of acceptance is a range of values. If the test statistic falls within the region of acceptance, the null hypothesis is not rejected. The region of acceptance is defined so that the chance of making a Type I error is equal to the significance level.

The set of values outside the region of acceptance is called the region of rejection. If the test statistic falls within the region of rejection, the null hypothesis is rejected. In such cases, we say that the hypothesis has been rejected at the level of significance.

One-Tailed and Two-Tailed Tests

A test of a statistical hypothesis, where the region of rejection is on only one side of the sampling distribution, is called a one-tailed test. For example, suppose the null hypothesis states that the mean is less than or equal to 10. The alternative hypothesis would be that the mean is greater than 10. The region of rejection would consist of a range of numbers located on the right side of sampling distribution; that is, a set of numbers greater than 10.

A test of a statistical hypothesis, where the region of rejection is on both sides of the sampling distribution, is called a two-tailed test. For example, suppose the null hypothesis states that the mean is equal to 10. The alternative hypothesis would be that the mean is less than 10 or greater than 10. The region of rejection would consist of a range of numbers located on both sides of sampling distribution; that is, the region of rejection would consist partly of numbers that were less than 10 and partly of numbers that were greater than 10.

Large & Small Samples

1. Reducing sampling error is the major goal of any selection technique.

2. A sample should be big enough to answer the research question, but not so big that the process of sampling becomes uneconomical.
3. Estimating sample size in general, you need a larger sample to accurately represent the population when:
   (a) The amount of variability within groups is greater, and
   (b) The difference between the two groups gets smaller.
4. In general, the larger the sample, the smaller the sampling error and the better job you can do.
5. If you are going to use several subgroups in your work (such as males and females who are both 10 years of age, and healthy and unhealthy urban residents), be sure your initial selection of subjects is large enough to account for the eventual breaking down of subject groups.
6. If you are mailing out surveys or questionnaire, count on increasing your sample size by 40% to 50% to account for lost mail and uncooperative subjects.

Independent T-Test for Two Samples

The independent t-test, also called the two sample t-test, independent-samples t-test or student's t-test, is an inferential statistical test that determines whether there is a statistically significant difference between the means in two unrelated groups.

Null and Alternative Hypotheses for the Independent T-Test

The null hypothesis for the independent t-test is that the population means from the two unrelated groups are equal:

$H_0: u_1 = u_2$

In most cases, we are looking to see if we can show that we can reject the null hypothesis and accept the alternative hypothesis, which is that the population means are not equal:

$H_A: u_1 \neq u_2$

To do this, we need to set a significance level (also called alpha) that allows us to either reject or accept the alternative hypothesis. Most commonly, this value is set at 0.05.

In order to run an independent t-test, we need the following:

- One independent, categorical variable that has two levels/groups.
- One continuous dependent variable.

Z Test

The Z-test is also applied to compare sample and population means to know if there's a significant difference between them. Z-tests always use normal distribution and also ideally applied if the standard deviation is known. Z-tests are often applied if the certain conditions are met; otherwise, other statistical tests like T-tests are applied in substitute. Z-tests are often applied in large samples (n > 30).

Comparison between T test and Z Test

1. Z-test is a statistical hypothesis test that follows a normal distribution while T-test follows a Student's T-distribution.
2. A T-test is appropriate when we are handling small samples (n < 30) while a Z-test is appropriate when we are handling moderate to large samples (n > 30).
3. T-test is more adaptable than Z-test since Z-test will often require certain conditions to be reliable. Additionally, T-test has many methods that will suit any need.
4. T-tests are more commonly used than Z-tests.
5. Z-tests are preferred than T-tests when standard deviations are known.

Anova

These days, researchers are using ANOVA in many ways. The use of ANOVA depends on the research design. Commonly, researchers are using ANOVA in three ways: one-way ANOVA, two-way ANOVA, and N-way Multivariate ANOVA.

One-Way

When we compare more than two groups, based on one factor (independent variable), this is called one way ANOVA. For example, it is used if a manufacturing company wants to compare the productivity of three or more employees based on working hours. This is called one way ANOVA.

Two-Way

When a company wants to compare the employee productivity based on two factors (2 independent variables), then it said to be two way (Factorial) ANOVA. For example, based on the working hours and working conditions, if a company wants to compare employee productivity, it can do that through two way ANOVA. Two-way ANOVA's can be used to see the effect of one of the factors after controlling for the other, or it can be used to see the **interaction** between the two factors. This is a great way to control for extraneous variables as you are able to add them to the design of the study.

N-Way

When the factor comparison is taken, then it said to be n-way ANOVA.

For example, in productivity measurement if a company takes all the factors for productivity measurement, then it is said to be n-way

ANOVA

ANOVA is used very commonly in business, medicine or in psychology research. In business, ANOVA can be used to compare the sales of different designs based on different factors. A psychology researcher can use ANOVA to compare the different attitude or behaviour in people and whether or not they are the same depending on certain factors. In medical research, ANOVA is used to test the effectiveness of a drug.

Chi-Square Test

The test is applied when you have two **categorical variables** from a single population. It is used to determine whether there is a significant association between the two variables.

For example, in an election survey, voters might be classified by gender (male or female) and voting preference (Democrat, Republican, or Independent). We could use a chi-square test for independence to determine whether gender is related to voting preference.

The chi-square goodness of fit test is appropriate when the following conditions are met:

- The sampling method is **simple random sampling**.
- The variable under study is **categorical**.
- The expected value of the number of sample observations in each **level** of the variable is at least 5.

This approach consists of four steps: (1) state the hypotheses, (2) formulate an analysis plan, (3) analyze sample data, and (4) interpret results.

1. State the Hypotheses: Every hypothesis test requires the analyst to state a null hypothesis (H_0) and an alternative hypothesis (H_a). The hypotheses are stated in such a way that they are mutually exclusive. That is, if one is true, the other must be false; and vice versa.

For a chi-square goodness of fit test, the hypotheses take the following form.

H_0: The data are consistent with a specified distribution.

H_a: The data are *not* consistent with a specified distribution.

2. Formulate an Analysis Plan: The analysis plan describes how to use sample data to accept or reject the null hypothesis. The plan should specify the following elements.

Significance Level: Often, researchers choose significance levels equal to 0.01, 0.05, or 0.10; but any value between 0 and 1 can be used.

Test Method: Use the chi-square goodness of fit test to determine whether observed sample frequencies differ significantly from expected frequencies specified in the null hypothesis.

3. Analyze Sample Data: Using sample data, find the degrees of freedom, expected frequency counts, test statistic, and the P-value associated with the test statistic.

Degrees of Freedom: The degrees of freedom (DF) is equal to the number of levels (k) of the categorical variable minus 1: DF = k - 1.

Expected Frequency Counts: The expected frequency counts at each level of the categorical variable are equal to the sample size times the hypothesized proportion from the null hypothesis

$E_i = np_i$

Where E_i is the expected frequency count for the *i*th level of the categorical variable, n is the total sample size, and p_i is the hypothesized proportion of observations in level *i*.

Test Statistic: The test statistic is a chi-square random variable ($\times^2$) defined by the following equation.

$$\mathbf{X^2 = \Sigma\ [(O_i - E_i)^2 / E_i]}$$

Where O_i is the observed frequency count for the *i*th level of the categorical variable, and E_i is the expected frequency count for the *i*th level of the categorical variable.

P-Value: The P-value is the probability of observing a sample statistic as extreme as the test statistic.

4. Interpret Results: If the sample findings are unlikely, given the null hypothesis, the researcher rejects the null hypothesis. Typically, this involves comparing the P-value to the significance level, and rejecting the null hypothesis when the P-value is less than the significance level.

Unit - IX

Corporate Strategy

Concept of Corporate Strategy

Corporate strategy encompasses a firm's corporate actions with the aim to achieve company's objectives while achieving a **competitive advantage**.

A corporate strategy entails a clearly defined, long-term vision that organizations set, seeking to create corporate value and motivate the workforce to implement the proper actions to achieve customer satisfaction. In addition, corporate strategy is a continuous process that requires a constant effort to engage investors in trusting the company with their money, thereby increasing the company's equity. Organizations that manage to deliver customer value unfailingly are those that revisit their corporate strategy regularly to improve areas that may not deliver the aimed results.

Corporate strategy is one, which decides what business the organization should be in, and how the overall group of activities should be structured and managed.

Porter has described it as the overall plan for a diversified business. The strategies are then evolved for each strategic business unit and strategic business area.

Strategic Business Unit: As the number and diversity of products increases, the structure is likely to be centered upon division called Strategic Business Unit (SBU). **SBU** are responsible individually for developing, manufacturing and marketing their own product or group of products.

Strategic Business Area (SBA): SBA is a distinctive segment of the environment in which the firm does want to do business. A company instead of trying to compete in all the area, it selects the area of its competitive advantage and invest its money. This helps the company to concentrate its strategies in a particular area and to reduce the unnecessary expenses in non-profitable area.

Components of Strategy Formulation

Formulation of strategies is a creative and analytical process. It is a process because particular functions are performed in a sequence over the period of time. The process involves a number of activities and their analysis to arrive at a decision. Though there may not be unanimity over these activities particularly in the context of organizational variability, a complete process of strategy formulation and implementation can be understood.

The process set out above includes strategy formulation and its implementation, what has been referred to as strategic management process. The same process can be applied to both strategy and policy. A brief discussion of each element is as follows:

- **(i) Organizational Mission and Objectives:** These are the starting point of strategy formulation. Mission is the fundamental unique purpose of an organization that sets it apart from other organizations and objective is the end result, which an organization strives to achieve. These together provide the direction for other aspects of the process.
- **(ii) Environmental Analysis:** The second aspect of the process is the environmental analysis. Since the basic objective of strategies is to integrate the organization with its environment, it must know the kind of environment in which it has to work. This can be known by environmental analysis. The process of environmental analysis includes collection of relevant information from the environment, interpreting its impact on the future organizational working, and determining what opportunities and threats-positive and negative aspects-are offered by the environment. The environmental information can be collected from various sources like various publications, verbal information from various people, spying, and forecasting. The process of environmental analysis works better if it is undertaken on continuous basis and is made an intrinsic part of the strategy formulation.
- **(iii) Corporate Analysis:** While environmental analysis is the analysis of **external factors**, corporate analysis takes into account the **internal factors**. These together are known as SWOT (strengths, weaknesses, opportunities and threats) analysis. It is not merely enough to locate what opportunities and threats are offered by the

environment but equally important is the analysis of how the organization can take the advantages of these opportunities and overcome threats. Corporate analysis discloses strengths and weaknesses of the organization and points out the areas in which business can be undertaken. Corporate analysis is performed by identifying the factors, which are critical for the success of the present or future business of the organization, and then evaluating these factors whether they are contributing in positive way or in negative way. A positive contribution is strength and a negative contribution is a weakness.

(iv) Identification of Alternatives: Environmental analysis and corporate analysis taken together will specify the various alternatives for strategy. Usually this process will bring large number of alternatives. For example, if an organization is strong in financial resources, these can be used in many ways, taking several projects. However, all the ways or projects cannot be selected. Therefore, some criteria should be set up to evaluate each alternative. Normally the criteria are set in the light of organizational mission and objectives.

(v) Choice of Strategy: The identification and evaluation of various alternatives will narrow down the range of strategies that can seriously be considered for choice. Choice is deciding the acceptable alternative among the several which fits with the organizational objectives. Normally at this stage, personal values and expectations of decision-maker play an important role in strategy because he will decide the course of action depending on his own likings and disliking. This happens because in one way the organizational objectives reflect the personal philosophy of individuals particularly at the top management level.

(vi) Implementation: After the strategy has been chosen, it is put to implementation, that is, it is put into action. Choice of strategy is mostly analytical and conceptual while implementation is operational or putting into action. Various factors which are necessary for implementation are design of suitable organization structure, developing and motivating people to take up work, designing effective control and information system, allocation of resources, etc.

Ansoff's Growth Vector

"The Ansoff growth matrix assists organizations to map strategic product market growth"

Ansoff's Growth Matrix Diagram

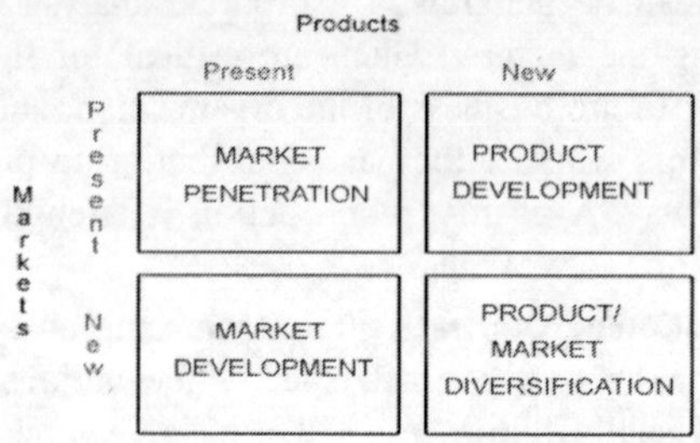

The Ansoff Matrix also known as the Ansoff product and market growth matrix is a marketing planning tool which usually aids a business in determining its **product and market growth**. This is usually determined by focusing on whether the products are new or existing and whether the market is new or existing.

The model was invented by **H. Igor Ansoff**. It is believed that the concept of strategic management is widely attributed to the great man.

The Ansoff Matrix has four alternatives of marketing strategies; market penetration, product development, market development and diversification.

Market Penetration

When we look at market penetration, it usually covers products that are existence and that are also existent in an existing market. In this strategy, there can be further exploitation of the products without necessarily changing the product or the outlook of the product. This will be possible through the use of promotional methods, putting various pricing policies that may attract more clientele, or one can make the distribution more extensive.

In market penetration, the risk involved in its marketing strategies is usually the least since the products are already familiar to the consumers in the established market. Another way in which market penetration can be increased is by coming up with various initiatives that will encourage increased usage of the product. A good example is the usage of toothpaste. Research has shown that the toothbrush head influences the amount of toothpaste that one will use. Thus, if the head of the toothbrush is bigger it will mean that more toothpaste will be used thus promoting the usage of the toothpaste and eventually leading to more purchase of the toothpaste.

Product Development

In product development growth strategy, new products are introduced into existing markets. Product development can differ from the introduction of a new product in an existing market or it can involve the modification of an existing product. By modifying the product one would probably change its outlook or presentation, increase the products performance or quality. By doing so, it can appeal more to the already existing market. A good example is car manufacturers who offer a range of car parts so as to target the car owners in purchasing a replica of the models.

Market Development

The third marketing strategy is market development. It may also be known as **market extension**. In this strategy, the business sells its existing products to new markets. This can be made possible through further market segmentation to aid in identifying a new clientele base. This strategy assumes that the existing markets have been fully exploited thus the need to venture into new markets. There are various approaches to this strategy, which include: new geographical markets, new distribution channels, new product packaging, and different pricing policies. In new geographical markets, the business can expound by exporting their products to other new countries. It would also mean setting up other branches of the business in other areas that the business had not ventured before. Various businesses have adopted the franchise method as a way of setting up other branches in new markets.

A good example is Guinness. This beer had originally been made to be sold in countries that have a colder climate, but now it is also being sold in African countries. The other method is via new distribution channels. This would entail selling the products via e-commerce or mail order. Selling through e-commerce will capture a larger clientele base since we are in a digital era where most people often access the internet. In new product packaging, it means repacking the product in another method or dimension. In different pricing policies, the business could change its prices so as to attract a different customer base or so create a new market segment.

Diversification

The last strategy is diversification. This growth strategy involves an organization marketing or selling new products to new markets at the same time. It is the most risky strategy among the others as it involves two unknowns, new products being created and the business does not know the development problems that may occur in the process. There is also the fact that there is a new market being targeted, which will bring the problem of having unknown characteristics. For a business to take a step into diversification, they need to have their facts right regarding what it expects to gain from the strategy and have a clear assessment of the risks involved.

There are two types of diversification. There is related diversification and unrelated diversification. In **related diversification**, this means that the business remains in the same industry in which it is familiar with. For example, a cake manufacturer diversifies into a fresh juice manufacturer. This diversification is in the same industry which is the food industry. In **unrelated diversification**, there are usually no previous industry relations or market experiences. One can diversify from a food industry to a mechanical industry for instance.

BCG Model

Boston Consulting Group (BCG) Matrix is a four celled matrix developed by BCG, **USA**. It is the most renowned corporate portfolio analysis tool. It provides a graphic representation for an organization to examine different businesses in its portfolio on the basis of their **related market share** and **industry growth rates**. It is a two dimensional analysis on management of SBU's (Strategic Business Units). In other words, it is a comparative analysis of business potential and the evaluation of environment.

According to this matrix, business could be classified as high or low according to their industry growth rate and relative market share.

The analysis requires that both measures be calculated for each SBU. The dimension of business strength, relative market share, will measure comparative advantage indicated by market dominance.

BCG matrix has four cells, with the horizontal axis representing relative market share and the vertical axis denoting market growth rate. The mid-point of relative market share is set at **1.0**. If all the SBU's are in same industry, the average growth rate of the industry is used. While, if all the SBU's are located in different industries, then the mid-point is set at the growth rate for the economy.

Resources are allocated to the business units according to their situation on the grid. The four cells of this matrix have been called as stars, cash cows, question marks and dogs. Each of these cells represents a **particular type of business**.

(i) **Stars:** Stars represent business units having **large market share** in a **fast growing industry**. They may generate cash but because of fast growing market, stars require huge investments to maintain their lead. Net cash flow is usually modest. SBU's located in this cell are attractive as they are located in a robust industry and these business units are highly competitive in the industry. If successful, a star will become a cash cow when the industry matures.

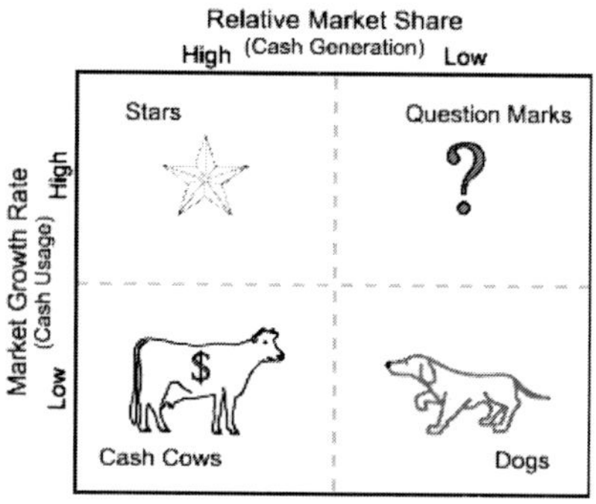

(ii) Cash Cows: It represents business units having a **large market share** in a mature, **slow growing industry**. Cash cows require little investment and generate cash that can be utilized for investment in other business units. These SBU's are the corporation's key source of cash, and are specifically the core business. They are the base of an organization. These businesses usually follow stability strategies. When cash cows lose their appeal and move towards deterioration, then a retrenchment policy may be pursued.

(iii) Question Marks: Question marks represent business units having **low relative market share** and located in a **high growth industry**. They require huge amount of cash to maintain or gain market share. They require attention to determine if the venture can be viable. Question marks are generally new goods and services which have a good commercial prospective. There is no specific strategy which can be adopted. If the firm thinks it has dominant market share, then it can adopt expansion strategy, else retrenchment strategy can be adopted. Most businesses start as question marks as the company tries to enter a high growth market in which there is already a market-share. If ignored, then question marks may become dogs, while if huge investment is made, then they have potential of becoming stars.

(iv) Dogs: Dogs represent businesses having **weak market shares** in **low-growth markets**. They neither generate cash nor require huge amount of cash. Due to low market share, these business units face cost disadvantages. Generally retrenchment strategies are adopted because these firms can gain market share only at the expense of competitor's/rival firms. These business firms have weak market share because of high costs, poor quality, ineffective marketing, etc. Unless a dog has some other strategic aim, it should be liquidated if there are fewer prospects for it to gain market share.

Limitations of BCG Matrix

The BCG Matrix produces a framework for allocating resources among different business units and makes it possible to compare many business units at a glance. But BCG Matrix is not free from limitations, such as-

(i) BCG matrix classifies businesses as low and high, but generally businesses can be medium also. Thus, the true nature of business may not be reflected.

(ii) Market is not clearly defined in this model.

(iii) High market share does not always leads to high profits. There are high costs also involved with high market share.

(iv) Growth rate and relative market share are not the only indicators of profitability. This model ignores and overlooks other indicators of profitability.

(v) At times, dogs may help other businesses in gaining competitive advantage. They can earn even more than cash cows sometimes.

(vi) This four-celled approach is considered as to be too simplistic.

Porter's Generic Strategies

The key strategic challenge for most businesses is to find a way of achieving a **sustainable competitive advantage** over the other competing products and firms in a market.

A **competitive advantage** is an advantage over competitors gained by offering consumers greater value, either by means of lower prices or by providing greater benefits and service that justifies higher prices.

The four strategies are summarized in the figure below:

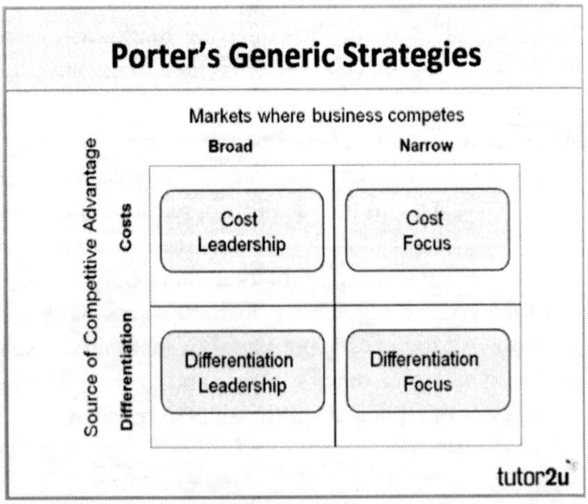

The **differentiation** and **cost leadership** strategies seek competitive advantage in a **broad range of market or industry segments**.

By contrast, the **differentiation focus** and **cost focus** strategies are adopted in a **narrow market or industry**.

Cost Leadership

With this strategy, the objective is to become the **lowest-cost producer** in the industry. The traditional method to achieve this objective is to produce on a large scale which enables the business to exploit economies of scale.

If the achieved selling price can at least equal or near the average for the market, then the lowest-cost producer will enjoy the best profits.

This strategy is usually associated with large-scale businesses offering standard products with relatively little differentiation that are readily acceptable to the majority of customers. Occasionally, a low-cost leader will also discount its product to maximize sales, particularly if it has a significant cost advantage over the competition and, in doing so, it can further increase its market share.

A strategy of cost leadership requires close cooperation between all the functional areas of a business. To be the lowest-cost producer, a firm is likely to achieve or use several of the following:

- High levels of productivity
- High capacity utilization
- Use of bargaining power to negotiate the lowest prices for production inputs
- Lean production methods (e.g. JIT)
- Effective use of technology in the production process
- Access to the most effective distribution channels

Cost Focus

Here a business seeks a lower-cost advantage in just one or a small number of market segments. Cost focus is a strategy that organizations implement by providing their products and services as low as consumers are willing to pay, thereby being competitive and realizing a volume of sales that allows them to be the leaders in the industry. Typical examples of cost leaders are Wal-Mart in the retail industry, McDonalds in the restaurant industry, and Ikea, the furniture retailer that offers low-priced, yet good quality home equipment by sourcing its products in emerging markets, thereby having a high-profit margin.

Differentiation Focus

In the differentiation focus strategy, a business aims to differentiate within **just one or a small number of target market segments.**

The special customer needs of the segment mean that there are opportunities to provide products that are clearly different from competitors who may be targeting a broader group of customers.

The important issue for any business adopting this strategy is to ensure that customers really do have different needs and wants. Differentiation focus is the classic niche marketing strategy. Many small businesses are able to establish themselves in a niche market segment using this strategy, achieving higher prices than un-differentiated products through specialist expertise or other ways to add value for customers.

Differentiation Leadership

With differentiation leadership, the business targets much larger markets and aims to achieve competitive advantage through differentiation across the whole of an industry.

This strategy involves selecting one or more criteria used by buyers in a market and then positioning the business uniquely to meet those criteria. This strategy is usually associated with charging a premium price for the product often to reflect the higher production costs and extra value-added features provided for the consumer.

Differentiation is about charging a premium price that more than covers the additional production costs, and about giving customers clear reasons to prefer the product over other, less differentiated products.

There are several ways in which this can be achieved, though it is not easy and it requires substantial and sustained marketing investment. The methods include:

- Superior product quality (features, benefits, durability, reliability)
- Branding (strong customer recognition & desire; brand loyalty)
- Industry-wide distribution across all major channels (i.e. the product or brand is an essential item to be stocked by retailers)
- Consistent promotional support often dominated by advertising, sponsorship, etc

Great examples of a differentiation leadership include global brands like Nike and Mercedes. These brands achieve significant economies of scale, but they do not rely on a cost leadership strategy to compete. Their business and brands are built on persuading customers to become brand loyal and paying a premium for their products.

Competitor Analysis

Usually competition analysis is done along with the industry analysis. This is so because competition and competitive forces are a part and parcel of industry structure. As a part of strategy formulation, the firm must analyze and size up all the forces that shape competition in the industry. Most of the firms suffered from what was referred to as '**strategic myopia**'. It was Michael Porter who gave a new thrust to the ideas associated with the competition.

Five forces model was created by M. Porter in 1979 to understand how five key competitive forces are affecting an industry. The five forces identified are:

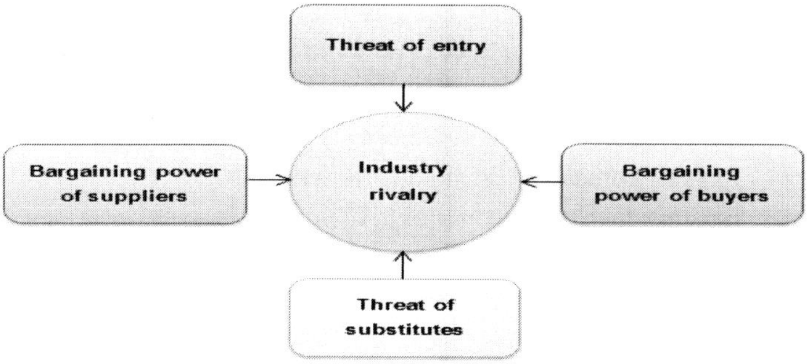

These forces determine an industry structure and the level of competition in that industry. The stronger competitive forces in the industry are the less profitable it is. An industry with low barriers to enter, having few buyers and suppliers but many substitute products and competitors will be seen as very competitive and thus, not so attractive due to its low profitability.

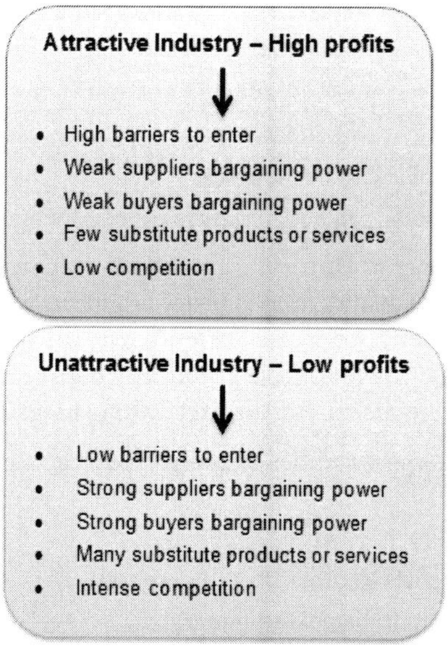

It is every strategist's job to evaluate company's competitive position in the industry and to identify what strengths or weakness can be exploited to strengthen that position. The tool is very useful in formulating firm's strategy as it reveals how powerful each of the five key forces is in a particular industry.

Threat of New Entrants: This force determines how easy (or not) it is to enter a particular industry. If an industry is profitable and there are few barriers to enter, rivalry soon intensifies. When more organizations compete for the same market share, profits start to fall. It is essential for existing organizations to create high barriers to enter to deter new entrants. Threat of new entrants is high when:

- Low amount of capital is required to enter a market;
- Existing companies can do little to retaliate;
- Existing firms do not possess patents, trademarks or do not have established brand reputation;
- There is no government regulation;
- Customer switching costs are low;
- There is low customer loyalty;
- Products are nearly identical;
- Economies of scale can be easily achieved.

Bargaining Power of Suppliers: Strong bargaining power allows suppliers to sell higher priced or low quality raw materials to their buyers. This directly affects the buying firms' profits because it has to pay more for materials. Suppliers have strong bargaining power when:

- There are few suppliers but many buyers;
- Suppliers are large and threaten to forward integrate;
- Few substitute raw materials exist;
- Suppliers hold scarce resources;
- Cost of switching raw materials is especially high.

Bargaining Power of Buyers: Buyers have the power to demand lower price or higher product quality from industry producers when their bargaining power is strong. Lower price means lower revenues for the producer, while higher quality products usually raise production costs. Both scenarios result in lower profits for producers. Buyers exert strong bargaining power when:

- Buying in large quantities or control many access points to the final customer;
- Only few buyers exist;
- Switching costs to other supplier are low;
- They threaten to backward integrate;

- There are many substitutes;
- Buyers are price sensitive.

Threat of Substitutes: This force is especially threatening when buyers can easily find substitute products with attractive prices or better quality and when buyers can switch from one product or service to another with little cost. For example, to switch from coffee to tea doesn't cost anything, unlike switching from car to bicycle.

Rivalry among Existing Competitors: This force is the major determinant on how competitive and profitable an industry is. In competitive industry, firms have to compete aggressively for a market share, which results in low profits. Rivalry among competitors is intense when:

- There are many competitors;
- Exit barriers are high;
- Industry of growth is slow or negative;
- Products are not differentiated and can be easily substituted;
- Competitors are of equal size;
- Low customer loyalty.

Competitor analysis is a critical part of a firm's activities. It is an assessment of the strengths and weaknesses of current and potential competitors, which may encompass firms not only in their own sectors but also in other sectors. Directly or indirectly, competitor analysis is a driver of a firm's strategy and impacts on how firms act or react in their sectors. Gluck, Kaufman and Walleck (2000) showed that competitor analysis is one of two components that give a firm a strong market understanding. This drives the formulation of a strategy and it applies whether a firm formulates a strategy through strategic thinking, formal strategic planning, or opportunistic strategic decision making. Competitor analysis, together with an understanding of major environmental trends, is a key input in strategy formulation and should be developed properly.

In utilizing competitor analysis as part of strategy formulation, firms are able to adapt or build their own strategies and be able to compete effectively, improve performance and gain market share in their businesses. In a large number of instances, firms are able to tap new markets or build new niches. For example, after European air travel was deregulated in the mid-1990s, Ryanair and Easyjet focused on the no-frills market and provided low-cost travel across Europe after figuring out through competitor analysis, where the opportunities were emerging.

Main Aspects of Competitor Analysis

The key objectives in competitor analysis are to develop a greater understanding of what competitors have in place in terms of resources and capabilities, what they plan to do in their businesses, and how the competitors may react to various situations in reaction to what the firm does. Michael Porter has defined a competitor analysis framework that focused on four key aspects: **competitor's objectives, competitor's assumptions, competitor's strategy, and competitor's resources and capabilities**. These four aspects of competitor analysis are the areas critical for a firm to understand and they should pursue this knowledge not only for current competitors but also for other potential competitors in the business.

This framework is broken into two parts. The competitor's objectives and assumptions drive the competitor while the competitor's strategy and resources and capabilities define what the competitor is doing or is capable of doing. Together, these four aspects define a competitor response profile which gives the firm an understanding of what actions a competitor may take. Taking this analysis across a firm's key competitors will give the firm a viewpoint on where the sector is heading, and provides the firm with a basis for developing their strategy and actions. The key aspects of competitor analysis and the resulting competitor response profile are defined further below.

Competitor's Objectives

In competitor analysis, there are two key factors to note in building knowledge of a competitor's objectives. The first factor is to know the actual objectives of a competitor. This could range from building market share in a specific market or overall business, entering a new market or even just maintaining profitability. This should also look at not only current competitors but also potential competitors.

The second factor is to know if the competitor is actually achieving their stated objectives. Looking at these two factors will provide a firm with an opinion on a competitor's potential actions to changes in the sector. As part of a comprehensive competitor analysis, firms should identify their key competitors and be able to define the objectives of each competitor and their likelihood of achieving their objectives.

Competitor's Assumptions

Another key aspect in competitor analysis is an understanding of competitors' assumptions about the overall market (trends in the market, products, and consumers). For example, competitors could define their actions based on what their assumptions are on the growth of the market. In a cyclical industry (say pulp and paper or shipping sectors), investments decided by players in the industry should be driven by when competitors expect the industry to be at their peak, as timing is critical for players in the industry to meet demand. However, this is not what usually happens. For a proper competitor analysis work, the assumptions made by competitors on the industry and other players should be indicated, but as seen in the example, the validity of these assumptions should be challenged.

Competitor's Strategy

A third aspect in competitor analysis is the understanding of a competitor's strategy. In most cases, this strategy will be defined and stated, particularly for public firms. In other cases, it may not be openly stated what competitors' strategies are but these can be understood by utilizing a number of sources available to firms from analyzing a competitor's behaviour in certain situations to discussing with industry experts to get their viewpoints.

Competitor's Resources and Capabilities

Finally, a competitor analysis should also include an understanding of a competitor's resources and capabilities as these would give a firm an idea of how a competitor can achieve its strategy and objectives, and also give a firm a timeline for when it would expect competitors to pursue certain activities.

Competitor Response Profile

The results of the analysis from the four aspects of competitor analysis, as defined above, lead to a competitor response profile. In this profile, a firm can define its thoughts on what actions competitors may purse depending on the understanding given by the competitor analysis. This provides a firm with a better grounding and preparation to react to competitor actions.

Strategic Dimensions & Group Mapping

It is a technique for looking at your position in your sector, field or market. Hunt coined the term 'strategic group' in 1972 when he noticed sub-groups of businesses with similar characteristics in the same market. Michael Porter then expanded the concept in the 1980s. There are a number of benefits to strategic group mapping:

- It helps to identify your direct and indirect competitors
- It can illustrate how easy it might be to move from one strategic group to another
- It helps to identify future opportunities or strategic problems
- It ensures you to take your customers' or beneficiaries' views into account when developing or assessing your strategy

Purpose

The purpose of strategic group mapping is to make sure you to take the needs or wants of your customers/beneficiaries into account. It encourages you to ask different questions about your future strategy, relationships with other businesses in your sector and your understanding of the people who ultimately benefit from your products or services.

The Tool

The tool helps you to assess the top five other players working in your field or sector. You then map the results on a matrix. You can do it on your own or with a group. It is most suitable for SMEs and larger businesses but can be adapted. It will take several hours to complete a detailed map.

Industry Analysis

In order to have a better understanding of the external environment, analyzing the industry in detail is critical. In conducting an industry analysis managers need to analyze seven aspects carefully:

(i) **General Features and Basic Conditions of the Industry:** General features/basic conditions of the industry include factors such as current size of the industry, product categories/sub categories, their relative volumes, performance of the industry in recent years, etc.

(ii) **Industry Environment:** Industries can be classified based on their settings/environment. Porter classified industries as fragmented, emerging, matured, declining and global industries.

(iii) **Industry Structure:** Industry structure essentially means the underlying fundamental economic and technical forces of an industry. Each company will have its own key structural features such as number of players, market size, relative shares of the player, nature of the competition, differentiation practiced by the various players in the industry, cost structure of the players, etc. These features determine the strength of competitive forces operating in the industry and thereby serve as direct indicators to the attractiveness or profitability of the industry.

(iv) **Industry Attractiveness:** The various determinants of industry attractiveness are industry potential, industry growth, industry profitability, future pattern of the industry barriers and forces shaping the competition in the industry.

(v) **Industry Performance:** Industry performance entails looking at production, sales, profitability and technological development.

(vi) **Industry Practices:** Industry practices refer to what a majority of the players do in the industry with respect to essential aspects of the business such as distribution, pricing, promotion, methods of selling, service field support, R&D and legal tactics.

(vii) **Emerging Trends and Likely Future:** The emerging trends/likely future pattern of the industry can be discerned by analyzing issues such as the product life cycle, stage of the industry, rate of growth, changes of buyer needs, innovation in product/process, entry and exit of firms and emerging changes in the regulatory environment governing the industry.

Strategies in Industry Evolution

Like other living creatures, industry also has its circle of life. The industry lifecycle imitates the human lifecycle. The stages of industry lifecycle include fragmentation, shake-out, maturity and decline.

Fragmentation Stage

Fragmentation is the first stage of the new industry. This is the stage when the new industry develops the business. At this stage, the new industry normally arises when an entrepreneur overcomes the twin problems of innovation and invention, and works out how to bring the new products or services into the market. For example, air travel services of major airlines in Europe were sold to the target market at a high price. Therefore, the majority of airlines' customers in Europe were those people with high incomes who could afford premium prices for faster travel.

Shake-Out: Shake-out is the second stage of the industry lifecycle. It is the stage at which a new industry emerges. During the shake-out stage, competitors start to realize business opportunities in the emerging industry. The value of the industry also quickly rises.

For example, many people die and suffer because of cigarettes every year. Thus, the UK government decided to launch a campaign to encourage people to quit smoking. Nicorette, one of the leading companies is producing several nicotine products to help people quit smoking. Some of its well-known products include Nicorette patches, Nicolette gums and Nicorette lozenges.

Maturity: Maturity is the third stage in the industry lifecycle. Maturity is a stage at which the efficiencies of the dominant business model give these organizations competitive advantage over competition. The competition in the industry is rather aggressive because there are many competitors and product substitutes. Price, competition, and cooperation take on a complex form. Some companies may shift some of the production overseas in order to gain competitive advantage.

For example, Toyota is one of the world's leading multinational companies, selling automobiles to customers worldwide. The export and import taxes mean that its cars lose competitiveness to the local competitors, especially in the European automobile industry. As a result, Toyota decided to open a factory in the UK in order to produce cars and sell them to customers in the European market.

Decline: Decline is the final stage of the industry lifecycle. Decline is a stage during which a war of slow destruction between businesses may develop and those with heavy bureaucracies may fail. In addition, the demand in the market may be fully satisfied or suppliers may be running out.

In the stage of decline, some companies may leave the industry if there is no demand for the products or services they provide, or they may develop new products or services that meet the demand in the market. In such cases, this will create a new industry.

Competitive Strategy &Corporate Strategy

Competitive strategy is about being different. It means deliberately choosing to perform activities differently or to perform different activities than rivals to deliver a unique mix of value. (Michael E. Porter)

The essence of strategy lies in creating tomorrow's competitive advantages faster than competitors mimic the ones you possess today.

Corporate strategy encompasses a firm's corporate actions with the aim to achieve company objectives while achieving a competitive advantage.

A corporate strategy entails a clearly defined, long-term vision that organizations set, seeking to create corporate value and motivate the workforce to implement the proper actions to achieve customer satisfaction. In addition, corporate strategy is a continuous process that requires a constant effort to engage investors in trusting the company with their money, thereby increasing the company's equity. Organizations that manage to deliver customer value unfailingly are those that revisit their corporate strategy regularly to improve areas that may not deliver the aimed results.

Transnationalization of World Economy

Transnationalization as an economic process involves the global reorganization of the production process, in which various stages of the production of any product can occur in various countries, typically with the aim of minimizing costs. Economic Transnationalization, commonly known as globalization, was spurred in the latter half of the 20th century by the development of the internet and wireless communication, as well as the reduction in global transportation costs caused by containerization. Multinational corporations could be seen as a form of Transnationalization, in that they seek to **minimize costs**, and hence maximize profits, by organizing their operations in the most efficient means possible irrespective of political boundaries.

Proponents of capitalists Transnationalization seek to facilitate the flow of people, ideas, and goods among regions. They believe that it has increasing relevance with the rapid growth of capitalist globalization. They contend that it does not make sense to link specific nation-state boundaries with for instance migratory workforces, globalized corporations, global money flow, global information flow, and global scientific cooperation.

However, critical theories of Transnationalization have argued that transnational capitalism has occurred through the increasing monopolization and centralization of capital by leading dominant groups in the global economy and various power blocs. Scholars critical of global capitalism have argued instead for a Transnationalization from below between workers and co-operatives as well as popular social and political movements.

Transnationalization as concept, theory and experience has nourished an important literature in social sciences. In practice Transnationalization refers to increasing functional integration of processes that cross-borders or according to others trans bordered relations of individuals, groups, firms and to mobilizations beyond state boundaries. Individuals, groups, institutions and states interact with each other in a new global space where cultural and political characteristic of national societies are combined with emerging multilevel and multinational activities. Transnationalization is a part of the process of capitalist globalization. The concept of Transnationalization refers to multiple links and interactions linking people and institutions across the borders of nation-states. Although much of the more recent literature has focused on popular protest as a form of transnational activism, some research has also drawn attention to clandestine and criminal networks, as well as foreign fighters, as examples of a wider form of Transnationalization.

Managing Cultural Diversity

From our increasingly diverse domestic workforce to the globalization of business, cultural competence is arguably the most important skill for effective work performance in the 21st century.

Culture refers to the values, norms, and traditions that affect the way a member of a group typically perceives, thinks, interacts, behaves, and makes judgments. It even affects perceptions of time, which can impact day-to-day scheduling and deadlines.

Cultural competence, in brief, is the ability to interact effectively with people from different cultures. This ability depends on awareness of one's own cultural worldview, knowledge of other cultural practices and worldviews, tolerant attitudes towards cultural differences, and cross-cultural skills.

Developing cultural competence results in an ability to understand, communicate with, and effectively interact with people across cultures, and work with varying cultural beliefs and schedules. While there are myriad cultural variations, here are some essentials to the workplace:

1. **Communication:** Providing information accurately and promptly is critical to effective work and team performance. This is particularly important when a project is troubled and needs immediate corrective actions. However, people from different cultures vary in how, for example, they relate to bad news. People from some Asian cultures are reluctant to give supervisors bad news – while those from other cultures may exaggerate it.
2. **Team-building:** Some cultures – like the United States – are individualistic, and people want to go it alone. Other cultures value cooperation within or among other teams. Team-building issues can become more problematic as teams are comprised of people from a mix of these cultural types. Effective cross-cultural team-building is essential to benefiting from the potential advantages of cultural diversity in the workplace
3. **Time:** Cultures differ in how they view time. For example, they differ in the balance between work and family life, and the workplace mix between work and social behaviour. Other differences include the perception of overtime, or even the exact meaning of a deadline. Different perceptions of time can cause a great misunderstanding and mishap in the workplace, especially with scheduling and deadlines. Perceptions of time underscore the importance of cultural diversity in the workplace, and how it can impact everyday work.
4. **Calendars:** The business world generally runs on the western secular year, beginning with January 1 and ending with December 31. However, many cultures use other calendars to determine holidays such as New Years or specific holidays. For example, Eastern Orthodox Christians celebrate Christmas on a different day from western Christians. For Muslims, Friday is a day for prayer. These variations affect the workplace as people require time off to observe their holidays.

Global Entry Strategies

Foreign market entry strategies differ in degree of risk they present, the control and commitment of resources they require and the return on investment they promise. There are two major types of entry modes: 1) non-equity mode, which includes export and contractual agreements, 2) equity mode, which includes joint venture and wholly owned subsidiaries. The market-entry technique that offers the lowest level of risk and the least market control is export and import. The highest risk, but also the highest market control and expected return on investment are connected with direct investments that can be made as an acquisition and Greenfield investments.

(i) Exporting and Importing: The first and the most common strategy to be an international company is: import and export of goods, materials and services. Exporting is the process of selling goods or services produced in one country to other countries. There are two types of exporting: direct and indirect. Indirect export means that products are carried abroad by other agents and the firm doesn't have special activity connected with international market, because the sale abroad is treated like the domestic one. For these reasons it is difficult to say that it is an internationalization strategy. In the case of direct exporting, the firm becomes directly involved in marketing its products in foreign markets.

(ii) Licensing: Licensing is another way to enter a foreign market with a limited degree of risk. The international licensing firm gives the licensee patent rights, trademark rights, copyrights or know-how on products and processes. In return, the licensee will produce the licensor's products, market these products in his assigned territory and pay the licensor fees and royalties usually related to the sales volume of the products. This type of agreement is generally welcomed by foreign public authorities because it brings technology into the country.

(iii) Franchising: Franchising is similar to licensing except that the franchising organisation tends to be more directly involved in the development and control of the marketing programme. The franchising system can be defined as a system in which semi-independent business owners (franchisees) pay fees and royalties to a parent company (franchiser) in return for the right to become identified with its trademark, to sell its products or services, and often to use its business format and system.

(iv) Joint Ventures: Foreign joint ventures have much in common with licensing. The major difference is that in joint ventures, the international firm has an equity position and a management voice in the foreign firm. A partnership between host- and home-country firms is formed, usually resulting in the creation of a third firm. This type of agreement gives the international firm better control over operations and also access to local market knowledge. The international firm has access to the network of relationships of the franchisee and is less exposed to the risk expropriation to the partnership with the local firm.

(v) Strategic Alliances: A strategic alliance is a term used to describe a variety of cooperative agreements between different firms, such as shared research, formal joint ventures, or minority equity participation. The modern form of strategic alliances is becoming increasingly popular and has three distinguishing characteristics:

(a) They are usually between firms in high - industrialized nations.

(b) The focus is often on creating new products and technologies rather than distributing existing ones.

(c) They are often only created for short term durations.

(vi) Technology Exchange: This is a major objective for many strategic alliances. The reason for this is that technological innovations are based on interdisciplinary advances and it is difficult for a single firm to possess the necessary resources or capabilities to conduct its own effective R&D efforts. This is also supported by shorter product life cycles and the need for many companies to stay competitive through innovation.

Global Financial System and Services

The global financial system is the worldwide framework of legal agreements, institutions, and both formal and informal economic actors that together facilitate international flows of financial capital for purposes of investment and trade financing. Since emerging in the late 19th century during the first modern wave of economic globalization, its evolution is marked by the establishment of central banks, multilateral treaties, and intergovernmental organizations aimed at improving the transparency, regulation, and effectiveness of international markets.

In the late 1800s, world migration and communication technology facilitated unprecedented growth in international trade and investment. At the onset of World War I, trade contracted as foreign exchange markets became paralyzed by money market illiquidity. Countries sought to defend against external shocks with protectionist policies and trade virtually halted by 1933, worsening the effects of the global Great Depression until a series of reciprocal trade agreements slowly reduced tariffs worldwide. Efforts to revamp the international monetary system after World War II improved exchange rate stability, fostering record growth in global finance.

Global Financial service is the interplay of financial companies, regulators and institutions operating on a supranational level. The global financial system can be divided into regulated entities (international banks and insurance companies), regulators, supervisors and institutions like the European Central Bank or the International Monetary Fund.

The system also includes the lightly regulated or non-regulated bodies. This is known as the "**shadow banking**" system. Mainly, this covers hedge funds, private equity and bank sponsored entities such as off-balance-sheet vehicles that banks use to invest in the financial markets.

Example

As banks lend money to governments, hedge funds and private equity firms, and central banks lend money to commercial and investment banks, the interrelationship between these loans creates the global "systemic" risk, which explains why a "local" crisis such as the US subprime meltdown in 2007 translated into a global financial crisis.

Managing International Business

The qualities that may work well when managing domestic business could possibly lead to failure when applied across cultures. Today's international business manager will utilize a skill set that draws upon his or her grasp of industry and standard best practices, outstanding cultural awareness and diplomacy, and sharp communication and negotiation skills.

Even business managers based in their home countries will sometimes need to manage teams, partners or suppliers and others. Learning the skills that multicultural business leaders need is a valuable asset for any manager working for an international concern. These skills can be obtained or honed by participating in professional business courses. Among them are:

(i) **Cultural Sensitivity:** International business managers know that adapting to different cultures enhances personal and business growth. It's important to appreciate and respect other cultures, and to understand how culture impacts business relationships. Learning how others interpret cues like tone of voice and body language, as well as how to appropriately use one's negotiation skills, is vital to moving and dealing successfully within a culture.

(ii) **Multilingual:** Successful international business managers are able to converse in more than one language especially that of their firm's largest client or trading partner. It's also important when communicating in English to speak so that non-native speakers can understand and comprehend clearly. Avoiding unfamiliar words and phrases, using shorter sentences and explaining concepts more thoroughly will help individuals of different cultures more quickly grasp the context of your communication.

(iii) **Global Management Philosophy:** Successful international business managers have the ability to formulate strategies and management systems to take advantage of international opportunities, as well as to respond to changes in a sometimes-volatile international marketplace.

Competitive Advantage of Nations

A competitive advantage is what makes you better than the competition in your customers' minds. The term was first applied to businesses, but it works for anyone, from employees to countries.

In 1985, Harvard Business School professor **Michael Porter** wrote **Competitive Advantage**. It is the definitive business school textbook on the topic.

Porter outlined the three primary ways through which companies achieve a sustainable advantage. They are cost leadership, differentiation and focus. Porter identified these strategies by researching companies.

Cost leadership means you provide reasonable value at a lower price. Companies do this by continuously improving operational efficiency. That usually means paying their workers less. Some compensate by offering intangible benefits such as stock options, benefits or promotional opportunities. Others take advantage of unskilled labour surpluses. As these businesses grow, they can use economies of scale and buy in bulk.

Walmart and Costco are good examples of cost leadership. But sometimes they pay their workers less than the cost of living. Higher minimum wage laws threaten their advantage.

Differentiation means you deliver better benefits than anyone else. A company can achieve differentiation by providing a unique or high-quality product. Another method is to deliver it faster. A third is to market in a way that reaches customers better. A company with a differentiation strategy can charge a premium price. That means it usually has a higher profit margin.

Companies typically achieve differentiation with innovation, quality or customer service. Innovation means you meet the same needs in a new way. An excellent example of this is Apple. The iPod was innovative because it allowed you to play whatever music you want, in any order.

Quality means you provide the best product or service. Customer service means going out of the way to delight shoppers.

Focus means you understand and service your target market better than anyone else. You can use either cost leadership or differentiation to do that. The key to focusing is to choose one specific target market. Often it's a tiny niche that larger companies don't serve. For example, community banks use a focus strategy to gain sustainable competitive advantage. They target local small businesses or high net worth individuals. Their target audience enjoys the personal touch that big banks may not be able to give. They are willing to pay a little more in fees for this service. These banks are using a differentiation form of the focus strategy.

A country can also create competitive advantage. It is called national competitive advantage or comparative advantage. For example, China uses cost leadership. It exports low-cost products at a reasonable quality level. It can do this because its standard of living is lower, so it can pay its workers less. It also fixes the value of its currency, the yuan, at a value lower than the dollar.

India started as a cost leader but is moving toward differentiation. It provides skilled, technical, English-speaking workers at a reasonable wage. Japan also changed its competitive advantage. In the 1960s, it was a cost leader that excelled at cheap electronics. By the 1980s, it had shifted up to differentiation in quality brands, such as Lexus.

America's comparative advantage is innovation. U.S. companies bring innovative products to market faster than other countries. A great example is Silicon Valley, America's innovative advantage. America is so innovative because it has a vast and affluent domestic consumer base. It is easy to test new product ideas and work out the bugs at home. Once successful, they're marketed throughout the world.

Restrictive Trade Practices (RTP)

From 21 July 1996, the restrictive trade practices provisions in **Part IV** of the Trade Practices Act **1974** apply to all areas of the Queensland Government that represent the Crown, so far as the Crown carries on a business, either directly or an authority of the state.

Part IV of the TPA will apply to all other organizations regardless of whether they carry on a business.

Part IV of the TPA prohibits restrictive trade practices. Restrictive trade practices include:

- **Exclusionary Provisions:** When competitors agree not to supply (or buy) goods or services to a particular person or class of persons, or when competitors agree to prevent or hinder the acquisition of goods or services from a particular person or class of persons.
- **Price Fixing:** A contract, arrangement or understanding with a competitor that has the purpose or the effect, or the likely effect, of fixing, controlling or maintaining prices, discount levels, allowances, rebates or credits in relation to goods or services.
- **Third Line Forcing:** It requires a customer to acquire goods or services from another person as a condition of the supply of your goods or services to that customer. It also includes refusing to supply because the customer has not accepted the condition to acquire goods or services from another, or setting prices according to

whether a customer has acquired goods or services from another person.

- **Resale Price Maintenance:** When a supplier sets a minimum price below which resellers must not resell goods.
- **Anti-Competitive Contracts:** The making or giving effect to general anticompetitive contracts, arrangements or understandings. These are any contracts, arrangements or understandings that have the purpose or likely effect of substantially lessening competition in a market.
- **Secondary Boycotts:** These provisions are primarily designed to combat union boycott activity.
- **Exclusive Dealings:** It prohibits specified conduct involving product exclusivity, tying arrangements and customer and territory exclusivity, in circumstances where the conduct results in a substantial lessening of competition in the relevant market.
- **Mergers and Acquisitions:** If the effect would be to substantially lessen competition in a market.
- **Misuse of Market Power:** When an entity that has a substantial degree of market power takes advantage of that power for one of the prescribed purposes. The prescribed purposes are eliminating or damaging a competitor, preventing a person from entering a market, or deterring or preventing a person from engaging in uncompetitive conduct.

World Trade Organization (WTO)

Objectives and Functions

The **Uruguay** round of **GATT** (1986-93) gave birth to World Trade Organization. The members of GATT singed on an agreement of Uruguay round in **April 1994** in **Morocco** for establishing a new organization named WTO.

It was officially constituted on **January 1, 1995** which took the place of GATT as an effective formal, organization. GATT was an informal organization which regulated world trade since 1948.

Conference	*Year*	*Place*
First	1996	Singapore
Second	1998	Geneva (Switzerland)
Third	1999	Seattle (USA)
Fourth	2001	Doha (Qatar)
Fifth	2003	Cancun (Mexico)
Sixth	2005	Hong Kong
Seventh	2009	Geneva (Switzerland)

Unit - X

Ethics and Management System

Ethical Management System

Meaning of Business Ethics

Business ethics deals with determining rules or behaviour of business enterprises. It determines rightness or wrongness of actions of businessmen. "It is the study of what is ethically permissible and of what is positively virtuous, in regard to business activity".

"Management Ethics is a concept closely related to the concept of social responsiveness of a firm. It is the discipline of dealing with what is good and bad, or right and wrong or with moral duty and obligation".

"It is the set of moral principles that governs the actions of an individual or a group". Business ethics is the application of ethical principles to business relationships and activities. It governs the way a business runs and carries its operations. It determines the **standard of behaviour** that guides managers in their work.

Features of Business Ethics:

1. It determines issues that business houses face in operating their activities.
2. It draws distinction between what is right or wrong, fair or unfair, just or unjust.
3. It is an important component of corporate social responsibility that demands business houses to engage in socially responsible behaviours.

4. It demands that corporate houses should not only be profit making units, they should be good corporate citizens also.
5. It demands that corporate houses should obey the law. Legal obedience is an ethical content that ensures long run survival and prosperity of business houses.
6. It defines not just what business managers do (descriptive ethics) but also why they should be doing so (normative ethics).
7. It is broader than law. There may be business activities that are ethical but illegal or, unethical but legal.

Some Examples of Business Ethics:

1. To give fair and equitable treatment to the employees.
2. To charge fair prices from the customers.
3. To use fair weights for measurement of commodities.
4. To pay taxes to government and other bodies honestly.
5. To earn reasonable profit.
6. To become a good corporate citizen.

Need for Ethics in Management

With the increased level of business scandals throughout the world, more and more people are emphasizing ethics in management. Need for ethics in management is due to the following reasons:

1. **Environmental Pressure:** Various organs of the environment put pressure on the organization to behave ethically. Such organs are customers, suppliers, franchisers, trade unions, and government. Therefore the organization has to refrain from unethical behaviour. Because of this in-built control mechanism of the society, there are more chances of ethical behaviour and less chances of unethical behaviour.
2. **Credibility:** Ethical behaviour helps in increasing credibility of an organization. Credibility of an organization is an essential phenomenon because through it, the organization protects its identity. Identity of an organization refers to what it is and what kind of perception people have about it. For an organization, building credibility is a long-drawn process but its tarnishing is a short one. High credibility can be maintained through continuous ethical behaviour.
3. **Moral Consciousness:** Every individual is morally conscious. Since an organization is a collectivity of individuals for certain specified objectives, it tends to behave ethically even if there is a pressure from external forces to behave unethically.

4. **Legal Pressure:** Ethical behaviour is evolved from the social system. Thus, ethical behaviour is evolutionary. In this evolution process, there is a probability that, sometimes, it may not be clear to people whether a particular behaviour is ethical or unethical. In order to avoid this dilemma, most of the societies enact laws which define ethical and unethical behaviour.

Ethical Issues and Analysis in Management

There are many different scenarios that could indicate an ethical issue during a hiring process that a manager of a small or large business might have to encounter. These ethical issues can be dealt with professionally with efficient education of business ethics and employment law. In hiring, ethics and law intertwine, and since very seldom is any law unethical, following equal opportunity employment laws would be the best way to manage any ethical issues that might arise. There are many different laws prohibiting discrimination which will be listed below. Many company rules also effect a manager's hiring process, which is, in some ways, just a process of elimination. A well-trained and educated manager will only have to abide by simple rules and regulations to be able to make an ethical choice while hiring employees. "A manager's most important responsibility is to bring good people into the organization and then manage in a way that makes those good people want to stay." (Trevino & Nelson, 2007, p.155)

Many ethical issues can arise for a manager when trying to make the important decision to hire an employee for the firm that they work for. It is the manager's most valuable duty to hire the right people for their company because a bad or unethical employee can have dire consequences. A manager must also read in between the lines during an interview and the whole hiring process. For example, if an applicant is being interviewed and is asked if the hiring company may contact a previous employer for a reference and they say no, but says that they had no problems or misconduct at the company, there might be an issue here with lying. Why else would the applicant not want the company to be contacted? It would be understandable if they were presently employed. Another ethical issue would be if the candidate was unattractive, obese, worn ethnical clothes, or even had strict religious rules to abide by. Everybody has some kind of bias opinion, but as a manager, they must overcome all predetermined thoughts of how the person may look or dress and base their decision solely on the applicant's ability to do the job correctly and with the most ease. These biases extend throughout the company and also into its customers, but a sensible person, whether it is a worker or customer, would set aside their problems and handle business appropriately. Since this is not always the case, a manager will have to realize that they cannot always please everybody at once, not even close. There are many different employment laws in place although some may vary from state to state, but most are the same. The main five acts that have been established are: Equal Pay Act, Civil Rights Act, Age Discrimination in Employment Act, Pregnancy Discrimination Act, and the Americans with Disabilities Act.

The Equal Pay Act states that no matter the gender the pay must be fair and equal for the work that employees do. The Civil Rights Act is where there can be no discrimination based on race, colour, religion, national origin, or gender. The Age Discrimination Act puts forth that the age of the applicant or employee cannot matter or make a difference in any business decision. If a woman gets pregnant or is pregnant when interviewing the Pregnancy Discrimination Act prohibits them from being seen as disabled or unavailable. According to the Americans with Disabilities Act, no applicant with a disability can be discriminated against as long as they can do the job duties listed to them "with or without reasonable accommodation." As long as the manager stays within these main regulations of hiring, few other ethical issues can come up.

When a person is placed as a manager, they might also be given company rules for hiring individuals. The desirable person might be a certain build or have a specific hair colour. From personal experience, the company Hooters, a restaurant chain, hires a different number of red, brunette, and blondes. They must have an assortment at all times.

Value Based Organizations

A values-based organization (VBO) is a living, breathing culture of shared core values among all employees. This is different from the traditional structure which is a more machine-like, business approach that focuses on an authoritarian type relationship or rigid organizational structure. A values-based organization is a culture shaped by a clear set of ground rules establishing a foundation and guiding principles for decision-making, actions and a sense of community. In a values-driven culture, employees find alignment between their personal values and the organization's values creating a unified and motivated workforce. Management and leadership set examples for their organizations and live the values they preach. Strongly held value-systems rarely change yet remain flexible to handle changes in strategy or outside influences such as competition or the economy. A strongly held values-based culture or purpose will remain more stable over time characterized by productivity and employee commitment.

Personal Framework for Ethical Choices

Decisions about right and wrong permeate everyday life. Ethics should concern all levels of life: acting properly as individuals, creating responsible organizations and governments, and making our society as a whole more ethical.

This document is designed as an introduction to making ethical decisions. It recognizes that decisions about "right" and "wrong" can be difficult, and may be related to individual context. It first provides a summary of the major sources for ethical thinking, and then presents a framework for decision-making.

Ethics provides a set of standards for behaviour that helps us decide how we ought to act in a range of situations. In a sense, we can say that ethics is all about making choices, and about providing reasons why we should make these choices.

Ethics is sometimes confused with other ways of making choices, including religion, law or morality. Many religions promote ethical decision-making but do not always address the full range of ethical choices that we face. Religions may also advocate or prohibit certain behaviours which may not be considered the proper domain of ethics, such as dietary restrictions or sexual behaviours. A good system of law should be ethical, but the law establishes precedent in trying to dictate universal guidelines, and is thus not able to respond to individual contexts. Law may have a difficult time designing or enforcing standards in some important areas, and may be slow to address new problems. Both law and ethics deal with questions of how we should live together with others, but ethics is sometimes also thought to apply to how individuals act even when others are not involved. Finally, many people use the terms morality and ethics interchangeably. Others reserve morality for the state of virtue while seeing ethics as a code that enables morality. Another way to think about the relationship between ethics and morality is to see ethics as providing a rational basis for morality, that is, ethics provides good reasons for why something is moral.

There are many systems of ethics, and numerous ways to think about right and wrong actions or good and bad character. The field of ethics is traditionally divided into three areas: **(i)** meta-ethics, which deals with the **nature** of the right or the good, as well as the nature and justification of ethical claims; **(ii)** normative ethics, which deals with the **standards and principles** used to determine whether something is right or good; **(iii)** applied ethics, which deals with the **actual application** of ethical principles to a particular situation. While it is helpful to approach the field of ethics in this order, we might keep in mind that this somewhat "top down" approach does not exhaust the study of ethics. Our experience with applying particular ethical standards or principles can inform our understanding of how good these standard or principles are.

Three Broad Types of Ethical Theory

Ethical theories are often broadly divided into three types: **(i)** Consequentialist theories, which are primarily concerned with the **ethical consequences** of particular actions; **(ii)** Non-consequentialist theories, which tend to be broadly concerned with the **intentions** of the person making ethical decisions about particular actions; and **(iii)** Agent-centered theories, which, unlike consequentialist and non-consequentialist theories, are more concerned with the **overall ethical status** of individuals, or agents, and are less concerned to identify the morality of particular actions. Each of these three broad categories contains varieties of approaches to ethics, some of which share characteristics across the categories. Below is a sample of some of the most important and useful of these ethical approaches.

(i) Consequentialist Theories

The Utilitarian Approach: Utilitarianism can be traced back to the school of the Ancient Greek philosopher Epicurus of Samos (341-270 BCE), who argued that the best life is one that produces the least pain and distress. The 18th Century British philosopher Jeremy Bentham (1748-1832) applied a similar standard to individual actions, and created a system in which actions could be described as good or bad depending upon the amount and degree of pleasure and/or pain they would produce. Bentham's student, John Stuart Mill (1806-1873) modified this system by making its standard for the good the more subjective concept of "happiness," as opposed to the more materialist idea of "pleasure."

Utilitarianism is one of the most common approaches to making ethical decisions, especially decisions with consequences that concern large groups of people, in part because it instructs us to weigh the different amounts of good and bad that will be produced by our action. This conforms to our feeling that some good and some bad will necessarily be the result of our action and that the best action will be that which provides the most good or does the least harm, or, to put it another way, produces the greatest **balance of good over harm**. Ethical environmental action, then, is the one that produces the greatest good and does the least harm for all who are affected—government, corporations, the community, and the environment.

The Egoistic Approach: In this approach, an individual often uses utilitarian calculation to produce the greatest amount of good for him or herself. Ancient Greek Sophists like Thrasymacus (c. 459-400 BCE), who famously claimed that might makes right, and early modern thinkers like Thomas Hobbes (1588-1679) may be considered forerunners of this approach. One of the most influential recent proponents of ethical egoism was the Russian-American philosopher **Ayn Rand** (1905-1982), who, in the book **The Virtue of Selfishness** (1964), argues that **self-interest** is a prerequisite to self-respect and to respect for others. There are numerous parallels between ethical egoism and laissez-faire economic theories, in which the pursuit of self-interest is seen as leading to the benefit of society, although the benefit of society is seen only as the fortunate byproduct of following individual self-interest, not its goal.

The Common Good Approach: The ancient Greek philosophers Plato (427-347 BCE) and Aristotle (384-322 BCE) promoted the perspective that our actions should contribute to ethical communal life. The most influential modern proponent of this approach was the French philosopher Jean-Jacques Rousseau (1712-1778), who argued that the best society should be guided by the "**general will**" of the people which would then produce what is best for the people as a whole. This approach to ethics underscores the networked aspects of society and emphasizes respect and compassion for others, especially those who are more vulnerable.

(ii) Non-consequentialist Theories

The Duty-Based Approach: The duty-based approach, sometimes called **deontological ethics**, is most commonly associated with the philosopher Immanuel Kant (1724-1804), although it had important precursors in earlier non-consquentialist, often explicitly religious, thinking of people like Saint Augustine of Hippo (354-430), who emphasized the importance of the personal will and intention to ethical decision making. Kant argued that doing what is right is not about the consequences of our actions but about having the proper intention in performing the action. The ethical action is one taken from duty, that is, it is done precisely because it is our **obligation to perform the action**. Ethical obligations are the same for all rational creatures, and knowledge of what these obligations entail is arrived at by discovering rules of behaviour that are not contradicted by reason.

Kant's famous formula for discovering our ethical duty is known as the "**categorical imperative**." It has a number of different versions, but Kant believed they all amounted to the same imperative. The most basic form of the imperative is: "Act only according to that maxim by which you can at the same time will that it should become a **universal law**." So, for example, lying is unethical because we could not universalize a maxim that said "One should always lie." Such a maxim would render all speech meaningless. We can, however, universalize the maxim, "Always speak truthfully," without running into a logical contradiction. In acting according to a law that we have discovered to be rational according to our own universal reason, we are acting autonomously (in a self-regulating fashion), and thus are bound by duty, a duty we have given ourselves as rational creatures. We thus freely choose to bind ourselves to the moral law. For Kant, choosing to obey the **universal moral law** is the very nature of acting ethically.

The Rights Approach: The Rights approach to ethics is another non-consequentialist approach which derives much of its current force from Kantian duty-based ethics, although it also has a history that dates back at least to the Stoics of Ancient Greece and Rome, and has another influential current which flows from work of the British empiricist philosopher John Locke (1632-1704). This approach stipulates that the best ethical action is that which protects the ethical rights of those who are affected by the action. It emphasizes the belief that all humans have a right to dignity. This is based on a formulation of Kant's categorical imperative that says: "Act in such a way that you treat humanity, whether in your own person or in the person of another, always at the same time as an end and never simply as a means to an end." The list of ethical rights is debated; many now argue that animals and other non-humans such as robots also have rights.

The Fairness or Justice Approach: The Law Code of Hammurabi in Ancient Mesopotamia (c. 1750 BCE) held that all free men should be treated alike, just as all slaves should be treated alike. When combined with the universality of the rights approach, the justice approach can be applied to all human persons. The most influential version of this approach today is found in the work of American philosopher John Rawls (1921-2002), who argued, along Kantian lines, that just ethical principles are those that would be chosen by free and rational people in an initial situation of equality. This hypothetical contract is considered fair or just because it provides a procedure for what counts as a fair action, and does not concern itself with the consequences of those actions. Fairness of starting point is the principle for what is considered just.

The Divine Command Approach: As its name suggests, this approach sees what is right as the same as what God commands, and ethical standards are the creation of God's will. Following God's will is seen as the very definition what is ethical. Because God is seen as omnipotent and possessed of free will, God could change what is now considered ethical, and God is not bound by any standard of right or wrong short of logical contradiction. The Medieval Christian philosopher William of Ockham (1285-1349) was one of the most influential thinkers in this tradition, and his writings served as a guide for Protestant Reformers like Martin Luther (1483-1546) and Jean Calvin (1509-1564). The Danish philosopher Søren Kierkegaard (1813-1855), in praising the biblical Patriarch Abraham's willingness to kill his son Isaac at God's command, claimed that truly right action must ultimately go beyond everyday morality to what he called the "teleological suspension of the ethical," again demonstrating the somewhat tenuous relationship between religion and ethics mentioned earlier.

(iii) Agent-centered Theories

The Virtue Approach: One long-standing ethical principle argues that ethical actions should be consistent with ideal human virtues. Aristotle, for example, argued that ethics should be concerned with the whole of a person's life, not with the individual discrete actions a person may perform in any given situation. A person of good character would be one who has attainted certain virtues. This approach is also prominent in non-Western contexts, especially in East Asia, where the tradition of the Chinese sage Confucius (551-479 BCE) emphasizes the importance of acting **virtuously** (in an appropriate manner) in a variety of situations. Virtue ethics is concerned with the entirety of a person's life. It takes the process of education and training seriously, and emphasizes the importance of role models to our understanding of how to engage in ethical deliberation.

The Feminist Approach: In recent decades, the virtue approach to ethics has been supplemented and sometimes significantly revised by thinkers in the feminist tradition, who often emphasize the importance of the experiences of women and other marginalized groups to ethical deliberation. Among the most important contributions of this approach is its foregrounding of the principle of care as a legitimately primary ethical concern, often in opposition to the seemingly cold and impersonal justice approach. Like virtue ethics, feminist ethics concerned with the totality of human life and how this life comes to influence the way we make ethical decisions.

Applied Ethics

Terms Used in Ethical Judgments

Applied ethics deals with issues in private or public life that are matters for ethical judgments. The following are important terms used in making moral judgments about particular actions.

Obligatory: When we say something is ethically "obligatory" we mean that it is not only right to do it, but that it is wrong not to do it. In other words, we have an ethical obligation to perform the action. Sometimes the easiest way to see if an action is ethically obligatory is to look at what it would mean not to perform the action. For example, we might say it is ethically obligatory for parents to care for their children, not only because it is right for them to do it, but also because it is wrong for them not to do it. The children would suffer and die if parents did not care for them. The parents are thus ethically "obligated" to care for their children.

Impermissible: The opposite of an ethically obligatory action is an action that is ethically impermissible, meaning that it is wrong to do it and right not to do it. For example, we would say that murder is ethically impermissible.

Permissible: Sometimes actions are referred to as ethically permissible, or ethically "neutral," because it is neither right nor wrong to do them or not to do them. We might say that having plastic surgery is ethically permissible, because it is not wrong to have the surgery (it is not impermissible), but neither is it ethically necessary (obligatory) to have the surgery. Some argue that suicide is permissible in certain circumstances. That is, a person would not be wrong in committing suicide, nor would they be wrong in not committing suicide. Others would say that suicide is ethically impermissible.

Supererogatory: A fourth type of ethical action is called supererogatory. These types of actions are seen as going "above and beyond the call of duty." They are right to do, but it is not wrong not to do them. For example, two people are walking down a hallway and see a third person drop their book bag, spilling all of their books and papers onto the floor. If one person stops to help the third person pick up their books, but the other person keeps on walking, we somehow feel that the person who stopped to help has acted in a more ethically appropriate way than the person who did not stop, but we cannot say that the person who did not stop was unethical in not stopping. In other words, the person who did not help was in no way obligated to help. But we nevertheless want to ethically praise the person who did stop, so we call his or her actions supererogatory.

Frameworks for Ethical Decision-Making

Making good ethical decisions requires a trained sensitivity to ethical issues and a practiced method for exploring the ethical aspects of a decision and weighing the considerations that should impact our choice of a course of action. Having a method for ethical decision making is essential. When practiced regularly, the method becomes so familiar that we work through it automatically without consulting the specific steps. This is one reason why we can sometimes say that we have a "moral intuition" about a certain situation, even when we have not consciously thought through the issue. We are practiced at making ethical judgments, just as we can be practiced at playing the piano, and can sit and play well "without thinking." Nevertheless, it is not always advisable to follow our immediate intuitions, especially in particularly complicated or unfamiliar situations. Here our method for ethical decision making should enable us to recognize these new and unfamiliar situations and to act accordingly.

The more novel and difficult the ethical choice we face, the more we need to rely on discussion and dialogue with others about the dilemma. Only by careful exploration of the problem, aided by the insights and different perspectives of others, we can make good ethical choices in such situations.

Three Frameworks

Based upon the three-part division of traditional normative ethical theories discussed above, it makes sense to suggest three broad frameworks to guide ethical decision making: The Consequentialist Framework; The Duty Framework; and the Virtue Framework.

Hence it is important to be familiar with all three frameworks and to understand how they relate to each other—where they may overlap, and where they may differ.

Ethical Pressure on Individual in Organizations

"Ethics involves the study of moral issues and choices. It is concerned with right versus wrong, good versus bad, and the many shades of gray in supposedly black-and-white issues. Moral implications spring from virtually every decision, both on and off the job. Managers are challenged to have more imagination and the courage to do the right thing to make the world a better place."(p. 23) Kinicki and Kreitner's statement accurately encapsulates how ethical concerns are of major importance within organizations. Ethical issues effect more than the immediate decisions and consequences we deal with on a minute by minute basis. They have far reaching and multidimensional consequences as well.

If a manager makes decision that even appears unethical to peers and subordinates, then that manager's reputation may be forever affected, even if no one decides to hold him formally accountable for his decision. Also, that decision may create an environment within the organizational culture which implies that unethical behaviour is both allowed and rewarded. Such apparent allowances can be very difficult to eradicate, as they tend to spread and erode the organizational structure, even reaching into future hiring practices.

The individual also faces internal and external influences within an organization. The internal organizational influences are as follows:

"Ethical codes, Organizational culture, Organizational size, Structure, Perceived pressure for results, Corporate strategy."

Some, such as ethical codes, corporate strategy, size and structure have a more foundational impact, while culture and perceived pressure can have secondary impact. It is important to note however, that if the secondary influences are pervasive enough, they may actually override the stated codes and strategies found within the organizational core.

A person is born with certain innate personality traits, and is shown examples of ethical and/or unethical behavior throughout his life. He then takes that existing data set to an organization, where both internal and external organizational influences continue to shape his ethical paradigm, whether toward good or bad ends. It is important to understand that ethical behaviour, while fluid in nature, is still a behaviour, and can therefore be difficult to change.

Ethical Dilemmas in the Workplace for Employees

Sexual Harassment

Sexual harassment is a form of sex discrimination. The legal definition of sexual harassment is "unwelcome verbal, visual, or physical conduct of a sexual nature that is severe or pervasive and affects working conditions or creates a hostile work environment."

A hostile work environment is defined as: sexual advances, requests for sexual favors, and other verbal or physical conduct of a sexual nature, when such advances, requests, or conduct have the purpose or effect of unreasonably interfering with an individual's work performance by creating an intimidating, hostile, humiliating, or sexually offensive work environment.

To show a hostile work environment, an employee must prove the following.

He/she was subjected to conduct of a sexual nature (e.g., inappropriate touching, sexual epithets, jokes, gossip, sexual comments, requests for sex, sexually suggestive pictures and objects, leering, whistling, sexual gestures).

The conduct was unwelcome.

The conduct had the purpose or effect of creating an intimidating, hostile, humiliating, or sexually offensive work environment. The conduct unreasonably interfered with the employee's work performance or altered the terms and conditions of employment.

Let's assume your boss threatens to stifle your career advancement unless you sleep with him. This is unlawful whether you submit and avoid the threatened harm or resist and suffer the consequences. Your first step should be to make it clear to your boss this is an unwelcomed advance. If the offensive behaviour persists, you should report it to the HR Department where Equal Employment Opportunity Commission (EEOC) matters are dealt with. You can also file a complaint with the EEOC and/or your state's fair employment agency.

Gender Issues

Gender bias is wrong in any form whether based on age, sex, or sexual orientation. The law has not caught up with the rights of transgender individuals but the spirit of the law should protect transgender people in the workplace. The workplace should be a welcoming environment and the culture one of inclusion.

Gender identity issues have surfaced recently because of the landmark opinion by the U.S. Supreme Court on June 26, 2015, that established same-sex couples can marry nationwide. It's not a leap to focus attention on the rights of the LGBT community. The basic ethical principal here is one of fair treatment. Each of us deserves respect for who we are. Discriminating against anyone based on gender identity is wrong.

Gender identity discrimination can include terminating a transgender employee after the employer finds out about the employee's gender identity or planned transition; denying a transgender employee access to workplace restroom facilities available to other employees; harassing a transgender employee; permitting and/or refusing to investigate claims of harassment by coworkers and supervisors; or any other negative employment action taken because of an employee's gender identity.

Discrimination based on gender identity is not specifically prohibited under federal law but there are legislative efforts to pass federal laws to make it explicitly illegal. There is also some case law interpreting sex discrimination laws to encompass gender identity in certain circumstances. Protection from gender identity discrimination is enforced by state or local anti-discrimination agencies in 18 states.

Cyber-Bullying

Workplace Bullying refers to repeated, unreasonable actions of individuals (or a group) directed towards an employee (or a group of employees), which are intended to intimidate, degrade, humiliate, or undermine, or which create a risk to the health or safety of the employee(s) including physical and emotional stress.

Workplace Bullying often involves an abuse or misuse of power. Bullying behaviour creates feelings of defenselessness and injustice in the target and undermines an individual's right to dignity at work. Bullying is different from aggression. Whereas aggression may involve a single act, bullying involves repeated attacks against the target, creating an on-going pattern of behaviour.

Cyber Bullying in the workplace usually looks like offensive emails or text messages containing jokes or inappropriate wording towards a specific race, nationality, or about sexual preference. In these cases, the words uttered have a direct effect on the target of the bullying act through threatening email being sent to the target anonymously or not.

Sharing embarrassing situations relating to the target with everyone online, being offensive and mean to the target on various social media websites and networks, spreading rumors or gossip online which could have a serious effect on a fellow co-worker, and downright mean-spirited actions are meant to harm the target whether on a personal or professionals level.

Cyber bullying can cause significant emotional distress and significantly lead to diminished workplace performance. The danger of cyber bullying in the workplace is that it follows you home after working hours. The target is put under constant harassment even when the working hours are over. The only way to avoid such harassment is having it reported to try and put an end to it.

Cyber bullying in the workplace needs to be addressed through promoting a work environment that refuses to nurture a bully. As with most actions in the workplace, the best way to prevent cyber bullying is to create an ethical culture in the organization. Top management must make it clear that any form of bullying will not be tolerated.

Ecological Consciousness

'Ecology may be defined as the scientific study of the relationship of **living organisms** with each other and with their environment.'

The term ecology was first coined in 1869 by the German biologist Ernst Haeckel. It has been derived from two Greek words, 'oikos', meaning home or estate and 'logos' meaning study. The emphasis is on relationships between organisms and the components of the environment namely a biotic (non-living) and biotic (living).

Ecology not only deals with the study of the relationship of individual organisms with their environment, but also with the study of populations, communities, ecosystems, biomes, and biosphere as a whole.

Ecological consciousness is the awareness that nearly every aspect of our way of life affects the environment so decisively that we now must choose whether to let the effects go unchecked, or we change the way we live in order to arrest the damage.

Nature and man do not share a common language; humans hear messages from the environment only in their own human languages. On top of this, whatever messages the environment transmits are necessarily filtered by the multiple cultures and belief systems, and varying systems of cognition that characterize human societies.

Thus, natural phenomena like unusual rainfall levels, strong typhoons, rising seas, droughts, tsunamis, volcanic eruptions, etc. are viewed in different lights and treated with varying degrees of concern by different societies. The responses they trigger are never the same. Indeed, even within the same society, these phenomena are not uniformly interpreted by the different institutional spheres of society.

Environmental issues do not have the same resonance in law, religion, the economy, and politics, as they often do in science. Not even the most modern society can be said to have a central nervous system that is specifically attuned to changes in environmental conditions, and can control societal response.

Indeed, even in an advanced country like the United States, the politicians and businessmen differ with the scientists in their appreciation of the urgency of global warming.

In view of this, it is a wonder how anyone can imagine that the 193 nations meeting in **Copenhagen** for the UN-sponsored summit on global climate change could arrive at any agreement on the dimensions of the problem, its causes and solutions, or, much less, on what every nation must do, when, and by what means, in order to confront the problem. It does not require any sophistication to think that every definition of the problem of climate change, every piece of knowledge that is advanced, far from being objective, is implicated in a system of power.

This is not to deny the existence of the problem. But if global warming were the self-evident and objective phenomenon it is supposed to be, there would be little negotiation about its magnitude, origins, and the shape and direction of the requisite global response. There would be no need to call urgent attention to its gravity. But the poor and the rich countries meeting in Copenhagen precisely cannot agree on what every nation needs to do to check global warming, and who will pay for the adjustments that must be made, because there is no common understanding.

The United States blames China for being the biggest producer of carbon dioxide emissions since 2006. China counters that America remains the largest CO_2 producer per capita and has been so since it became an industrial power. American scientists charge that massive deforestation occurring in the poor countries is releasing more CO_2 into the atmosphere than all the combined vehicles and industrial plants in the world. Taking their cue from this, rich countries are offering money to help the poor countries stop deforestation. On the surface, this looks like an altruistic solution to a global problem. But critics have accused rich nations of trying to buy their way out of binding commitments to slash their own carbon emissions. Climate change is clearly not a simple scientific issue. It is embedded in political and economic questions, and is routinely used by countries as a proxy in the global struggle for political and economic supremacy.

Yet none of this diminishes the value of ecological consciousness. Indeed, it only highlights the need for every nation and every individual, as citizens of this planet, to examine their respective ways of life with a view to altering those practices that destroy the earth's long-term viability as a place in which to live.

Environmental Ethics

Environmental ethics is a branch of ethics that studies the relation of human beings and the environment and how ethics play a role in this.

Environmental ethics believe that humans are a part of society as well as other living creatures, which includes plants and animals. These items are a very important part of the world and are considered to be a functional part of human life. Thus, it is essential that every human being respect and honor this and use morals and ethics when dealing with these creatures.

As per Nature.com, "Environmental ethics is a branch of applied philosophy that studies the conceptual foundations of environmental values as well as more concrete issues surrounding societal attitudes, actions, and policies to protect and sustain biodiversity and ecological systems."

According to Wikipedia, "Environmental ethics is the part of environmental philosophy which considers extending the traditional boundaries of ethics from solely including humans to including the non-human world. It exerts influence on a large range of disciplines including environmental law, environmental sociology, theology, ecological economics, ecology and environmental geography."

Social Responsibility of Business

We all know that people engage in business to earn profit. However, profit making is not the sole function of business. It performs a number of social functions, as it is a part of the society. It takes care of those who are instrumental in securing its existence and survival like- the owners, investors, employees, consumers and government in particular and the society and community in general. So, every business must contribute in some way or the other for their benefit. For example, every business must ensure a satisfactory rate of return to investors, provide good salary, security and proper working condition to its employees, make available quality products at reasonable price to its consumers, maintain the environment properly, etc.

However, while doing so two things need to be noted to view it as social responsibility of business. First, any such activity is not charity. It means that if any business donates some amount of money to any hospital or temple or school and college etc., it is not to be considered as discharge of social responsibility because charity does not imply fulfilling responsibility.

Secondly, any such activity should not be such that it is good for somebody and bad for others. Suppose a businessman makes a lot of money by smuggling or by cheating customers, and then runs a hospital to treat poor patients at low prices; his actions cannot be socially justified. Social responsibility implies that a businessman should not do anything harmful to the society in course of his business activities.

Thus, the concept of social responsibility discourages businessmen from adopting unfair means like black-marketing, hoarding, adulteration, tax evasion and cheating customers, etc. to earn profit. Instead, it encourages them to earn profit through judicious management of the business, by providing better working and living conditions to its employees, providing better products, after sales-service, etc. to its customers and simultaneously to control pollution and conserve natural resources.

Responsibility towards Different Interest Groups

After getting some idea about the concept and importance of social responsibility of business. Let us look into the various responsibilities that a business has towards different groups with whom it interacts. The business generally interacts with owners, investors, employees, suppliers, customers, competitors, government and society. They are called as interest groups because by each and every activity of business, the interest of these groups is affected directly or indirectly.

Responsibility of Business towards Different Interest Groups

(i) Responsibility towards Owners: Owners are the persons who own the business. They contribute capital and bear the business risks. The primary responsibilities of business towards its owners are to:

(a) Run the business efficiently,

(b) Proper utilization of capital and other resources,

(c) Growth and appreciation of capital,

(d) Regular and fair return on capital invested.

(ii) Responsibility towards Investors: Investors are those who provide finance by way of investment in debentures, bonds, deposits, etc. Banks, financial institutions, and investing public are all included in this category. The responsibilities of business towards its investors are:

(a) Ensuring safety of their investment,

(b) Regular payment of interest,

(c) Timely repayment of principal amount.

(iii) Responsibility towards Employees: Business needs employees or workers to work for it. These employees put their best effort for the benefit of the business. So, it is the prime responsibility of every business to take care of the interest of their employees. If the employees are satisfied and efficient, then only the business can be successful. The responsibilities of business towards its employees include:

(a) Timely and regular payment of wages and salaries,

(b) Proper working conditions and welfare amenities,

(c) Opportunity for better career prospects,

(d) Job security as well as social security like facilities of provident fund, group insurance, pension, retirement benefits, etc.,

(e) Better living conditions like housing, transport, canteen, crèches, etc.,

(f) Timely training and development.

(iv) Responsibility towards Suppliers: Suppliers are businessmen who supply raw materials and other items required by manufacturers and traders. Certain suppliers, called distributors, supply finished products to the consumers. The responsibilities of business towards these suppliers are:

(a) Giving regular orders for purchase of goods,

(b) Dealing on fair terms and conditions,

(c) Availing reasonable credit period,

(d) Timely payment of dues.

(v) Responsibility towards Customers: No business can survive without the support of customers. As a part of the responsibility of business towards them the business should provide the following facilities:

(a) Products and services must be able to take care of the needs of the customers,

(b) Products and services must be qualitative,

(c) There must be regularity in supply of goods and services,

(d) Price of the goods and services should be reasonable and affordable,

(e) All the advantages and disadvantages of the product as well as procedure to use the products must be informed do the customers,

(f) There must be proper after-sales service,

(g) Grievances of the consumers, if any, must be settled quickly,

(h) Unfair means like under weighing the product, adulteration, etc. must be avoided.

(vi) Responsibility towards Competitors: Competitors are the other businessmen or organizations involved in a similar type of business. Existence of competition helps the business in becoming more dynamic and innovative so as to make itself better than its competitors. It also sometimes encourages the business to indulge in negative activities like resorting to unfair trade practices. The responsibilities of business towards its competitors are:

(i) Not to offer exceptionally high sales commission to distributers, agents etc.,

(ii) Not to offer to customers heavy discounts and /or free products in every sale,

(iii) Not to defame competitors through false or ambiguous advertisements.

(vii) Responsibility towards Government: Business activities are governed by the rules and regulations framed by the government. The various responsibilities of business towards government are:

(a) Setting up units as per guidelines of government,

(b) Payment of fees, duties and taxes regularly as well as honestly,

(c) Not to indulge in monopolistic and restrictive trade practices,

(d) Conforming to pollution control norms set up by government,

(e) Not to indulge in corruption through bribing and other unlawful activities.

(viii) Responsibility towards Society: A society consists of individuals, groups, organizations, families, etc. They all are the members of the society. They interact with each other and are also dependent on each other in almost all activities. There exists a relationship among them, which may be direct or indirect. Business, being a part of the society, also maintains its relationship with all other members of the society. Thus, it has certain responsibilities towards society, which may be as follows:

(a) To help the weaker and backward sections of the society,

(b) To preserve and promote social and cultural values,

(c) To generate employment,

(d) To protect the environment,

(e) To conserve natural resources and wildlife,

(f) To promote sports and culture,

(g) To provide assistance in the field of developmental research on education, medical science, technology, etc.

Corporate Governance and Ethics

Good Corporate Governance is a formal system of accountability and control of ethical and socially responsible decisions and use of resources. The following are the chief characteristics of Good Corporate Governance: It is

1. Participatory
2. Consensus Oriented
3. Accountable
4. Transparent
5. Responsive
6. Effective and Efficient
7. Equitable and Inclusive and
8. Follows the Rule of Law

Corporate Governance and Business Ethics

The national codes emphasize the ethical nature of good corporate governance. Special emphasis is placed on the fact that good governance is based on a number of cardinal ethical values. Topping the list of the values that should be adhered to in good governance are the values of transparency, accountability, responsibility and probability. These values should permeate all aspects of governance and be displayed in all actions and decisions of the board. The various aspects of governance, such as board complication and functional reporting, disclosure and risk management, are seen as instrumental in realizing these cardinal values of good governance.

Index